PRAISE FOR

The Third Pole

NPR BOOKS WE LOVE 2021 SELECTION

ONE OF THE 57 MOST ANTICIPATED BOOKS OF 2021 —*ELLE*

SUMMER'S MOST TRANSPORTING BOOKS LIST —*NEWSWEEK*

ONE OF 5 ACTION-PACKED NEW NONFICTION BOOKS FOR SUMMER —*AARP*

ULTIMATE SUMMER READING LIST PICK —*E!*

"[A] vivid, heart-pounding dispatch from the top of the world."

—Liz Baker, NPR

"A hold-your-breath story that features the author's own hazardous journey and exploration of the motives behind climbers' obsession with reaching dangerous heights."

—*AARP The Magazine*

"Captivates with mystery and adventure."

—*National Parks Traveler*

"The book is a fascinating tale and forces the reader to constantly ask themselves, *What would I do?* in each situation."

—*Fodor's*

"Mark Synnott's new book . . . is as rewarding as any Everest book can be, with history and geography wonderfully woven into the author's own climb, in 2019."

—*Air Mail*

"As in his previous book, the author's writing comes alive when he recounts life on the mountain. . . . This is a must-read for outdoor enthusiasts and readers of Everest and exploration history."

—*Library Journal*, starred review

"[A] hair-raising mountaineering story . . . A fine tale of adventure and exploration sure to please any fan of climbing and Everest lore."

—*Kirkus Reviews*, starred review

"Synnott weaves back and forth between the early climbing pioneers' experiences and his 2019 expedition, harrowing in its own right. A gifted storyteller, he proves firsthand the irresistible lure and perilous dangers of climbing Mount Everest."

—*Booklist*

"*The Third Pole* is an elegy of extremes, a white-knuckle tale of obsession and survival. From the archives of London's Royal Geographical Society to a tent battered by howling winds on the edge of the Death Zone, Mark Synnott puts it all on the line in his quest to solve Mount Everest's most enduring mystery."

—Susan Casey, author of national bestsellers *The Wave* and *Voices in the Ocean*

"A hundred-year-old detective story with a new twist. A high-altitude adventure. The best Everest book I've read since *Into Thin Air.* Synnott's climbing skills take you places few will ever dare to tread, but it's his writing that will keep you turning pages well past bedtime."

—Mark Adams, author of *Tip of the Iceberg* and *Turn Right at Machu Picchu*

"Join Mark Synnott on a quest for an artifact that could change Everest mountaineering history. Part detective story, part high adventure, Synnott engages obsessed historians, dodges Chinese bureaucrats, and ultimately risks his life high on the mountain's North Face. As the tension rises, he discovers astounding strengths in his fellow climbers, tragic frailty, and an ineffable truth he never imagined."

—Andy Hall, author of *Denali's Howl*

THE THIRD POLE

Mystery, Obsession, and Death on Mount Everest

MARK SYNNOTT

DUTTON

DUTTON
An imprint of Penguin Random House LLC
penguinrandomhouse.com

Previously published as a Dutton hardcover in April 2021

First Dutton trade paperback printing: April 2022

A portion of this work was originally published in the July 2020 issue of *National Geographic*

THE LIBRARY OF CONGRESS HAS CATALOGED THE HARDCOVER EDITION OF THIS BOOK AS FOLLOWS:
Names: Synnott, Mark, author.
Title: The Third Pole : mystery, obsession, and death on Mount Everest / Mark Synnott.
Description: New York : Dutton, Penguin Random House LLC, 2021. | Includes index.
Identifiers: LCCN 2020048322 (print) | LCCN 2020048323 (ebook) | ISBN 9781524745578 (hardcover) | ISBN 9781524745585 (ebook)
Subjects: LCSH: Mountaineering expeditions—Everest, Mount (China and Nepal) | Irvine, Andrew, 1902-1924. | Synnott, Mark. | Mountaineers—Great Britain. | Mountaineers—United States. | Mount Everest Expedition (1924) | Mountaineering—Everest, Mount (China and Nepal)—History. | Everest, Mount (China and Nepal)—Description and travel.
Classification: LCC GV199.44.E85 S96 2021 (print) | LCC GV199.44.E85 (ebook) | DDC 796.522092—dc23
LC record available at https://lccn.loc.gov/2020048322
LC ebook record available at https://lccn.loc.gov/2020048323

Dutton trade paperback ISBN: 9781524745592

Printed in the United States of America
2nd Printing

For Tommy, Lilla, Matt,

Will, and Hampton

CONTENTS

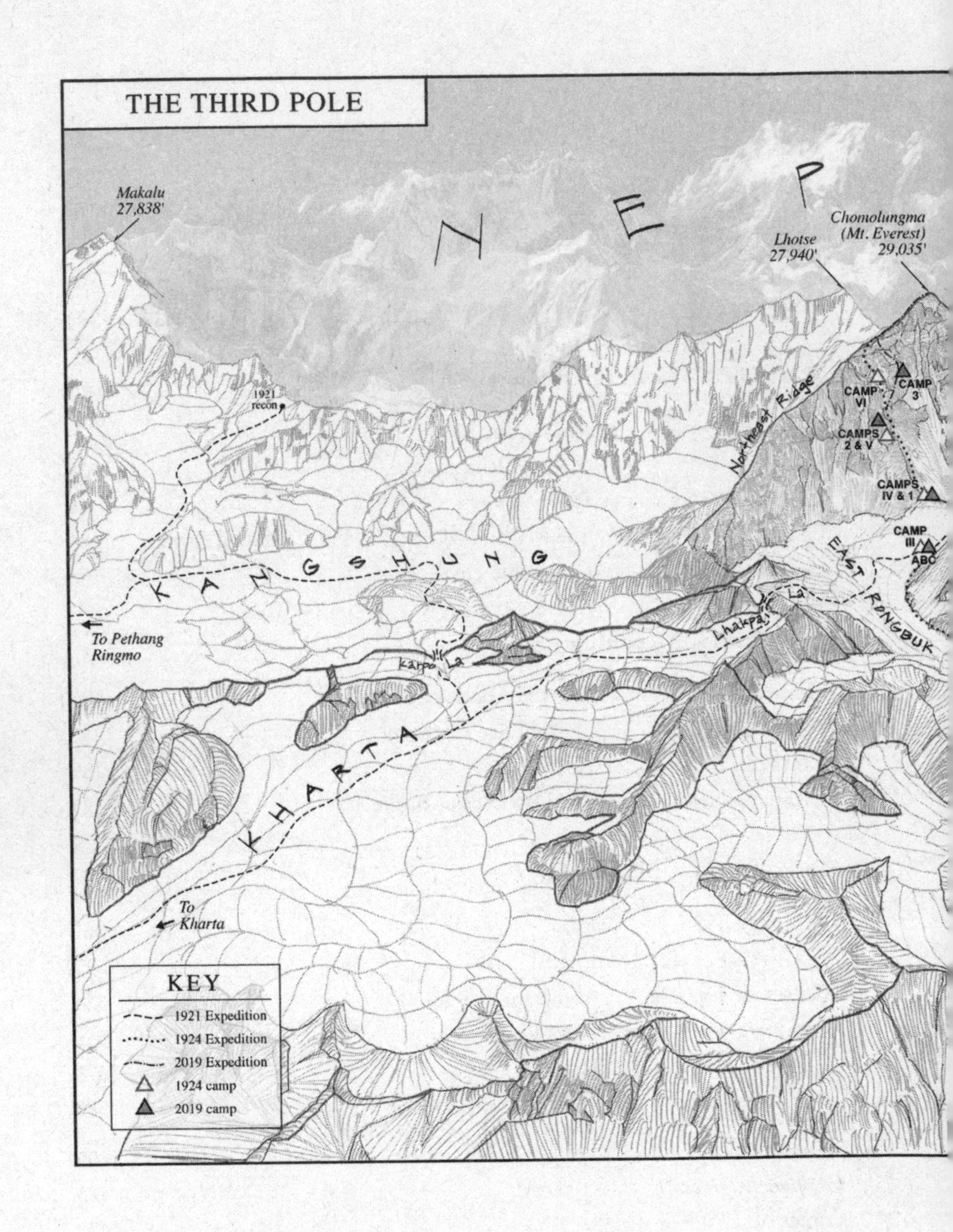
THE THIRD POLE
Makalu
27,838'
N E P
Lhotse
27,940'
Chomolungma
(Mt. Everest)
29,035'
1921
recon
Northeast Ridge
CAMP
VI
CAMP
3
CAMPS
2 & V
CAMPS
IV & 1
CAMP
III
ABC
KANGSHUNG
EAST RONGBUK
Lhakpa La
Karpo La
To Pethang
Ringmo
KHARTA
To
Kharta
KEY
1921 Expedition
1924 Expedition
2019 Expedition
1924 camp
2019 camp

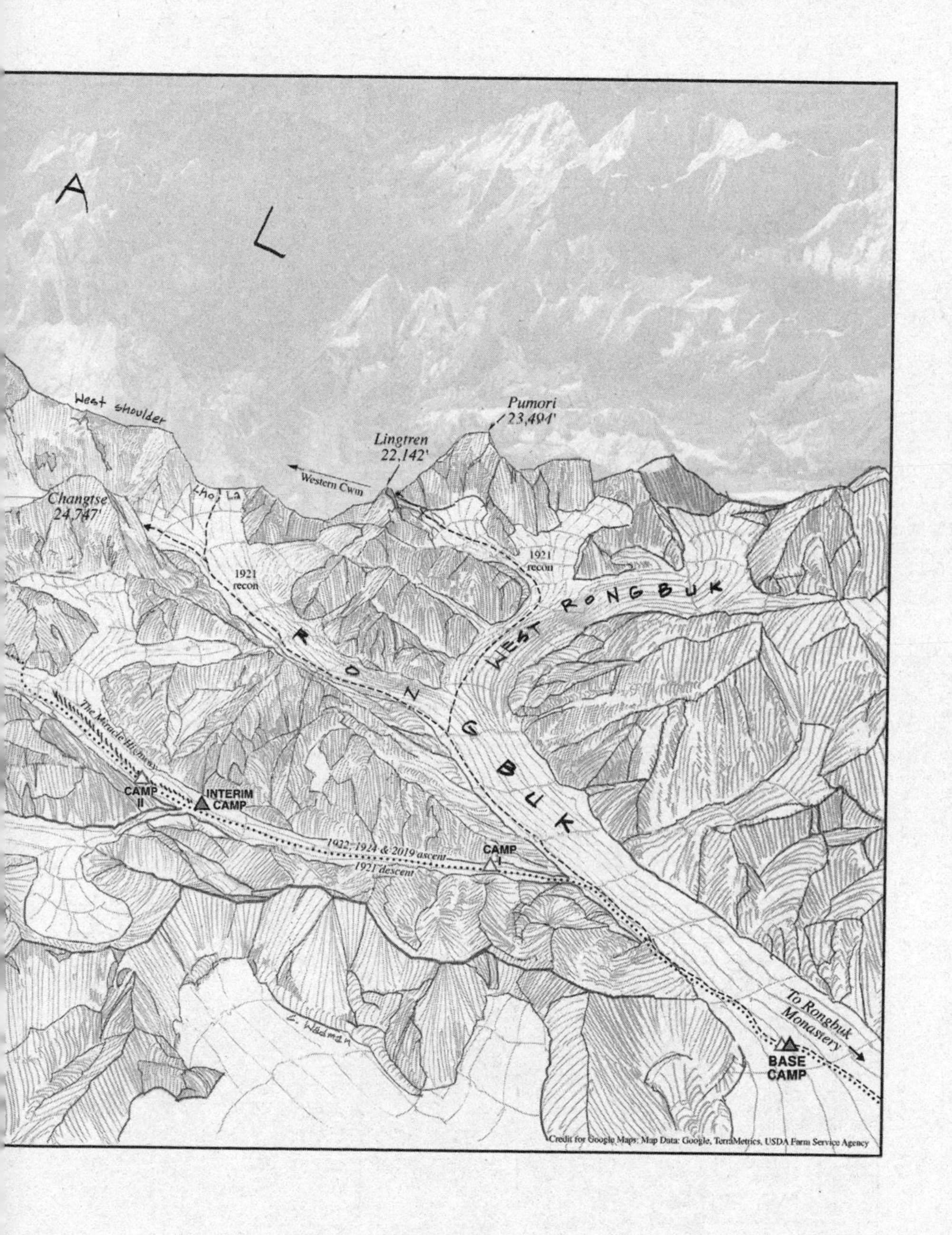

A
L
West shoulder
Pumori
23,494'
Lingtren
22,142'
Western Cwm
Changtse
24,747'
Lho La
1921
recon
1921
recon
WEST RONGBUK
RONGBUK
WEST
The Miracle Highway
CAMP
II
INTERIM
CAMP
1922, 1924 & 2019 ascent
1921 descent
CAMP
I
To Rongbuk
Monastery
BASE
CAMP
Credit for Google Maps: Map Data: Google, TerraMetrics, USDA Farm Service Agency

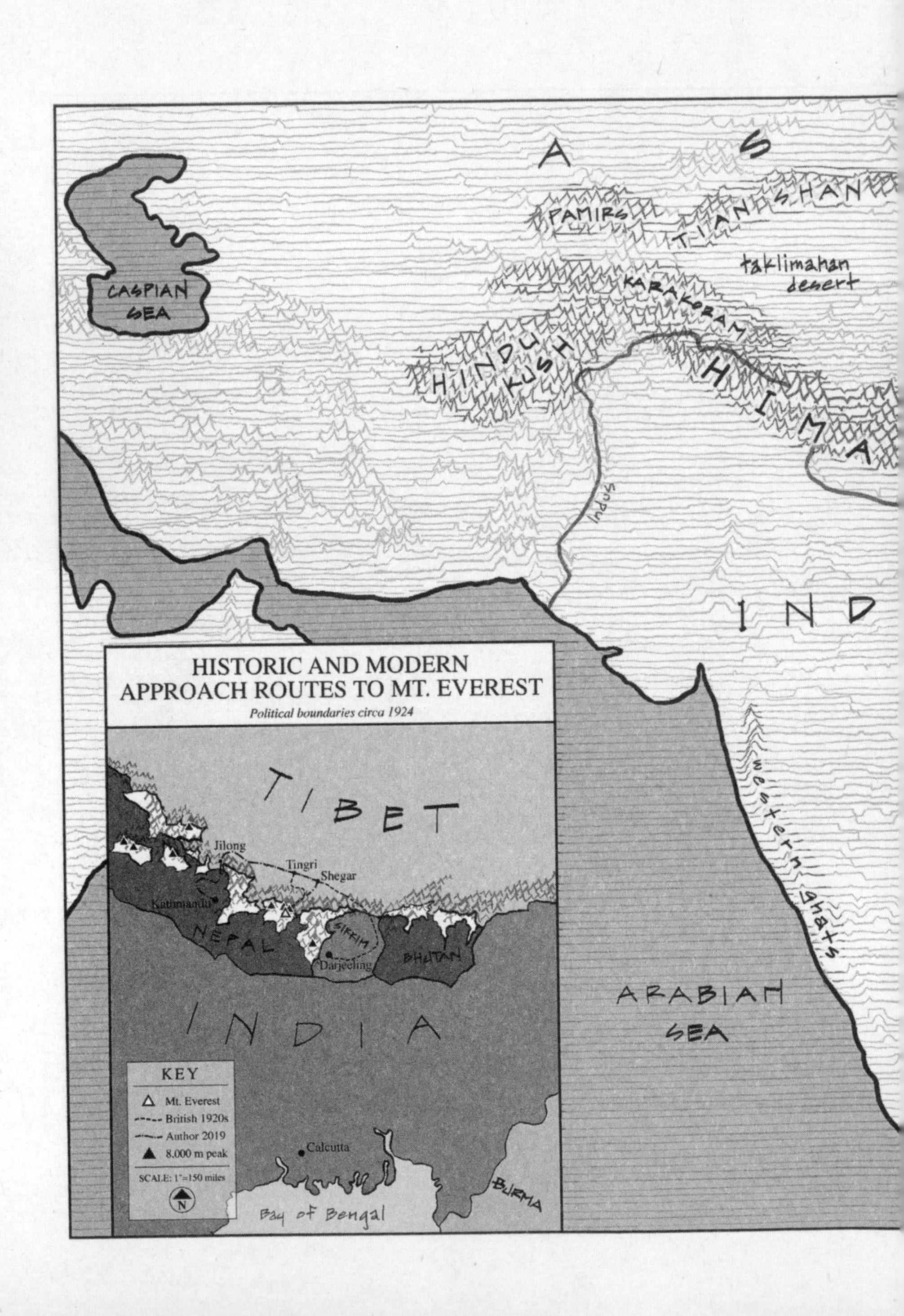
A S
TIAN SHAN
PAMIRS
taklimakan desert
KARAKORAM
CASPIAN SEA
HINDU KUSH
HIMA
Indus
IND
western ghats
ARABIAN SEA
HISTORIC AND MODERN APPROACH ROUTES TO MT. EVEREST
Political boundaries circa 1924
TIBET
Jilong
Tingri
Shegar
Kathmandu
NEPAL
SIKKIM
Darjeeling
BHUTAN
INDIA
KEY
Mt. Everest
British 1920s
Author 2019
8,000 m peak
SCALE: 1"=150 miles
N
Calcutta
BURMA
Bay of Bengal

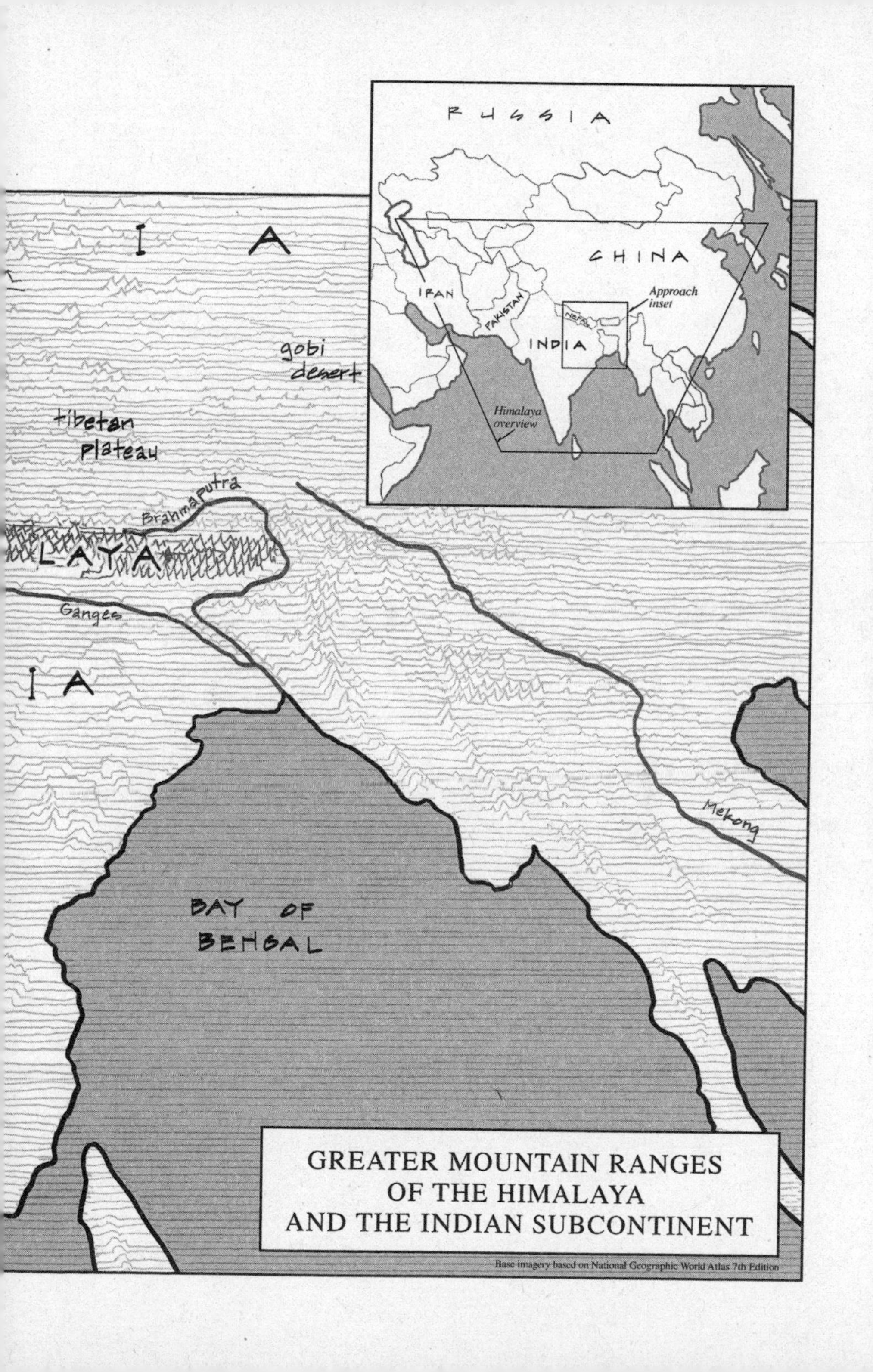

GREATER MOUNTAIN RANGES
OF THE HIMALAYA
AND THE INDIAN SUBCONTINENT

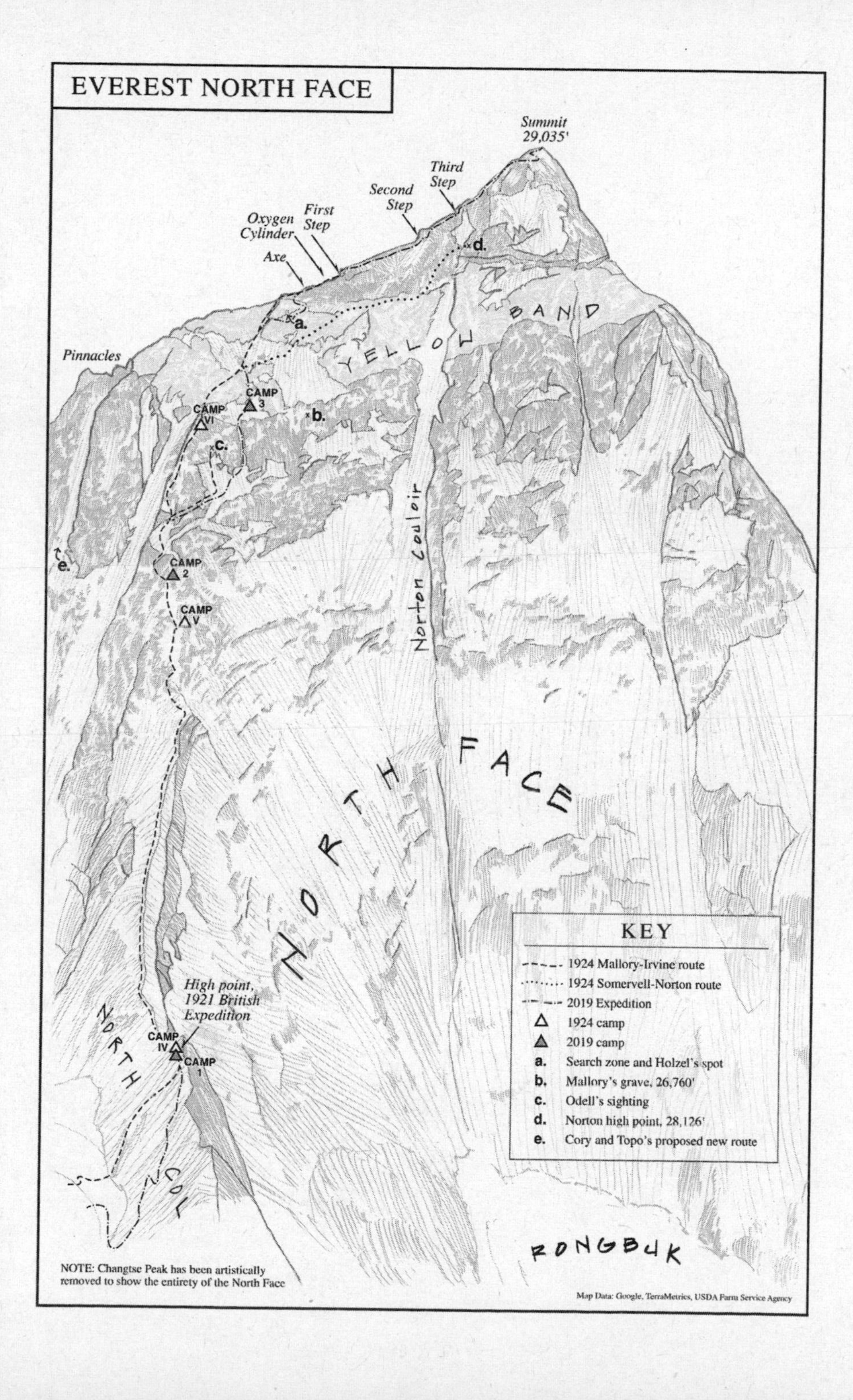

EVEREST NORTH FACE
Summit
29,035'
Third
Step
Second
Step
First
Step
Oxygen
Cylinder
Axe
d.
a.
YELLOW BAND
Pinnacles
CAMP
3
CAMP
VI
b.
c.
Norton Couloir
e.
CAMP
2
CAMP
V
NORTH FACE
High point,
1921 British
Expedition
CAMP
IV
CAMP
1
NORTH COL
KEY
1924 Mallory-Irvine route
1924 Somervell-Norton route
2019 Expedition
1924 camp
2019 camp
a. Search zone and Holzel's spot
b. Mallory's grave, 26,760'
c. Odell's sighting
d. Norton high point, 28,126'
e. Cory and Topo's proposed new route
RONGBUK
NOTE: Changtse Peak has been artistically
removed to show the entirety of the North Face
Map Data: Google, TerraMetrics, USDA Farm Service Agency

PROLOGUE

IT MUST HAVE been a little after 2 A.M. The wind had been building steadily through the night, and the tent fabric was flapping so violently that I thought it would tear apart. The noise made communication with my climbing partners impossible, even though the three of us were tightly pressed against each other in the darkness. There was nothing to say anyway.

My head throbbed and nausea tickled the back of my throat. I felt like I was suffering from the flu and a terrible hangover at the same time. I tried to calm my churning stomach by inhaling deeply, but the supercooled air bit hard into my chest and set off a dry, rattling cough that was impossible to control.

Earlier, after a ferocious gust flattened the tent for the third or fourth time, Jim had struggled out of his sleeping bag and put on his boots. He was preparing for the worst. I had just lain there, watching him. Trapped in a deadly storm at 23,000 feet on the North Face of Mount Everest, I couldn't imagine where he thought he would go, or how he would get there without being blown off the mountain.

I turned on my headlamp. Ice particles danced in the beam like the inside of a snow globe. Then, from high above, came a sound unlike anything I had ever heard in the mountains before—a deep, menacing rumble, like a rocket taking off. Seconds later, a furious gust of icy wind flattened our tent, and I was pressed so hard into my air mattress that the ice beneath it seared into my cheek. The tent poles cracked and our tiny shelter collapsed around us. I prayed that the thin bamboo stakes securing us to the slope would continue to hold as the wind picked up speed.

When the sun finally rose, I struggled to sit up. The crumpled tent was draped over my aching head. Jim lay next to me, curled up in a fetal position. I bumped his leg to make sure he was still alive. He groaned. Matt, his beard sheathed in ice, looked up at me with glowing red eyes.

I found the door, unzipped it, and crawled outside. The camp was devastated. Every tent I could see had been smashed or broken. I looked up and saw a tent flying, inexplicably, hundreds of feet above us in the still-swirling wind. I sucked in a breath and was immediately doubled over with another coughing spasm.

It had taken me months of constant work to get here. I had leveraged the goodwill of my family, flown 8,000 miles across the globe, and helped haul in over two tons of gear to camps across the mountain. Now all I could think was: *What the hell am I doing here?*

NEARLY A CENTURY EARLIER, another group of climbers wrestled with their own doubts. It was 1924, and the third British expedition to Mount Everest was not going well. A deep low-pressure system, which had stalled to the west of the Himalayas, had been pummeling the mountain for weeks with high winds and heavy snowfall. One storm in particular was so severe, porters had been forced to drop their loads along the icy path to Camp III, scattering the team's essential supplies.

The British had established a staging camp on the North Col, not far from where our battered tents were now. By the beginning of June, they had made two attempts to reach the summit. Both were valiant efforts, but each had failed, neither getting higher than 28,126 feet—still almost 1,000 vertical feet shy of the top. They were running out of time. Would the summer monsoon hold off long enough for one final assault?

The youngest member of the British team, Andrew "Sandy" Irvine, had taken ill. He was suffering from diarrhea and a face badly burned and chapped by the strong sun and relentless wind. And yet, when George Mallory, the team's best climber, invited Irvine to join him for the last go at the summit, he rallied. Equipped with the newfangled oxygen sets that Irvine had been tinkering with for weeks, the pair set off from a high camp on the morning of June 8. Later that day, a teammate spotted them "going strong" for the top, high on the Northeast Ridge.

They were never seen alive again.

EVER SINCE THAT DOOMED EXPEDITION, all climbers who challenge Everest have faced the unforgiving and brutal realities of the peak. As a veteran of the Battle of the Somme in the First World War, George Mallory can be taken at his word when he wrote that climbing Mount Everest was "more like war than sport."

Over the ensuing decades, hundreds of men and women have perished on the mountain's slopes, most in the aptly named "Death Zone" above 8,000 meters (26,247 feet). Many of their bodies still litter the standard climbing routes. Every single dead climber was drawn to Everest for their own reasons—be it vanity, money, or some other obsession. Wouldn't every one of them have asked at some point: *Why am I here?*

My own answer was multilayered. There was personal ambition, of course, which always has something to do with vanity and ego. But my team had another mission. We were on assignment for National Geographic, searching for a ghost. George Mallory's body was discovered on Everest's North Face in 1999, but his partner, Sandy Irvine, had never been found. We were searching for his final resting spot, and the ancient Kodak camera that he may have carried. It was like looking for a needle in a frozen haystack. But if we could find the camera and the film was salvageable, it just might hold an image that would rewrite history.

I know it sounds crazy.

We weren't the first to do this. A number of other teams had searched for that camera over the years. All had come up empty. But we were armed with new evidence, powerful new technology, and a solid plan to scour the mountain in a way that no one had before.

And I suppose it's not surprising that I found something I wasn't expecting on the roof of the world. Everest turned out to be a window on the best of humanity. And the worst.

PART ONE

PATHS TO OBSESSION

CHAPTER ONE

Among the Dead

THE BODY LAY facedown and partly embedded in the gravel, as if it had fallen into a slab of wet concrete. The head was partly covered in the remnants of a leather bomber's cap, fringed with orangey yellow hair. Much of the drab, earth-toned clothing had long ago been torn away by the wind, but bits of fabric still clung to the arms and around the waist. The entire back was exposed, the skin so clean and virgin white it looked like a marble statue. The buttocks and thighs had been chewed away by Himalayan ravens, and the holes gave the body the appearance of a plaster mannequin that had been cracked open with a hammer.

There were obvious signs of suffering. The arms were outstretched, long thin fingers clawed into the slope. The backs of the hands were the color of leather—in stark contrast to the rest of the skin, which had no color at all. The right foot, inside a leather hobnailed boot, was bent at an unnatural angle, where the leg had broken above the boot top. The left leg was crossed over the right, as if protecting the injured limb. This small, undeniably human gesture is what struck me most. Whatever had happened to this climber, it seemed he arrived at his final resting place conscious of his plight.

I looked over at my twelve-year-old daughter, Lilla, sitting next to me in the lecture hall, gripping the armrests of her seat. I put my hand on top of hers. "Are you okay?" I whispered. She looked up at me with a blank expression and nodded slightly. I hadn't known this slideshow would be R-rated, and I realized this must be the first time she had seen a photograph of an actual dead body. I was familiar with the photo. It had made the rounds on the internet when this long-lost climber, George Mallory, had been discovered high on the North Face of Mount Everest almost twenty years earlier.

Standing on the stage between a mannequin wearing a yellow one-piece down suit and an orange tent adorned with a New Hampshire license plate that read *29035* (the elevation in feet of Mount Everest) was my friend Thom Pollard. His gray hair belied a spryness in his manner and movements. His dress, like his speech, was typically peppered with nouveau bohemian flourishes, including the string of Tibetan prayer beads around his neck. But on this night, he wore a navy blue blazer, a tan pair of chinos, and dress shoes. His beard was trim, his hair combed neatly in place, the dome of his head shining under the stage lights. My hippie friend was transformed into something like a college professor on this October evening in 2017, and he carried himself as such, strolling casually from one side of the stage to the other.

I had known Thom since the 1990s, having first met him through mutual acquaintances shortly after he moved to North Conway, New Hampshire. We both had young children around the same age, and in a lot of ways, we were living parallel lives, struggling to make a living doing what we loved. He worked as a cameraman and filmmaker, and I as a professional climber, mountain guide, and journalist. Our wives were also friends, who shared a bond that was likely forged from the unique challenges posed by husbands who frequently traded family duties for global adventures—leaving them to raise young children in the sticks of New Hampshire, alone. Years later, Thom and I would each end up paying the predictable price for willfully chasing our dreams. Heartbroken and dazed, our scripts converged when both of our divorces were finalized at the same court hearing.

As it turned out, Thom was wise to dress up. His talk, titled "Lessons Learned in Pursuit of Everest," had drawn a crowd of nearly four hundred people. In 2016, a year earlier, he had summited Mount Everest for the first time at age fifty-four. It was his third attempt.

Truth be told, I wasn't interested in Mount Everest at all. I saw the mountain as a place overrun with inexperienced climbers who stacked the odds in their favor by outsourcing the most significant risks to the climbing sherpas, who carried the weight of everyone's egos on their shoulders—and frequently paid with their lives. The American alpinist Mark Twight summed up the sentiment of many climbers and pundits alike when he wrote, "I think posers have polluted mountaineering. They replace skills and courage with cash and equipment. They make the summit, not the style, the yardstick of success . . . Now I'm embarrassed to call myself a climber, because close on the heels of the admission some dilettante will ask whether I've read *Into Thin Air* or done Everest." For me and many other climbers of my generation, the world's highest mountain was not a worthy objective.

But it hadn't always been that way.

When I first started climbing at age fifteen, I quickly became fascinated with climbing lore. One of the first books I read was *All 14 Eight-Thousanders*, which told about Reinhold Messner and Peter Habeler's groundbreaking oxygenless ascent of Mount Everest in 1978. Medical experts had warned them that it was impossible to climb to 29,000 feet without supplemental oxygen. Even attempting to do so, they said, would cause permanent brain damage. So Messner and Habeler climbed as fast as they could, then practically ran down the mountain after they reached the summit. When they arrived in Base Camp, even they were surprised to find themselves perfectly healthy and mentally intact. After I read his book, Messner promptly replaced Evel Knievel as my idol. Who cared about jumping the Snake River Canyon in a rocket car when the roof of the world was waiting for you?

The first commercial client on Everest was Dick Bass, a Texas oilman and rancher who cofounded the Snowbird ski resort in Utah. In 1985, David Breashears and Ang Phurba Sherpa led the fifty-five-year-old Bass to the summit via the South Col route, making him the oldest person at the time to climb the mountain and also the first to climb the highest peaks on each continent—now a popular quest called the Seven Summits. Unwittingly, Bass had opened Pandora's box, and by the early nineties, several companies were selling guided Everest ascents. Two of the most successful Everest guides were Scott Fisher and Rob Hall, both of whom died while guiding clients on the mountain during the tragic 1996 season. The storm that killed them claimed the lives of six other people and was soon after memorialized in Jon Krakauer's *Into Thin Air.* While Krakauer decried the growing trend of well-heeled Everest clients who had not earned their mountaineering spurs, his book only brought into the mainstream the idea that you could buy your way to the top of the world.

As a preamble to his Everest talk, Thom had taken us on a quick spin around the globe, from the French Alps and Denali to Gasherbrum II, an 8,000-meter peak in Pakistan. The story I loved most was his attempt to sail across the Pacific Ocean—simply to prove it could be done—on a ship that he and a few companions constructed from 2.5 million totora reeds they cut from the shores of Lake Titicaca in Peru. Without a motor, the sixty-five-foot sailboat eventually drifted into the doldrums between South America and Easter Island, where it bobbed for weeks on the glassy water, making no progress toward its destination. The expedition's official line was that Thom had bailed onto a Chilean navy vessel after fifty-six days because of a family emergency. But the emergency, he later told me, was that his wife had threatened to leave him if he didn't get home immediately.

I looked again from the corner of my eye at Lilla. She still seemed uncomfortable, but Thom certainly had her full attention.

"IT IS ALMOST UNTHINKABLE with this plan that I shan't get to the top," Mallory wrote to his wife, Ruth, before his team reached Mount Everest in 1924. "I can't see myself coming down defeated."

The question of whether he and his climbing partner, Sandy Irvine, might actually have reached the summit twenty-nine years before the official first ascent in 1953, by Sir Edmund Hillary and Tenzing Norgay, has haunted mountaineers ever since. The last person to see the two men alive was their teammate, Noel Odell. Early on the afternoon of June 8, 1924, Odell turned his gaze toward the summit, 3,000 feet above his own position, where Mallory and Irvine were attempting to reach the top. A swirling veil of clouds had enveloped the upper reaches of the North Face that morning, but as Odell looked on, the churning cloud cap began to lift. High on the Northeast Ridge, at what he later approximated to be 28,200 feet, Odell spotted two tiny silhouettes "moving expeditiously" toward the summit. "My eyes became fixed on one tiny black spot silhouetted on a small snow crest," he would write on June 13 or 14 in an official dispatch. "The first then approached the great rock step and shortly emerged on top; the second did likewise. Then the whole fascinating vision vanished, enveloped in cloud once more."

The dream of climbing Everest had captivated the British elite for years. At a time when the Himalaya was still terra incognita to

Westerners, the idea of scaling the world's highest peak was no less daring than a modern spaceflight to Mars, with all the pressures and dangers that would come with it. In 1905, Lord Curzon, the viceroy of India, proposed an expedition to the mountain in a letter to Douglas Freshfield, an accomplished mountaineer and former president of the Alpine Club. "It has always seemed to me a reproach that with the second highest mountain in the world for the most part in British territory and with the highest in a neighboring and friendly state, we, the mountaineers and pioneers par excellence of the universe, make no sustained and scientific attempt to climb to the top of either of them . . . I would be prepared to lend every aid the government can give to a thoroughly well-appointed climbing party, comprised of trained experts with Swiss guides . . . Ought we not be able to do this?"

It wasn't until after World War One, in 1921, that the Alpine Club, in conjunction with the Royal Geographical Society, formed the Mount Everest Committee. The committee correctly reasoned that an assault on the world's highest mountain would require a multiyear effort involving reconnaissance, further surveying, and an army of porters. These logistical considerations became more complicated when the Nepali government, intent on preserving its isolation, replied with a firm no to Lord Curzon's request for a permit to approach the mountain from the south through the Khumbu Valley. Tibet was the only other possibility, but the secretary of state for India, John Morley, a myopic, "dry as dust" bureaucrat nicknamed "Aunt Priscilla," was worried about aggravating tensions with the Chinese and Russians. He forbade Britons from traveling in Tibet. Access remained the primary obstacle to Everest until the First World War.

In a further affront to the nation's dignity, British exploration was no longer on the leading edge. A series of British expeditions had been beaten in races to the Northwest Passage and to both poles of the Earth.

In 1848, while seeking a shortcut to the Pacific Ocean, two British ships—the HMS *Erebus* and HMS *Terror*—mysteriously vanished in the Canadian Arctic, with 129 men on board. In 1909, the American Robert Peary claimed the North Pole. Two years later, a scrappy, self-funded Norwegian explorer named Roald Amundsen—who had finally solved the enigma of the Northwest Passage in 1906—beat the Brits at their own game, once again. When the doomed British Antarctic expedition led by Robert Falcon Scott arrived at the South Pole, they were greeted by a flapping Norwegian flag firmly planted in the snow.

Mount Everest, which some had dubbed the "Third Pole," offered a last hope for British vindication after the Great War. The final obstacle, the permit to approach the mountain through Tibet, was granted by the Dalai Lama in December of 1920. The news broke in British newspapers shortly thereafter. Francis Younghusband, the president of the Royal Geographical Society, who had led a disastrous military incursion into Tibet in 1904, believed that for the Everest expedition to be successful, it needed to capture the imagination of the British public. During an address to the membership of the RGS, he said that he wanted to get the idea of ascending Mount Everest "enshrined in the very heart of society."

"Our forefathers were terrified of mountains," he said, "and called the most ordinary peak inaccessible. Nowadays, we refuse to admit that the highest mountain in the world cannot be scaled, and the man who first stands on the summit of Mount Everest will have raised the spirit of countless others for generations to come." Indeed, with the help of British newspapers, the first Mount Everest expedition soon grew into a popular crusade.

By the spring of 1921, the Mount Everest Committee had organized an exploratory expedition to reconnoiter a route up the mountain. No Westerner had been within forty miles of the peak, and no one had the foggiest idea how to get to the base, let alone climb it. They did know that a labyrinthine maze of almost unimaginably huge glaciers guarded access to its slopes. Even if they could find a way through them, techniques of high-altitude mountaineering were in their infancy. Climbers of that era used thin ropes made of hemp and other natural fibers, more similar to clothesline than modern climbing rope. These cords were easily severed and generally used as a token last-ditch safety measure, the way a guardrail might—or might not—prevent a bus from plummeting down an embankment. Climbers and mountaineers made a point to never actually put their ropes to the test. Crampons—metal spikes used for traction on snow and ice—were practically unworkable because the straps that were used to fasten them to the leather boots restricted circulation to toes. The all-essential carabiner, a kind of snap shackle used in almost every imaginable climbing situation, had only recently been invented and had not yet come into widespread use.

No one knew if it was even possible for a human to survive at 29,000 feet, and indeed, many physiologists of the day were adamant that it was not. The precedent set in 1875 by three French scientists who took off in a hot-air balloon, hoping to set a new altitude record, was not encouraging. When the balloon landed in a field several hours after takeoff, the instruments showed that it had reached an altitude of 28,000 feet. But two of the three men were dead, with their faces blackened and mouths filled with blood. The third, who somehow survived, had gone deaf. Today, it is obvious that the French scientists died because they had utterly failed to acclimate to the altitude—a process that can take weeks. At the time, there was very little awareness of this physiological reality.

Despite these unknowns, George Mallory and his teammates on the first British Mount Everest expedition in 1921 made significant advances. Overcoming many obstacles, he and his climbing partner,

Guy Bullock, reached a high point of 23,000 feet on a glacial col separating the North Ridge of Everest from an adjacent 7,000-meter peak called Changtse. The men turned back 6,000 feet below the summit, but they had discovered a feasible route. A year later, Mallory was back. Using supplemental oxygen sets for the first time in mountaineering history, two of his teammates set a new altitude record of 27,300 feet. But on the team's final bid for the summit, the climbers were caught in an avalanche, resulting in the deaths of seven local porters who had supported the expedition. Many held Mallory, who had led this final assault, responsible for the tragedy. But when he returned home, the Mount Everest Committee nonetheless shipped him off to the United States on a lecture tour. And it was on this visit, when a reporter from the *New York Times* asked Mallory why he wanted to climb Mount Everest, that he quipped, "Because it's there."

From hard experience in 1921 and 1922, the Mount Everest Committee had concluded that packing its teams with veteran mountaineers who had held high-ranking commands during the Great War, men now in their forties and fifties, was not working. These men may have had decades of alpine experience and more than proven their valor in battle, but they were simply too old to climb at elevations above 25,000 feet. In '21 and '22, Mallory had been considered the young gun, chosen primarily for his technical climbing talent as well as the fact that he had distinguished himself as a lieutenant in the Royal Garrison Artillery during the Great War. Now the committee decided that Mallory was almost too old himself, at age thirty-seven, and that they should find him a younger partner. The committee settled on a tow-headed twenty-one-year-old rower and chemistry student from Oxford University. Andrew "Sandy" Irvine was a precocious engineer and outstanding athlete. He impressed the committee with his evident pluck, even if he had almost no mountaineering experience and had never been higher than 5,500 feet above sea level.

So, WHAT EXACTLY HAPPENED to Mallory and Irvine on June 8, 1924? Was it possible that they were the first people to stand on top of the world? Seventy-five years after the third British Expedition ended in tragedy, an international team led by Eric Simonson, a veteran climber and guide from Seattle, who had summited Everest via the Northeast Ridge in 1991, set out for Tibet to find the answer. The team included several strong American mountaineers as well as a German mountaineering historian named Jochen Hemmleb. The expedition had come about through a collaborative effort among Hemmleb, Simonson, a publishing executive named Larry Johnston, and a Briton named Graham Hoyland—a journalist for the BBC who was the great-nephew of 1924 expedition member Howard Somervell. A deal was struck in which the expedition would be filmed by both the BBC and Nova, the PBS science-based documentary television series. Thom Pollard was hired by Nova as one of the expedition cameramen.

The 1999 Mallory and Irvine Research Expedition focused on finding the camera that Mallory and Irvine carried as they disappeared into the clouds—the same object that would become the source of my own obsession nearly twenty years later. On June 5, 1924, Howard Somervell reported loaning his Vest Pocket Kodak (VPK) to George Mallory in Camp IV on the North Col. Somervell had just returned from his own historic summit attempt, during which his partner Edward Norton, the expedition leader, had reached 28,126 feet (8,572 meters) without the use of supplemental oxygen. The notoriously absentminded Mallory, who was staging for his own final bid with Sandy Irvine, had forgotten his camera in one of the lower camps.

Before departing for China, Simonson had contacted experts to see if it might be possible to develop film from the camera. Technicians at Eastman Kodak told him that if the VPK body was intact, the film, which would have been deep-frozen for decades, might still be salvageable. They recommended carrying desiccant, a foil bag, and a cooler of dry ice for transporting the film home.

Their hope was to find the camera and develop the film. If it showed Mallory or Irvine standing triumphantly on the summit, the history of the world's tallest mountain would have to be rewritten.

The team historian, Jochen Hemmleb, though only twenty-seven years old, was one of the world's leading authorities on the Mallory and Irvine mystery. By piecing together all the various clues, he had narrowed the search zone to an area the size of ten football fields (about thirteen acres) near the top of the North Face. One of the most important pieces of evidence was the eyewitness account of a Chinese climber named Wang Hongbao, who had reported finding the body of an old "Engish, English" dead at 26,576 feet, when he had wandered off the Northeast Ridge route in 1975 in search of a missing teammate. At the time, no other bodies were known to be that high on the north side of the mountain, so the corpse Hongbao had seen could only be one of the lost British climbers.

By examining aerial photographs and maps of the mountain, Hemmleb had determined that the approximate location where Hongbao had seen this body was almost directly in the fall line from where an ice axe, believed to be Sandy Irvine's, had been found in 1933 on the Northeast Ridge. The British made several more unsuccessful attempts to climb the mountain in the 1930s, and during the first of this second round of expeditions, climber Percy Wyn-Harris found the axe at 28,000 feet on a slab of rock 60 feet below the crest of the ridge. The 1933 team assumed that this location marked the scene of a fatal accident. In his book, *Everest 1933*, the leader of the expedition, Hugh Ruttledge, speculated that the axe was either "accidentally dropped when a slip occurred or that its owner put it down possibly in order to have both hands free to hold the rope." He went on to explain that the slabs below the axe's location are not steep, but the rock is smooth and much of it is covered in loose pebbles. If a slip happened, it could easily have proved catastrophic. If Ruttledge's theory is correct, and Mallory and Irvine were roped together at the time, it's possible that one of them fell from this location and pulled the other off with him.

But even more important to Hemmleb was fixing the location of the Chinese Camp VI from which Hongbao had wandered in 1975 in search of his missing teammate. By orienting the search team relative to this camp, Hemmleb believed he could put the searchers in Hongbao's footsteps. Everything pointed to a snow terrace on the lower end of the Yellow Band, a distinctive layer of yellowish-brown limestone that encircles the mountain like a golden ring between 26,000 and 28,000 feet.

ONE OF THE SEARCHERS was the American alpinist Conrad Anker. On the first day of searching, May 1, 1999, Anker looked up toward the skyline of the Northeast Ridge, more than 1,000 feet above him, to the approximate area where Irvine's ice axe had been found. *If a body fell from up there, where would it end up?* It appeared to Anker that there was a natural catchment basin to his west, in the direction of a deep snow gully known as the Norton Couloir. He soon found a badly mangled body in a purple down suit, but it was immediately obvious from the clothing and modern clip-on crampons that it wasn't Mallory or Irvine. Soon thereafter, Anker found another body, this one also contemporary and similarly crumpled, with its head hanging downhill. When Anker leaned in close to see the face, he found himself staring into the empty eye sockets of a skeleton—birds had eaten away all the flesh.

Anker continued searching the basin. A few minutes later, he felt something strange, sort of like déjà vu. He'd later tell me that it was probably just the delay between what he saw in the periphery of his vision and when his oxygen-starved brain processed the information, but he said he definitely experienced a moment when he sensed the body before consciously seeing it. Over to his right, about forty feet away, was something the color of "alabaster, a light absorbing white, like matte rather than gloss at the paint store." When he was ten feet away, he realized he was looking at the bare backside of a long-deceased man. One glance at the body and he knew that this was no modern climber. The clothing, most of which had disintegrated, was obviously very old—but the leather hobnailed boot told Anker this was a climber from the earliest British Everest expeditions. *This is it*, he said to himself. *This is Sandy Irvine.*

Jake Norton, a twenty-five-year-old mountain guide from Massachusetts, was the first to arrive. When he was about twenty feet away, he stopped to take a photo of Anker standing over the body. There seemed to be no doubt that the body lying before them was the same one that Hongbao had discovered in 1975. And since it lay below the location where the ice axe was found in 1933, it was presumed to be Irvine. The man's hair was bleach blond and this gave them more certainty; Irvine had been nicknamed "Sandy" because of his light-colored hair. Norton was so convinced that he sat down and began pecking out a tombstone on a chunk of shale that read: SANDY IRVINE 1902–1924.

When Andy Politz and the other searchers, Tap Richards and Dave Hahn, finally arrived, they were initially speechless. Everyone had been hopeful of finding something, on account of the strength of Hemmleb's research and the fact that the mountain had less snow that year than anyone had ever seen on the north side. But still, they all knew that the odds of a successful outcome were long. And yet here they were, less than ninety minutes into the search.

The first clue as to what might have happened was the fifteen-foot length of flax rope tangled around the body. Norton noticed bruising and rope-imprinted indentations on the left side of the torso. Closer inspection revealed broken ribs.

Most of the clothing was shredded by decades of exposure to ultraviolet rays, but the collar of the shirt was still intact. Curious about what brand it might be, Norton turned out the collar and discovered a laundry label that read: G. MALLORY. "Wait," he said, "this is George Mallory!"

To which Dave Hahn replied breathlessly, "Really!? Oh my God, oh my God!"

IT WAS FORTUITOUS THAT Mallory was lying facedown. Technicians at Eastman Kodak had speculated that the best-case scenario for viability of the film would be if the body had shielded the camera from cosmic rays. The problem was that over the ensuing decades, the corpse had practically become one with the slope. Richards and Norton began chipping away at the rock-hard matrix of ice and gravel around the perimeter of the body, while Anker pulled upward from the legs. The frozen-stiff corpse finally creaked and broke free from the slope. Dust wafted around the team as more of the natural-fiber clothing disintegrated.

While Anker held the lower half of the body in the air, Richards and Norton reached under the torso and began checking the various pockets. Unlike the backside, where most of the garments had been stripped away, the chest was still fully clothed. Mallory and Irvine had set off for the summit that day wearing four layers on their legs and six on their upper bodies: silk underwear, wool pants with puttees, a wool sweater, and as outerwear, a gabardine coat. Norton was rifling through the pockets when his hand closed around something square and hard in a small pouch hanging from the neck. "I think I've found something," he said. A jolt of electricity went through the group. Could this be the VPK? The pouch didn't want to come loose, so Norton cut it open with his knife. A second later, he held the item in his hand for everyone to see. Alas, it was not the camera but a tin of "savoury meat lozenges"—the 1920s version of an energy bar.

Richards and Norton continued sifting through the pockets, bringing forth a trove of artifacts. After an hour or so, Norton pulled out a handkerchief from an inside chest pocket. Decorated with a floral burgundy, blue, and purple pattern, the initials *GLM* were embroidered on its edge in blue thread. Wrapped inside it were three letters, all addressed to George Mallory. One of them was from Mallory's wife, Ruth, and another from his brother, Trafford. The third was from a woman named Stella Cobden-Sanderson. This was undeniably Mallory's body, not Irvine's.

Norton pulled forth an altimeter, checking to see if it might miraculously have stopped recording at 29,000 feet. But it was smashed and missing its front glass and needle. The other items included a sewing kit, a bone-handled jackknife, a box of still operational Swan Vestas—"the smoker's match"—a tube of zinc oxide, a small pair of scissors, and the stub of a pencil, which Mallory had used to make notes on the back of one of the envelopes about the oxygen levels in each of their cylinders.

The most interesting item was a pair of goggles with dented aluminum frames, wire mesh side shields and wine-bottle-green lenses. Politz recognized that this was an important clue. The fact that Mallory was carrying these in his pocket suggested that the fall probably took place late in the day, perhaps even at night.

Another clue as to what might have happened on June 8, 1924, was what the search team didn't find. According to Mallory's family, he carried a photograph of Ruth with him on the mountain, and he had made it known that if he managed to stand on top of the world, he would leave her picture on top. Was it possible that the reason they didn't find it wrapped in that floral-patterned handkerchief was because Mallory had indeed left it on the summit earlier that day?

There was also no sign of the camera. Howard Somervell had reported handing the VPK to Mallory, but there is a rationale that it may have ended up with Irvine. He was the better photographer and would more likely be the one taking the summit photo rather than posing for it.

So, where was Sandy Irvine? The severed rope still knotted to Mallory's waist suggested that he had been tied to his young partner when he came to grief. And the injury to his torso seemed a sure sign that at some point, Mallory had come up hard on that rope. Perhaps Irvine had let go of his ice axe while trying to arrest Mallory's fall and then the rope had parted as the pair tumbled a thousand vertical feet down through the Yellow Band. But if that was the case, Mallory's body should have been more badly damaged, like the other bodies the team had found on the snow terrace. In all likelihood, repeated impacts from such a fall would have killed him before he came to rest at this spot. The arrangement of his body and limbs—head uphill, arms outstretched above his head with fingers clawed into the slope, one leg crossed over the injured other—suggested that he was conscious, and desperately trying to save himself when he reached this spot.

The team could only conclude that the answer to how these two men met their demise wasn't as simple as a single fall from the ice-axe location.

WHEN ANKER FOUND Mallory's body, Thom Pollard was on his way down to Advanced Base Camp (ABC). Earlier that morning, he had filmed his teammates as they set off from Camp II at 25,200 feet in the early morning alpenglow. It was only after stowing his camera that he had noticed a problem with his oxygen apparatus. He had yelled to Jake Norton, who was about 300 feet above him, but Norton never heard him above the wind, and Thom didn't have a radio. So Thom reluctantly headed down the mountain, not up with the rest of the team.

After the discovery, the search team had gone quiet on the radio. They knew that other teams were monitoring their transmissions, so a decision was made to cease all communication. So Thom and Simonson didn't know exactly what had transpired, only that it was something big. Hahn's last words over the radio before signing off had been: "Thanks, Jochen. You're going to be a happy man."

When Anker and the others later strolled into camp, Simonson looked at them expectantly. But no one said anything because there were strangers nearby. After zipping themselves into the dining tent, Hahn, Norton, and Politz began pulling artifacts out of their packs. The first one they handed to Simonson was an old faded envelope. It was addressed to Mr. George Leigh Mallory in fancy cursive handwriting. Simonson's face lit up with a huge smile.

The next morning, the whole team was relaxing in the dining tent. It was a warm sunny day, so the door was tied back. Thom sat near the opening, gazing out at the trail that ran straight through their camp. A man walking by looked into the tent and called out to them.

"Hey, congratulations."

"What are you talking about?" asked Thom.

"The discovery. You guys found Mallory."

"How do you know about that?"

"I was listening to the BBC and there was an interview with Ed Hillary congratulating you guys."

Unbeknownst to Thom, Simonson and Dave Hahn had posted a

dispatch the night before, announcing the discovery on a website called Mountain Zone that specialized in real-time coverage of Everest and other high-altitude expeditions. The post included a digital image of Mallory's corpse lying facedown in the gravel. Hahn had divided the image into a dozen pieces to get it small enough to be transmitted through the modem on their satellite phone. Simonson says he hadn't wanted to announce the discovery so soon, but a producer for Nova named Liesl Clark, who was in Base Camp, had posted her own dispatch on the Nova website and had quoted Hahn telling Jochen, "You're going to be a happy man." Word was already spreading fast and since Mountain Zone was supposed to have the exclusive on any breaking news from the expedition, Simonson felt he had no choice but to go public.

Within minutes of the dispatch going live, Mountain Zone's site logged a million hits per hour. George Mallory's body became front-page news around the world. The fact that the men who had found Mallory were still on the mountain and planning to head back up to search for Irvine and the camera added the element of real-time suspense and drama of the story, turning it into a global sensation.

So far, the only photograph of Mallory that had been published was the tiny 100-kilobyte file that Hahn had spent an entire night uploading. Hahn, who had been submitting dispatches and photos throughout the expedition, was shooting with a digital camera, but most of the others were using 35-millimeter film. Back in Base Camp, Simonson collected everyone's film, as agreed upon before the expedition, so it could be carried back to the US by a trekker and submitted to a stock agency that would control the distribution of the images to the media. Within twenty-four hours of the first dispatch, a bidding war had erupted among several publications, including *Time, Newsweek, Life, National Geographic*, and various British tabloids and newspapers. *Life* and *National Geographic* had even offered a six-figure payment, *in advance*, for the photos from the Kodak VPK—which hadn't even been found yet.

Thom says that numbers were discussed and that he was told his share could be $10,000, possibly more. "People were scrabbling for whatever money they could get," says Thom. "I'm not proud of the fact that I was one of them." On the surface, everyone was being civil, but according to Thom, the team was breaking into factions and "there was a war brewing underneath" about who would control the story and the windfall now in the offing.

On May 8, Hahn's low-res digital photo of Mallory was published in the *Sun*, a British tabloid owned by Rupert Murdoch. Anker, for one, was appalled. He had advocated strongly for the photo to be sold to *National Geographic* magazine, since he believed the editors there would handle its publication tastefully. Apparently, they had been outbid.

Meanwhile, Simonson had been emailing with Mallory's grandson, George Mallory II, who lived in Australia. Before the expedition, Simonson had asked the family for permission to obtain a DNA sample if his team happened to find the body. Anker had used his knife to cut a small piece of flesh from Mallory's arm. When George Mallory II heard that his grandfather had been found, he initially sent an email to the team expressing his "heartfelt thanks." But that was before he had seen the photo in the *Sun*. According to Thom, on May 8, Mallory sent another email, this time conveying his deep disappointment that the effort to find his grandfather might have been motivated by money. In an interview that same day with the *Observer*, he said, "Frankly, it makes me bloody angry."

As word spread that the team had sold the photo to the highest bidder, the backlash was swift and furious. Sir Chris Bonington, who led the British expedition that made the first ascent of Everest's Southwest Face in 1975, told the *Observer*: "Words cannot express how disgusted I am. These people don't deserve to be called climbers."

Thom took some time to himself that night to record these events and his thoughts about them in his journal. "The drama . . . of the expedition, as if it couldn't heighten any more, appears to be taking off into orbit."

TWO WEEKS AFTER the discovery, the entire team was back up on the mountain amidst a swirl of controversy. The original plan had been to search for Irvine and the camera on this second rotation, but a storm on May 8 had blanketed the mountain with snow. The team decided that in the mountain's current condition, searching further for Irvine would be futile.

That same storm had caught three Ukrainian climbers on their descent after they had summited without supplemental oxygen. One of the men had disappeared. His partners thought he had broken through a cornice and fallen down the remote and seldom-climbed Kangshung Face, on the east side of the mountain. The other two, suffering from frostbite and high-altitude cerebral edema, spent a night in the open above 27,000 feet. In the morning, they were barely able to move. Most of the other expeditions mobilized for the ensuing rescue, including several members of Simonson's team. Anker and Hahn helped lower the Ukrainians down from the North Col in makeshift litters. They eventually made it down safely. Anker and Hahn's efforts, in addition to those of many other climbers on the mountain, most certainly saved their lives. When the surviving Ukranian climbers finally reached a hospital, their frostbitten fingers and toes were amputated. Their lost companion was never seen again.

The effort had cost Simonson's team time and energy—commodities that are always in limited supply on Mount Everest. He decided to split the team into two parties, making the most of what was left. Anker, Hahn, Norton, and Richards would go for the summit, searching for any signs that Mallory and Irvine might have reached the upper section of the Northeast Ridge. Along the way, Anker would try to free climb a notorious feature known as the Second Step to ascertain whether Mallory could have done it with his rudimentary equipment—a subject that had been fiercely debated for decades.

The Northeast Ridge has three distinct rock crags, known as the First, Second, and Third Steps. Of the three, the Second Step is by far the most difficult. It has long been held that if Mallory and Irvine could have surmounted it, as Odell originally reported they had, there would have been no further technical difficulties to stop them from summiting. In 1975, the Chinese installed an aluminum ladder on the Second Step, and ever since, climbers have used it to clamber past the most difficult section of this vertical cliff. Anker planned to forgo the ladder and climb the rock itself, as Mallory and Irvine would have done.

A second party, which included Thom, would return to the site of Mallory's final resting place to search the body again. In the days since the discovery, the team had decided that the first searchers hadn't completely exhausted the possibility of finding the camera. By bringing along a metal detector, they now hoped to conduct a more thorough search of the area.

On May 16, both teams arrived at Camp III at 27,200 feet. While Anker and the others set up camp, Thom and Politz set off to find Mallory. They traversed west, descending as they maneuvered across a 35-degree slope interspersed with sections of firm snow and loose plates of stone that skittered out from under their crampons. They climbed unroped, fully aware that if either of them slipped or stumbled, the next stop would be in a gaping crevasse at the base of the North Face—6,000 feet below.

Thom caught up with Politz after the pair had descended about 500 feet. Politz was standing on a rubble-covered ledge, looking confused. "I can't find him," he said. "Let's split up and meet at that rock. If we haven't found him by then we'll bail and come back tomorrow." Half an hour later, Thom saw Politz staring intently at the ground. Moving closer, he noticed a mound of rock with a bone-white lower leg sticking out of it. Not knowing whether anyone would be coming back, the first search team had attempted to pay its respects to the legendary climber by piling rocks on top of the body.

Up until that moment, Thom had thought of the expedition as simply a "gig" and Mallory as an historical figure. But now, as he and Politz uncovered the man's remains, Thom saw Mallory as a fellow climber, and he was struck by a feeling of kinship.

The original party had done the heavy work of digging the body out of the frozen slope, so it took only a few minutes for them to dismantle the makeshift grave and lift Mallory's body into the air. As it came loose from the gravel, Thom had to cover his mouth to avoid breathing in dust from Mallory's pulverized clothing.

They lifted Mallory by the legs. As rigid as a plank of wood, the corpse hinged off the arms, which meant the entire front of the body, including the face, was free of the slope. Thom slid his fingers into Mallory's pants pocket and immediately found a round-faced watch with a thin leather band, an important artifact that had been overlooked by Jake Norton and Tap Richards. The crystal and minute hand were missing, but Thom noted that the hour hand (which would fall off later, when they were carrying it off the mountain) was pointing between one and two. Thom dug around in the pocket to see if there was any broken glass, but he found nothing, suggesting the crystal had broken somewhere along the climb. This meant that Mallory must have been doing okay at the time, as he would have had to remove his heavy wool mittens to take off the watch and place it in his pocket. Thom thought about the crux of the Second Step, which he knew to be a six-inch-wide crack running vertically up the cliff. If Mallory had climbed it, he surmised, he likely would have jammed his left arm into that crack. Noel Odell had reported seeing Mallory surmounting this feature at 12:50 p.m., so the timing matched up, more or less. Was this how the watch crystal had broken?

After going through all the pockets and finding nothing else, Thom decided that he wanted to look at Mallory's face, which the first team had chosen not to do. Maybe he would see something that couldn't be detected by feel. Maybe this *was* Irvine, who for some reason was wearing his partner's clothing. Politz was getting tired from holding the corpse, so Thom used his ice axe like a brace to prop the body in the air. He then got on his back and shinnied underneath headfirst, like a car mechanic slipping under a vehicle. Sharp rocks dug into his back. He worried he was tearing his down suit.

Thom initially got so close to Mallory's face that he actually had to back off a bit to bring it into focus. The nose was slightly flattened from decades of being pressed into frozen gravel, but otherwise, the impossibly handsome face that Mallory's friend Lytton Strachey once described as "the mystery of Botticelli, the refinement and delicacy of a Chinese print, the youth and piquancy of an unimaginable English boy" was perfectly preserved. His eyes were closed. His chin was covered in black stubble, which Thom touched with the tip of his finger, noting that it felt like three-or-four-days' worth of growth. There was no sign of frostbite in any of the telltale spots—the tip of the nose, cheeks, earlobes. But above his right eye, Thom insists that he saw a horrific wound, a hole about the size of a half-dollar that went right through the skull, with jagged edges rimmed with bits of bone and blood. "I actually felt a sense of relief when I saw it," says Thom, "because it was clearly a mortal wound. Whatever had caused it, Mallory could not have lived long afterwards." Thom considered taking a photo of Mallory's face, but after the photo that had been published in the *Sun* and all the outrage that had rained down on the team as a result, he balked.

He would later regret his decision not to document the wound he saw in Mallory's head. Politz never saw it (he was searching the surrounding area—to no avail—with the metal detector at the time), and eyewitness accounts at high altitude are notoriously unreliable. When they were back at their tent that night and Thom brought it up, Politz didn't remember any mention of the wound while they were examining the body. Thom remains adamant that the wound was real and not a figment of his imagination, or a play of shadows on his altitude-addled eyes. And he did record it in his journal shortly afterward. Most Everest historians have accepted his account. But the fact is that he and Politz did not flip the body over, so they never got a clear view of Mallory's face. And the existence of a gaping hole in the head potentially conflicts with the conclusions of others (including my own) that Mallory must have been conscious and still struggling to save himself before he succumbed.

When they had finished searching the body, Thom and Politz covered it with rocks as well as they could. As they hiked down the mountain toward Camp II, Thom stopped and looked back at the gravesite—now about seventy-five feet above him. It wasn't a proper burial, as there simply weren't enough stones in the vicinity to fully bury the body. This fact bothered Thom more than anything else.

THOM CALLED ME a few days after his lecture to get a critique, and it was during this conversation that he filled in a lot of details he had left out that night in Maine. "That image of his leg sticking in the air, it still haunts me to this day," he said. "I've always felt that if I ever went back to the north side of Everest, I would finish the job."

"Are you thinking about going back someday?" I asked. Thom had already been to Everest three times. I assumed now that he had finally made the summit, he would retire from high-altitude mountaineering. After all, he was fifty-six years old. Why would he want to go back again?

"I thought you knew," Thom said. "I've been trying for years to get funding for another expedition to look for Sandy Irvine and the camera. And I've always wanted to summit from the north."

I was aware that subsequent teams had gone looking for Irvine on several occasions in the years since Mallory had been found. Most of the 1999 team, except Thom and Anker, had taken part in a second search expedition in 2001. They had found Mallory and Irvine's final camp at 26,700 feet on the North Ridge, where a few more artifacts were unearthed—a sock with the name Norton on it, a piece of rubber tubing and two leather straps with buckles—but nothing that gave them any more clues about what happened the day Mallory and Irvine disappeared. Norton and Hahn had tried again in 2004, and that same season another team led by the veteran Sherpa Chhiring Dorje was also looking around in the Yellow Band. Most recently, Hemmleb led two more Irvine search expeditions in 2010 and 2011. Despite all this effort and resources, not a trace of Irvine had been found.

I was skeptical. "You don't think you could actually find him, do you?"

"What if I had a critical piece of information that no one else has had?" Thom replied.

"Like what?"

He paused for a few seconds.

"Like the exact location of the body."

CHAPTER TWO

Moscow Rules

On a chilly December evening in 2018, Thom and I stood in the driveway of the Westleigh condominium complex in Litchfield, Connecticut. Thom gestured toward the back bumper of the white Subaru Outback parked in the driveway. The Connecticut plate read *29002*.

"I don't get it," I said. "Isn't Everest 29,035 feet high?"

"It is now, but back in the 1920s, it was thought to be 29,002."

I'd known since a freshman geology class that the Himalaya, the world's youngest and tallest mountain range, is still pushing upward as the Indian subcontinent crashes into Asia proper. I had always liked the idea that the most ferocious mountains on Earth, rising to altitudes barely attainable by even the strongest mountaineers, have yet to reach their full stature. Geologists aren't in perfect agreement as to the exact growth rate, but the consensus seems to be about half a centimeter per year. If the mountain has grown at this rate as an average, it may have increased in height by approximately sixteen feet over the past millennia.

Thom and I had driven more than six hours to Litchfield to visit Tom Holzel, a seventy-eight-year-old entrepreneur, inventor, and

Everest enthusiast who has devoted considerable time over the past forty years to solving the Mallory and Irvine mystery.

Thom and I had been talking about Everest almost every day since he first dangled the possibility that he knew the exact location of Sandy Irvine's body. It was Holzel, an old friend of Thom's, who had supposedly figured it out. And, as Thom had recently told me, Holzel hoped to recruit some climbers that could be his boots on the ground to continue his detective work up on the mountain. A few days earlier, he had texted Thom a "top secret" set of GPS coordinates.

My bookshelf included the stories of James Cook, Ernest Shackleton, Roald Amundsen, and many other great explorers like them. But I had overlooked Mallory and Irvine. I suppose I just hadn't taken much interest in the history of Everest due to the mountain's modern stigma.

But in the weeks following Thom's slideshow and our subsequent conversation, as the story of Mallory and Irvine percolated through my mind, I came to see these early Everest pioneers in a new light. Their attempt to claim the Third Pole at a time before equipment and clothing were up to the task was as noble and courageous as any of the other exploratory exploits that had long fascinated me.

Eventually, I gave in and ordered half a dozen books on the subject: *Into the Silence*, *Fearless on Everest*, *The Wildest Dream*, *Detectives on Everest*, *The Lost Explorer*, *The Mystery of Mallory and Irvine*, and *The Fight for Everest 1924*.

So was I now coming under the Everest spell? Initially, I had dismissed Thom's claim of knowing the exact location of Irvine's body; it held little relevance for me. But now that I had cracked open the lid, the Everest box would not close. Thom's implicit invitation to join him on what he hoped would be another expedition began to intrigue me. Then it built into something more.

SEVERAL MONTHS EARLIER, on a balmy summer evening, my wife, Hampton, and I were having dinner at a restaurant near our home. By now, I'd read most of those Everest books, and I couldn't stop thinking about the idea of joining Thom in trying to find Sandy Irvine. Up until a moment ago, when I had mentioned the possibility of mounting an Everest expedition to look for a nearly 100-year-old dead body, we had been enjoying a rare date night.

"Everest?" she said. "Really? That seems so unoriginal and not *you*. Hasn't everyone already been there and done that?"

I launched into a detailed explanation of the Mallory and Irvine mystery, and how this wasn't going to be your typical Everest expedition. By the time I got to the part about the camera, and the possibility that I might one day find myself in a darkroom watching as images taken on June 8, 1924, materialized in the developing tray, I could tell by Hampton's posture and the light in her eyes that she was intrigued.

"But I thought you weren't interested in climbing mountains like Everest and K2," she said. "You told me you were retired from Himalayan climbing when we first started dating."

"Well, at the time, I truly didn't think I would ever *want* to go to Everest. And technically, I'm not actually climbing the mountain. I'm doing high-altitude archaeology. Also, at this point this is only an idea."

Hampton took a sip of her drink and stared back at me, chewing the inside of her cheek. I had put her in an awkward position, and we both knew it. In the decade before she met me, she hadn't lived in the same town for more than a year and had even spent a couple seasons working in New Zealand, during which she racked up nearly seven hundred consecutive ski days. She made the decision to quit her job in the outdoor industry when our son, Tommy, was born in 2016, and the transition from having a successful career and an adventure-driven lifestyle to being a stay-at-home mom had not been easy. The upshot, though, was that with her newfound freedom, she and Tommy had been able to join me on many of my trips. Tommy already had stamps in his passport from three continents and had been to Japan twice. Unfortunately, that model wouldn't work this time. Base Camp on the north side is at 17,000 feet—no one in their right mind would bring a toddler to that elevation.

I'd had many conversations similar to this one with my first wife, Lauren. She and I were together for almost all of my professional climbing career—during which time I went on more than thirty international expeditions that kept me away from home for weeks or months at a time. We had three children who were now eighteen, fifteen, and twelve (Lilla, the youngest, had accompanied me to Thom's lecture). While I always asked Lauren for her blessings before going on a big trip, and she had never once overtly withheld them, I knew all along that she yearned for the day that I would decide to step away from expedition climbing and focus instead on our growing family.

Over the years, a quiet resentment built up. It got old, those pitying looks from other parents at the grammar school when Lauren went to parents' night alone, or the hundredth person asked at the post office, "So, where's Mark this time?" On the gray days when she had the flu, or the car was broken, or the kids were melting down, I was happily ensconced in the middle of nowhere, chasing my dreams of adventure.

"Who's getting anything out of these climbs other than you?" she once asked me.

In the fall of 2012, after a monthlong exploratory sailing and climbing expedition to the Musandam Peninsula in Oman, I came home to a particularly frosty reception. The kids were excited about their souvenirs, but Lauren was distant.

"Aren't you glad I'm home?" I finally asked.

"Honestly, I was happier when you weren't here," she said.

We started seeing a counselor. Then one day she handed me a manila envelope with the name of a law firm stickered onto the front.

Now, looking over at Hampton, I wondered if I was following the same patterns that had already ruined one marriage. Was this too big an ask? After all, I was pushing fifty. I had a hernia and a bum knee. And I didn't have life insurance. As a professional climber, it was impossible to get a policy we could afford.

Hampton was leaning back in her chair, looking relaxed with her legs crossed and a predinner gin and tonic in her hand. Just as I started to worry that I had ruined our night, she looked up at me. "If this is something you really want to do," she said, "then you should definitely do it." As I sat there wondering if she really meant it, a smile came over her face. "But if you're going to Everest next year, Tommy and I are going big too."

HOLZEL'S DOG, a Sheltie named Tuckerman, went berserk when Thom and I stepped inside the front door. He ran around in circles, barking as I shook hands with his owner, who was looking well for a guy just shy of eighty. Holzel stood over six feet tall and had a full head of light brown hair barely tinged with gray. His eyes, though, were red-rimmed and rheumy, framed by purplish bags that looked almost like bruises. I wondered if this was the price you pay for spending decades poring over old journals, maps, and black-and-white photos from the 1920s.

Holzel had dusted off the mystery of who first summited Everest in a controversial article he wrote for the UK's *Mountain* magazine in 1971. He posited that Mallory could have summited by taking Irvine's remaining oxygen and sending him back down alone. This speculation raised the hackles of the British mountaineering establishment, whose members generally revere Mallory. Abandoning one's partner in this way would have been decidedly unsporting. Holzel also asserted that the mystery could be solved by searching the snow terrace below where Irvine's ice axe was found in 1933, but, again, it wasn't the British way to go looking for the bodies of long-dead mountaineers. When the *Sunday Times* ran a story on Holzel's article, it prompted weeks of angry letters. And the recriminations never quite died out. One Holzel hater in 2007 warned against letting "Americans with an electronic thesaurus on their computers near topics and people they simply don't understand . . . It's like seeing a drunk using post boxes as supports as they stagger erratically down the street."

Holzel first became interested in the Mallory and Irvine mystery after reading a brief account of the 1924 climb in the *New Yorker*. This led him to the New York Public Library, where he found *The Fight for Everest 1924* as well as two Mallory biographies. He puzzled over why none of these books had undertaken a detailed analysis of the accident that must have befallen the two climbers.

In May 1975, Holzel drafted a letter to the United States Liaison Office in Peking, China, asking if the US government could help him to secure a permit for a Mallory and Irvine search expedition. He still has the reply, which he says is one of his most prized possessions. "I have read with great interest your letter of May 1st concerning the Atlantic Alpine Clubs desire to explore the fate of the two British climbers, Mallory and Irvine. It is a fascinating project, but one, I fear, that faces many obstacles. As I am sure you are aware, the

People's Republic of China has never allowed foreign climbers to operate from the Chinese side of the Himalayan mountain chain. Although I could be wrong on this, it is my recollection that the Chinese have never even publicly acknowledged that foreign climbers have reached the summit of Mount Everest. Finally, the region of southwest China, and particularly Tibet, has been closed to foreigners for many years . . . The entire area is one of great political and military sensitivity for the Chinese." The letter was signed, "With Best Regards, George Bush, Chief U.S. Liaison Office." In the margin, handwritten in black ink, Bush senior had added, "Your letter was as fine a letter as we've ever gotten here. Wish I could help."

A decade later, however, the Chinese had softened their position toward Western climbers. The first ascent of Everest's north side by a non-Chinese team occurred in 1980 when a Japanese team climbed a direct route up the North Face via the Hornbein Couloir. In 1986, Holzel put together a well-funded Mallory and Irvine search expedition. But he and his co-leader, Audrey Salkeld, an author and fellow Everest historian, hoping to have the mountain to themselves, slated the expedition for the fall, and an unusually heavy monsoon had left the mountain buried in snow. The climbing team, led by filmmaker David Breashears, never got above 25,000 feet. If conditions had been better, they might have found Mallory. According to Holzel, when Conrad Anker discovered Mallory's body, the location was within roughly 100 feet of where Holzel had speculated it would lie.

After tossing our stuff in adjacent guest rooms, we made for the living room, where Holzel was waiting for us. In the hallway outside the kitchen, I stopped to admire a framed black-and-white portrait of George Mallory and his wife, Ruth. I'd seen it before. The photo was taken in 1917 when Mallory was home on leave from his garrison on the Western Front—a snapshot from the days before their lives would be taken over by Mallory's obsession with Everest. Mallory is in the foreground, wearing his army uniform. Ruth is behind him, her face partly shaded and slightly out of focus. Both of them are staring intently into the camera, their eyes wide, mouths unsmiling.

We didn't know exactly what Holzel drank but wanted to come bearing gifts, so Thom and I had brought a bottle of Tito's vodka, some Japanese whisky, and a twelve-pack of Stella Artois. Holzel wanted none of it. "I'm a Beck's man," he said, heading for the kitchen. He returned a few minutes later with his preferred beer and three glasses. "No drinking out of the bottle in this house," he said.

We sat around a glass-topped coffee table upon which Holzel had laid out three copies of a typewritten document. I picked one up and read the title page:

CONSIDERATIONS IN RECOVERING THE VPK CAMERA
[Practice "Moscow Rules"]

Holzel saw the quizzical look on my face and explained that the Moscow Rules were developed during the Cold War by American spies working in the Soviet Union. There were ten. The last one was: *Keep your options open.*

I leafed through Holzel's "manifesto," as Thom had already dubbed it. The document read like a legal brief, with numbered points, lettered subpoints, and so on. Line one read:

> OPERATIONAL SECRECY IS PARAMOUNT. Any suggestions of an imminent VPK camera search will cause an immediate rush of hangers-on wanting to join the search, reports to media, government agencies etc.—any of which may alert Chinese authorities—and cause cancellation of your permit.

I looked over at Holzel, who was reclined on the couch with his legs crossed, beer held high. "Are you saying that if we tell the Chinese that we're looking for Sandy Irvine, they won't give us a permit?"

"Absolutely, and if they discover that you found the camera, they will want it; $400,000 was the last bid and that was in 1999. Imagine how much it's worth now."

Thom reckoned a million.

"The best thing to do is just say you're climbing; you've got a cameraman who likes to do sunsets. Just make up any bullshit you want. You've got to keep this thing hermetic because if anybody finds out, by the time you get to Kathmandu, there will be a goddamn reception committee at the airplane wanting to join the expedition."

"If we can't tell anyone what we're doing, how are we supposed to get this funded?" asked Thom.

"You know the old quote, right?" said Holzel. "'To succeed, you have to break the rules.' You have to understand that there are some questionable legalities. I don't mean you're going to do anything that's overtly illegal, but this whole issue is fraught with people who want to sue."

"Over what?"

"Ownership of the camera, of course. Read point number four."

Thom slipped on his glasses and read aloud: "If the VPK camera is found, say a prayer to your favorite god because you are going to be in for a whirlwind of shit."

"You have to understand that there are half a dozen parties who claim ownership of the camera and any photos that might be on it," Holzel said. "Years ago, the senior copyright lawyer at Microsoft, who was an amateur climber, did an interesting study on this question, and he basically said that it's a complete quagmire. The copyright laws have changed two or three times since [1924], you have

British law versus American law, and the fact that all of the people directly involved are now dead. This guy is one of the top legal minds in the country and he essentially said that he had no idea how it would be adjudicated. And you know what that means, it means that muscle is what wins. Not law."

"Why did he take this up?"

"For the same reason that I did, because it's fun."

"To avoid all this, we were thinking we could go to England to tell the family and people like Chris Bonington about our expedition and hopefully get their buy-in," I said.

"For God's sake, don't do it," Holzel said. "There's absolutely nothing to be gained and everything to be lost. The entire British mountaineering establishment will be aflame with this news. Go to page three."

We all flipped forward in the document to an April 15, 2001, headline from the *Guardian*: OUTRAGE AS CLIMBERS BID TO FIND EVEREST HERO'S BODY. I would later pull up the story. The subtitle summed up the gist of it: "Eric Simonson's team was accused of grave robbing after he sold pictures of Mallory's corpse on Everest. Now he's back to find the second body, disgusting many who believe Sandy Irvine should rest in peace."

HOLZEL'S THEORY AS TO the whereabouts of Irvine's body, I would learn that night, was based on two eyewitness accounts. One was a Sherpa named Chhiring Dorje who reported stumbling upon an old dead body wearing faded green "army-colored" clothing at 8,400 meters on the Northeast Ridge in 1995. The other account was from a Chinese climber named Xu Jing, who claimed he saw a body high on the North Face of Mount Everest on May 24, 1960. Xu was the deputy leader of the Chinese expedition that claimed the first ascent of Everest's north side. Like seemingly every other clue to have surfaced in the Mallory and Irvine mystery, however, Xu and Chhiring's purported sightings are fraught with vagaries and inconsistencies.

In August of 2001, Eric Simonson and Jochen Hemmleb were in Beijing researching the 1960 Chinese Everest expedition. The pair had recently returned from the second Mallory and Irvine Research Expedition, which, unlike the 1999 effort, failed to find anything of real significance. At the headquarters of the Chinese Mountaineering Association, the pair sat down with Xu Jing and other members of the 1960 team. Xu explained, through a translator, that he was supposed to go to the summit with the four other climbers of the summit team. But shortly after setting off from high camp at almost 28,000 feet, he had turned back because he wasn't feeling well. Oxygen deprived, borderline hypothermic, and barely functioning, he began his retreat off the mountain. Almost immediately, Xu veered off the established route onto what he thought might be a shortcut down through the Yellow Band. Hemmleb recalls that as Xu described his harrowing descent in Chinese, he suddenly became animated and pressed his arms to his side to describe an outstretched body. Hemmleb and Simonson turned anxiously to the translator to find out what Xu was talking about. In the translator's words: "At that time, he looked . . . there is a body . . . in a sleeping bag. That person is frozen there."

According to the transcript of the interview, which Hemmleb shared with me, Xu described the location as "a slight ditch on the ridge." Xu picked up a book, opened it, and ran his finger down the gutter, to show that he had seen the body inside a crevice-like feature. (Two years later, in an interview with the *Sunday Times*, Xu was more precise: "I found his body in a crack one meter wide, with steep cliffs on both sides. He was in a sleeping bag, as if he was taking shelter, fell asleep and never awoke. His body was intact but his skin (face) was blackened. He was facing up.")

Hemmleb pulled out a photo of the Northeast Ridge and asked Xu to point out where he had seen the body. Xu indicated that the body he had seen was at approximately 8,300 to 8,400 meters. Hemmleb then pointed out where they had found Mallory on the 8,200-meter snow terrace. Xu looked up and said, "Where's Irvine?" According to Hemmleb, it was at this moment that Xu realized that he had discovered the remains of Sandy Irvine.

This was the first time anyone in the Western world had directly queried the Chinese about finding traces of the early British expeditions. But how much stock should we put in Xu's account? It had been more than four decades since the Chinese expedition, and by his own admission—quite understandably—Xu's memory was a bit fuzzy on a lot of the details. High altitude has an insidious way of muddling one's mind, blurring the line between real and imaginary. In particular, the detail about the body being in a sleeping bag seems to discredit the sighting. The sleeping bags used by Mallory and Irvine weighed about ten pounds, and we can be reasonably certain that they did not carry one on their dash for the summit. They were already burdened enough by the clunky oxygen sets, and no other summit parties during the 1920s expeditions carried bivouac gear. Holzel thinks that this detail may well have been a conflation with the earlier sighting in 1960 of the remains of Maurice Wilson. Wilson was a British eccentric and self-described mystic who declared in 1933 that he would fly to Mount Everest and then climb the mountain alone—despite the fact that he had no experience as an aviator or a mountaineer. No one knows exactly how he met his demise, but his remains were found by the 1935 British expedition, wrapped in a sleeping bag, at 22,000 feet below the North Col. The body was buried in a crevasse.

At the time of the interview, Xu insisted that he had never told anyone before then that he had spotted an old dead body high on Everest. And that probably would have remained an accepted fact were it not for one fanatical researcher who came across another reference to Xu's sighting while digging through decades-old newsletters from the St. Petersburg Alpine Club.

In 1965, the Russian Geographical Society, based in what was then Leningrad, invited Wang Fuzhou, another member of the 1960 team and one of the three who summited, to give a lecture about the first ascent of Everest's North Face. Toward the end of his presentation, Fuzhou remarked: "At an altitude of about 8,600 meters we found the corpse of a European." According to a translation of the newsletter, Fuzhou's remark set the audience aflame. The Russians knew their Everest history and understood immediately that Fuzhou was sharing something sensational—the first sighting of the lost British climbers. At the conclusion of the lecture, the floor was opened to questions. The very first one was: How did they know the body was that of a European?

"He was wearing braces," replied Fuzhou.

Braces, of course, is the British term for suspenders. There is a well-known photograph of Sandy Irvine, standing outside the Shekar Dzong Monastery in April of 1924, as the team neared the end of its 300-mile overland trek to the mountain. Irvine, wearing a felt hat and a long-sleeve button-down flannel shirt, stands in front of a lean-to with his hand resting on one of the oxygen sets. Hanging from his waist, dropped from his shoulders, is a pair of suspenders.

I held up my hand to stop Holzel, who was into his second Beck's. "Wait a second. So it was known in 1965 that the Chinese had found an old body high on the mountain, but then this sighting was lost to obscurity until 2001?"

"That's right. I mean, who reads the *St. Petersburg Alpine Club Journal*?" said Holzel.

"Well, you, apparently."

WHEN THE CHINESE made the first ascent of Everest's North Face in 1960, no one had set foot on that side of the mountain for more than twenty years. After the tragedy of 1924 and a subsequent strain on relations with Tibet, the British took a nine-year hiatus before launching four more Everest expeditions between 1933 and 1938. Despite strong teams stacked with legendary climbers like Percy Wyn-Harris, Eric Shipton, Frank Smythe, and Bill Tilman, no one was able to best Edward Norton's oxygenless high point from 1924. It was almost as if there were an invisible ceiling at 28,000 feet, protecting Everest's throne room from the scrabbling hands of mortal man. With each failed attempt, the mountain's mystique grew.

Nazi Germany's invasion of Poland on September 1, 1939, put Great Britain's Everest ambitions on hold for the next decade. By the time the Mount Everest Committee was ready to start ramping back up for another attempt, the geopolitical situation was drastically altered and the People's Republic of China, under the leadership of Mao Zedong, had taken control of Tibet and closed its borders to foreigners. Soon after, the British gained access to Everest's south side via Nepal, which offered a route deemed easier than the Northeast Ridge. And so, Westerners all but gave up on climbing the mountain from the Chinese side.

China is surrounded by mountain ranges that define its borders with neighboring countries, many of which were unfriendly in the years following World War Two. Taking a cue from the Soviets, the Chinese began organizing training camps with an eye toward developing a corps of elite mountain troops. In 1955, the Chinese adopted mountaineering as an official government-sanctioned sport, like gymnastics or track and field, and began organizing state-funded climbing camps. Both the Chinese and the Soviets had their eye on the ultimate prize, the first ascent of Everest's North Face. Plans were laid for a joint Sino-Soviet reconnaissance expedition in 1958 as a precursor to a full-blown attempt in 1959. To help bring China's best mountaineers quickly up to the level of their Russian counterparts, a number of Chinese were invited to attend Soviet training camps in the Caucasus Mountains and the Pamirs. At these camps the Chinese were trained by expert Russian climbers, including Vitaly Abalakov, the legendary mountaineer and inventor who had been arrested by the Soviet Ministry of Internal Affairs in the late 1930s for being a propagandist of Western climbing techniques.

The reconnaissance took place in November of 1958, but the expedition slated for the following year was scuttled after an uprising in Lhasa and the Dalai Lama's subsequent exile from Tibet. By the time the expedition was launched in the spring of 1960, relations between the Chinese and Soviet governments had soured. The team that showed up on the Rongbuk Glacier via a new 248-mile road was a purely Chinese affair. It was a quasi-military operation comprising 214 people, a third of whom were Tibetans. Most of the climbers on the team had only two years of mountaineering experience.

According to the official expedition report, four climbers set off on the morning of May 24 from their high camp at 8,500 meters (27,887 feet). (The report makes no mention of Xu Jing, probably because he turned back almost immediately.) The team included a lumberjack, a fireman, a geologist, and a Tibetan soldier. They soon arrived at the base of the Second Step, a sheer wall of vertical rock. Liu Lienman, the fireman, took the lead. As he had been taught by the Russians, he reached above his head and hammered a piton into a small fissure in the limestone. After clipping his rope to this anchor with a carabiner, he grappled with an icy, six- to eight-inch-wide crack capped with an overhanging block. Four times in a row, the crack spit him out and he swung onto the piton, which creaked as it took his weight but held firm. Defeated and utterly exhausted, Liu handed the lead to Qu Yinhua, the lumberjack. Qu managed to secure a second piton, but he too was soon foiled. Wang Fuzhou, the geologist, also had a go but fared no better.

Stymied less than 800 vertical feet from the summit, Liu had an idea. They would try a technique he had learned in fireman school. Qu took off his crampon-clad boots and stepped onto Liu's shoulders. According to the published account, Liu "trembled all over, short of breath, but he clenched his teeth and steadily stood up, with much heroic effort." From this shoulder stand, Qu could now step on the highest piton with his right foot and wedge his left leg into the crack. In this precarious position, with the cold steel searing through his stockings, Qu spent an hour hammering a foot-long piton into a horizontal crack at the limit of his reach. Using this anchor to tension his way around the overhang, he clawed onto a small ledge and then scrambled to the top of the Second Step. After tying his rope to a horn of rock, he slipped his frozen feet back into his boots, which he had pulled up with his rope. The Second Step, a mere three body lengths of climbing, had taken three hours to surmount. It was now 3 P.M. and the gauges on their oxygen cylinders indicated they were almost out of gas.

But merely running out of daylight or oxygen would not deter the Chinese from pushing on. Far too much was at stake. They had to continue, "knowing it was a matter of honor for the whole nation, which was watching us closely," recounts Fuzhou in the book *Footprints on the Peaks: Mountaineering in China*. "We would rather die than retreat like cowards." Gazing upward, they surveyed what now lay between them and the top of the world. The ridge here was broad and mostly devoid of snow, having been picked clean by the relentless blasting of the jet stream. Ahead lay one more small rock step above which rose a triangular snowfield gleaming in the sun.

The point of the triangle, which they assumed to be the summit, stood out starkly against the blue sky. The top was tantalizingly close. Then, another snag. Liu, utterly spent from his efforts to surmount the Second Step, was faltering, falling to the ground every few steps. His partners faced a stark dilemma: Abandon the summit and the hopes and dreams of an entire nation or leave Liu at 28,500 feet with nothing for shelter but the clothes on his back. They didn't speak about it, but all four men knew that he would almost certainly die from exposure during the night. In the end, Liu saved his friends from the burden of signing his death warrant by insisting that he would stay behind while they continued to the summit. From his open bivouac below the Third Step, he watched his teammates clamber upward until they disappeared in the dark.

Without headlamps or lanterns of any kind, Fuzhou, Qu, and Gonbu, the Tibetan soldier, groped their way forward, sometimes on their hands and knees, guided by nothing more than the twinkling of the star-filled sky above. The wind was light, but the temperature had dropped to minus 30°C. When the snow slope steepened just below the ridge, they traversed west around a shoulder, then picked their way up a wall of loose rock. At 28,970 feet, less than 100 feet from the summit, their oxygen ran out. Fuzhou turned to his teammates. "We are shouldering the glorious task of storming the summit. Can we turn back?"

"Press on," urged Qu and Gonbu.

At 2:20 A.M., the three men staggered onto an "oval-shaped crest between rock and snow." The ground dropped away in every direction. "The top!" shouted Gonbu. "Another step and we're down in Nepal." In the dim light cast by the Milky Way, they could see that every peak surrounding them was lower than where they now stood. It had been nineteen hours since they left their high camp. They had not ingested a single morsel nor a sip of water beyond some dried mutton and ginseng soup taken for breakfast the previous day. In the darkness, it seemed pointless to attempt a photo. Fuzhou pulled his diary from inside his coat and scribbled a few words with the stub of a pencil that he gripped in his bare, frozen fingers: "Wang Fuzhou, Gonbu and Qu Yinhua of the Chinese Mountaineering Team topped the world's highest peak at 4:20 A.M., May 25, 1960" (the Chinese used Beijing time on their expedition, despite being two time zones to the west, a practice they still follow today). Gonbu reached into his pack and withdrew a plaster bust of Mao Zedong, which he wrapped in the Chinese national flag and placed, along with the page from Fuzhou's diary, under a rock. Somewhere in the vicinity of the summit, they grabbed nine small rocks to bring back to Peking as souvenirs for Mao and then headed down.

At first light, the three exhausted men were inching their way down the triangular snow slope above the Third Step when they spotted Liu below. He saw them too, raised his arm and waved. It took the summiteers another hour to reach their comrade, who, though wretchedly cold, was still very much alive and overjoyed to see his teammates. Everyone hugged and when Liu heard that they had made the summit, tears filled his eyes. Wang Fuzhou, Qu Yinhua, and Gonbu were similarly moved, even more so when they saw the note that Liu had scribbled in the middle of the night.

"Dear Comrade Wang and others, I'm sorry for not having fulfilled my duty. Here are the candies and some oxygen for you on your way back. Hoping people will hear of your victory soon. Goodbye!"

Liu had saved what little food he had and barely used his oxygen during the night, even though it might save his life, because he knew that his partners would need it when they returned from their ordeal.

Now that it was light enough to see, Qu pulled a small movie camera from his pack and shot a few frames, including a panorama of the surrounding peaks and the view looking back toward the summit, the only photographic documentation from the entire summit push.

THE CHINESE ANNOUNCED to the world that they had placed three men on the summit on May 25, 1960, thus completing the third ascent of Mount Everest (the Swiss, who had almost summited in 1952, had put four men on top from the south side in 1956). The first ascent of the North Face, also known to the British as Mallory's Route, had finally been completed—thirty-nine years after it was first attempted. The news was initially celebrated in England. Lord Nathan, president of the Royal Geographical Society, wrote: "The Chinese ascent of Chomo Lungma has aroused the admiration of all, not only in this country but throughout the world, for the splendid skill and courage of the Chinese mountaineers. It is an achievement which will remain forever a landmark in the history of mountain exploration."

But when the official account of the expedition was published, laced as it was with nationalistic chest thumping, the typically understated British climbing establishment was less enthusiastic. The Chinese report stated that "we must in the first place attribute our victory to the leadership of the Communist Party and the unrivalled superiority of the socialist system of our country. Without all this, we, the ordinary workers, peasants and soldiers, could never have succeeded in climbing the world's highest peak. The victory of the Chinese mountaineering expedition is also due to the fact that we had followed the strategic thinking of Mao Tze-tung, that is to scorn difficulties strategically, while paying full attention to them tactically."

In an editorial about the Chinese ascent in the *American Alpine Journal*, G. O. Dyhrenfurth wrote, "One must never forget that nowadays, unfortunately, the summit of Mount Everest lies on the front of the Cold War." A few British pundits took things a step further by casting doubt on the veracity of the Chinese claim to have actually attained the summit, which lacked photographic proof. Today, most Everest historians are more willing to give the Chinese the benefit of the doubt. Analysis of the film has verified that the climbers were within 500 feet of the top, above the Second Step. "When you read the original testimony of the summit climbers from 1960, it tallies very well with what we know about the terrain," says Hemmleb. "So there's a very good probability that they did indeed summit."

In the hearts and minds of the Chinese people, the first ascent of Everest's North Face occupied the same sacred psychic space as the moon landing would for America. The *People's Daily*, one of the largest newspapers in China, and a key promoter of propaganda for the Communist Party, ran a thirty-page special supplement about the expedition. The only other story ever given this much attention was in 1964, when China tested its first atomic bomb. At the time, Western pundits casting doubt on the 1960 ascent would have galled the Chinese bitterly and provoked even greater nationalist fervor. Hemmleb never asked the Chinese climbers specifically how they felt about their epic climb being doubted, but he says the men projected "a certain aura of self-assurance." They knew what they had done. But the fact that the Chinese laid plans for a follow-up expedition in 1967, on which they specifically planned to reach the summit in daylight hours, suggests that they had not entirely shrugged off the criticism.

Throughout the ensuing decades, the Chinese have maintained a proprietary claim on the north side of Everest, not only because it lies within China's geographical boundaries but, more important, because it represents for them a triumph of Chinese culture and the communist system. Even before the climb, China and Nepal were embroiled in a bitter territorial dispute over ownership of the roof of the world. Both nations claimed Mount Everest as sovereign territory. As George H. W. Bush referenced in his letter to Tom Holzel, the Chinese had never officially acknowledged the British first ascent of Everest in May of 1953.

So closely does China guard its 1960 achievement that the Chinese Mountaineering Association (CMA), now known as the Chinese Tibet Mountaineering Association (CTMA), has repeatedly denied that any old dead bodies were found in 1960, even though two members of the Chinese expedition, Xu Jing and Wang Fuzhou, have said otherwise. The Chinese "have always been extremely sensitive to the Mallory and Irvine scenario," says Holzel, "because if they [the British] got there first, it would relegate the Chinese to being second. And this is totally unacceptable."

A member of Holzel's 1986 expedition, an American who wishes to remain anonymous (to avoid getting blacklisted by the Chinese government) spoke with a Chinese official who flatly denied the existence of any prewar British bodies high up on the mountain. But later, when the official was out of earshot of his superiors, he quietly admitted that it was CTMA policy to discourage speculation about finding a British body on the mountain because it was known that Mallory or Irvine probably had a camera, and if so, it could prove that the Chinese were not the first to summit from the north.

In 2008, Qu Yinhua recounted his story of climbing the Second Step in his stocking feet to Jochen Hemmleb. At the end of the interview, Hemmleb asked Qu if he could see his feet. Qu, who was then in his mid-seventies (he died in 2016), removed his sneakers and socks. His feet were devastated. He had lost all ten toes and parts of his heels, leaving little more than stumps that he had been hobbling around on for almost fifty years. The old scars had broken apart, leaving the wounds raw and in need of constant care. "He must have been in a lot of pain," Hemmleb says.

On a research visit to China in 1998, Audrey Salkeld asked Qu if he thought Mallory and Irvine could have climbed Everest in 1924. Qu said no but that he wished they had. "If the British had climbed the Second Step in 1924," he said, "I would not be in this condition today."

HOLZEL HANDED ME the nearly 100-year-old camera. "This is the Kodak VPK," he said. "I bought this on eBay twenty years ago for twenty-six dollars."

I had been taking pictures of Holzel and his Everest artifacts with my own camera—an electronic gizmo called the Sony RX 100. When I brought the two cameras together, one in each hand, they were about the same size and weight. The big difference between the two was that the ancient VPK was entirely mechanical. It had no battery and was therefore impervious to the cold and, according to Holzel, nearly impossible to break. He grabbed the camera back from me and pulled outward on its front face. "Check this out," he said to Thom and me. The VPK opened like an accordion, revealing the bellows, a flexible, paper-like material that allowed the lens to be properly positioned. Holzel flipped the camera over and showed us another neat feature, an "autographic" flap on the back through which caption information could be engraved directly onto the negative with a tiny metal stylus.

Holzel had brought us down to his basement, where a giant

bookcase covered one of the walls. The middle shelves were stacked with vintage hardcover Everest books, many of which were first editions: *Everest: The Unfinished Adventure*; *Through Tibet to Everest*; *Mount Everest: The Reconnaissance, 1921*; *The Assault on Mount Everest, 1922*; *The Fight for Everest 1924*; *Everest 1933*; *Everest 1938*, to name a few. An old pair of straight-sided Rossignol skis framed an arch between two more bookcases that sat perpendicular to the walls on either side. Ducking under the skis, he led us over to a gun rack that leaned against the back wall. Above it, on a shelf, sat an old rusted oxygen cylinder and a scrappy-looking stuffed crow that I had to ask him about.

"Have you ever heard the saying 'eating crow'?" asked Holzel.

"Yeah, of course," I said.

"Do you know where the saying comes from?"

Thom and I both shook our heads.

"It comes from the fact that crow tastes horrible—at least, that's what everyone says. But I hate this kind of thing, where something becomes fact, just because someone says it. So, I shot a crow, plucked off its feathers, and fried up the breast."

"And . . . ?"

"It tasted like shit."

THOM HAD TOLD ME a bit about Holzel's legendary photograph of Everest's Yellow Band, the primary reason for our visit to his home. The black-and-white print was eight feet long and three feet tall and stretched across one wall of the basement. Holzel had obtained the image from BSF Swissphoto. It was taken in 1984 from a Learjet that flew over Mount Everest at 44,500 feet during a mapping project organized by Bradford Washburn, an esteemed mountaineer and longtime director of Boston's Museum of Science. Swissphoto made Holzel a scan of the negative, which he then took to a large-format printing facility. The reproduction hung on the wall in front of us.

I could see the Yellow Band clearly. It is composed of various layers of limestone that formed eons ago on the bed of an ancient ocean called the Tethys Sea. From the air, it looks like a layer cake, with horizontally banded walls of rock sandwiched between snow-covered ledges. Holzel's photo doesn't show it, but the angle of the face is about as steep as a 12/12-pitch roof, which is 45 degrees and too steep to walk on without ropes or scaffolding. In a few key spots, vertically oriented gullies incise the horizontal layers. These gullies allow climbers to move from one ledge system to the next.

Scouring his photo with a magnifying glass, Holzel painstakingly charted out every possible route that Xu Jing could have taken on his descent through the Yellow Band in 1960. Then, using a process of elimination, he crossed out the lines that pinched off above cliffs or appeared to lead in directions inconsistent with Xu's account. In the end, he was left with a single line through the Yellow Band that offered the most likely direct route back down to the Chinese Camp VI.

The resolution of Holzel's print wasn't high enough to actually see a body in the terrain, but there were obvious human-scale shapes in the pixelated black-and-white image, small as they were even on this large print. After days of bleary-eyed study with a microscope, Holzel had what he calls a eureka moment. Inside a twenty-foot-long concavity, which he assumed to be the gully described by Xu, he spotted a feature that he named "the Red Slash." It was five millimeters long, which on his print scaled up to the height of a man, and it was oriented in a manner consistent with the account given by Xu. Could this be the long-lost body of Sandy Irvine?

I moved in closer to see if I could discern the Red Slash. Sure enough, there it was, a fuzzy dark blob. Thom had told me about this "blob" a few weeks ago, and I had dismissed it then as nothing more than the product of an old man's overactive imagination. Looking at it now, it was still a blob, indistinguishable from thousands of other similar-looking anomalies strewn about the photo.

"The Red Slash must be taken with a grain of salt," Holzel said.

Maybe more than a grain, I thought to myself.

But I had to credit Holzel for identifying a possible route that Xu might have taken through the Yellow Band on his descent in 1960. At the least, it highlighted an area that seemed worthy of a thorough search. Holzel insisted that, to date, no Mallory-Irvine searchers had ever been to the exact location of the Red Slash. And it was this location for which Thom and I now had precise GPS coordinates.

"What odds are you giving that he's actually here?" I asked.

"He can't *not* be there."

THE NEXT MORNING, Thom and I sat in my car in Holzel's driveway. We had a long drive ahead of us, but for some reason we just sat there, staring into a forest of white pines behind the condo complex. I looked over at Thom, who was slumped over in the passenger seat. One of my last recollections of the night was Holzel, still eschewing our liquor, grabbing a crystal decanter of pinot grigio from his liquor cabinet. In the bottom of the carafe floated a vibrant green, star-shaped leaf with long pointy petals. Holzel said it was woodruff, a hallucinogenic herb he harvests from the same patch of woods we were staring into now. "It's an old German folk recipe," he explained. Not long afterward, Thom started talking about how he was going to channel the spirits of Mallory and Irvine to help solve the mystery—and, if we did find the camera, how he would smuggle it out of China in his ass.

In the car, Thom broke the silence. "I'm getting the feeling that you're not going to be able to walk away from this." He locked me with his hooded, bloodshot eyes, and held out his hand. I nodded slowly and took it.

CHAPTER THREE

Haut Monde

THE BATTLEGROUND WAS a twenty-mile-long strip running along the banks of the Somme River in northern France. Nearly 300,000 troops were faced off across an apocalyptic no-man's-land, with the Imperial German Army hunkered down in a deeply fortified, three-tiered system of trenches protected by miles of barbed wire on the eastern side of the front. The Allies were similarly dug in to the west, a few miles outside the village of Albért.

It was the last week of June in 1916 and George Mallory's unit, the 40th Siege Battery, had been bombarding the Germans for days to pave the way for Britain's first major offensive in the Great War. "It was very noisy—field batteries again firing over our heads (of course there are plenty in front of us too) and most annoying of them a 60 pounder which has a nasty trick of blowing out the lamps with its vigorous blast," Mallory wrote to his wife, Ruth, on June 25. Mallory was "full of hope" that the weeklong bombardment had cowed the Germans.

The order to attack came at 7:30 on the morning of July 1. As 120,000 Allied troops—including regiments from England, Scotland, France, Australia, New Zealand, India, South Africa, and Canada—swarmed out of their trenches in wave after wave, Mallory's six-inch howitzer fired a lifting barrage intended to prevent the Germans from resupplying their front line. From the clay bank where Mallory's battery was positioned, it was difficult to see what was happening on the battlefield apart from general chaos. Mallory described his vantage to Ruth as "the rim of a seething cauldron."

As the battle raged around him, Mallory worked in bits and spurts on a long letter to Ruth. They had been married now for almost two years, and their daughter, Clare, born in September of 1915, was less than a year old. Mallory and Ruth had met at a dinner party in 1913, and not long afterward, they acted alongside each other in a community play. "It was more than love at first sight," writes Wade Davis in *Into the Silence*. "For Mallory it was as if a dam had burst and the impounded emotions of a young lifetime had found immediate release." Ruth's father, a widower and successful architect, invited Mallory to join his family (Ruth was the middle of three sisters) on an Easter vacation to Venice in the spring of 1914 and Mallory proposed soon thereafter. "It's too too wonderful that you should love me and give me such happiness as I never dreamt of," wrote Mallory at the time.

The subject of Mallory's letter on this day, though, was not his love for Ruth or his experience fighting on the Western Front, but rather the religious upbringing of their daughter Clare. "Firstly, what is religion?" he scribbled as the earth shook with the incessant din of battle. "How soon, I wonder, would a child of ordinary intelligence ask the question, if left to itself, 'What happens to us when we die?'"

Ruth was herself a devout Christian, having turned to religion at age fifteen after losing her mother to pneumonia. When she was eight months pregnant with Clare, Ruth wrote to Mallory, "I wonder dear how much we shall keep up with the times and be able to be proper companions for our children. Let's try and remember that they must educate us as well as we educating them then I think we may not go so far wrong, we mustn't hate every new thing that comes along until its got old."

While Mallory was contemplating existential questions, the Royal Newfoundland Regiment, stationed nearby at Beaumont-Hamel, awaited its orders while watching the slaughter of the first two infantry waves. The no-man's-land in this section of the front was incised with a Y-shaped ravine that naturally favored the enemy, and it soon became clear that the battle-hardened German army had come through the bombardment more or less unscathed. The trenches on the Allied side that led to the front were now so clogged with the dead and dying that when the Newfies were ordered to attack at 8:45 A.M., they had no choice but to advance on the surface. "The wire had been cut in our front line and bridges laid across the trench the night before," wrote Private Anthony Stacey. "This was a death trap for our boys as the enemy just set their sights of their machine guns on the gaps in the barbed wire and fired."

Most of the Newfies died within minutes of leaving their trenches. The few who did manage to make it down the grassy slope leading to the no-man's-land headed for the only cover they could see—a ragged apple tree. They had no way of knowing that their bodies would be silhouetted as they approached the tree, making them easy targets for the Germans. Only a handful of brave men made it past "Danger Tree" to reach the German trenches, where they discovered that the barbed wire was still intact, contrary to what they had been promised. Most of the men who made it this far were gunned down as they became entangled in the wire.

By late morning, wounded troops began to pass through gaps in the artillery line all around Mallory's position, but the true extent of the bloodbath was not yet clear. All told, 20,000 Allied troops would lose their lives that day—one in six who crawled out of the trenches. At the height of the massacre, a dozen men were killed every minute. But no unit paid a higher price than the Royal Newfoundland Regiment. Of the 780 Newfies who took part in the advance, 324 were killed or reported missing and another 386 were wounded—a casualty rate of 91 percent. At roll call the next day, only 68 men could muster for duty.

MALLORY DIDN'T SHARE MUCH about his feelings as the Battle of the Somme continued and finally ground itself out, but the experience surely hardened him to death. "I don't object to corpses so long as they are fresh," he wrote to Ruth shortly before the battle ended on November 18, 1916. (All told, the five-month-long battle would inflict more than a million casualties, during which time the Allies would push their front line forward by a mere six miles.) Mallory had seen so much death that he told Ruth he sometimes spoke with the dead: "'Between you and me is all the difference between life and death. But this is an accepted fact that men are killed and I have no more to learn about that from you, and the difference is no greater than that because your jaw hangs and your flesh changes color and blood oozes from your wounds.'"

When the Armistice was declared two years later, on November 11, 1918—symbolically timed to coincide with the eleventh hour of the eleventh day of the eleventh month—Mallory celebrated at an officers' club in Cambrai, France, with his older brother, Trafford, who had served as a squadron commander in the Royal Air Force. "Life presents itself very much to me as a gift," he wrote to his father a few days later. "If I haven't escaped so many chances of death as plenty of others, still it is surprising to find myself a survivor." Mallory had avoided the first two years of the war because Frank Fletcher, the headmaster at Charterhouse, a boarding school where Mallory taught history and mathematics, had full discretion over his military eligibility and refused to let him go. Fletcher, who rock climbed himself and was thus well aware that Mallory ranked among England's finest practitioners of the sport, may well have saved his life.

During the deadly spring offensive of 1918, during which nearly every soldier who could stand was ordered to the front, Mallory was assigned to an artillery training course in Lydd, England, where he lived with his family in a cottage by the seaside for more than half a year. That spring and summer, as the Allies, bolstered by the newly arrived Americans, fought to repel a massive attack by the Germans in Belleau Wood and Aisne, France, Mallory and Ruth went on a climbing holiday to the isle of Skye in Scotland. When he was finally sent back to France, he was assigned to a unit well back from the front lines, where he remained until the end of the war.

While plain luck certainly played into Mallory's survival of the war, he might have had more than one guardian angel looking out for him. Wade Davis speculates that it may have been Eddie Marsh, an explorer, polymath, scholar, translator, and patron of the arts who served for many years as Winston Churchill's private secretary. Marsh, who was an influential member of London's underground homosexual community, first met Mallory in 1912 and immediately fell under his spell. "Besides the great beauty of face, I think he has enormous charm of mind and character," he would later write to the poet Rupert Brooke. According to Davis, Marsh was responsible for the fact that Mallory was assigned to the 515th Siege Battery, well back from the front line, for the final months of the war.

When he first met Marsh, Mallory had recently graduated with a history degree from Cambridge University. At the time, he had fallen in with the Bloomsbury set, a group of London intellectuals and writers who would often gather on weekends at Pen-y-Pass in Wales, where they would climb the surrounding cliffs, then retire to a local inn to drink, smoke their pipes, and philosophize deep into the night. By most accounts, Mallory struggled to keep up intellectually with the fertile minds that made up the Bloomsbury set. Lytton Strachey described Mallory's intelligence as "unremarkable," but he was a star amongst them nonetheless because he climbed like a god and looked like one too. Strachey evidently had a massive crush on Mallory. In a letter to some friends, he wrote: "Mon Dieu—George Mallory—When that's been written, what more need be said? . . . I'm wafted over seas of amaranth, plunged up to the eyes in all the spices of Arabia, and lulled in the bosom of eternal spring."

Like many of his contemporaries in the Bloomsbury set, Mallory aspired to be a writer, and in 1912 he was struggling to complete his first book, a biography of James Boswell. The book opens with the following passage: "The responsibility for upwards of 300 pages in print is a burden which my unaccustomed conscience cannot easily bear, and by accepting it I lose for ever the unassailable dignity of private criticism . . . I shall not apologise for writing a dull book by explaining in what manner it is interesting. I had thought of doing something of the sort, but at the present moment that course presents insuperable difficulties." *Boswell the Biographer* did not win a large audience when it was published later that year.

AFTER THE ARMISTICE, in the spring of 1919, Mallory was back at Charterhouse. He found the environment suffocating; those who had not fought in the war could never understand the trauma of soldiers who had, a fact that tore British society apart. Mallory found his orientation, as he always had, in the vertical world, and he was soon climbing regularly again at Pen-y-Pass in Wales. In the summer of 1919, he was back in the Alps after a seven-year hiatus, where he had first cut his teeth as an alpinist during his secondary-school years.

That spring, Captain John Noel had captured the imagination of the British mountaineering establishment during a lecture at the Royal Geographical Society in which he recounted a clandestine expedition to Tibet in 1913 that brought him to within forty miles of the base of Mount Everest. Noel said to the assembled crowd, "Now that the poles have been reached . . . the next and equally important task is the exploration and mapping of Mount Everest."

Mallory wasn't at the meeting, but through his Alpine Club connections, he was undoubtedly well aware that plans for an Everest reconnaissance expedition were now underway. When the Mount Everest Committee was formed in January of 1921, Percy Farrar, president of the Alpine Club, immediately put forth Mallory's name. "It looks like Everest will really be tried this summer," he wrote Mallory on January 22. "Party would leave early April and get back in October. Any aspirations?"

Mallory was looking for his ticket out of Charterhouse, but what about Ruth and his young family? When the war ended, he had written to Ruth: "What a wonderful life we will have together. What a lovely thing we *must* make of such a gift. I want to lose all harshness of jagged nerves, to be above all gentle." Ruth had also recently given birth to their third child, John—the son Mallory had always wanted. Clare was now five, Beridge was three, and Ruth was feeling less than generous about giving up her husband for yet another dangerous enterprise that would take him away from home for half a year. Mallory was unsure himself and reluctant to put such a burden on his young family, until his old friend and climbing partner, Geoffrey Winthrop Young, visited him and Ruth at their home in Godalming and impressed upon them how Everest could be the springboard for Mallory's next career as a professional explorer, writer, and lecturer. After a brief twenty-minute pitch, Ruth relented and gave Mallory her blessing to go.

LOWTHER LODGE, a sprawling three-story redbrick Victorian-era compound festooned with oversize chimneys, presides over Hyde Park and the Albert Memorial in London's Kensington district. The building has been home to the Royal Geographical Society for more than a century.

When the RGS added a new wing in 2004, it chose to vitalize its public image with a striking, avant-garde glass pavilion. And it was through this new portal on Exhibition Road that I entered the world's most venerable geographical institution on a sunny January morning in 2019.

I found my way to the Foyle Reading Room, where I was greeted by Jan Turner, a chipper fiftysomething librarian in a purple down vest. When I walked through the door, she was reading a membership ledger that had *1880* written on its cover. Turner handed me an application. "Depending on how long you're going to be here, perhaps it might make sense to join the society," she said. The society has Fellows—she didn't know how many—who vote and go to annual meetings and such. To become a Fellow, one must do "important work in the field of geography or exploration" and be recommended by at least two current Fellows. But there are also about 14,000 nonvoting members whose ranks she was inviting me to join.

Turner said that many of the original Fellows of the society, which was founded in 1830, were naval and military officers who explored and surveyed in their spare time while posted in far-flung corners of the British Empire. The RGS has never been an academic institution per se, but it was directly responsible, through its long history of sponsoring exploratory expeditions and geographical research, for filling in many of the remaining blanks on the map. (Of course, Western "exploration" of the world often came at considerable cost to local populations in Africa, Australia, and many other parts of the British Empire.) Today, the mission of the RGS is to advance our collective knowledge of world geography and to support geographers across the world. The headquarters also serves as a repository for the society's Special Collection, which includes 250,000 books, a million maps, and countless photos, diaries, letters, and artifacts. All of these items are available to view five days a week by anyone who walks in off the street and is willing to pay the £10 admission fee.

When I told Turner what I was looking for, she handed me a thick, spiral-bound notebook with a sticker on its spine that read:

Archives
Special Collection
Everest Expeditions
1920s, 1930s, 1950s

Page after page, the notebook listed the items in the Everest special collection. I found my way to the 1924 expedition and made my own inventory of half a dozen boxes of photos, various correspondence of the Mount Everest Committee, and all the artifacts recovered following the discovery of Mallory's body in 1999. As directed, I handed my list to another librarian, an older, gray-haired man named David McNeil who was standing at a large table studying maps of Liberia. He seemed slightly annoyed when I handed him the list, but he took it and headed out a door in the back of the room.

While I waited, I took a closer look around. The room was U-shaped and dominated by a bank of outward-tilting windows, which made me feel like I was standing on the bridge of a ship. The view, rather than of the sea, was of a sunken courtyard fringed with greenery that dangled from some kind of hanging garden above. Below the windshield on a long shelf sat busts of famous explorers and geographers, including David Livingstone, Richard Burton, Claudius Ptolemaeus, Gertrude Bell, and Ernest Shackleton. On the wall hung a magnificent black-and-white photograph of Makalu, the world's fifth-tallest mountain. In its corner, written in pencil, was a photo credit—*George Mallory*. The room was oddly quiet, considering it lay adjacent to a busy London street. Besides me, there were only two other patrons, both white-haired old men sitting on either side of a table with books and maps fanned out around them.

McNeil soon reappeared pushing a wheeled cart covered in gray paperboard boxes. One by one he placed them on the metal table in front of me, then pulled out a pair of white cotton gloves. He slipped them on, opened the lid of the biggest box and ceremoniously lifted out what may be the world's most famous boot.

"Wow, is that Mallory's?"

McNeil nodded.

"Can I hold it?"

McNeil peered at me over his glasses, as if to say, *Why do you think I'm wearing these special gloves?* But said nothing.

I shook my head, marveling at the idea that anyone would have tried to climb the highest mountain on Earth in this boot. It was leather, and apart from a thick layer of felt sandwiched between the sole and the upper, it appeared to have no insulation. In fact, it looked almost identical to a pair of Dachstein hiking boots I wore on summer jaunts in the Adirondack and White Mountains. The toe was curled slightly upward and the sole rimmed with special V-shaped "boot nails" hammered into the leather to give traction on snow and ice. The side of the boot had a green, copper-colored tint, which I thought might be mold. "That's chromium metal," said McNeil, who had noticed me studying it. "They used it back in those days as a leather preservative." I wondered if Mallory had applied it himself after he purchased the boots. The stuff must work well, because apart from a scuff mark on the inside of the toe, the leather was in remarkably good condition.

What struck me most, though, was that it looked to be my size. I wanted to slip it on and see how it felt. Then, of course, I pictured McNeil chasing me in his white gloves as I clodhopped across the room, the nails clippity-clopping on the floor. We moved on to another box. McNeil removed more items, including a leather sheath that once covered the pick of Mallory's ice axe, a bone-handled pocketknife, and a plexiglass case containing a round-faced watch rimmed with tiny dimples. This, I realized, was the watch that Thom found in Mallory's pocket in 1999 when he and Andy Politz had returned to the body. There were rust marks on the face where the hour and minute hands used to lie. Everest historians have debated these markings ad nauseum, but I don't think most of them know that Thom took a photo of the watch before the hour hand fell off. I had seen the image, which showed clearly that the time was around 1:25—but A.M. or P.M., no one could know. McNeil explained that the watch had to remain in the case because it was radioactive. The face was coated in radioluminescent paint containing radium-226. McNeil said that if we turned the lights off, the watch would still glow a milky green.

There was one last box of artifacts, but McNeil wasn't authorized to show it to me. He passed me off to another guy with a beard, who didn't give his name but identified himself as "the conservator."

"There's nothing too interesting in here," he said, putting his hand on top of the box where *Handle with Care* was written in bold type. "Why don't we skip this one." His reticence only made me more keen to see what was inside.

I played my best role as a pushy American climber, and after a few minutes, the conservator donned his own pair of special white gloves. Clearly annoyed, he daintily peeled back layers of tissue paper before lifting out some random bits of string and a clothing label that read *W. F. Paine 72 High Street Godalming*, and beneath, in small red letters, *G. Mallory*. Next came a pair of heavily rusted nail scissors, and then in the bottom of the box, a short length of thin white rope.

"This was tied to George Mallory when they found him," he said solemnly. "It's very delicate."

Indeed, I could see tiny white flecks flaking off the rope as he laid it on the table in front of me. Now I understood why he had been reluctant to show it to me: The rope was disintegrating before our eyes. It was about as thick around as a pencil and comprised of three braided strands with a red thread woven inside, which I could only presume was a wear marker. Jochen Hemmleb had told me that the rope was made of flax and was originally 100 feet long. (After his 2010 Irvine search expedition, Hemmleb had a rope company create a replica and test its tensile strength, with appalling results.)

I simply couldn't imagine using something this flimsy, even brand-new, to climb anything—let alone, technical rock above 8,000 meters on Mount Everest.

THREE AND A HALF DAYS LATER, I staggered out of the RGS with a pile of notes and a mild headache. Jumping on the Tube, I headed across London to the headquarters of the Alpine Club. I knew I had found it when I saw what looked like a storefront with a bank of picture windows covered in bracing photos of mountaineers on high peaks. One of the windows was filled with the organization's logo, which was just *Alpine Club* and *1857* written above in small type. Most countries with mountains have a national alpine club—there's the American Alpine Club, the Japanese Alpine Club, the New Zealand Alpine Club, etc.—but in the UK, where alpinism was invented, it's just Alpine Club. The club's mission, more mountaineering specific than that of the RGS, is to support its members in the active pursuit of exploratory climbing objectives throughout the world's great ranges.

I had called ahead, but I still caught the librarian, Nigel Buckley, in the middle of his lunch. Buckley was a bookish young man with a neatly trimmed hipster beard and wire-rimmed glasses. I could tell at a glance that he was a climber, simply by the way he held himself—loose-limbed, his shoulders slightly hunched. He was tall and thin, with long arms, and wore a tight-fitting burgundy cashmere sweater. "So what can I help you with?" he asked. I told him I was visiting from the States and had long been a fan of the club. I was doing some historical research on the early Everest expeditions and had heard that it had some Everest artifacts, including Sandy Irvine's ice axe. I had seen a photo of the tool online, hanging up on the wall in a glass case.

"Well, you've caught me at a good time," said Buckley. "Let's have a look around and see what we can find."

Our first stop was the lecture hall. "Check this out," he said, leading me to an old oxygen cylinder hanging from a wooden stand. "This is one of the original 1924 oxygen bottles. We signal the start of every lecture like this." Buckley took a wooden mallet and struck the metal cylinder. The sound that reverberated through the room reminded me of a Tibetan singing bowl. When it was quiet again, I told him about the hands-off policy at the Royal Geographical Society.

"Sometimes I'm a little embarrassed at how lax we are here," he said, "but that's why we have this stuff, so people can enjoy it." As Buckley looked on, I stroked the oxygen cylinder. Just because I could.

"Who sleeps down here?" I asked as we entered a bunk room in the basement of the building.

"Whoever," replied Buckley. "You could if you want." As I contemplated whether I could get out of my hotel reservation, Buckley disappeared into what looked like a storeroom and emerged two minutes later holding an ancient-looking ice axe. Then, without ceremony or even a hint of squeamishness, he handed it to me. Just like that, and without any white gloves, I was holding the ice axe that Sandy Irvine had carried on June 8, 1924. The axe was heavy, maybe five pounds or so, and about three-and-a-half feet long. The wood was dark and grainy and speckled with cuts and nicks. I could feel the vertical striations under my hand where the high-altitude ultraviolet rays had eaten away the wood along its annular rings during the nine years it sat out on the Northeast Ridge. The head of the axe was tarnished, but I could still make out the maker's mark: WILLISCH OF TAESCH.

Buckley pointed to a spot on the shaft where three nicks, each spaced about a centimeter apart, had been deeply carved into the wood. "Those hatch marks are how they eventually figured out it was Sandy's axe," said Buckley. Lower on the shaft, about eight inches above the metal spike on the end, Buckley pointed out another nick. "We think he carved this one to remind himself where to hold the axe when he was swinging it."

I spent the rest of the afternoon in the Alpine Club's library, rooting around in its archives, where I eventually found the personal papers of Noel Odell. Odell was the one member of the early British Everest expeditions with whom I had long felt a personal affinity. In 1927, three years after he had last seen Mallory and Irvine questing into the unknown, he was invited to serve as a visiting geology lecturer at Harvard University. For the next three years, he lived in Cambridge, Massachusetts, and in addition to his teaching duties, he served as a mentor to the fledgling Harvard Mountaineering Club. On weekends he would take students on climbing trips up to New Hampshire, and in winter their destination was often Mount Washington, where he taught them how to ice climb in Huntington

Ravine. Odell's Gully, to this day, remains a classic ice route, and it was a touchstone climb for me when I was cutting my teeth as a young alpinist.

As the last person to see Mallory and Irvine alive, Odell's name is inextricably linked with Everest's greatest mystery. However, there is little in the written record about his long and varied life as a geologist, climber, and explorer. A one-page obituary written by Charles Houston, the renowned American high-altitude physiologist and mountaineer who first met Odell as an undergrad at Harvard states, "He was a gentle man. Generous, mild, modest and seldom ruffled or angry . . . of the old school of climbers, tweedy, casual, low-key and more concerned with joy than triumph . . . Though he never sought fame and fortune he was known and loved all over the world as a distinguished father figure, far more interested in others' activities than in talking of his own." The obituary ends with a story from 1975 when Odell, at eighty-four, spoke to a mountain medicine symposium in Yosemite. He projected glass slides of the 1924 Everest expedition—without ever mentioning his own role in the story.

Odell's papers were organized into folders by year. The first folder I opened was full of letters concerning the ice axe I had just held. Percy Wyn-Harris brought the tool back to London in 1933, and it found a home at the Alpine Club, where it has resided ever since. Odell examined it shortly afterward, and according to his notes, he was the first to notice the three hatch marks. At the time, no one knew if the tool belonged to Mallory or Irvine. Odell, a mentor for young Sandy, was determined to find out. He wrote to both Ruth Mallory and Willie Irvine, Sandy's father, in February of 1934. The originals of their replies were in the folder. On a piece of yellowed stationery that read WESTBROOK, GODALMING in red type across the top, Ruth wrote: "As far as I know, George never marked his things with three lines"—here she drew the three horizontal lines one over the other—"or with any other mark. So I should think it very probable that the axe was Irvine's." Ruth went on to say that her daughter Clare, who was now eighteen, was becoming "a very promising climber" and was leading others up many of the easier routes in Wales.

Willie Irvine apologized for taking so long to respond (ten days), explaining that the delay was because he had been investigating the matter. "Both Hugh and Evelyn think that Sandy used the triple nick III, but they are not certain. I, too, have a feeling that it is familiar—on the other hand, this may simply be an example of 'suggestion'!" Willie goes on to say that he had searched through Sandy's things, including his skis, the ice axe he used on an expedition to Spitsbergen, and his dairies, but could find no example of the marking. He said that his son generally used a monogram, which he drew on the page. It was clear from his letter that Willie was keenly interested in determining if the axe was indeed his son's.

SEVERAL INCHES OF wet snow had fallen overnight. The pavement was slick as I pulled off the motorway, heedful that I was driving on the wrong side of the road in a subcompact rental car that I was downshifting with my left hand. Despite the dreariness of this cold February morning, Oxford was bustling with people onto whom I couldn't help projecting a certain scholarly aura. At a complicated intersection in the town center, I went the wrong way in a roundabout, drawing honks and dirty looks from pedestrians. I got straightened out and entered High Street, Oxford's main thoroughfare, lined with bookstores, pubs, and shops, and ancient-looking buildings that crowd the street so tightly my GPS stopped working. After several scenic but time-consuming wrong turns, I eventually found Merton Street, a nondescript, cobblestoned side road, and parked (illegally, I would later discover) along the side of a long stone wall.

Merton College, one of Oxford University's thirty-eight constituent colleges, is one of the oldest and most storied academic institutions in the world. It was founded in 1264 by Walter de Merton, who would serve as chancellor to two kings of England—Henry III and Edward I—and then later as the Bishop of Rochester. It has educated bishops, parliamentarians, and Nobel laureates. Notable alumni of the last century include the writer T. S. Eliot; Roger Bannister, the first man to run a sub-four-minute mile; author J. R. R. Tolkien, who was an English professor at Merton in the 1940s and '50s; and Sandy Irvine, who enrolled to study chemistry in 1922.

Inside the Porter's Lodge, I met Dr. Julia Walworth, a bespectacled, middle-aged librarian with curly brown hair. After exchanging pleasantries and learning how unlucky I was with the weather—"It hardly ever snows in Oxford," she insisted—Walworth led me through an archway into a quadrangle hemmed by medieval stone buildings with slate roofs, tiny dormers, and ivy-clad walls. The campus, like most of Oxford's colleges, is made up of a series of interlinking quads. This one, which serves as the main hub for the campus, is paved with slabs of gray limestone and small cobbles that have been worn smooth over the centuries. A few students were milling in the entry of a dining hall, but otherwise the place felt oddly quiet for a college campus.

"It's a small place," said Walworth. "Currently, there are about six hundred students enrolled." We ducked into a stone tunnel that led us to a smaller quad. This one, Walworth said, was called "the Mob" and was the oldest part of the college. The buildings that surrounded us on four sides were whitish yellow, built with the same Jurassic limestone from which most of Oxford has been constructed. A church towered above us to the east. In the north wall of the quad, a small wooden door opened into the oldest continuously functioning academic library in the world. The Merton College Library is long and narrow with a runway of green carpet running down the center of the room. A few students looked up from their work as I passed by, but overall the place felt deserted. We arrived at a large wooden table where Walworth had arranged for me to look through the Sandy Irvine archives. Then she pointedly asked what exactly my project was about.

"I'm doing research on the early Everest expeditions," I said. Her face pinched, and I could tell she wanted more detail. I changed the subject by handing her my phone. "Check this out." I had pulled up a vintage photograph of the Merton College lawn tennis team from 1930. The black-and-white, sepia-tinted image showed six men, three seated and the others standing behind, dressed in white suits with crossed tennis rackets embroidered onto their breast pockets. Each man, hair cut short and perfectly coiffed, wore a scarf tied in an ascot knot around his neck and held a wooden tennis racket. Their names were inked in at the bottom of the photograph. Seated in the middle was H. F. Moseley, my grandfather. When my first request for access to the Sandy Irvine archives was denied due to scheduling conflicts, I played the "my grandfather was a Mertonian" card. Walworth had responded by emailing me a PDF of my grandfather's entry in the college register. It contained a lot of information I never knew about a man I had met only a few times before he died in 1984. Fred Moseley had attended Merton on a Rhodes Scholarship, arriving in 1927 and graduating three years later with a degree in physiology. After Merton, he moved on to St. Thomas' Hospital in London to study surgery. He married in 1934 and my mom was born two years later in London. All told, my grandfather lived in England for nine years before moving back to Montreal in 1938, where he wrote surgery textbooks as a professor at McGill University.

"This photo was taken right over there," said Walworth, pointing out the window. "Do you see the pine cones on top of the spikes?" A wrought iron fence stood forty feet away. Every few feet, the spikes were adorned with a greenish blob that looked like a mini pineapple. I glanced at the photo and saw that the fence had the same little blobs. "There used to be a two-hundred-year-old chestnut tree in that yard," said Walworth, pointing to the greenery hanging over my grandfather's head. "They cut it down four years ago, worried it was going to fall on someone." In its place, someone had planted a sapling about two inches in diameter, held up by stakes. It was snowing again, and its tiny branches were covered in a thin white frosting.

THE SANDY IRVINE archive at the Merton College Library consists of twenty-five boxes, plus a few additional items. I decided I might as well start with box number one, at which point Walworth wished me luck and passed me off to a younger librarian named Harriet. Harriet didn't put on white gloves, but she did open the box and hand me the items one by one. The first thing she pulled out was a photograph of Sandy outside the Shekar Dzong monastery in 1924. I had seen the photo before, the one in which he's wearing the telltale suspenders.

Harriet then handed me a series of drawings that Sandy had made of an oxygen apparatus shortly after he was invited to take part in the 1924 Everest expedition. One of the pages depicted the original design of the apparatus used in 1922: four tanks, with the valves on the top, hoses coming off to a regulator and mask. The next page was Sandy's drawing of the redesign he had fashioned after completely dismantling one of the original sets. The thrust of Sandy's work was to make the oxygen sets lighter, less cumbersome, and less prone to malfunction.

Sandy surely understood that his own life might depend on this still-untested design. I pictured him at his bench in the chemistry lab here at Oxford, lost in the meticulous detailing of pressure valves, regulators, and the copper piping. He had even shaded the underside of the shoulder straps with little hatch marks to make them look more realistic. These drawings, Harriet told me, were reproductions. The originals were sealed in a vacuum tube that was strictly off-limits. But the next set of documents she pulled out of the box, seven pages of notes handwritten in blue pencil, were originals. One was written on the back of a leaflet called the *Bishop's Register*.

> With the present form of the Mount Everest Oxygen Apparatus the cylinder valves are at the top of the back & so can only be turned when the apparatus is standing on the ground. This arrangement also requires that 2 auxiliary valves be carried in such a position that the climber can easily turn from one cylinder to the other. The weight of the auxiliary valves is quite a consideration & might be eliminated if the cylinders were inverted, so putting the cylinder valves in a convenient position to be used by the climber wearing the apparatus.

SANDY'S APTITUDE AS AN ENGINEER and designer first came to light at age eleven when he built a scale model of a racing yacht the family had sailed while summering on the Isle of Man. The hull was fashioned with the slats from a venetian blind, and the model came complete with cloth sails and string for rigging. Sandy had a workshop in a shed behind the family home in Birkenhead, where he worked on his models and fixed anything that broke around the house.

When the war broke out in 1914, Sandy was twelve years old. The following summer, he and his siblings were shipped off to Newbold, a small village in England's Peak District, to stay with their bachelor uncle. At the end of the summer, on a trip to Glasgow with his sister Evelyn, Sandy had his first exposure to the war effort. "We saw on the Clyde about 20 cruisers and 15 Torpedo Destroyers being built, and a light cruiser seemed to be guarding the mouth," he wrote to his mother. "We are going to have a game of golf after dinner. Everybody is telling you second or third hand about the Russians."

In September of 1916, at age fourteen, Sandy entered Shrewsbury, a prestigious secondary school that had already educated generations of his relatives. The school was a perfect fit for him, and he quickly came into his own now that he was finally out from under the rigid rule of his mother. Sandy was thrilled to discover that Shrewsbury placed a heavy emphasis on athletics, and he soon began to shine in cross-country, track and field, and, most important, rowing.

His academic performance at Shrewsbury was less impressive, although he did excel in chemistry and engineering. His mentor was C. J. Baker, an inventor and chemistry master who recognized and nurtured Sandy's interest in the sciences. In 1917, Baker gave Sandy access to a German machine gun that had been brought back from the front. Sandy stripped it down and spent weeks studying its design and making intricate notes about its various mechanisms. It was well known at the time that a deadly problem faced by the British troops was the tendency of their machine guns to jam. Through his study of the German gun, which was similar to those used by the Allies, Sandy determined that it wasn't the guns but the ammunition that was causing the problem. In the process of manufacturing millions of rounds, the dies used to cast the bullet casings would slowly distend, resulting in bullets that were slightly too large for the gun barrels.

Sandy next turned his attention to a couple of urgent problems plaguing the British effort to wage war in the air. He'd heard about these issues from his older brother, Hugh, who had enlisted in the Royal Air Force. In 1917, working in one of the labs at school, Sandy designed a synchronization gear that made it possible for a machine gun mounted on the nose of a single-engine aircraft to fire through the spinning propeller without hitting the blades. He followed this up with a design for a gyroscopic stabilizer that used inputs from the airplane's instrument panel to automatically control its stability and heading—the first autopilot. With encouragement from Baker, Sandy submitted his designs to the War Office. Both of his inventions had been preempted by the work of one of England's preeminent engineers, but only barely. The War Office sent Sandy a letter commending him on his work and encouraging him to continue.

Around this same time, Sandy was introduced to rowing. His latent talent for the sport was quickly recognized by the Captain of Boats and soon Sandy was training five days a week on the river Severn. Shrewsbury's headmaster, intent on raising the school's profile in the rowing world, had recently hired a new coach from Oxford named Everard Kitchin. "Kitch's great talent was that he could bring out the best in a rower and Sandy responded to that," writes Julie Summers in *Fearless on Everest*. "He knew from his own experience, what it felt like to get it right: and he had the ability to convey this to his crews. He and Sandy had similar physiques and were both notably fair-haired, but they also shared the understanding of the difference between rowing hard and rowing flat out. Sandy had the confidence to do the latter, giving 110 percent of himself in the full knowledge that he would not crack up."

The pinnacle of public school rowing in those days was the Henley Royal Regatta, which had been held annually on the river Thames since 1839. The regatta had been suspended during the war, but in the summer of 1919, the stewards of the race reinstated it as the Henley Royal *Peace* Regatta. The various trophies were renamed for the occasion and several races were established specifically for crews made up of veterans who had fought in the Great War. It was a seminal event set up to celebrate not only the Treaty of Versailles, which had just been signed a few weeks earlier, but also the spirit of competition and the joy that could be found in sport.

Sandy hadn't fought in the war, but his crew was selected to compete in the Peace Regatta's Elsenham Cup. In the quarter finals, Sandy went head-to-head with his brother Hugh, who had survived the war and was now rowing for Magdalen College. Shrewsbury, rowing against older, more experienced university students, won the race by three-quarters of a length and went on to win the cup, a victory that gave Sandy his first taste of real glory. In a letter to his mother, he recounted the final race: "It was the most awful race I have ever rowed, because Bedford were such a colossally strong crew, though they had an ugly style but weight was all on their side. We were determined that it would be too disgraceful to let them win."

When the boys arrived at the Shrewsbury train station at 5:30 A.M. the morning after their win, they discovered that most of the town had turned out to celebrate their victorious homecoming. Sandy recounted that "it was nearly as bad as Armistice Day" and that the school bell was broken in the pandemonium.

SANDY'S CLOSEST FRIEND was a shy young man named Richard Summers, who went by Dick. They met on the handball court at Shrewsbury, where they were drawn together, in part, through their mutual fascination with motorcars. Dick came from a wealthy family—his father was a steel magnate—but his life had taken a tragic turn early on when his mother died from septic pneumonia. In 1917, around the time that Sandy was tinkering with his inventions at Shrewsbury, Dick's father, Harry, married a spirited chorus girl named Marjory Thomson, who was thirty-three years his junior.

Sandy was a frequent visitor to Cornist, the Summers's estate in

North Wales, and it was here that he met his best friend's stepmother for the first time. Photos of Sandy at the time show a tall, handsome, tow-headed young man with an easy, winning smile. As one of the best oarsmen in England, he was by now a minor celebrity. Marjory, who was the same age as Harry Summers's oldest child, quickly decided that she could have a lot more fun with the kids than with her middle-aged, balding husband. Harry Summers was often away on business, so Marjory would entertain herself, taking Dick and Sandy on picnics and to the theater in the family's Rolls-Royce. She loved music and dancing and in the course of the many wild parties she threw at Cornist, she taught young Sandy the foxtrot.

BY JANUARY OF 1922, Sandy had enrolled at Merton College. It had been touch and go as to whether he would be admitted. Initially, he was declined a spot at Oxford's Magdalen College due to his less than stellar academic record. Baker, who was an alumnus of Merton and personally knew the warden, pulled a few strings and Sandy was offered a spot, provided he could pass an examination called the responsions, a requirement for all Oxford undergrads. So poor was Sandy's knowledge of Latin, Greek, and French, that it would take him four attempts before he finally passed the exams in the autumn of 1922. Within days of taking up residence at Merton, he was offered a seat in the Oxford University boat, a rare honor for a first-year student.

In early April, as George Mallory and his teammates set off on their second attempt to climb Mount Everest, Irvine was once again rowing his heart out, this time in the 74th edition of the Boat Race, an annual head-to-head competition between Oxford and Cambridge Universities. A few days before the race, Noel Odell, who was teaching geology at Oxford, joined the crew for a dinner at the

Putney Hotel in London. As a newly minted member of the Oxford Mountaineering Club and an obvious athletic talent, Sandy had caught the attention of Odell, who was looking for recruits for an upcoming expedition to Spitsbergen, an island in the Svalbard Archipelago in the Norwegian Arctic. Sandy and Odell had met two years before at the top of a 3,000-foot peak in Wales called Foel Grach. Odell and his wife were taking in the view from the summit when an "intrepid young motorcyclist" came bouncing up the trail, pulled to a stop in front of them, and asked for directions. It was the first time anyone had taken a motorbike into these mountains, and several newspapers later wrote about the feat. Sandy loved motorbiking perhaps even more than rowing, and he carried one of the newspaper clippings in his wallet for the rest of his short life.

At the time, Odell was one of the UK's leading climbers, well known for his numerous feats in the Alps and, most notably, a ropeless ascent in 1919 of a 450-foot-tall rock climb called Tennis Shoe on the Idwal Slabs in Snowdonia, Wales. Today, the climb is rated at a moderate level of 5.7, but at the time of Odell's ascent, this was only one notch below the hardest routes of the day.

Sandy made a strong impression on Odell that night. Odell would later recount that Sandy "seemed at once to typify all that I was looking for and all that is so essential in the make-up of one that is to be not merely useful, but also a genial companion under the trying conditions of the Arctic." Shortly afterward, he invited Sandy and another member of the crew, named Geoffrey Milling, to join the expedition to Spitsbergen.

The goal was to complete an east-west traverse of the island via an unexplored route through the heart of its heavily glaciated interior. Along the way, Odell would collect rock samples while others would study the flora and fauna. There was even a harebrained plan for the expedition to capture a live walrus for the Zoological Society of

London. More realistically, they intended to climb as many peaks as possible, using the summits as survey stations for mapmaking. In the spirit of the British Everest expeditions, the team would also file dispatches with a newspaper back home. After the impressive but ultimately unsuccessful attempt in 1922, the Mount Everest Committee had decided to take a year off before launching the next bid for the Third Pole. So, in the summer of 1923, the Spitsbergen expedition had taken Everest's place in the British media, which was hungry for anything that might distract from the grim state of affairs in gutted postwar England.

IN THE MONTHS leading up to the expedition, Sandy continued to pay regular visits to Cornist, and it was during this time that his relationship with Marjory blossomed into something more than mere friendship. To the shock of the Summers children and Sandy's sister Evelyn, Marjory made no effort to hide the fact that she intended to seduce her stepson's best friend. It's not clear exactly when the relationship became romantic, but it was soon known to everyone—except perhaps Harry Summers—that Sandy and Marjory were having regular trysts.

When it came time for the Spitsbergen expedition to sail for Norway, Marjory announced that she and her friend Dora would tag along for the first part of the voyage to Tromsø. The team could afford cabins only in steerage, but Marjory had booked a first-class cabin for herself. This was fortuitous for Sandy, who complained in his diary that his own bunk was "hard as nails" and smelled "like a badger house." He was seen by his teammates throughout the voyage making frequent visits to Marjory's cabin.

A week into the Spitsbergen trek, Sandy and Odell were dragging their sledge across an expanse of mushy wet snow when the area around them collapsed and they found themselves mired in a gloppy morass. They eventually freed themselves, but the sledge was hopelessly marooned, leaving them no choice but to abandon it and continue on to their next camp, four miles distant. The next day, Sandy and Geoffrey Milling headed back to see whether they might retrieve the sledge. The thin runners, which had worked beautifully on hard-packed frozen snow and ice, were useless in the unconsolidated slush. Sandy came up with the idea of sliding their own hickory skis under the sledge. It was still tough going, but with Sandy's inventiveness, they got the load moving again. Hours of mind-numbing manual labor later, they straggled into camp. Odell was delighted.

It's unclear whether Sandy knew that the Spitsbergen expedition was a tryout for his possible inclusion on the upcoming Everest expedition, but he was certainly aware that Odell had been appointed as the head oxygen officer. After the trip, when Odell would formally recommend Sandy to the Mount Everest Committee, he used the story of the abandoned sledge to promote his young friend. Odell knew that the committee was looking for what they were calling a "superman," a young athlete with extraordinary lung power, not to mention grit and determination. Sandy had all of these qualities. But he was also a gifted engineer, as evidenced by the endless repairs he facilitated over the course of the Spitsbergen expedition. During the many days that Odell and Sandy were tent-bound during bad weather, the older man shared drawings of the oxygen apparatus with his young apprentice. And they spent hours discussing the design and how it could be improved.

SHORTLY AFTER RETURNING from Spitsbergen, Sandy got caught red-handed sneaking out of Marjory's room at Cornist in the wee hours of the morning, by a friend of her husband. Summers, no longer able to turn a blind eye, filed for divorce, which at the time was still a rarity.

The official invitation to join the 1924 Everest expedition arrived in Sandy's mailbox in October of 1923—right as the scandal was blowing up. The last spot on the climbing team had been offered to a twenty-one-year-old chemistry student who had virtually no climbing experience and had never been higher than 5,500 feet above sea level. Sandy, anticipating this day, had already asked his parents' permission to go. They had read the accounts of the first two Everest expeditions in the *Times*, and, surely, they were well aware of the dangers Sandy would face in Tibet. But they didn't discourage their son's enthusiasm.

And, of course, it must have occurred to everyone in Sandy's orbit that the sooner he could get out of town, the better.

AFTER LUNCH, Julia Walworth moved me to a different room on the other end of the Merton Library, where I dug into box five, which was filled with receipts for Sandy's Everest kit. I had recently sourced some of my own gear for the mountain, and it had all seemed relatively soulless in comparison to how Irvine and Mallory had outfitted themselves. Many of my purchases were made online; I got emailed receipts that I could print out or view later on my credit card bill. Signatures, handwriting of any kind, were not recorded. These receipts, on the other hand, were works of art. From Hookham and Company, Irvine had ordered twelve pairs of socks (three "fancy"), gray flannel trousers, best white serge trousers, a Myrmidons tie (Myrmidons was a Merton College dining club), two cellular vests, two pairs of drawers, and khaki shirts. Each item was handwritten on the invoice in meticulous cursive. From Purnell, Phipps Purnell, a Leander costume tie and muffler, along with a handwritten note: "Sir, we think it hardly fair to deduct 5% considering the cost of carriage or case." James S. Carter, Alpine Bootmaker and Tourist Outfitter, had supplied a pair of climbing boots, felt-lined, that were "made to measure." The cost was five pounds, two shillings, and six pence, which works out to about $350 today. I assumed these were the same as the boot I had seen at the Royal Geographical Society. There was an order for a Primus stove with three number 127 burners, seven number 128 burners, and two manometers (devices used to measure pressure). From Burberry's, an "Everywhere coat" and fur mittens, and from Benjamin Eddington, canvas covers for his suitcases, a Verdun chair, a folding candle lamp, a rucksack, a six-and-a-half-foot-long bed and a "kapok" pillow. (Kapok "fluff," which comes from the seedpods of the Ceiba tree, was a precursor of today's synthetic fibers.)

I dug next into a box filled with family photographs. The black-and-white images, each sealed inside a clear polyester sleeve, were ordered more or less chronologically, starting with a shot of the Irvine family fishing from some lichen-covered rocks on the bank of a fast-flowing river. A fair-haired young boy, aged four or five, sat on a large boulder, holding a homemade fishing rod. Willie Irvine, Sandy's father, leaned over him with his hand on his shoulder. Flipping through these images was like watching a slideshow of Sandy's life: Sandy, maybe five years old, stood beside a three-wheeled ice-cream cart; Willie Irvine sitting in a garden with a huge tome open in his lap; Sandy and Evelyn, now teenagers, holding golf clubs; Sandy, smiling, in a trench coat beside a motor car.

Deeper in the box, I found a portrait of Marjory Summers. She had dark curly hair and a dimple in her left cheek. She wore a coy smile. Next was a shot of Marjory and Sandy sitting on a wooden bench alongside Evelyn and Maude Summers, Dick's sister. Marjory has her arm over Sandy's shoulder and a newspaper in her lap. They're both smiling, legs crossed toward each other. Marjory's foot is touching Sandy's.

After I had sifted through a number of boxes, Walworth passed me off to my third handler of the day, a man roughly my age with thinning gray hair and a barrel chest who introduced himself as Julian Reid, the college archivist. The Irvine archive listed a number of unboxed items, including the hickory skis Sandy had used on the Spitsbergen expedition and a "swagger stick," a small cane or riding crop that was in vogue with military officers until World War Two. I had read somewhere that this swagger stick was marked with three hatches, similar to those on the ice axe that I had seen at the Alpine Club, and so I was curious to make my own comparison. "I'm afraid those items are not available," said Reid apologetically. "They're too fragile and so we don't ever bring them out. But I can show you Sandy's Everest diary, if that would be of interest."

Reid returned a few minutes later carrying the book and a V-shaped block of foam that he set on the table as a viewing stand. The diary had a black leather cover and was about eight inches tall by four inches wide. When Willie Irvine died in 1962, Sandy's older brother, Hugh, found three of his brother's diaries amongst his father's papers. Hugh gifted them to Merton College, writing to the warden that Sandy "expected to have to 'show them up' sometime and so has not written them in his raciest vernacular . . . he has obviously been hampered in his expressions by the thought of publication and so the diary is far more pedestrian than would seem natural to you and me." Reid opened the diary and began slowly flipping through the pages. The entries were short and to the point. Most were a paragraph or two in length. Almost every day contained reference to the oxygen apparatus that Sandy had been working on throughout the approach to the mountain.

"Hold it there, please," I said, when Reid flipped to the entry for April 24, 1924. I remembered this as being on or about the day the photo was taken of Irvine in his suspenders outside the Shekar Dzong Monastery.

> Oxygen apparatus all day: very dusty. I chased a crowd of Tibetans with a loudly hissing cylinder of oxygen. I've never seen men run so fast—they must have thought it a devil coming out.

A day later, Sandy recounted the team's arrival at the Rongbuk Monastery, a few miles down valley from Base Camp, where he gifted the head lama two oxygen cylinders he had polished for the occasion.

> They made two fine gongs of different tones. We also told him there was a devil inside whose breath would kindle a spark—we showed him on incense. The temple was most interesting, and in pretense of worshipping Buddah [*sic*] I took three photos—I hope they come out.

As Reid flipped through the entries, I cross-referenced them with the pile of Sandy's letters that I had pulled from one of the other boxes and which now sat on the table next to me. The letters were mostly written to his mother and began shortly after he left England on the SS *Sardinia* in February of 1924 and continued until May 26. Their style was more effusive than the diary and they contained greater detail about the experiences he was having en route to the mountain. Some of the letters included detailed sketches of notable landmarks and other oddities, including a wooden Ferris wheel in one of the villages on the Tibetan Plateau. The April 24 letter contained more detail about the visit to the Rongbuk Monastery.

Grandfather will never own me as a grandson again because I bow down before a colossal Buddah [*sic*] about 20 feet high with an altar covered with most brilliant jewels. I had to make a great pretense to worship in order to get a photograph from a camera concealed in my coat as I had to give a 70 sec. exposure in the very dim light of the holy of holies—my devotions had to be very prolonged!!

Reid kept flipping forward until he came to the last two pages. These were the last words Sandy ever wrote.

June 4th

. . . After an early tiffin [mid-afternoon snack] George and I put the worst aspect on things, and we decided to go up to the N.C. [North Col] and be ready to fetch sick men down, or make an oxygen attempt ourselves a day later. We took exactly three hours going up, which included about a quarter of an hour at the dump selecting and testing oxygen cylinders. I breathed oxygen all the last half of the way and found that it slowed my breathing down at least three times (using 1½ litre/ min). George and I both arrived at the Camp very surprisingly fresh. Odell, who had been deserted by Hazard in the morning, had failed to pick up anything with the glasses. George believes he has seen their downward tracks some 700 ft. below the summit. I hope they've got to the top, but by god, I'd like to have a whack at it myself . . .

June 5th

My sore face gave a lot of trouble during last night. Somervell still very exhausted, but started for Camp III before tiffin.

> Norton is badly snow blind and can't be moved down just yet. We covered his tent with sleeping bags to keep it dark—he's had a pretty miserable day of it—it has been very trying for everyone with a freezing air temperature and a temperature of 120 in the sun, and terribly strong reflection off the snow. My face is perfect agony. Have prepared 2 Oxygen apparatus for our start tomorrow morning.

IT WAS DUSK when I exited the library. The snow had stopped, but the clouds hung low, and the air was saturated with a cold mist that gave me a shiver. I set off to try and find Irvine's memorial before darkness fell. Reid's directions led me around the back of the library, past the pine cone fence and onto a narrow path covered in splotches of wet snow and bits of broken branches. I was about to turn around, thinking I had gone the wrong way, when I saw it. A gray limestone obelisk about eight feet high, topped with a sculpture of an eternal flame, sat in the middle of a terrace that was tucked into the corner of an L-shaped building with darkened windows. I stepped forward to read the inscription carved into its face as water dripped from the trees overhead.

ANDREW
COMYN
IRVINE

1902 1924

PERISHED
NEAR THE
SUMMIT

OF MOUNT

EVEREST

JUNE

1924

Weeds grew from the chinks between the lichen-covered stones beneath my feet. There was no body buried in this spot. Whatever remained of Sandy Irvine still lay somewhere on the cold North Face of Mount Everest, perhaps even at the coordinates we had been given by Holzel. I knew that even if we could find him, there was zero chance to bring the body down and back to his family. I hoped, though, that we might be able to give him some form of burial on the mountain. And if he still carried the camera in his pocket, we might just figure out what happened on the day that he and George Mallory disappeared.

CHAPTER FOUR

The Redheaded Stepchild of Product Testing

On the morning of July 10, 2018, a Balti cook at K2 Base Camp in Pakistan was looking through his binoculars toward Broad Peak, five miles away, when he spotted something that looked like a body. The cook shared his discovery with Bartek Bargiel and his brother Andrzej, members of a Polish expedition hoping to make the first ski descent of K2, the world's second-highest mountain. At first, the Poles thought they were looking at a dead body. But after a while, they saw movement. It was a man in distress, trying to claw his way up the mountain. There was no communication between the two Base Camps, so they immediately dispatched one of their teammates, who ran five miles down the glacier to the other camp.

When he got there, they learned that the climber in trouble was the legendary British alpinist Rick Allen, who had set off on a solo attempt to push a new route up the mountain. His team at Broad Peak Base Camp hadn't seen or heard from him for thirty-six hours. Bartek immediately thought of the recreational drone that he had brought with him to film his brother skiing down K2. It was a consumer-grade device called the Mavic Pro that weighed only one and a half pounds and fit in the palm of his hand. As far as he knew, no one had ever flown a small drone at such a great distance and altitude. But he figured it was worth a try. If he could somehow reach Allen's position, roughly 2,000 feet below the summit, he might be able to see what was happening.

Bartek had recently learned how to make a critical hack to the drone's flight control software. Off the shelf, the Mavic Pro limits flight to only 1,640 feet above the launch point. This obviously wasn't going to work for filming a skier descending from the summit of K2. Luckily, the manufacturer of the drone, a Chinese company called Dà-Jiāng Innovations, or DJI, left a development debug code in one of its applications that gave Bartek a back door into the software.

Bartek quickly launched the drone, which sped over the glaciers toward Allen. When the drone was about three miles out, it suddenly stopped in midflight, turned around, and began flying home. Bartek realized that while he had unlocked the drone's height ceiling, the security controls on the battery now overrode his commands and directed the drone back home so that it wouldn't run out of power midflight. While Allen languished at around 24,300 feet, Bartek plugged the drone into his computer and worked on hacking into the battery's security system.

His hack worked, and Bartek launched the drone again. Minutes later, he found Allen's position on the steep slope and took a series of photos from about 100 feet away. The images showed Allen lying on his chest, hanging from his ice axe by both arms. A short distance below him, a gaping crevasse cut across the slope at the lip of a horrific 6,000-foot wall of sheer ice cliffs. Bartek recorded Allen's location with the drone's GPS and radioed the coordinates to Broad Peak Base Camp to guide the rescue team. It turned out that none of the climbers on Broad Peak had a working GPS device, so Bartek flew the drone back to K2, loaded in a fresh battery, and started flying back and forth between Allen and the rescuers, showing them the way, until they found him.

As I write this, the aerial footage shot during Allen's rescue can still be found on the website Planet Mountain. It opens with the drone hovering in the air above two rescuers who wave with their axes. Then it turns around and flies in and out of clouds across a vertiginous wilderness of snow and ice. Many hundreds of feet above, the drone homes in on a tiny figure in a blue suit. Allen was eventually found by the rescuers and helped down the mountain to safety.

Ten days after Allen's epic, when Andrzej clicked into his bindings on the summit of K2, that same Mavic Pro was hovering in the air 200 feet above his head. Bartek had launched it from Base Camp, 10,000 feet below, just a few minutes earlier. When Andrzej looked up and saw the drone overhead, he smiled, knowing that his brother was with him, at least virtually. According to Bartek, despite the modifications he had made to the drone's software, the machine somehow still sensed that it was operating way outside its parameters, and all it wanted to do was fly home. "I had to fight the drone every inch of the way," he told me many months later at a film festival in Canada. At one point, Bartek knew that he had pushed the drone too far and didn't have enough battery power left to fly all the way back to Base Camp. If he crashed the drone somewhere on the flank of the mountain, the drone and the precious memory card containing his dramatic footage would be lost forever. Bartek eventually managed to crash-land the drone on the summit, near his brother, who grabbed it and stuck it in his pack.

Over the next six hours, while Andrzej successfully skied down the sheer slopes of K2, Bartek flew a total of seven more flights, using his backup drone. In the end, the crux wasn't the flying or the filming at such extreme altitudes, but, rather, figuring out how to keep the miniature aircraft supplied with power. "If it wasn't for the generator we had carried to Base Camp, I never could have pulled it off," he told me.

Bartek Bargiel's drone footage became an instant sensation in mountaineering circles. So, when Thom Pollard first suggested to me that we could mount a credible search for Sandy Irvine, I wondered if we could utilize drones too. With a handheld drone, we could investigate Tom Holzel's Red Slash at 27,700 feet without ever having to leave camp. If we could pull it off, this would give us the ability to quickly and safely search acres of terrain that would be nearly impossible (and possibly deadly) to cover on foot.

As yet, no one had flown drones this high on Everest, but the Bargiel brothers had shown that it was possible, and it was probably just a matter of time before someone did it. The more I thought about it, the more I became convinced that using drones to do the bulk of the searching wasn't just a novel idea, it was essential to the success of the whole endeavor.

THE ENTRANCE TO National Technical Systems (NTS), on the outskirts of Anaheim, California, is marked by a sheet of four-by-eight plywood with a haphazard array of various metal signs.

Dangerous area, trespassers will be prosecuted

Notice All Vehicles leaving this facility are subject to Search

Danger Never Fight Explosives Fires

Warning no photographic equipment is allowed on this facility. The taking of photographs by any means, long range, aerially etc., is prohibited due to national security

Duly advised, we proceeded up a gravel road in our SUV, which was chock-full of photographic equipment. We drove past barbed-wire pens filled with industrial detritus and pulled into a small lot outside a one-story metal office building. Our visit had been arranged by Taylor Rees, a filmmaker and climber who specializes in environmental storytelling. Rees's friend, Christine Gebara, a Jet Propulsion Laboratories (JPL) engineer who works on satellite and spacecraft systems, had pulled some strings to get us access to NTS. As the two women worked on getting us signed in to the facility, Rees's husband, Renan Ozturk, an old friend and climbing partner of mine, started unloading the vehicle. Meanwhile, our tech guru and driver, Rudy Lehfeldt-Ehlinger, pulled a drone from one of the cases and began snapping on the blades.

A few minutes later, a jovial walrus of a man with a massive potbelly, impressive jowls, and a thick gray mustache pulled up in a golf cart. He chuckled at our small mountain of Pelican cases. "Welcome to NTS," he said. "I'm Randy."

Randy Shaw, department manager and senior test lead, would be our handler for the day. As we introduced ourselves, a tractor trailer pulled into the parking lot.

"Ah, looks like we're getting a missile today."

"There's a missile on that truck?" I said.

"Just a cruise missile."

Shaw went on to explain that NTS was essentially the military version of Underwriters Laboratory. Scattered across the 160-acre campus of barren desert were various pressure chambers, centrifuges, drop towers, and shakers. Shaw pointed to a building large enough to park three Greyhound buses inside, and told us he could lower the temperature to as low as –200°F. In another area, he boasted about shooting two-by-fours through a wall at 100 miles an hour to simulate a hurricane and of a device that could measure the shock wave that goes through the space shuttle when its rocket boosters ignite. It was clear that Shaw took obvious delight in the incredible mayhem that he and his staff are capable of whipping up.

"Think of us as the redheaded stepchild of product testing," he said.

While most of NTS's clients are aerospace companies like Lockheed Martin, Northrop Grumman, JPL, and various NASA divisions, the facility can test virtually anything. It was once hired by a law firm to determine if tennis balls perform differently after being shipped in an unpressurized aircraft cargo hold. Shaw guessed that it was probably for some famous tennis player who lost a big match. (They didn't.) A Mexican potato chip manufacturer wanted to determine how many bags of chips it could cram into a box without having them pop open during shipment. In a crowning moment in 2017, NTS tested the module in which a Kentucky Fried Chicken Zinger sandwich was launched into space. Some of the tests can take months of painstaking work to set up and last only tenths of a second. Others take years to complete.

As we spoke, one of his technicians in a building about 300 feet away was preparing to test a 1,000-pound warhead on a mechanical shaker that would lift the weapon up and down, 100 times a minute, for days or weeks to see what might pop loose. All of this would take place in a concrete bunker buried 20 feet underground, just in case. That afternoon, another technician planned to test the newly arrived cruise missile on a drop tower. The missile would be strapped to a magnesium plate and then released from 40 feet in the air. Shaw's guy would conduct the test, repeatedly, from inside a heavily armored bunker.

But Shaw was most proud of a contraption that he and a crew of engineers, machinists, and welders had recently built themselves. A 25-foot mechanical arm, festooned with various hydraulics, was attached to an engine the size of a small car. When turned on, the arm would swing around in circles at 60 revolutions per minute generating centrifugal forces in excess of 30g. This world's deadliest carnival ride is used to test all manner of gear and equipment that must withstand high g-forces, and it had just been used to thrash a new design of the self-inflating life rafts used by Air Force pararescue specialists on marine missions.

Shaw turned and looked at me poker-faced. "I haven't had anyone in my department die in a few years, so I'm pretty happy about that." After a few beats, he burst out laughing. "I'm sure you're anxious to see the pressure chamber. I've put you guys in the corner of the facility to keep you as far away as possible from any explosives." I caught his eye and waited for him to start guffawing again. But he climbed back onto the golf cart and, without another word, motioned for us to follow him.

The chamber was located at the end of a paved alleyway between a large metal building and a chain-link fence. It was cube-shaped, sky blue on the outside, and about ten feet square. The entire front of the chamber was a massive door with a circular glass opening in its center that looked like a porthole on a ship. The inside was polished steel, much of which looked like it had been recently run over with a grinder. Two round steel plates the size of manhole covers were bolted to the outside of the right wall. Numbers were handwritten next to each bolt—torque settings, I'd later learn.

"What are these giant plates for?" I asked.

"No one here has any idea," said Shaw. "We can only guess. This chamber is a Cold War baby. All we know is it was built for a big aerospace company." He said he thought the chamber was used to test engines for the SR-71, also known as the Blackbird. Used as spy planes back in the 1960s, only about twenty-five of these aircraft were built. They flew so high and so fast they could outrun any antiaircraft missile of the day.

Shaw now explained that within minutes he could depressurize the inside of this chamber to the equivalent atmospheric pressure of

85,000 feet above sea level and cool it down to –100°F. The walls had to be solid steel a foot thick so the chamber wouldn't implode.

"Have you ever seen a gas can left out in the sun that collapses once it goes into the shade?" asked Shaw. "That's called oil canning. It's caused by uneven stresses. It's what you don't want your chamber to do. By the way," he added, "I still don't know what you guys are doing."

"We want to fly a drone to the top of Mount Everest," I told him.

"Really? Well, you've come to the right place." Shaw went on to describe, in certain vague terms, how NTS tests all manner of military drones up to the size of regular aircraft. He would later tell me, conspiratorially, that he had recently tested a capsule "the size of a tractor trailer" that attaches to the wing of a drone.

AMERICANS FIRST BECAME widely aware of drones in 2002 when the CIA used a Predator drone in an assassination attempt on Osama Bin Laden, the first-ever targeted killing via Unmanned Aerial Vehicle (UAV). The Hellfire missile found its target in Khost, Afghanistan, but it turned out not to be Bin Laden. According to journalists on the ground, the victim was an innocent bystander who was in the area collecting scrap metal.

By 2006, as military drone technology began trickling into the private sector, the Federal Aviation Administration (FAA) issued its first commercial drone permits. At the time, you couldn't buy a drone on the open market, but private companies and individual enthusiasts were now building their own. Over the next seven years, the FAA issued only about a dozen of these permits. Then Jeff Bezos announced that Amazon was looking at drones as a possible delivery method for packages. By 2015, the FAA had issued 1,000 drone permits in total. A year later, that number had tripled, and consumer drones were being used in myriad and previously unimagined applications—aerial photography and filmmaking, inspections, surveillance, surveying, crop spraying, wildlife tracking, forest fire detection, and the delivery of medicine to remote areas. The FAA then introduced the Remote Pilot Certificate, which anyone operating a drone for commercial purposes is required to obtain. Obtaining the license involves a background check, an online course, and passing a knowledge test. The rule also states that any drone weighing over .55 pounds must be registered with the FAA. As of 2018, over 100,000 Remote Pilot Certificates had been issued.

THE NIGHT BEFORE the drone test at NTS, I met the crew at a rented house in a suburb of Los Angeles. When I walked in, Renan was standing in the middle of the living room looking a bit bewildered amidst a sea of complicated-looking camera and drone equipment. He was wearing jeans, a long-sleeve button-down, and his usual close-cropped beard. I noticed for the first time that his tousled, brown curly hair was beginning to thin a bit in the front. His eyes were bloodshot, and his skin was pale. But when he saw me, his face lit up.

After our usual handshake and back slaps, he asked after my wife and kids. He then put his hands in his pockets and surveyed the chaotic mass of gear strewn across the parquet floor. He could see what I was thinking. "I know it seems crazy," he said, "but we actually use all this stuff." He and Rudy Lehfeldt-Ehlinger were in the midst of back-to-back shoots and Taylor was working on her own film about lithium mining in Chile's Atacama Desert. After NTS, he and Rudy were off to the French alps for Turkish Airlines, then Namibia for an iPhone commercial. And Taylor was heading back to Chile.

"It sounds great, but honestly, I feel like I'm drowning," he said. "My life has no balance."

When the drone idea had struck me a few months earlier, I had immediately set about recruiting Renan for a possible expedition. Not only is he easy to get along with and a rock-solid mountaineer with numerous Himalayan summits under his belt, he's also by far the best drone pilot I know. But I wasn't sure he would bite. I knew that Renan wanted nothing to do with Everest, for all the same reasons that I had long recognized. So, I pitched the project as the "anti-Everest expedition." I told him that Thom and I might not even try for the summit. It was all about solving a 100-year-old mystery, not conquering the mountain ourselves. As it turned out, I needn't have downplayed our own prospects for climbing the mountain. Within days, Renan was running with the idea of directing a feature-length documentary film for National Geographic that he was calling *The Greatest Mystery*.

But Taylor was worried about Renan going to Everest. He was juggling multiple productions, managing half a dozen employees, spending hours a day on his phone, and staying up until the wee hours of the morning staring at computer screens in their studio in Park City, Utah. He was self-medicating with pot and alcohol to manage the stress, and it was all beginning to take a toll on his thirty-nine-year-old body. "I know he could do anything he sets his mind to," she said. "No one believes in him more than I do. But this is *fucking Everest*."

RENAN AND I met in 1997 at Colby College in Maine. He was a sophomore, and I was a guest of the outing club presenting a slideshow about a first ascent I had made that summer in Pakistan. Renan had dabbled with climbing in high school, and at Colby he committed himself to excelling at the sport. He liked its counterculture ethos because he had always self-identified as a bit of a misfit, never thriving in team sports like baseball or soccer. Growing up on the shore of Narragansett Bay in Rhode Island, he had taken to sailing and spent summers racing small dinghies.

Renan was born in Germany in 1980. His mother, an American from the south shore of Massachusetts, was working on a master's degree in music in Berlin when she met Renan's father, a Turkish law student. Renan was one year old when his parents divorced. His mother moved back to the US, remarried, and had two more children. Renan's grandparents on his mother's side were Jews who had fled Nazi Germany. In the twenty-plus years I've known Renan, he has never shared much about his youth, but his childhood best friend, Ben Phipps, told me that Renan had grown up "very Jewish," attending Hebrew school every week.

Renan's best friend at Colby was a religion studies major from Lincoln, Massachusetts, named Hal Hallstein, who is now an investment advisor in Boulder, Colorado. Hallstein found himself drawn to Renan's intensity, which he wasn't finding in other people. "When I was with Renan," says Hallstein, "I felt like I was part of . . . I don't want to say an environmental underground, because it wasn't overtly that, maybe more like a parallel lifestyle that was focused on much more important and meaningful things like alpine spires, deep conversations, art, and music. He was very suspect of mainstream America."

By the end of his sophomore year, Renan had burned out on the small-town New England college scene. In search of taller mountains and bigger horizons, he transferred to Colorado College. After he graduated in the spring of 2003 with a degree in biology, he bummed a ride with some friends to a famous climbing area in Utah's Canyonlands called Indian Creek. It was raining when they dropped him off with a duffel bag of climbing gear and a few hundred dollars in his pocket. That night he camped in an abandoned mining shack.

Before long, he fell in with a group of hard-core rock climbers who called themselves the Stone Monkeys. For the next few years, Renan and a revolving crew of other Monkeys followed the seasons across the western US, climbing full-time, camping in the dirt, and scrounging to stay clothed, fed, and outfitted with gear. Spring and fall were typically spent in Yosemite, summers in Squamish, British Columbia. In winter, the Monkeys would migrate to Indian Creek or Joshua Tree. Renan climbed as much as possible, working only enough to sustain the most frugal and barest of lifestyles. He doubts he put together more than $5,000 a year during this time.

Renan had taken an art class during his senior year at Colorado College, and in the years since, he continued to draw and paint. His ethos in those days was to create art with found materials. A "canvas" might be a cardboard box he pulled out of the trash, his paint natural pigments he dug from the earth or ink he squeezed from the pens given away at the Yosemite visitor center. When he traveled into the mountains, he would often carry bolts of canvas cloth that he would pin to the ground with rocks. He also liked to combine photographs with pen and ink, watercolors, and pastels, incorporating a riot of Day-Glo colors that gave his work a psychedelic touch. The canvases ended up wrinkled and smudged with dirt. Some of his pieces have water streaks from the storms that he painted through. One of them, of Shipton Spire in Pakistan, hangs on the wall in my daughter Lilla's bedroom.

In the spring of 2004, Renan was hired as a rigger by a film team that was following a couple of climbers on a trip through the Canyonlands. One of the routes they climbed was a striking line called the Lightning Bolt Cracks on a 350-foot sandstone spire called North Six Shooter. When the shoot was over, Renan found himself standing at the base of the tower staring up at the eponymous crack zigzagging up the sandy-colored rock to a spindly summit high above. He had never set foot on the route. On a whim, he decided to free solo it right then and there, with no rope or protection of any kind. The cameramen were still in position, so they started rolling. Renan's ropeless ascent of North Six Shooter later became a segment in an award-winning climbing film called *Return 2 Sender*, which I saw at a climbing festival outside Las Vegas in the spring of 2006. At the time, I was hanging out with the manager of the North Face Athlete Team. She turned to me and said, "We need to sign this guy." Shortly thereafter, she did.

Over the next few years, Renan achieved renown within the climbing community and beyond for his painting, but his primary focus soon became film and photography. In 2008, he teamed up with the veteran climber Conrad Anker and burgeoning filmmaker Jimmy Chin for an attempt to climb a fang of sheer granite known as the Shark's Fin on Mount Meru in the Indian Himalaya. After a harrowing nineteen days on the climb, they turned back 500 feet below the summit. (Three years later, they would return and successfully claim the first ascent. The film about their multiyear quest to climb this iconic last great problem of Himalayan climbing—called *Meru*—won numerous awards. Renan added drama to the final ascent when he suffered a severe brain injury from a skiing accident just months before the successful ascent).

By 2009, camera technology had evolved to the point where it was possible to shoot Hollywood-movie-quality HD video with affordable handheld digital cameras. Renan came to believe filmmaking was "the ultimate art form" and, conveniently, one that also pays the bills. After years of living hand to mouth and getting around by bicycle and hitchhiking, Renan suddenly had a six-figure salary.

I visited him around this time at the bungalow he was renting with his girlfriend in an upscale neighborhood on a hill above the

University of Colorado campus in Boulder. His new car was parked out front. It was a little hard wrapping my head around this sudden change in Renan's circumstances. The last time I'd checked in with him, he was crashing at a friend's mobile home outside Bishop, California, using a window for ingress and egress since he didn't have a key.

SHAW NODDED TOWARD a young man in a Carhartt jacket who was packing putty into a small opening in the side of the chamber through which Rudy had fed several wires. "This guy is one of the best corkers in the business," he said. There was a camera set up inside the chamber and it was connected via these cables to a monitor sitting on a table outside. The corker had welded two rings onto the floor of the chamber, to which Rudy tightly lashed the drone with parachute cord to keep it from going haywire and flying into the wall during the test.

The flying machine guyed to the floor was an Inspire 2 quadcopter, which Renan described to me as the Mavic Pro's big brother and one of the world's most advanced drones. It weighs eight pounds and has carbon fiber arms that rise up like an eagle lifting its wings. It has a built-in heater that allows it to fly in extreme cold, and two batteries that give it a fly time of twenty-seven minutes. Its top speed is 58 miles per hour, as compared to the Mavic Pro's 41 mph. The main advantage of the Inspire over the Mavic is that it comes with a more powerful camera that has better "dynamic range," which means it can expose for a variety of lighting conditions, enabling it to capture details, particularly in low light, that might be missed by a less sensitive camera. The Inspire is superior to the Mavic in every respect, except portability, and it was for this reason that Renan was unsure whether it would work for us on Everest. "I just don't know if we can even carry it up there," he said, pointing to its case, which was four feet square and a foot and a half thick.

But more troubling was the fact that the Inspire 2 is lethally dangerous. Its long, stout blades, spinning at 8,000 revolutions per minute, are like mini Samurai swords. Since becoming a drone pilot, Renan has lost track of how many stitches he's had from mishaps with drone propellers. The closest he ever came to death by drone was in 2014, during a shoot in Iceland. He was filming surfers at night under the northern lights with a large prototype drone that still had some kinks to work out. Renan doesn't know how it happened, but he reached for the controller and right then the drone leapt at him like a crouching tiger. "It was like a flying chain saw," he says. He reacted instinctively, swatting the machine out of the air. The drone went down and, in the rush of adrenaline, Renan initially thought he had come through unscathed. Then he looked down at his legs. The props had cut into the meat of his thighs like Ginsu knives, just missing his femoral artery. Blood was pouring into his boots.

"A Mavic can fuck you up pretty good," said Renan, "but an Inspire can kill you."

Due to the lack of flat landing surfaces on Everest, Renan had decided someone would have to catch the drone each time it came in for a landing. "With the wind and other factors we'll be dealing with . . . I'm honestly kind of terrified," he said.

Shaw motioned for me to follow him around to the back of the chamber. Here, on a concrete slab, sat several pieces of heavy machinery. There was a boiler used to pump steam, a refrigeration unit, and two giant vacuum pumps connected to the back of the chamber with rusty four-inch pipes. Shaw hit a few buttons and the pumps came to life, filling the air with heavy engine noise. "When I'm running both the boiler and the pumps at the same time, it's a full-on battle," he yelled. "One machine is pumping steam into the chamber while another one is trying to suck it out." The original vacuum pump was a giant diesel motor that spewed so much black smoke they called it the African Queen. Then one day, Shaw was watching the television show *How It's Made.* One of the stories was about the poultry industry. "The chickens were going into this machine and they were vacuum bagging them *wet*!" Shaw looked at me with an expression of total incredulity on his face, as if I should understand how impressive it was that an industrial vacuum pump could bag a chicken *wet.* When the show ended, he got on the internet, found the company that makes the pumps, and ordered two at $75,000 each.

As Shaw's pumps sucked air out of the chamber, a numeric display recording barometric pressure began ticking downward. Renan and I peered through the porthole over Rudy's shoulder as he worked the joystick on the controller like a teenager going for his high score on *Grand Theft Auto.* The drone veered wildly from side to side and snapped against its tethers like an angry junkyard dog. When the ticker hit 11.61 inHg—the equivalent of 24,000 feet—the drone went into a death wobble and flipped upside down. The propellers hit the metal floor and blew apart, spraying chunks of black plastic into the air like shrapnel. The Inspire 2 lay twitching on its back like a wounded animal.

"Shut down!" yelled Renan.

The test had only taken three or four minutes, but in that brief time Rudy had pushed the drone as hard as it would go. "As far as I could tell, it had plenty of thrust, which was the main thing I was worried about," he said.

"Why did it crash?" I asked.

"I'm not totally sure," said Rudy, "I think the motor overheated because it was tied down. It was really straining."

The good news was that the drone had made it to 24,000 feet before it crashed. It was the highest Rudy and Renan had ever flown. The bad news was that the drone had flown *only* to 24,000 feet—4,000 feet below Holzel's Red Slash.

When the chamber had depressurized, Shaw unlatched the door and Renan dashed in. He bent over and picked up his injured drone, pinching the body between his thumb and fingers like someone might hold a lobster. He stood there in the center of the chamber, shoulders slumped, staring at his baby with a forlorn expression. He didn't say anything, but I suspected he was thinking the same thing I was: We had based our proposal to National Geographic on our ability to fly a drone to the highest point on Earth. Drones would allow us to bring modern technology to bear on Everest's greatest mystery. They would also allow Renan to capture artful, high-altitude cinematography of the top of the world. A company called Teton Gravity Research had shot aerial footage of Everest's south side from a helicopter flying at 24,000 feet in 2014, but as far as we knew, no one had ever documented the Chinese side in this way. Renan's hope was that we would fly up the north side of Everest and go right over the summit, capturing photos and footage from a totally new and unique perspective. He had been counting on demonstrating conclusively here at NTS that we could do it.

Shaw had been standing by my side this entire time. He did not seem surprised in the least by the outcome.

"How often do your tests fail?" I asked him.

"Unofficially? About fifty percent of first articles fail—although we don't use that word here. Most customers just pick up the pieces and go back to their cubicles for a while, wait for a week to see if they get fired. If they don't, they do the stress analysis to see why the thing failed."

All four props had disintegrated, which wasn't the end of the world—Renan and Rudy had spares. But the hubs where the spinning blades attach to the drone were also broken, and this was more serious. The drone, which had cost about $20,000 with all its accessories, would have to be shipped back to DJI for repairs, a slow and expensive process. National Geographic had not yet committed to funding our trip, so Renan and Taylor had paid for this experiment out of their own pockets.

"At this point, I can't say I'm feeling great about our chances of pulling this off," Renan said. "Even if things had gone perfectly today, we'd still have no idea how the drone will react in high winds. If it's updrafting strongly, will I be able to get the drone back down?"

Renan, Taylor, and I were standing in the chamber watching Rudy as he scooped up the pieces of the crippled drone. A burnt smell filled the air. The entire premise upon which we now hoped to fund the expedition remained in doubt, but there was another nagging question we hadn't yet answered: Would the Chinese even allow us to fly drones at the top of the world?

"Even if we hadn't gotten our butts kicked today, we still don't have a permit from the Chinese to even do this," I said. "What if they grab all our drones at the border?"

CHAPTER FIVE

Damnable Heresy

I WAS ON MY back, an open book resting on my chest, when the tent began to shake. Startled, I turned and shined my headlamp into Hampton's face. I could see only the outline of her features through the crinkled vinyl. Her mouth was moving, but I couldn't hear anything until I pulled out the earplugs and lifted the foot of the tent, which was weighted with lead beads.

"What's going on in there?" she said. "It's like you're in another world. I was practically yelling your name."

"Oh, sorry. The sound of the pump is driving me nuts so I'm wearing earplugs. What's up?"

"I was just trying to say good night."

"Oh, well, good night. I love you."

"Love you too," said Hampton, smiling wanly as she rolled over on her side of our king-size bed.

I lay back down and wondered if this whole altitude tent thing was worth the aggravation. Aside from the noise, the HEPA filter next to my head was intermittently blowing cold air onto my neck, and the environment inside felt stale and clammy. I'd started sleeping in this tent a week ago and already I had awoken a few times in a claustrophobic panic in the middle of the night, not knowing where

I was. A digital gauge attached to the filter read 14.5—the percentage of oxygen in the air inside the tent. Over the past week, I had been slowly ratcheting it down, working my way from the equivalent of 7,000 feet above sea level to 10,000. My goal was to be sleeping at 18,000 feet, roughly the height of Base Camp on the north side of Everest, by the time I left for the expedition.

I had decided to use an altitude tent to pre-acclimatize for our expedition on the recommendation of Adrian Ballinger. Ballinger, an old friend, is one of the world's most accomplished high-altitude mountaineers and guides. He has climbed Everest six times (once without supplemental oxygen), K2 (also without oxygen), and has skied from the summit of two 8,000-meter peaks (Manaslu and Cho Oyu). I first met him in 2006 when we were both taking an exam to become internationally certified mountain guides. In the years since, Ballinger's company, Alpenglow Expeditions, has quickly grown into one of the most respected guides services in the world.

Ballinger says he first heard about people using special tents to pre-acclimatize for high-altitude expeditions in 2012. He was drawn to the idea because he figured he might be able to cut down on the amount of time he was spending away from home. In 2016, after pre-acclimatizing in such a tent, he and his partner, Emily Harrington, speed-climbed Cho Oyu, the world's sixth-tallest peak. All told, the expedition took only two weeks, door to door, from their home in Lake Tahoe, California—less than half the time it typically takes to climb this mountain.

A year later, Ballinger went all in and began marketing a whole new way to climb Mount Everest that he calls Rapid Ascent. The program combines pre-acclimatization with state-of-the-art training, precise logistics, weather forecasting, and small team sizes to cut the typical two-month duration of a guided Everest climb in half. In 2018, Ballinger guided a team of three highly trained clients—North

Face athlete Jim Morrison, former guide Neal Beidleman (who was on Everest in 1996 and is a central character in *Into Thin Air*), and Walmart board chair Greg Penner—to the tops of both Cho Oyu and Everest in twenty-three days door to door.

When I spoke with Ballinger in the fall of 2018, he told me that for the upcoming season, he was offering an even more ambitious Everest itinerary that he had dubbed Lightning Ascent. The goal was to summit Everest in fourteen days, door to door. He has since talked of climbing Everest in only a week. "Imagine how many more people would be interested in climbing Everest if they could get it done in days instead of weeks," he said.

My "head tent" was about the size of a doghouse and covered the top half of my body. Constructed of clear plastic draped over a frame of PVC pipe, it was connected to a control unit that looked like a freestanding air conditioner via plastic tubing similar to what I used to make beer funnels with in college.

When the unit arrived at the house, I called the manufacturer, Hypoxico Altitude Training Systems, and chatted with its CEO, Brian Oestrike. He helped me figure out how to set it up and also explained a bit about how the system works. While tents like this are often called altitude tents, strictly speaking, they don't create a high-altitude environment like we had done in the chamber at NTS. Rather than sucking air out with a vacuum pump, the Hypoxico system works by running ambient air from the room through a molecular sieve that separates oxygen and nitrogen. The compressor then pumps an oxygen-reduced, nitrogen-dense blend into the tent. The tent has no floor, so air leaks out through small gaps where the vinyl is weighted down to the bed. This keeps the pressure inside almost the same as it is outside; there's just enough positive pressure in the tent to prevent the relatively oxygen-rich ambient air from leaking in. An O_2 sensor inside the tent monitors the oxygen so that the control unit can maintain the desired level.

The tent does, however, effectively simulate higher altitude by creating a hypoxic, which is to say low-oxygen, environment. I could set the machine so that with each breath, I would be inhaling an amount of oxygen similar to what would be available at any given altitude. And the effect on my body would be largely the same. When exposed to low-oxygen air, whether due to low pressure or because of a reduced oxygen ratio as in my tent, our cells produce a protein called hypoxia inducible factor, or HIF-1. This protein stimulates adaptive responses in several ways that help our bodies better transport and utilize oxygen.

HIF-1 production is a response that helps us survive the onset of hypoxia, which can occur for a variety of reasons, not just going into low-oxygen environments. There are many diseases, including cancer, that inhibit the transfer of oxygen from our lungs to our cells. In the critical care unit of a hospital, hypoxia often marks the beginning of the end for a terminally ill patient. Ultimately, what kills them is organ tissue cells not getting enough oxygen. One by one, critical organs shut down, and death follows swiftly.

For decades, sports physiologists have understood that the responses our bodies evolved to stay alive under hypoxic conditions can also provide a competitive advantage when training for endurance sports like distance running. Research has demonstrated that living and training at altitude for an extended period of time boosts the production of erythropoietin hormone, or EPO. Anyone who follows professional cycling knows that EPO is a hormone that promotes the formation of red blood cells in our bone marrow. As many former competitors have testified, doping with synthetic EPO—originally developed for cancer patients—was rife within the peloton throughout the Lance Armstrong era. Red blood cells are the prime oxygen transporters in our bodies. More red blood cells mean more oxygen for our muscles, which translates directly into higher athletic performance. According to Dr. Joe Vigil, a former coach of the USA Track and Field Team, 95 percent of Olympic and world championship medals in endurance running events since 1968 have been won by athletes who trained at altitude. For this reason, the US Olympic Committee moved its headquarters to Colorado Springs, which is 6,000 feet above sea level, in 1978. And it's been there ever since.

Brian Oestrike told me that hypoxic training works so well that the World Anti-Doping Agency (WADA) reviewed the use of hypoxic tents in 2007 to determine if they should be banned as illegal performance-enhancing devices. After an extensive analysis, WADA chose not to prohibit "artificially induced hypoxic conditions" because this would create a disadvantage for athletes who don't have the ability to train at elevation.

While many of Hypoxico's customers are athletes of one kind or another, it also sells the system to medical researchers and practitioners. The Harvard Medical School has been using Hypoxico in its research on spinal cord rehab patients. One ongoing study involves patients breathing low-oxygen air before physical therapy sessions, and the results suggest improved function. Researchers speculate that hypoxia may be exciting nerve endings, helping to make important connections in the nervous system that hadn't previously existed. Some of Hypoxico's customers are also just people who believe that sleep in a hypoxic environment will help them live longer, healthier lives.

I have to assume most of these folks don't have a two-year-old.

A FIRM KICK in the leg from Hampton roused me out of my fitful night's sleep. My head throbbed and my mouth was dry and pasty.

Only after I removed the earplugs could I hear her yelling at me, "TURN OFF YOUR ALARM!"

Hampton is not a morning person.

"How'd you sleep . . . ?" I asked.

"I didn't," she croaked. "Tommy woke up at one A.M., but I didn't hear him over all this racket until he was screaming hysterically. He lost his bink. By the time I found it, he was beside himself. It took me over an hour to get him back to sleep."

"Oh, that sucks. I'm sorry."

"You were dead to the world," she said.

The Hypoxico website touts the Head Tent as "Perfect for athletes who have a partner that's not interested in altitude training. You can get your altitude training done while still sharing the bed!" There are other options, including a bigger tent that covers the entire bed. Knowing that the larger model would be more comfortable for me, Hampton had generously offered to get that one and sleep inside it as well. But I didn't want her to suffer from the headaches and general malaise associated with acclimatization. Neither of us, though, had quite realized what a pain in the ass this was going to be.

"Maybe I should move this whole shit show down to the guest room," I said.

Hampton didn't hesitate. "No, we're not doing that. But let's see if we can get a longer tube for the compressor so we can move it into the bathroom or a closet or something. It's so loud. And I can't wear earplugs like you. I won't hear Tommy."

I'D BEEN READING ABOUT the tribulations of George Mallory's personal life in the months leading up to his expedition to Everest in 1924. David Robertson, Mallory's son-in-law, had published a biography of the climber in 1969. Robertson had married Mallory's second daughter, Beridge.

By the time Mallory returned to England from the 1922 Everest expedition, he had been gone for half a year. Clare was now six years old, and during her short life, her father had spent years away from home, first fighting on the Western Front and then on two back-to-back Everest expeditions. It was the same for Beridge, who was now four. John, nearly two years old, may not have recognized his father at all when he arrived home in the late summer of 1922.

But the Mount Everest Committee was not about to let Mallory rest. By now, he was very much the public face of the British Everest enterprise. His celebrity was needed to help fundraise for the next attempt to claim the Third Pole, tentatively planned for the spring of 1924. He was soon on a lecture circuit crisscrossing the UK. He arrived home shortly before Christmas, spent a brief but happy two weeks with the family, and then in early January set sail for America, where he would spend the next several months sharing Everest tales with audiences across North America.

But by the time Mallory arrived in New York Harbor, his agent had managed to lock down only three venues. At his first lecture, a matinee in Washington, DC, on January 26, Mallory landed with a thud. He wrote to Ruth that night that "they were the most unresponsive crowd I ever talked to—never a clap when I meant them to applaud and almost never a laugh." Nevertheless, in Philadelphia, he drew audiences of 1,500 people two nights in a row to rave reviews. Back in New York, he felt good about his performance at the Broadhurst Theatre on Broadway, later writing to Ruth that the audience went away "fizzing." But half the seats were empty and the show lost money. The *Times* ran a story the next day, leading with the headline, SAYS BRANDY AIDED MT. EVEREST PARTY—A SWIG 27,000

FEET UP "CHEERED US ALL UP WONDERFULLY," MALLORY TELLS AUDIENCE.

CLEARLY, THE BRITISH quest to claim the Third Pole had failed to capture the imagination of the American public. It was no match for the distracting entertainments and upheavals of the Roaring Twenties. Except for one thing. It was in New York that Mallory supposedly uttered the most famous line in the history of mountaineering, his pithy retort to the question of why he wanted to climb Mount Everest:

"Because it's there."

As Tom Holzel discovered when studying microfiche at the Philadelphia Public Library, the quip to which we now attach such mystical gravitas first appeared in the *New York Times* on March 18, 1923. The 1,500-word article is titled CLIMBING MOUNT EVEREST IS WORK FOR SUPERMEN. It begins:

> "Why did you want to climb Mount Everest?" This question was asked of George Leigh Mallory, who was with both expeditions toward the summit of the world's highest mountain in 1921 and 1922, and who is now in New York. He plans to go again in 1924, and he gave as the reason for persisting in these repeated attempts to reach the top, "Because it's there."
>
> "But hadn't the expedition valuable scientific results?"
>
> "Yes. The first expedition made a geological survey that was very valuable, and both expeditions made observations and collected specimens, both geological and botanical. The geologists want a stone from the top of Everest. That will decide whether it is the top or the bottom of a fold. But these things are by products. Do you

think Shackleton went to the South Pole to make scientific observations? He used the observations he did make to help finance the next trip. Sometimes science is the excuse for exploration. I think it is rarely the reason.

"Everest is the highest mountain in the world, and no man has reached its summit. Its existence is a challenge. The answer is instinctive, a part, I suppose, of man's desire to conquer the universe."

When Mallory returned from the US, he was unemployed and dead broke. Ruth had been struggling to make ends meet during his absence. Over the winter, she had worried about having enough coal to keep the family warm. The only thing keeping the Mallory family above water was the allowance Ruth got from her father.

At this critical juncture in Mallory's life, Arthur Hinks, a Cambridge University astronomer and the secretary of the Mount Everest Committee, worked a connection through an old friend and helped Mallory secure a job as traveling lecturer for Cambridge University. The position came with a generous salary and the promise of a secure income for the foreseeable future. Essentially, it was a way for the committee to keep him on retainer and ready for the next go at Everest. The Mallorys put their home in Westbrook up for sale and bought a small estate in Cambridge called Herschel House.

But by the fall of 1923, Mallory was equivocating about joining the Everest expedition, torn between his family and the highest point on Earth. In the midst of the 1922 expedition that cost seven porters their lives, he had written to David Pye that Everest was "an infernal mountain, cold and treacherous . . . the risks of getting caught are too great; the margin of strength when men are at great heights is too small . . . It sounds more like war than sport—and perhaps it is." According to his daughter Clare, Ruth was firmly against another expedition. Mallory's marriage was certainly strained, and there has long been speculation about whether he was unfaithful to Ruth during this time. When his body was found in 1999, one of the three letters in his pocket was from a woman named Stella Cobden-Sanderson. Mallory had met her in New York while on his lecture circuit, although she was British and nominally connected to Mallory through her former husband, a climber. The letter, which is reported to be part of a longer correspondence, is signed, "Your affectionate Stella."

We know from his letters that Mallory was open with Ruth about his friendship with Cobden-Sanderson, but the same can't be said for another relationship he had with a nineteen-year-old British woman named Eleanor Marjorie Holmes. Mallory's correspondence with Holmes began after she sent him a fan letter in 1923, and it continued up through his departure for the 1924 expedition. We don't know whether Mallory ever actually met Holmes—there's no indication he did—but he certainly contrived to hide the correspondence from Ruth. He instructed Holmes to mark the letters she sent to his office "personal" and those mailed to his home, "George Mallory Esquire." Her letters have never come to light, but Mallory's were found by her son in her personal papers when she died in 1978. They were auctioned off and their contents made public in 2015.

"Your letter, kept in my pocket during the busy day was read at length in bed last night," reads one. "Why should a letter from you have strange effect on me? Strange effect? Well, only this, that after reading it I wanted to kiss you." And in another, penned while sitting by a crackling fire in a Cambridge pub: "Guess what might happen if another spark glowed there in the chair opposite. Would two sparks make a fire? Suppose the other spark were you Marjorie? What is it all about this fire always wanting to blaze up? Shall we see it blaze or shall we hold the snuffer on it?"

Mallory's correspondence with Ruth was decidedly less romantic. "I fear I don't make you very happy," he wrote in a letter penned aboard the TSS *California*, nine days after it had departed Liverpool on Leap Day of 1924 for the last and fateful expedition. "Life has too often been a burden to you lately, and it is horrid when we don't get more time to talk together. Of course, we have both had too much to do and I have hated thinking that it must fall upon you to do the car, for instance, which has often been an unpleasant grind, when you might otherwise have been painting china, or one thing or another more profitable for your soul."

Ruth had written to Mallory four days earlier, laying bare the pain she felt at being left to fend on her own once again. "I know I have rather often been cross and not nice and I am very sorry but the bottom reason has nearly always been because I was unhappy at getting so little of you. I know its pretty stupid to spoil the times I do have you for those when I don't."

There is a story about the day Mallory set sail for Everest. Ruth had joined a large crowd on the Liverpool quayside to bid bon voyage to the steamer of the Anchor Line. As smoke billowed from its stack, Ruth waved to Mallory standing on deck. But the ship was pinned to the dock by a powerful wind that prevented the tugs from pulling it out to sea. Ruth must have felt her own tug to get home to the children because she eventually decided she had waited long enough, gave one last wave, and turned her back on her husband. Mallory's last image of Ruth was of her walking away and disappearing into the city.

"So how worried should I be?"

Hampton stood facing me across our kitchen island. I had now committed to making this trip happen, and she had made her own plans to do some traveling in France with Tommy during the same time period. My computer was open in front of me on the kitchen counter. I was reading from a paper entitled "Effects of Age and Gender on Success and Death of Mountaineers on Mount Everest." I had gotten the paper, among many others, from Dr. Peter Hackett, a leading physician in the field of high-altitude physiology. On my way out to NTS in California earlier in the month, I had stopped in Colorado, where I visited him at his ranch in the San Juan Mountains.

One of the things I asked Hackett, who had himself climbed Everest's South Col route in 1981, was what advice he would give me if I were his own son. He replied that he would want me to stick to one of the standard routes (check), to use supplemental oxygen (check), to be in top physical shape (check), and to have a personal sherpa climbing guide (check). Finally, he firmly suggested I climb a 7,000-meter peak (23,000 feet) as a stepping-stone to gauge how my body would react to high altitude (no check). The highest I had ever been was 6,280 meters, and that had been twenty years ago. Our outfitter, a Nepali-owned company based in Kathmandu called Expedition Himalaya, had asked for my climbing résumé, which it had submitted to the Chinese authorities for review. I had listed dozens of climbs and expeditions and that I was certified by the International Federation of Mountain Guides Association, but as yet, I hadn't heard whether I had passed muster. There was no getting around the fact that I was taking a shortcut.

"According to this, my odds of dying on Mount Everest are about 1.3 percent," I told Hampton.

I would later dig deeper into this subject through the Himalayan Database, which catalogs a staggering amount of data about expeditions from the present back to 1905. A nonprofit organization, it was founded and managed for fifty years by Elizabeth Hawley, an indomitable Kathmandu-based journalist who made it her mission in life to keep track of virtually every climb ever undertaken in the Himalaya. Hawley passed away in 2018 at the age of ninety-four, but for decades you couldn't pass through Kathmandu without the requisite grilling from Hawley. She was a meticulous chronicler of details, and with Everest in particular, if she didn't sign off on your ascent and include your name on the list of summiteers in the database, then your climb effectively didn't count.

According to the database, as of spring 2018, a total of 24,772 people had attempted to climb Mount Everest, and of those, 293 had met their demise on the mountain. The vast majority died in what's called the Death Zone, the rarefied area above 8,000 meters where the air is only one-third as dense as at sea level. It's called the Death Zone not out of morbid sensationalism, but because when climbers go this high in the atmosphere, they are quite literally dying. In 2007, a project hoping to identify a gene that predisposes an individual to perform well at altitude studied blood samples taken from more than two hundred climbers on Everest. Above 8,000 meters, there was so little useful oxygen in the samples that the only equivalent the researchers could find was in people near death. No human can survive prolonged exposure to this altitude, so the trick is to get up to the top and back down before the process of dying is complete.

"Keep in mind," I told Hampton, "these are the odds for everyone, including people who've never used an ice axe or crampons and who have no business being on the mountain. I've been doing this stuff for decades."

The paper I was sharing with Hampton had a graph that showed statistical probabilities of summiting and dying based on age and sex. Five percent of all Everest aspirants have been women, and they have fared just as well as men. Age is a different story, however. One graph showed age on one axis, the chance of dying on the other. The line is more or less flat up until one's late fifties, then it goes exponential. A sixty-year-old is roughly twenty times more likely to die than a thirty-year-old. The authors put it like this: "Youth and vigor trump age and experience"—an inversion of the quote by playwright David Mamet: "Old age and treachery will always beat youth and exuberance."

Another paper cataloged the various ways that people come to grief on the mountain. Deaths fall into several categories: disappearance, avalanche, getting hit by falling rock and ice, high-altitude illness, hypothermia, falling into a crevasse, and "sudden death."

Hampton spun around from the sink. "What the hell is sudden death?"

I had posed the exact same question to Hackett when he first mentioned it to me. According to him, stories of sudden death typically follow a similar plot. A climber is on their way up or down from the summit when, without warning, they drop dead—probably due to an irregular heart rhythm or heart attack. But even more worrisome was another fatal scenario he described in which climbers rapidly deteriorate neurologically, for no apparent reason. One minute they're literally on top of the world, the next they're sitting in the snow, unable to speak or to perform even basic motor functions. At that point they are done for, because a sobering truth about climbing in the Death Zone is that the conditions are so extreme that even a team of the strongest climbing sherpas won't be able to muster enough strength to get you down should you lose the ability to move under your own power. Hackett says that these deaths, which are poorly understood, are inconsistently included under cerebral edema, unclassified, or disappearance.

Perhaps the scariest thing about both of these causes of death on Mount Everest is that they typically happen to people who were otherwise performing well. And in the case of those who melt down neurologically, the onset of symptoms may be sudden, but the process of dying is not. These people ultimately succumb to a combination of hypothermia, hypoxia, and exhaustion.

Hampton was now frowning and seemed, for the first time,

legitimately scared. After a short pause she said, "So, you're telling me that you could do everything right and still die for no reason? What else don't I know about this?"

A WEEK LATER, I landed in Denver on a foggy morning. I was back in Colorado to give a talk as part of a book publicity tour. The next morning, I would be off to Ohio. On the taxi ride to Boulder, I texted my old friend Cory Richards, a climber and *National Geographic* photographer, in the hope he might be around. He hit me back immediately, suggesting I join him for a training hike.

An hour later, the two of us were staring at a computer screen in his office. "Check this out," said Cory. He was leaning against his standing desk, using his finger to trace the line for a new route he was hoping to climb on the North Face of Everest that coming season. "Right in here is what I call the event horizon," he said, pointing at a menacing, triangular-shaped wall of dark rock that was partially obscured by a small cloud. "I've stared at this thing from every angle possible, and there's no way to see what the terrain looks like in there. It's a total unknown. It could be more straightforward gully climbing or it could be vertical death choss [dangerously loose rock]. I guess that's all part of the adventure, right?"

Cory had summited Everest twice, once without oxygen. He's also taken his fair share of licks in the mountains. In 2011, while descending from the first winter ascent of Gasherbrum I, an 8,000-meter peak in Pakistan, a storm moved in with heavy snow and high winds. Cory and his teammates, an Italian named Simone Moro, and a Kazakh named Denis Urubko, were roped together, wading through thigh-deep snow in a whiteout, when they heard a rifle crack—the sound of a massive block of ice breaking free somewhere above them. When the ice chunk hit a snow slope below, it triggered a huge avalanche that swept toward the three helpless men. "Avalanche," Cory screamed, seconds before it hit them. Cory was hurled through the air, then pummeled inside a hurricane of snow and ice. When the slide finally stopped, Cory was buried up to his neck in snow that had instantly set firm like fast-acting concrete. He couldn't move and he knew his partners were most likely entombed in the debris field or already dead from traumatic injury.

Just as panic seized him, Moro appeared and began frantically digging him out of the snow. Urubko, who also survived, came to his aid as well. The entire episode had lasted only three or four minutes, but there had been what felt like an eternal moment when Cory was being dragged down into an abyss. His world went pitch-black and he could sense the immense weight pressing down above him, as if he had fallen into deep water with a cinder block shackled to his ankles. Many avalanche victims are buried alive. Those who have been rescued describe an unimaginably terrifying claustrophobia. I've been caught twice in avalanches myself, and I can attest that dying in this way is every mountaineers' worst nightmare.

Now, sitting on the surface of the snow, still in shock, struggling to process the fact that he wasn't suffocating, Cory began to sob uncontrollably. Then he pulled out his camera, held it at arm's length and took a selfie. The image landed on the cover of *National Geographic* magazine.

A year later, Cory was on Everest, part of an expedition commemorating the fiftieth anniversary of the first American ascent in 1963. Back then, two teams had climbed to the summit, one via the South Col and the other up the West Ridge. Cory and Conrad Anker were hoping to repeat the latter, a challenging route that had been attempted many times since but never successfully repeated. Cory and Anker were at 23,000 feet, on their way down from their first attempt, when a rock the size of a suitcase came whistling toward them. It was an unseasonably warm day and Anker says the near miss confirmed that they had made the right call to descend.

On the way back to Base Camp, Cory began to hyperventilate. Dr. Luanne Freer, who evaluated Cory when he got to camp, later told *Outside* magazine that Cory's eyes "were as big as dinner plates" and that "he looked terrified." She gave him Valium intravenously, and his heart rate and breathing immediately stabilized. An hour later, when a helicopter landed in Base Camp, Cory walked out of the medical tent, climbed aboard, and flew back to Kathmandu, without talking to Anker. The official report held that Cory had been evacuated from the mountain "after suffering a possible, though as yet undiagnosed, pulmonary embolism." Cory says that he thinks he suffered a panic attack. After a few days in Kathmandu, he was feeling better and decided that he wanted to rejoin the expedition. But National Geographic, the sponsor of the climb, had a policy requiring that an evacuated grantee abandon the expedition.

Humiliated and ashamed, Cory went home to Boulder, where he reunited with his wife, Olivia Hsu, a yoga instructor and professional rock climber. They had been married for less than a year. Hsu says that she saw a side to Cory that summer she hadn't previously known.

Cory was drinking heavily. He started breaking his five o'clock rule. First it was at 3 P.M., then it was 1 P.M. Soon, he was drinking in the morning. Cory had been diagnosed as bipolar when he was fourteen years old and had been on medication ever since. But as his life began to unravel, he often forgot to take his meds and his moods swung from crazy manic highs to crippling lows that were so bad he contemplated taking his own life.

Cory says that he began to suffer from disassociation, as if he was hovering above himself looking in on his life. He was beginning to detach from reality, and when he'd reconnect, there were gaps in his memory. "I felt myself withdrawing further and further into this very deep sense of loneliness, and at a certain point the darkness inside of me erupted and began to fill the world around me."

When Cory was up, he was an unstoppable force of nature. At the North Face Athlete Summit in the fall of 2012 in Sayulita, Mexico, I spent time with him, and like the couple of dozen other athletes attending, I had no idea that my charming, witty friend, who had just been named National Geographic's Adventurer of the Year, was projecting a facade that masked alcoholism, bipolar disorder, and severe depression. Nor did I know that his storybook marriage to Olivia, who was also a North Face athlete, was a farce. Cory was cheating on her. A lot. He says now that he had fallen into a vicious pattern of using alcohol to drown the shame of his infidelity and the affection of other women to sooth the shame of his alcoholism.

When Olivia found out what was going on, she left Cory. Her therapist told her that Cory met the classic definition of a narcissist. "A narcissist is not what you think," says Olivia. "It's someone who has a huge ego, but actually hates themself. They think they're a piece of shit, so they have to prove that they're not, that they're awesome. It becomes a vicious cycle. Cory wasn't like that when I first met him. As his fame grew, the cracks got bigger and bigger."

Cory, meanwhile, began researching his symptoms—disassociation, fear, anxiety, memory loss, loneliness, emotional detachment. One day he typed them into Google and got a hit he remembers vividly—Post-Traumatic Stress Disorder (PTSD). At the time, he immediately flashed to the avalanche on Gasherbrum I. His heart fluttered and he made a connection. Perhaps, when he and Anker had nearly been hit by that rock on Everest, it had triggered the memory of the avalanche on Gasherbrum, and this, in turn, had caused the panic attack.

Cory read everything he could find about PTSD and learned that anywhere from 10 to 20 percent of people who suffer a near-death experience are haunted by it afterward, and also that people who have previously suffered psychological trauma are more likely to experience PTSD. He realized that his inability to resolve the experience on Gasherbrum probably had a lot to do with the psychological trauma he had suffered as a youth.

His parents were ski bums who had met while working at Alta Ski Resort in Utah. Cory's mom took him to a psychologist when he was one year old. "I had a sense that things weren't joyful for him," she says. Cory says that his youth was characterized by an almost unbearable sadness, the source of which he could never pinpoint. But despite the darkness he felt inside, he achieved at a high level as a student and athlete. He skipped two grades and enrolled in high school at age twelve, the same year he was diagnosed with severe depression. Soon he was partying with eighteen-year-olds. He took his first hit of acid at age thirteen. At fourteen, his parents pulled him out of school and admitted him into a juvenile psych program where part of his treatment was to shuffle around the facility, with older kids holding him by his belt loops.

"The place was absolutely awful," says Cory. "The only thing I learned in there was that I was a screw-up, a feeling which I've never been able to shake to this day."

Cory ran away from the program three times in eight months. His parents told him that it was the psych ward or the highway. So, at age fifteen, he hit the streets of Salt Lake City. He was constantly on the move, sleeping in parks and on the couch at his drug dealer's house. When he ran out of money, he broke into his parents' home, took what he could find, and left notes saying he was sorry.

By the time he was seventeen, he was living with an uncle in Seattle, who was a climber. Cory began making regular forays into the

Cascades, where he discovered a sense of peace that had eluded him in the horizontal world. "The mountains were a place where I felt secure and knew who I was," says Cory. "It was climbing that helped get me through those dark years of my adolescence."

ALL THESE YEARS LATER, after multiple stints in rehab, Cory was sober, attending weekly AA meetings, and seriously back in the game. His girlfriend, Melissa Schneider, was sitting a few feet away, talking to someone on the phone about a branded Instagram post. Next to her on the wall was a framed photograph of a group of Pakistani soldiers wearing camouflage, holding AK-47s, on a rubble-strewn glacier in the Karakoram. Cory likes to joke that he has so many Pakistani friends on Facebook, including the five soldiers in the picture, that he's on the TSA watch list.

He pulled up another photo on his computer screen for me that showed a profile of the face on Everest he wanted to climb. From this angle, I could see that it was about as steep as a double-black-diamond ski run—for 6,000 vertical feet. I'd been studying similar photos for months and had become well acquainted, at least virtually, with the architecture of Everest's north side. Cory's proposed route would ascend a wall called the Northeast Face, which lies to the east of the route I would soon be attempting. At 27,000 feet, Cory's line could join the standard route, but rather than clip into the fixed ropes at that point, Cory hoped to cross over the main route by traversing a small catwalk and then follow a seldom-climbed snow gully to the summit. Some have speculated that this traverse, which avoids the Second Step, may have been a way that Mallory and Irvine could have summited in 1924.

The rock buttress at the top of the Northeast Face, what Cory was calling the "event horizon," was part of an infamous feature known as the Pinnacles. It was here that two of the world's most accomplished alpinists, Peter Boardman and Joe Tasker, disappeared while attempting the first ascent of the five-mile-long Northeast Ridge in 1982. Ten years later, a joint Japanese-Kazakh expedition found a body below the second Pinnacle, which was later identified by its clothing as Boardman. Tasker has never been found, and no one has figured out what happened to them—apart from the fact that they were pushing hard into uncharted terrain without oxygen or sherpa support when a storm blew in.

Cory and his partner for this project, Esteban "Topo" Mena, an accomplished Ecuadorian alpinist who climbed Everest without oxygen in 2013, were planning to climb in the same purist style as Boardman and Tasker. Their goal was to scale the new route in a single push from Advanced Base Camp, carrying everything they needed for the climb in their packs and bivouacking wherever they could along the way. By necessity, they would need to free solo most, if not all, of the climb. The intensity of the terrain demanded that they move quickly and forgo the weight of ropes, pitons, and ice screws, and the luxury of safety belays. Cory told me that the climb would take anywhere from four to eight days. There would be no fixed ropes, no support from climbing sherpas, and no supplemental oxygen.

Of the many thousands of climbers who have stood on the summit of Everest, a little more than two hundred have done so without the aid of bottled oxygen. Cory made his first oxygenless ascent of Everest via the Northeast Ridge in 2016 and, in doing so, joined an elite club of mountaineers. But attempting to join their ranks came with enormous risk. Since Messner and Habeler first climbed Everest without supplemental oxygen in 1978, those who have endeavored to repeat the feat have died at a rate six to seven times higher than the average climber. For those who actually make it to the summit without oxygen—a minority of aspirants—the death rate on the descent is a staggering 40 percent. As the numbers bear out, summiting Everest "by fair means" (as stated by Messner), is to walk a knife edge between life and death.

The ethical debates around using supplemental oxygen to "murder the impossible," as Messner so famously put it, go all the way back to the British Everest expeditions in the 1920s. On their first attempt in 1921, the British chose not to use supplemental oxygen, in part because most of the team saw it as cheating and beneath the dignity of a proper English sportsman. In any event, they never got high enough on the mountain that year for it to come into play. When oxygen sets were included in the kit in 1922, Mallory famously called their use a "damnable heresy," and Arthur Hinks wrote that anyone who didn't climb to at least 25,000 feet without the apparatus would be a "rotter."

Cory and I would be climbing practically side by side on Everest, but we might as well have been practicing different sports. The first three-quarters of his proposed route was terra incognita. Climbing the remaining 2,000 feet to the summit without fixed ropes or oxygen would push him and Topo to the outermost limit of human endurance. You could hardly take a bigger bite from the Everest apple. The route that I would be following has by now been ascended thousands of times, by climbers of all abilities and experience, and it is intensively managed. We wouldn't even be allowed to set foot on the mountain until the CTMA authorities confirmed that their rope-fixing teams had strung it top to bottom with fixed lines.

Everest has about 20 different established routes, but 99 percent of the 5,000-plus people who have summited the peak have done so via its two standard routes—the South Col route through Nepal and the Northeast Ridge through China or, more specifically, Tibet. According to the Himalayan Database, only about 265 people have attempted to climb Everest via any of its nonstandard routes. And of those, approximately 80 died in the process. By the numbers, Cory's odds of dying on Everest this season were close to 1 in 3—the equivalent of playing Russian roulette with two bullets instead of one.

An hour later, Cory and I set off up a mud-and-ice-slicked trail on the shady east face of Flagstaff Mountain. He set a brisk pace, which made me glad I had caught him on what he was calling a "recovery day." We were ten minutes up the trail when he first checked his heart rate.

"What is it?" I asked.

"One-twenty. Perfect. I'm trying to stay in zone one, which is anything below one-thirty-three." I wasn't wearing a heart rate monitor, but I did have an app on my phone that measured my pulse by shining a light into the tip of my finger. I tried it as we walked, and it pegged mine at 128.

For the past year, Cory had been working with a company called Uphill Athlete, which specializes in training people for high-altitude mountaineering. Cory's coach, Scott Johnston, a former member of the USA Nordic Ski Team, is one of the company's founders. Cory said that Johnston gave him a detailed schedule at the beginning of each week and that they were in constant contact with each other. During a typical week, Cory would train five or six days, for a total of twenty to twenty-five hours. Most days he trained without weight, but at least one day a week he would fill his pack with four or five gallons of water (a total of thirty to forty pounds) and crank out 6,000 vertical feet in Boulder's Flatirons, the rock formations on the eastern edge of Green Mountain. On rest days, he would go for hikes like the one we were doing.

As we scooted up the trail, Cory helped fill in the gaps in my knowledge about what made for effective Everest training. When I first got serious about going to Everest, I bought a book cowritten by Scott Johnston and mountaineer Steve House called *Training for the New Alpinism*. A quick perusal told me that my upcoming expedition would require a different kind of training from the relatively high-intensity exercise I was accustomed to getting. For years, I've done a lot of cross-country skiing in the winter to maintain my fitness. A typical workout was to skate ski hard for an hour or so and call it good. Likewise, for the average person who is simply looking to lose weight or build muscle, a CrossFit or Peloton workout can be quite effective. But if you're trying to prepare for an ultra endurance event like a high-altitude mountaineering expedition, this type of training will offer you almost no benefit—and might even hinder your performance. Accordingly, I started skiing longer, for several hours most days, knowing I needed to build my aerobic base. But I didn't fully understand exactly why this was so important until Cory explained some of the physiology to me.

Our bodies produce most of the energy we need to live by way of aerobic metabolism, which uses oxygen to break down primarily fats and carbohydrates with a small contribution from amino acids (protein). Protein is almost never a good source of energy because it consumes tissue such as muscle, which the body generally does only as a last resort under conditions of starvation. Carbohydrate or sugar delivers the most intense energy of all three sources—think of it as the body's high-octane fuel—but must be constantly replenished, as we can only store about an hour's worth in our bloodstream. As I was soon to learn, a high-altitude, low-oxygen environment dramatically suppresses one's appetite, and as a result, Everest climbers struggle to take in enough calories. As it turns out, fat is the essential fuel for a long-duration event like an Everest climb because our bodies can store many days' worth of it. Cory's exercise regimen focused on retraining his body to feed off its intermuscular fat stores. Accordingly, Johnston had prescribed that many of his biggest workouts were to be done over many hours at a low intensity—on an empty stomach.

This gets to the reason I was doing much longer ski sessions. There was little benefit in pushing my body past its aerobic threshold—or, in other words, past a level of effort that I could sustain more or less indefinitely. When this threshold is crossed, the body activates its anaerobic circuit, which is a form of metabolism that produces energy without oxygen. The typical hour-long workout will have both the aerobic and anaerobic circuits operating simultaneously. (An effort of extreme intensity, one that requires the body to go "fully anaerobic," can be sustained only for a maximum of about two minutes.) When the anaerobic circuit is in play, two things happen: First, muscles produce and accumulate lactic acid, which makes them feel heavy and, eventually, useless. Second, the body begins to deplete stores of sugar in the bloodstream, as the high-octane sugar is the only fuel our anaerobic circuit can utilize.

Johnston and House note that four out of five people who sign up with Uphill Athlete have what they call Aerobic Deficiency Syndrome. These are people who look and feel fit but have long neglected their aerobic base. Often, they have highly tuned anaerobic thresholds from years of short-duration, high-intensity exercise. They can bench press a respectable weight or turn in a decent 10k time in part because they've never had to venture far from the refrigerator or convenience store. But their well-trained anaerobic circuits don't translate to success on big Himalayan climbs, which require several days' worth of effort in the absence of sustained caloric intake. In fact, this kind of athlete has a tendency to get themselves into trouble. Thinking they should be strong performers, and no strangers to pain, they're more likely to push themselves well past the point of exhaustion. What's actually needed is the ability to forestall activating the anaerobic circuit while still exerting oneself—all day long. This kind of fitness can be achieved only by racking up hours and hours of low-intensity exercise. As Cory observed with some embarrassment, training had become almost his full-time job.

THE SUN WAS SETTING when we pulled up in front of my hotel on Pearl Street in downtown Boulder. Cory slumped back in his seat and stared vacantly out the windshield. He didn't seem to be in a rush to head off to whatever was next on his agenda. I wondered whether he had considered his odds of not returning home this coming summer. I've often dismissed the idea that climbers and other extreme athletes might do what they do because they have a death wish. But here was a guy who had suffered from severe depression for years, had at one time seriously contemplated suicide, and who now intended to throw himself at a climb on which he had roughly a 30 percent chance of dying. I didn't get the sense that Cory consciously wanted to kill himself. But I did wonder what kind of self-destructive impulse might be driving him.

"Why are you doing this?" I said. "With everything you have to offer the world through your photography and storytelling, is this route really worth the risk?"

"I think about dying every day, and it's horrifying," replied Cory. "I'm battling with superstition and fear, and I can't help but wonder if I'm preparing to go out into battle and that maybe this is it, and I'm going to die up there. And it's fucking exhausting to have these kinds of thoughts running through your head over and over. But I keep pushing forward because the quest for the unknown and my curiosity is stronger than the fear. And I've done this enough to know that these dark thoughts are part and parcel of the experience. This happens every time I go into the mountains. And every time so far, knock on wood, I've come home alive."

He hadn't quite answered my question.

PART TWO

ASCENDING

CHAPTER SIX

Into the Abode of Snow

OUR DUST-SMEARED MAHINDRA Scorpio SUV lurched up a serpentine gravel road above the Trishuli River, swollen with mid-April snowmelt. Lush valleys with terraced fields and dense forests of walnut, alder, and spruce rose into the misty hills around us. Somewhere up ahead of us was a box truck stuffed with all the gear for the 2019 Sandy Irvine Search Expedition. Immediately behind was another SUV filled with our sherpa support team.

Like much of Nepal, the villages we passed were still rebuilding from the 7.9-magnitude earthquake that had devastated the country in 2015. Many of the homes and shops lining the road were partly demolished, or still under construction. The same tectonic forces that push the Himalaya ever higher make this one of the most seismically active regions in the world. The traditional hewn-stone-with-earthen-mortar construction methods couldn't be more ill suited to the shaking forces of an earthquake. Everywhere we looked were crumbled walls, caved-in roofs, and makeshift repairs. Most of the nine thousand people who died in the earthquake were crushed under the rubble of their own homes. The area we were passing through was only thirty miles from the epicenter.

The leader of our expedition, Jamie McGuinness, was explaining in his thick Kiwi accent that this corridor had been a trade route for more than eight hundred years. Tibetans would bring down wool and salt to trade for rice, flour, and butter brought up from the lowlands. The Nepali tribes in this area were middlemen between the Tibetans and Hindus. In addition to commerce, this valley was a conduit through which knowledge and culture flowed from the Indian subcontinent up onto the Tibetan Plateau.

Jamie, a fit, fifty-three-year-old mountain guide and Everest veteran, had spent a good chunk of his life exploring the Himalaya. His knowledge of this region, which he had been sharing via a stream-of-consciousness travelogue ever since we had left Kathmandu that morning, seemed boundless. He had his back to me, but I could see his face in the rearview mirror. He wore a big toothy smile beneath wire-rimmed glasses and a military-style crew cut.

I looked around the vehicle, taking in the guys I would be spending the next two months with. In addition to Jamie, Thom, and Renan, we had three more recruits who would be working with Renan to produce the documentary film for National Geographic, which they had renamed *Lost on Everest.* Jim Hurst, a tall, lanky climber and mountain runner in his mid-fifties, was the sound guy. I had met him a few years ago when he was working in Morocco on the film *Free Solo.* I remembered him as thoughtful, erudite, and well mannered, the latter trait not necessarily typical of career climbers. Thom, who had recently met him for the first time, had already nicknamed him "Sir James."

Matt Irving, thirty-five, and Nick Kalisz, thirty-one, sitting in the third row behind me, were codirectors of photography. Matt, a mustachioed and irreverent Utahan, was an accomplished climber and endurance runner. We first got to know each other on an exploratory climbing expedition on the south coast of Newfoundland in 2011.

Nick and I had met for the first time a few days earlier. His status as the youngest member of our team was exaggerated by the curly blond hair that hung over his eyes. I'm always nervous to sign up for a trip like this with someone I've never met, as chemistry can be a tricky thing on an extended expedition. But right off, his quick smile and quiet, self-deprecating demeanor put me at ease.

As we gained elevation, the valley narrowed dramatically, and we began switchbacking up the steep, eastern wall of the infamous Trishuli Gorge. The road was rough and poorly maintained, if at all. This is one of the most dangerous sections of highway in all of Nepal, and only one of two roads that cross the border with Tibet to the north. In 2015, a bus careened over the same cliff I was looking down out the rear window of our vehicle, killing thirty-five people.

Our Nepali driver, who was in his early twenties, was either blessed with extrasensory perception or else just tired of living. He gunned the overloaded SUV up the narrow track with wanton disregard for oncoming traffic. At each blind hairpin corner, he mashed the accelerator and the horn and yanked hard on the steering wheel. The truck skidded around the bends, Starsky and Hutch–style. I watched as gravel sprayed from our tires over the edge of the yawning precipice. Eventually, I decided that if I wasn't going to get out and walk the remaining twenty miles to Tibet, I should just put my head down and stare at the beaded seat cover in front of me.

As we neared the border, we began passing dozens of garishly painted Indian-built Tata trucks parked off the side of the road. They sported Bollywood quotes and slogans, many in English, like SPEED CONTROL, TURST IN GOD [*SIC*], and NO GIRLFRIEND—NO TENSION. Many of the drivers were living in their vehicles, waiting for their turn to load goods brought in from China. The wares were ordinary consumer goods for the Asian market: smartphones, ramen noodles, colorful blankets, and the like. Being a truck driver in Nepal is a tedious and dangerous job, but a good driver can make up to $500 a month—a decent wage in a country where the annual per capita income is $700.

Nepal's economic woes are evidenced by the long line of empty trucks driving up the valley to receive goods. Hardly any trade flows out of the country. Nepal's considerable trade deficit with India and China is one of the main factors that keeps the country consistently ranked amongst the world's poorest. Landlocked and almost completely lacking in natural resources, the country must import virtually everything it cannot grow or dig out of the earth.

THE OFFICIAL CUSTOMS OFFICE on the Nepal side was a shack made of corrugated tin with a folding table out front. A sign in Nepali warned against smuggling animal products like pangolin scales, deer musk, and tiger bones, lucrative contraband that can fetch a premium as ingredients for traditional Chinese medicines. After a cursory look through our packs by the Nepali officials, we stepped onto a steel bridge high above the Trishuli River. Straddling the roadway ahead of us towered a monolithic structure with Doric columns and multistory, tinted plate-glass windows. The road ran directly *through* the building via a large square opening, above which hung a massive red-and-gold emblem of the Chinese Communist Party, all the more intimidating against the façade of stark-white stone.

A liaison officer from the CTMA met us outside the building, arranged us in alphabetical order—climbing sherpas first, then foreigners—and ushered us inside. I looked around, taking in the high ceilings, stainless steel stanchions, security cameras, and overhead digital monitors. In the middle of the room sat a row of custom booths surrounded by plexiglass shields. Thom stood in front of me, and I noticed that his canvas duffel was dripping some sort of brownish liquid. When I pointed it out to him, he opened his bag and began muttering under his breath, "Fuck, fuck, fuck . . ." The bottle of whisky he had purchased in Kathmandu must have broken and was now emptying onto the polished marble floor of China's newest customs post. I hoped that no one would notice, because we certainly didn't want to draw attention to ourselves.

AT OUR FIRST TEAM MEETING back in Kathmandu, Jamie had confessed that he might have blown our hopes of flying drones on Everest. He had formally requested permission from the CTMA to use drones for filming. In his proposal, he had included a photo of a large commercial drone he had found online, instead of the smaller Mavic Pro that Renan had settled on using. "The Chinese weren't even thinking about drones, but now the army is aware of their potential in a security situation," he had told us. "They haven't officially said no, but they haven't said yes either . . . Whether they're going to be looking for drones at the border, I don't know."

Jamie had no desire for an incident of any sort with Chinese customs officials. Back in the late 1990s, he had crossed from Tibet into Nepal with a group of "crystal healers" from Colorado. They had just completed a trek around Mount Kailash, the most sacred peak in Tibet. In a stroke of bad luck, his permit contained a typo: The return date was printed as May 8 instead of May 18. When they got to the border, they were officially ten days overdue. Overstaying a visa in China is a serious offense in the best of times, but ten days earlier, during the NATO bombing of Yugoslavia, the US had accidentally hit the Chinese embassy in Belgrade, killing three Chinese journalists. President Clinton had profusely apologized, but the Chinese were outraged and had issued a statement labeling the attack a "barbarian act."

The Chinese border guards said to Jamie, "No problem, just pay a ten-thousand-dollar fine for each American and you can pass." Jamie grabbed the passports off the official's desk and scooted to the nearest police office to get the mistake corrected. When he showed the border guards that the problem had been fixed, they let everyone through—except Jamie, whom they detained for two more days.

Nevertheless, Jamie understood the importance of drones to our project, and since the Chinese had never officially told us we couldn't bring them, he agreed that our only option was to take our chances at the border.

My heart rate spiked as I got closer to the front of the line. I was worried about the drones and the stern warning Jamie had given us to be sure that our computers were clear of anything to do with the Free Tibet movement. He said it was not unknown for Chinese customs officials to open a laptop and type "Dalai Lama" into the search bar. Even a single photo could get you denied entry into the country. I had searched my machine to make sure I didn't have anything pro-Tibet in my files, but I did have hundreds of documents and photos related to the search for Sandy Irvine—a search that could possibly prove that the Chinese weren't actually the first to summit Mount Everest from the north.

When it was my turn, I gave the young woman my best smile and handed her my passport. In front of me was a little screen that invited me to rate my experience. I immediately gave her five stars. She looked me over with shrewd eyes, then stamped my passport.

Minutes later, we were zipping along a perfectly manicured highway in two new minivans supplied by the CTMA. The rutted donkey track of death we'd endured in Nepal had been replaced by a smooth strip of blacktop, with painted lines and much-appreciated concrete barriers along the sides. Half an hour later, we crested a small pass. A densely forested valley stretched before us, hemmed in on three sides by shimmering snowcapped peaks with fluted faces of snow and ice and soaring rock walls. The Himalaya.

AFTER LOSING THE American colonies in 1783, Great Britain shifted its imperial ambitions toward Asia and the Pacific. By 1803, the British East India Company ruled a huge swath of India with a private army numbering more than a quarter million soldiers. The British Empire would enjoy more than a century of unrivaled dominance in Asia—during which time it grew by roughly ten million square miles. By the early twentieth century, its colonies, protectorates, dominions, and territories—"the empire on which the sun never sets"—encircled the globe and covered nearly a quarter of the planet's land surface. One in four human beings on Earth was a British subject.

Among its vast portfolio of colonies, India was the crown jewel. From the moment Great Britain solidified its hold on this valuable territory, it began scheming to protect and buffer it from Russia, which would compete with Britain for control of Central Asia throughout much of the nineteenth century. The towering, 1,500-mile-long mountain range that separated the Indian subcontinent from Asia proper was still completely uncharted. The country that could effectively control the Himalaya would have a distinct upper hand in the contest to maintain and expand its colonial footprint.

The project that would eventually lead to mapping the Himalaya began in 1802, under the auspices of Lieutenant Colonel William Lambton. Lambton had approached the East India Company the year before with a proposal for what he called a "Great Trigonometrical Survey." The project, which Lambton predicted would take five years, would ultimately span seven decades. Not until the end of this endeavor was the highest mountain on Earth conclusively identified.

Lambton's ambitious plan addressed an important scientific question that lay at the heart of cartography and navigation. In 1672, a French astronomer named Jean Richer did an experiment in which he proved that a pendulum clock in French Guiana, latitude 4 degrees north, kept different time than the same clock in Paris, latitude 48 degrees north. Not long after, in his *Principia Mathematica*, Isaac Newton theorized that the Earth was not a perfect sphere, but rather an *oblate ellipsoid*—a sphere that is slightly fatter around its middle due to the centrifugal force of its rotation. Richer's experiment with the clock was evidence that the force of gravity is slightly weaker near the equator than at other points on Earth, which would be the case if Newton's theory were correct and the equator is indeed farther from the planet's core than elsewhere on the globe.

But in 1718, the Frenchman César-François Cassini de Thury, based on the results of geodetic surveys undertaken by him and his father, proposed that the Earth was a *prolate ellipsoid*—a sphere that is slightly smaller about its middle. To prove Cassini's theory, a group of French scientists set sail for South America in 1735 to measure a 3-degree arc of the meridian. One year later, another French expedition set sail for Sweden for the same purpose. The results proved Newton's theory, but only nominally, because the measured arcs of meridian were too short to be of any real value to the field of geodesy.

Lambton's goal was to determine the exact degree of this theoretical squishing of the Earth. Latitude and longitude (and the map datum on which this coordinate system is based) would never be perfectly accurate until the exact shape of the Earth's ellipsoid could be determined. Newton had proposed a straightforward method for determining the degree of this deflection: Survey an arc of longitude—a line running perfectly north-south—somewhere on the Earth's surface (the exact length and location didn't matter) and compare its actual measured length with its theoretical length derived from celestial observations at both endpoints. The theoretical length presumes that the Earth is a perfect sphere, so the discrepancy could be used to compute the planet's true shape. Simple and elegant in concept, given the rudimentary methods for measuring distance at the time, Newton's experiment would prove logistically cumbersome in the extreme. Lambton now proposed to do just that by measuring a 1,500-mile-long arc of longitude from the southern tip of the Indian subcontinent right up to the foothills of the Himalaya. The Indian Great Arc of the Meridian, as he called it, would also greatly aid the Survey of India, the ambitious British project to accurately map the entire Indian subcontinent and the mountains to the north. This would, in turn, open this vast territory to road building, railways, and eventual settlement and dominion.

Lambton's project was an epic effort. Supported by hundreds of laborers, he and his team of surveyors spent years triangulating their way north through malarial jungle infested with poisonous snakes and tigers. In places where the land was too flat to see any appreciable distance, the team built a series of thirty-foot-tall towers of brick and masonry and then hauled to the top a thousand-pound telescope-like device called a theodolite (the nineteenth-century equivalent of the guy in an orange vest on the side of the road with a tripod-mounted transit). Distances were measured with precisely calibrated chains that stretched for miles.

When Lambton died in 1823, his work was picked up by his assistant, George Everest. In his book *Into the Silence*, Wade Davis describes Everest, whose name was actually pronounced *Eve-Rest,* as a "miserable man, venomous and cantankerous" who made "few friends in India, in part because of his disregard for ancient religious monuments, which he considered temples of idle and pagan superstitions, mere impediments to his work." Indeed, Everest wouldn't hesitate to obliterate anything that stood in the way of his measurements. Villages were razed; sacred monuments were dynamited into oblivion—whatever it took to keep the Great Arc slicing north.

By all accounts, though, the monomaniacal Everest was a brilliant surveyor. The accuracy of his measurements can barely be improved upon with the latest GPS technology. Each calculation required that he correct for light refraction due to elevation and haze in the atmosphere, and every distance measurement also had to account for temperature; a 1-degree change caused the chains to expand or contract by approximately a third of an inch per mile. And every inch mattered.

Everest retired in 1843, at which point the Great Arc was nearly complete. It was left to his successor, Andrew Waugh, to continue it north and into the Himalaya. Waugh repeatedly asked the Nepal government for permission to enter its territory, but he was summarily turned down. This forced him to map the Himalaya from a lowland belt of marshland and forest on the Indian plain, south of the Himalayan foothills. As he couldn't directly measure distances to various points over the border, he had to derive them by triangulating from several different observation points.

In 1846, using survey stations whose coordinates were established by the Great Trigonometrical Survey, a team triangulated an unassuming smudge on the horizon, 140 miles to the west of a peak in the northeastern corner of Nepal called Kangchenjunga. At the time, Kangchenjunga, which had been calculated to be approximately 28,000 feet high, was believed to be the highest mountain on Earth (at 28,169 feet, it is actually the third-tallest). Calculations of the height of the new peak, which was dubbed XV, wouldn't begin until 1854 when the data was handed to a young Indian mathematician named Radhanath Sikhdar. Sikhdar would spend two years crunching the numbers, endlessly double-checking the various deviations, before eventually deducing that XV was 29,002 feet high. Today, Everest's official height is 29,035 feet. If the mountain has been growing at half a centimeter per year, it would have been approximately three feet shorter in 1856. Using the rudimentary tools available to them at the time, the Great Trigonometric Survey had come within a few dozen feet of Everest's true height.

When it came to naming the various geographic features they encountered and mapped, Lambton and Everest had honored the tradition of using local names. Waugh generally did the same. But the tallest mountain on Earth, he felt, needed a name more befitting its preeminent status—a decidedly British name. In an 1856 letter to the Royal Geographical Society, Waugh proposed that Peak XV be named in honor of his predecessor, who might otherwise have ended up—like he and Lambton—as little more than a historical footnote. The suggestion met with considerable resistance, even from Mr. Everest himself, who argued that locals would have trouble pronouncing his name. But Waugh was determined, and after nine years of relentless lobbying, the RGS announced in 1865 that the highest mountain in the world would henceforth be called Mount Everest.

Everest died a year later, in 1866. It is likely that it would have disappointed him to know that his name would forever be linked with a single mountain, and not, in the end, with the Great Indian Arc of the Meridian, which he called "the greatest scientific undertaking of the kind that has ever been attempted." In the *The Great Arc*, John Keay notes that "other than as convenient trig stations, mountains barely featured in [Everest's] life . . . He saw the Himalayas only towards the end of his career and he hailed them then only as a fitting conclusion to the Great Arc. There is nothing to suggest that he was particularly curious as to their height."

Between 1839 and 1841, not long before Everest handed the reins to Waugh, more than 3,000 astronomical observations were made from stations at both the northern and southern ends of the arc. The theoretical length of the arc was compared to its actual length, and the on-the-ground measurement was slightly shorter.

Using non-Euclidian geometry, Everest calculated that our planet's diameter across the equator is 26.34 miles longer than it is from pole to pole. With current GPS technology, scientists today peg the difference at 26.5 miles, which means Everest was off by 0.16 miles, or a mere 845 feet. Nevertheless, as meticulous as Everest was, he never would have accepted work this sloppy. And to his credit, recent work shows that this error was due to the gravitational pull of the Himalaya—the great mass of the mountains caused slight perturbations in the instruments that were used to find baseline level. This deviation ("deflection of the vertical") was reflected in his measurements and simply couldn't be accounted for with the technology of the time. Given his fanaticism for accuracy and disinterest in mountains, it's ironic (and fitting) that the number he devoted his life to finding was thrown off by the mountain that would forever bear his name.

EVEN THOUGH WE COULD see the Himalaya, we were still three days by road from Everest Base Camp. Our first night was spent in Jilong—a sleepy little border town at 9,200 feet with one foot in the past and another in the future. After checking into an austere, communist-style hotel with no heat, Thom and I headed out to have a look around. In an alleyway, we spied a vending machine. Hoping to find some snacks or maybe even a beer, we made a beeline for it. But to our surprise, the machine was filled with sex toys, including a life-size blow-up doll that we briefly considered purchasing and sticking in Matt's seat in the minivan.

Jilong felt as if it had been built overnight. Everywhere we looked, there were newly constructed cement-block buildings, shops, hotels, and restaurants—most of which sat deserted. We passed through an intersection with working stoplights—something we never saw in Kathmandu, where they are desperately needed—but no vehicles. The only people we saw were three Tibetan women who followed us, trying to exchange our dollars for yuan.

Thom and I soon found ourselves wandering down a freshly laid concrete highway complete with sidewalks and a row of streetlamps with wires sticking out of the bases. After about half a mile, the road ended in a cul-de-sac, beyond which lay a small meadow where a few goats grazed. A tattered string of prayer flags fluttered from a pine tree.

At dinner, Jamie explained that all the construction was in anticipation of a new rail line. The Chinese had recently completed the section connecting Beijing to Lhasa, and the next phase was to continue it across the Tibetan Plateau and up and over the Himalaya via the exact route we were following. The project was behind schedule, but eventually, trains will wind their way down through the Trishuli Gorge via a series of elaborate tunnels and bridges and then on to Kathmandu and, ultimately, India—a country predicted to have a larger population than China by 2027.

It is all part of an ambitious multitrillion-dollar infrastructure project launched by Xi Jinping, president of the People's Republic of China, called the Belt and Road Initiative (BRI), but more popularly known as the New Silk Road. Xi's vision, already well underway, is to finance and build a transportation and trade network connecting mainland China with the rest of Asia, the Middle East, Europe, Africa, and the Americas. This ambitious project is the modern equivalent of the land and sea routes of the ancient Silk Road. In his book of political theories entitled *The Governance of China*, Xi writes about what he calls "the Chinese Dream." His ambitious vision is for China to supplant the United States as the world's preeminent superpower by 2049—the one hundredth anniversary of the founding of the People's Republic of China—by outmaneuvering the US economically, geopolitically, and culturally. The New Silk Road is a clear indication of China's intentions to expand its sphere of influence on a global scale.

In exchange for Nepal's unwavering support for China's claim on Tibet, Xi has begun to pour money into Nepal. In June of 2019, the two countries signed a $2.4 billion trade agreement committing China to help Nepal develop major infrastructure projects. As we bounced our way up the Trishuli Gorge in Nepal two days earlier, we passed a massive hydroelectric complex that included a four-kilometer-long tunnel bored straight through a mountain. This was being constructed by a subsidiary of the China Three Gorges Corporation—the Chinese state-owned power company that built the world's largest hydroelectric dam on the Yangtze River.

IN THE MORNING, our group continued north along smooth blacktop that led us through thick forests of blue pine, fir, and spruce. As we gained elevation, the trees became smaller and scragglier until they petered out at around 13,000 feet. The road now led us through a desert canyon lined with sand-colored hills. Several hours later, after crossing a 17,000-foot pass, we descended a long series of switchbacks onto the Tibetan Plateau.

We had successfully crossed over the Himalaya. From a pullout by the side of the road, we stared in awe at the vast landscape spread before us. Grassy plains, vibrant with the green shoots of spring and braided with meandering rivers and creeks, stretched as far as we could see to the north, east, and west. The Tibetan Plateau encompasses an area the size of the entire western US, and in some ways it resembles the American Great Plains. Yet, with an average elevation of 14,800 feet—higher than the tallest peak in the Rocky Mountains—there is something otherworldly about Tibet that you just don't feel in Nebraska or Montana. It may be the quality of the light, which was in full display as we stood there shooting photos and admiring the view. Between the near hills and a swirling bank of dark clouds, a thin band of radiance glowed on the horizon. Through this, sunbeams illuminated patches of ground, as if, like George Everest once said, these places were "a little nearer the stars than that of any other." Directly in front of us, the seventeen-mile-long Lake Peiku, with water the color of the Caribbean Sea, glowed like an aquamarine gemstone in a basin surrounded by reddish-brown, low-lying hills. A white frosting of salt fringed the lake's shoreline—the same salt that Tibetan nomads have exchanged with Nepali traders for almost a millennium.

To the east, in the direction of Mount Everest, I traced the contours of the lofty peaks bordering this million-square-mile expanse. Shishapangma, the world's fourteenth-tallest mountain, and the only 8,000-meter peak to sit entirely within Tibet, shimmered like a mirage in the sky, its summit wreathed in clouds and blanketed in snow that never melts.

Tibetan nomads wandered these plains for millennia, grazing herds of sheep, cattle, goats, and yaks, following the seasons to fresh pastures and calling home wherever they pitched their yak-hair tents. But starting in 2006, the Chinese government began a program of resettling nomads under a policy called Comfortable Housing, which it says will increase rural Tibetans' standard of living and boost the local economy. We saw signs of this with increasing frequency as we made our way across the plateau toward Mount Everest. Jamie had told us that the proliferation of these housing projects has increased dramatically since the launch of the New Silk Road in 2013.

According to Human Rights Watch, at least two-thirds of Tibetan nomads, which amounts to hundreds of thousands of people, have been forcibly moved into housing projects along main thoroughfares like the "Friendship Highway" we were now following.

Families that move into these projects often find themselves forced to work in shops or on road construction crews, cast adrift from everything they have ever known. While the houses might be new and heavily subsidized, the price these people pay is the loss of an ancient way of life. Among former nomads, high rates of depression, alcoholism, and suicide have been reported.

Ever since the incorporation of Tibet into the People's Republic of China in 1950, critics of the Chinese government have accused it of subordinating Tibetan culture to Chinese ways. In the early years after its annexation, Tibet was able to maintain much of its autonomy, and the ancient culture continued to thrive. But by the mid-1950s, Chinese rule had become more oppressive and Tibetans began to chafe. An armed uprising in 1959 led the Dalai Lama, the spiritual leader of the Tibetan people, to flee Tibet to a new home in Dharamsala, India, where he has resided ever since. During China's Cultural Revolution, from 1966 to 1976, more than six thousand monasteries across Tibet were destroyed by Mao Zedong's Red Guards. Monastic life, the pillar of Tibetan culture for centuries, was eradicated or driven underground. Monks and nuns who resisted were killed or imprisoned. In the 1980s and '90s, China encouraged the migration of Han Chinese from the eastern lowlands into Tibet by offering housing subsidies, favorable loans, and cash bonuses. When I first visited Lhasa in 2002, the city was surrounded by farmland and still had an old-world Tibetan feel. Today, Lhasa has been rebuilt in the image of China. The streets are lined with Chinese restaurants, hotels, and shops. Business is booming, construction projects abound.

AFTER TWO NIGHTS acclimatizing at 14,200 feet in a gritty little town called Tingri, we set off on the final leg of our journey to Base Camp. We drove east on the Sino-Nepal Friendship Highway along the northern fringe of the Himalaya for an hour before turning off at the entrance of the Chomolungma Nature Reserve (Chomolungma, the Tibetan name for Mount Everest, means goddess mother of the world) now finally joining the route followed by the British during their seven attempts to climb Mount Everest from the north between 1921 and 1938. Without access to Nepal, the British had entered Tibet through Sikkim, far to the east of where we crossed over the Himalaya. Back then, of course, there were no roads, and the entire three-hundred-mile approach, which took almost two months, was done completely on foot and horseback, alongside a train of donkeys numbering in the hundreds.

The Everest Road, as this last section is called, has been continuously improved over the sixty years since its initial construction to support the 1960 Chinese expedition. In 2017, it was finally paved. This year, we rode on smooth pavement almost directly into Base Camp. The Everest Road serves as one of many poignant examples of the difference between the two faces of the mountain today. On the Nepal side, climbers must still take a sketchy flight to the "world's most dangerous airport" in Lukla, and then hike for ten days through the foothills of the Himalaya to reach Everest Base Camp on the Khumbu Glacier. On the north side, if you pre-acclimatize with Hypoxico or a similar system, you could fly to the city of Shigatse and be in Base Camp a few hours later. (We had chosen the longer overland route from Kathmandu because our outfitter and many of our sherpa support team were based there.) I wondered if Xi Jinping had visited Yosemite or Yellowstone, because the experience of driving toward Base Camp on smooth blacktop reminded me of how the US National Park Service funnels visitors into a cookie-cutter, curated experience designed to pump the masses through in a way that is easy, safe, and profitable.

Had we continued another twenty minutes east on the Friendship Highway, we would have reached the town of Shegar, where the finishing touches were being put on a monumental new mountaineering center the size of five Walmart Supercenters. The complex purportedly includes an Everest museum, a medical clinic, a travel agency, guide services, equipment rentals, accommodations, restaurants, and a helicopter base. Plans are underway to add a stop in Shegar along the New Silk Road high-speed rail line.

After crossing the final pass on the Everest Road, we descended into a wide river valley. Out on the Tingri plateau, villages had been few and far between, but here, in the shadow of Mount Everest, we passed small hamlets every few minutes. A typical village had a dozen or so homes built around a central courtyard, with thick, dry-stacked stone or mud-brick walls painted in whitewash. Jamie said these villages supply all the yaks that are used on the mountain to ferry supplies from Base Camp to Advanced Base Camp, and indeed we saw many herders moving yak trains along the banks of a shallow, braided river that ran down the middle of the valley. It was planting season and women and children were working in the fields, sowing barley and winter wheat. Near the side of the road, I watched two women working together to move a pile of dirt. One held the end of a shovel handle while the other yanked on a rope tied near the spade. We were now heading due south, with Everest looming above us, but dark clouds hung low and obscured any view of the peak. The sky was beginning to spit small flecks of snow.

Renan wanted some aerial footage to illustrate our approach, so we stopped on the outskirts of a small village where he launched one of the Mavic Pros—thankfully, all of the drones had made it over the border with no issues. Ever since our trip to NTS, Renan had been trying to hack the drones. But DJI had apparently fixed the software glitch that had provided clever and determined users backdoor access to disable the altitude governor. So far, Renan had failed to unlock the drones. This was a serious problem for the expedition, and one we currently did not have a solution for. But here it didn't matter because he only wanted to buzz low over the village.

We were zooming down the highway, with the drone in the air above the vehicle, when I looked up and saw a rope across the road just ahead.

"Uhh, I think we might have just rolled up on a police checkpoint," I said.

"Oh shit," said Renan. "Hold on, I'm going super high." He mashed the joystick and took the drone straight up into the sky. But just as it reached its height ceiling of 500 meters, the controller in Renan's hands, the guts of which was actually his iPhone, began beeping loudly while a robotic female voice said: "Battery level is low, the aircraft will fly to its home point in ten seconds."

"Oh my god, we're fucked," yelled Renan.

Matt was hovering over Renan's shoulder. "Let me take this," he said. Matt is also a professional drone pilot. Renan passed the controller to the back seat without another word. By now the drone was near the ground, so Matt flew it down the middle of the road ahead of us. The camera was pointing straight down, so the viewfinder showed nothing but gray pavement. Matt later told me that it suddenly dawned on him that he should pan up to see what was ahead. When he did, he instantly yelled, "Fuuuuuuuuuuck!" The drone was about to go through the windshield of an oncoming SUV. Matt would later say that he probably missed hitting the vehicle by about five feet. Were it not for his quick reflexes, our trip might have ended right there with an international incident. The four white Toyota Land Cruisers were some kind of government or military convoy. Each had red and blue lights flashing in the grill, and dark tinted windows. For all we knew, Xi Jinping himself was in one of them. A few minutes later, our driver jumped back in with our passports in his hand. A short way down the road, we stopped and picked up the drone where Matt had discreetly landed it next to a street sign.

At four in the afternoon, we passed through the final checkpost outside the famous Rongbuk Monastery where the British had first asked for the head lama's blessing in 1921. From the vintage photos I had seen in various books, the place didn't appear to have changed one bit over the past century. The cubist buildings, flat-roofed and built of whitewashed mud bricks, were similar to those we had been driving past for days, there were just more of them, stacked on top and beside each other somewhat haphazardly, across the base of a barren gray hillside. A giant stupa (Buddhist shrine), capped with a golden obelisk and ringed with prayer flags, sat commandingly in the front courtyard.

The road now finally turned to dirt. We crested one last hill and drove out onto a gravel plain at 17,000 feet. In front of us lay a veritable city across which hundreds of tents of every conceivable size, shape, and color were strewn.

So, this is home for the next six weeks, I thought, somewhat dejectedly, as I stepped out of the vehicle into a squall that was quickly coating the ground in wet snow. My first impression of the place was similar to what Sandy Irvine had written in his diary upon arrival here in April 1924.

"The Base Camp looked a very uninviting place."

CHAPTER SEVEN

The Miracle Highway

WE HAD PULLED up in an alleyway between half a dozen army-style tents. Prayer flags strung between their peaks whipped overhead in a stiff breeze blowing down off the glacier. Steam poured from the door of one of the tents. From within emerged a stout-looking Sherpa* in his mid-fifties. Walking up and taking both of my hands, he said, "Welcome to Base Camp, I'm Dawa." Jamie had already told us about Dawa, one of the directors of Expedition Himalaya, the Nepali outfitter we had hired. As a younger man, Dawa had

* Sherpa, which means "eastern person," is a specific ethnic group of people who migrated from eastern Tibet into Nepal's Solukhumbu District in the fifteenth century. Since the earliest days of Western exploration of the Himalaya, Sherpas have worked as support staff, porters, and guides. In the 1920s and '30s, the porters on the early Everest expeditions also included Tibetans, Bhutias (Sikkimese people of Tibetan descent), and Gurkhas (some of whom were from India). Today, *sherpa* is used ubiquitously for any native support staff on the mountain, be they Sherpa, Tibetan, Tamang, Rai, Gurung, Indian, or Chinese. In recent years, some have advocated dropping the term as a catchall out of cultural sensitivity and a recognition that there are many different ethnicities that work as guides and porters in the Himalaya. However, the moniker is still widely used on Mount Everest and, as far as I know, has entirely positive connotations amongst most climbers and Sherpas. I've chosen to use the term *sherpa* or *climbing sherpa*, lowercase, to denote anyone in the job or role of support staff on the mountain—guides and porters alike—and *Sherpa*, uppercase, in the instances where I refer to the ethnic group or as a proper name. In Nepal, it is common for Sherpa to use their ethnic identity as a last name. I have tried to avoid using the term "his sherpa," due to its colonial association, but where I have been unable to avoid it, please note that this is intended to be understood as the equivalent of writing, "his guide." In the historical narrative, I have followed the British example of calling their local support staff porters. For more on this subject, please see the Notes on Sources at the end of this book.

climbed many 8,000-meter peaks, including Everest several times. But he was now retired from high-altitude climbing and would serve as our Base Camp manager. His son, Sonam, who had driven with us from Kathmandu, was one of the dozen high-altitude climbing sherpas who would support us on the mountain. It was Sonam's first Everest expedition. In fact, like me, he had never climbed any other 8,000-meter peaks. Dawa had arrived a week earlier with half of our climbing sherpas, a cook, and two Tibetan kitchen hands, all of whom we would get to know well in the coming weeks.

Dawa led us to our bright yellow dining tent. Most of it was taken up with a long table flanked by folding lawn chairs. The floor was made of interconnecting foam tiles with a fake grass print. Over biscuits and tea, Dawa updated us on the latest news from the mountain. Our camp was set up right next to a Chinese expedition, which was not a coincidence. In the end, the CTMA had given us tacit permission to film on the mountain. Part of the agreement that Jamie, Dawa, and the other principals of Expedition Himalaya had worked out with the CTMA was that we would employ four CTMA-supplied climbing sherpas. Although it was not stated explicitly, we understood that apart from helping us on the mountain, these four would be keeping an eye on us for the Chinese.

We also learned that a Chinese production company was currently in Base Camp shooting for a Hollywood-style film about the first ascent of Everest's Northeast Ridge in 1960. I had read about this film, called *The Climbers*, on the Hollywood Reporter website back in March. It would star Jackie Chan. According to Dawa, Chan was in Base Camp right now, and the Chinese and other expeditions had been flying drones all over the place.

I spent the next couple of hours getting situated in my own personal four-man tent, a bombproof black-and-yellow dome made by the North Face, called the Bastion. A luxury I hadn't anticipated was that my tent had electricity, supplied by a wire connecting to the local power grid. A light hung from the ceiling and there was an electrical outlet—an expedition first for me. Another novelty was the halfway decent LTE signal. Apparently, communicating with Hampton and the rest of my family was not going to be an issue—at least not in Base Camp, my new home away from home.

Dawa had supplied each of us with a three-inch-thick foam mattress. And as this was not my first rodeo, I had brought my own pillows from home. With the mattress and three fluffy pillows, my bed was actually a bed. Next to my mattress, I placed a plastic chair I had bought in Tingri, which I deemed essential for all the reading, journaling, and studying I planned to do over the coming weeks. It was a bit too tall, so I borrowed a saw from the cook staff and hacked the legs down and used pieces of cardboard to keep them from cutting through the floor.

I had just plopped into my chair when Thom called from outside. "Hey, Synnott, get your ass out here, now." I slipped on a pair of down booties and crawled out through the vestibule. Thom and Renan were standing about ten feet away, flanked by Nick and Matt, who had their cameras out. Jim was a few feet farther back holding a boom mike with a big fuzzy thing on the end. The squall had passed, and the clouds had lifted. Right in front of us stood Mount Everest.

The sun was setting. Everything was in the shade except the upper section of the North Face, which was bathed in golden rays of alpenglow. The mountain was blanketed in a white mantle, but I could see the horizontal striations of the Yellow Band and the distinct vertical gash of the Norton Couloir. And above it all, hovering in the blue-black sky, was the ethereal summit.

George Mallory wrote extensively about the first time he saw Mount Everest, describing it as "a prodigious white fang." In a letter to Ruth on June 15, 1921, he wrote:

> Suddenly our eyes caught glint of snow through the clouds; and gradually, very gradually, in the course of two hours or so, visions of great mountainsides and glaciers and ridges . . . appeared through the floating rifts . . . little by little, the lesser to the greater until, incredibly higher in the sky than imagination had ventured to dream, the top of Everest appeared . . . The problem of its great ridges and glaciers began to take shape and to haunt the mind.

Sandy Irvine left little in his diary or his letters home in the way of impressions of the mountain. Flights of fancy weren't his style. On April 21, 1924, Irvine wrote about climbing a small hill where he and Mallory examined the upper pyramid with a pair of binoculars from about thirty miles away: "The whole mountain, or what we could see of it, gave the impression of tremendous bulk."

As assistant to the head oxygen officer, Irvine had taken it upon himself to refine the design of the apparatus as soon as he had been invited to join the expedition. He submitted detailed drawings and instructions to Siebe Gorman, the manufacturer. It wasn't until he unpacked the crates of oxygen equipment in Calcutta that he realized, to his great dismay, that Siebe Gorman hadn't incorporated any of his suggestions. Even worse, he discovered that many of the sets were damaged. Of the ninety cylinders the team had shipped to India, fifteen were empty and another twenty-four were leaking. "They unfortunately haven't taken my design," wrote Sandy to his Spitsbergen partner, Geoffrey Milling, ". . . what they've sent is hopeless—breaks if you touch it—leaks & is ridiculously clumsy and heavy."

Fortunately, Irvine had brought with him a full set of tools and replacement parts, including copper tubing, pressure valves, rivets, a soldering gun, screwdrivers, hammers, chisels, and wrenches. One of the only times the other expedition members saw Irvine lose his cool was when he discovered that Siebe Gorman had given him the wrong information on the type of threads used on the oxygen sets. Despite meticulous planning of his tool kit, which weighed upward of sixty pounds, he had brought the wrong size taps and dies to Tibet.

By the time the expedition reached Base Camp, Irvine was putting the finishing touches on what he called the Mark IV, his fourth redesign of the system. One reason bottled oxygen had not been used more on the 1922 expedition was that the contraption weighed more than thirty pounds and was so cumbersome that the men found it almost impossible to climb with it on their backs. Irvine discovered that if he inverted the oxygen cylinders so that the valves were on the bottom, he could eliminate a pressure gauge and much of the piping, the most fragile part of the apparatus.

Irvine's tent became the expedition workshop, and it was here, ensconced in oiled canvas that flapped incessantly in the strong winds blowing off the glacier, that he worked from sunup until midnight and sometimes later, every single day. In addition to working on the oxygen sets, the young Mr. Fix-It was also busy repairing and redesigning a host of other items, including the expedition cookstoves, Bentley Beetham's camera, Odell's tripod, Mallory's cot, and his own watch. He also fashioned tin shades for the kerosene lamps they used to illuminate their tents.

Irvine's role as the team engineer had become so demanding that he worried he wouldn't be able to leave his workshop to begin climbing the mountain. On the approach, the relative novice had been thrilled to learn that he would be teamed up with Mallory on the summit bid, which was planned for late May. Edward "Teddy" Norton and Howard Somervell would comprise the other summit team. In his diary that night, Irvine had written: "I'm awfully glad that I'm with Mallory in the first lot, but I wish ever so much that it was a non-oxygen attempt."

Our first night in Base Camp was a long one. My eyes wouldn't focus on my book, and it was too cold to hold it anyway, even with gloves. To stay warm, I burrowed deeply into my –40°F sleeping bag, only to realize that my flatulence, which had been building since we arrived in Base Camp, had turned the inside of my bag into a gas chamber.

In the morning, I staggered over to our dining tent, where the rest of the team was circling a steaming espresso maker. I plopped into a chair, exhaling loudly as my breath froze in the air around me. The sun had yet to hit camp and the temperature was probably in the single digits. Dawa had set up a propane heater in the corner, but it hardly took the edge off. I guessed it was leaking because there was a strange odor in the air.

"How do you feel?" asked Thom.

I told him about how I had nearly asphyxiated myself. "Ahh, you've got HAFE, high altitude flatulence emission." I thought this was just a clever joke on Thom's part, but when I later looked it up, I learned that it's a real thing. Scientists have even studied it—why, I'm not sure. A 2013 paper in the journal *Medical Hypotheses* found that HAFE (which actually stands for high-altitude flatus expulsion) is caused not by the expansion of gases in your intestinal tract but, rather, from the "diffusion of CO_2 into the intestinal lumen from the bloodstream."

Apparently, I was the only one suffering from this affliction, but Thom said that his head was pounding, and he had no appetite. Matt, who had given us a scare two days earlier when he passed out while exiting the minivan, said he felt okay and only had a slight headache. I was listless and had actually winded myself walking over from my tent, but I was pleased not to have any trace of a headache. It appeared that my time in the altitude tent back home was paying off.

Or maybe it was the Diamox. I'd taken my first dose two days earlier as we were approaching the final 17,000-foot pass before the Tibetan Plateau. Diamox, aka acetazolamide, is a prescription medicine that was developed in the early 1950s for the treatment of glaucoma and epilepsy. In a landmark study conducted in 1975 in the Khumbu Valley, Dr. Peter Hackett tested Diamox on trekkers and proved it was also effective in the prevention and treatment of altitude sickness. A study that showed the drug worked as a respiratory stimulant and raised oxygen levels in hypoxic dogs had tipped him off. Diamox works by acidifying the blood, which increases respiration and therefore oxygen levels, and it also counteracts retention and edema in the brain. Climbers and trekkers going to altitude have used it ever since. I had taken the drug on several previous expeditions, and once again I was suffering from one of its common side effects, known as paresthesia, a tingling and numbness in my toes and fingers.

Jamie, who had spent more time at altitude than all of us combined, was the only one who seemed unfazed. He turned his laptop toward me so I could see the brightly colored image he had pulled up on a website called Storm Surf. "This is my secret weapon," he said. He was studying a computer model of the jet stream, which undulated like a brightly colored snake across the display. On Everest, life revolves around the weather. It was Jamie's job to interpret the forecasts and, like a game of chess, plot our movements on the mountain accordingly. In simple terms, you advance when the weather is good and retreat when it's bad, and you hope like hell you never checkmate yourself by ending up in the wrong place at the wrong time. Back in Mallory and Irvine's day, weather forecasting consisted of checking the barometer and looking out the door of the tent, but nowadays, every expedition on the mountain works with a professional meteorologist. Jamie had signed up with a company called Everest Weather, run by a private meteorologist and amateur mountaineer from Redmond, Washington, named Michael Fagin. Fagin, who provides weather forecasting for farms and vineyards in addition to mountaineering expeditions, emailed Jamie a detailed forecast every day.

The big picture, Jamie explained, was that things were not looking good. It had been an unusually snowy winter and spring, and the mountain was currently buried in snow. The conditions could not have been worse for searching. Paradoxically, what we needed now, more than anything, was for the jet stream to pummel the upper reaches of the mountain with hurricane-force winds. Above 8,000 meters, the snow never melts, so our only hope for drier conditions was for the Yellow Band to be swept clean by the broom of the mountain gods.

Mount Everest is so tall that its top actually sticks up into the jet stream. For all but a handful of days every year, the summit is raked by gale-force winds. But when the monsoon begins to build, the subtropical jet stream tends to weaken, while the polar jet stream pushes north. For complex reasons having to do mostly with temperature differentials at different elevations in the atmosphere, there is often a short window of time when the wind dies on the upper reaches of Mount Everest—normally in late May, just before the monsoon pushes up against the Himalaya. This is when you go for the summit. Everest also has a brief post-monsoon weather window in September or October, but due to the cold, this season is much less popular with climbers.

While it is hard to imagine, Everest has been summited fifteen times in the winter—the first in 1979, and the last all the way back in 1993. In 1987, the late Ang Rita Sherpa summited Everest on December 22 without supplemental oxygen. Today, winter ascents of 8,000-meter peaks represent the extreme limit of modern-day alpinism. There have been unsuccessful attempts at a solo, winter, oxygenless ascent of Everest. The long-sought-after first winter ascent of K2 was finally achieved in January 2021 by a team of ten Nepali climbers. The first British expedition to Mount Everest in 1921 ran straight through the summer monsoon season, and it was thus they learned the hard way that this is a bad time for climbing due to frequent storms and heavy precipitation.

Nonetheless, Reinhold Messner's unsupported, oxygenless solo ascent of the North Face took place in July 1980, during the height of the monsoon. This was perhaps the most ambitious Everest ascent to date. Messner knew it was a snowy time of year, but he chose it specifically because there would be no one on the mountain, and the deep snow would cover the upper rock bands in the Norton Couloir, making them easier to climb.

According to Jamie, it's feasible to climb Everest in wind speeds up to 25 miles per hour and ideal if they stay below 15 mph. With winds higher than 25 mph, the wind-chill factor elevates the risk of frostbite and hypothermia to an unacceptable level. In a typical season, wind speeds below 25 mph might last only for three to five days, so forecasting when the lull will begin and end is critical. Once you're acclimated and your camps are in place, it takes three or four days to summit from Advanced Base Camp (the itinerary is roughly the same from the north or south side) and another day or two to descend. If you err one way or the other, even by a day, you could find yourself high on the mountain when the jet stream reappears—a potentially fatal mistake.

There are some years, though, when the summit window is longer. In the spring of 2018, it lasted for eleven consecutive days. The jet stream gave teams on Everest such a wide berth that all the various expeditions on both sides of the mountain were able to work together to stagger their summit bids and avoid the crowds that seem to be the bane of today's Everest climber. That was a good year. Only five people died.

As Jamie now explained, our plan was to spend the next four days in Base Camp acclimatizing to our present altitude. He recommended that we stay hydrated, and if we could muster it, some short hikes in the surrounding hills would probably be good for our constitutions. We planned to set out for our first rotation up the mountain on April 26. The tentative itinerary had us taking five days to reach the North Col, where we'd sleep for two nights at 23,000 feet, then descend all the way back to Base Camp for rest and recovery. Those two oxygen-deprived days on the North Col would further activate the acclimatization response of our bodies, boosting the proportion of red blood cells in our bloodstream and making other adaptations. Only then would we be physiologically prepared to venture up into the Death Zone.

If Renan could figure out how to hack the drone in the meantime, we hoped to do some flights from the North Col to get some high-resolution photos of the search zone, which we could later analyze in the comfort of Base Camp. Then, if we found something promising with the drone, either at Holzel's spot or somewhere else, we could climb to that location and investigate firsthand. Nothing was said about the summit. At this point, the search was all that mattered.

A WEEK EARLIER, during our first evening in Nepal, we had settled in with a round of beers in the Hotel Tibet's rooftop bar, five stories above the chaos of downtown Kathmandu.

"Let's have a show of hands," Jamie said. "Who wants to summit Mount Everest as part of this expedition?"

Thom shot his arm in the air. I was next, then Jim. Matt and Nick raised their hands simultaneously, albeit a bit sheepishly. Renan, sitting directly across from me, hesitated for so long that I thought maybe he would demur, but then his hand came up too. Jamie was the only one who didn't raise his hand. He had agreed to lead this trip because he wanted to help write the final chapter in the Mallory and Irvine saga—not because he wanted to stand on the summit one more time. Jamie pursed his lips and slowly moved his gaze from one of us to the next.

"You guys are way more experienced than the average group I guide up Everest," he said, "but the thing you need to understand is that the window of time you get high on the mountain is very short. Yeah? The jet stream usually only lifts off for a limited time, and you're at your physical limit up there. There are very few people who can spend a second or third night at Camp Three. So, I really think it's going to be searching or summiting, but not both. I'm not totally dashing hopes, but I wanted to get this out there."

It made sense, of course. Any time we spent on a summit bid was time we could be searching instead. The more we searched, the better chance we had of finding Irvine and the camera. National Geographic had by now committed nearly seven figures toward our expedition. What would our sponsor think if we got up high on the mountain and then gave short shrift to the search because we all got summit fever?

I had always known that it would likely be an either-or proposition. When this project first germinated through those early conversations with Thom, forgoing the summit seemed plausible. Assuming Renan would be philosophically opposed to joining the herd of Everest summit seekers, I actually concocted as a selling point something about how cool it would be if we had the summit within our grasp, only to turn our backs on it. At the time, I half bought into the idea myself. As I got deeper into the planning stages of the trip, however, the prospect of coming all the way to Everest and not trying for the summit felt less and less appealing.

Now that I was in Base Camp, the question of what I was really doing here began to gnaw at me.

Resting in my tent after breakfast, I realized how critical the drones had become to this whole enterprise. If we could conduct a thorough search from the North Col during our acclimatization rotation, then we might just be able to have our cake and eat it too. If we could find what looked to be a body with the drones, we would only have to detour off the route to that exact location, which might still give us time to reach the summit. But so far, Renan had been stymied in his efforts to hack the altitude governor. Like the constantly tinkering Sandy Irvine, he was spending hours every day trying every possible thing he could think of to unlock his machines.

IN THE AFTERNOON, Renan, Matt, Jim, and I went to see Cory Richards, who was staying in the Alpenglow Base Camp, which was somewhere out amongst the sea of Day-Glo nylon that surrounded us. The mountain was mostly obscured in clouds, but the visibility down here was good enough for me to study the lay of the land. The first camp we passed was Transcend Adventure. Jamie had already warned us about this team. It was an Indian expedition that included eleven teenagers with very limited mountaineering experience. Off to our left, up against the gravel mounds marking the snout of the Rongbuk Glacier, was a cluster of white dome tents. This was the home base of the Seven Summits Club, a Russian outfit run by Alex Abramov. Abramov organizes expeditions to the Seven Summits, most of the other 8,000-meter peaks, and the North and South Poles.

What struck me as we shuffled our way through Base Camp was the cleanliness of the place. I didn't see a single scrap of trash anywhere. We had paid a $1,500-per-person environmental levy to cover the removal of our trash. Sure enough, two days later, a garbage truck would pull into camp, just like they used to do in the Boston suburb where I grew up.

We found Cory sitting in the middle of camp in a gigantic orange geodesic dome tent owned by Alpenglow Expeditions. Cory, who had eventually secured financial backing for his expedition from Nikon and a Swiss watch company called Vacheron Constantin, had purchased spots on Alpenglow's permit for him and his partner, Topo. The tent had a wooden door and a coat room that led into a cavernous space about thirty feet across, with a ceiling half as high. It was double-walled, with an inner layer that looked like a white down comforter and a large plastic window on the south side through which the view was undoubtedly epic on clear days. The floor was covered wall to wall in a maroon indoor-outdoor carpet with smaller oriental rugs scattered on top of it. The place was palatial compared to our camp and reminded me of a sultan's encampment in the desert, complete with an L-shaped inflatable couch where Cory lounged alongside Topo.

Cory was looking well. His face was tanned, and his dirty-blond hair was stylishly tousled, as it always seems to be. Cory jumped off the couch and greeted us enthusiastically.

"What can I get you?" he offered. "Coffee? Sparkling water? We have cans and soda stream." Unlike the last time we had hung out, Cory seemed buoyant and excited. Maybe it was finally being in the thrall of the objective for which he had been training nonstop for the past year. Cory and Topo had been in Base Camp about a week. They had been doing acclimatization hikes and their plan was to head up to ABC in a few days.

"The Chinese came by yesterday," said Cory. "They tried to tell us that we couldn't do our route."

"What? Why? You have a permit for it, don't you?"

"Yeah, of course. We worked all that out months ago. Still, they tried to talk us out of it, saying it was too dangerous. I guess they just needed to have their say. Once they did, it was okay."

I suppose I could understand where the Chinese were coming from. It was hard to say what was more dangerous, climbing a new route on Everest or climbing Everest without oxygen. But combining the two was just about the most dangerous thing I could imagine doing. And apparently the CTMA, which takes great pride in the fact that fewer people die on its side of the mountain, agreed. According to Alan Arnette, an American climber and respected Everest blogger, a total of 284 people were expected to climb the north side of Everest this season—equally divided between paying customers and the supporting climbing sherpas. The number on the south side was 772 (382 members, 390 support). All told, 1,136 people would be trying to climb the peak. And of those, Cory and Topo were the only two people attempting a nonstandard route. They were also the only ones on the north side eschewing bottled oxygen, while just a handful were planning to do the same on the South Col route.

When I asked Cory why he wanted to climb without oxygen, he waved his hand like he was shooing a fly away. Matt was filming, and Jim was holding a boom mike over Cory's head, just out of the frame. "I think Topo should answer that question," said Cory. Topo had been listening to our conversation with a thoughtful expression on his face, but he had barely spoken so far. Notwithstanding the jeans and hoodie, his dark hair, black-rimmed glasses and quiet demeanor gave me the distinct impression of an Ecuadorian Clark Kent.

He now looked at me directly and spoke matter-of-factly. "Climbing Everest with oxygen is like doing the Tour de France on a motorbike. You still enjoy the views. It's fun. But it's not like riding the bike."

Topo had climbed Everest four times. The first was his own personal quest, and he did so without using oxygen. Then he climbed the mountain three more times working as a guide, when he used it. He said that all the people he had guided to the summit would not have been able to do it if they hadn't used "a lot" of oxygen. But he quickly hedged, maybe because he realized that we were using oxygen. He said he didn't think there was a right or wrong way to climb Everest. "I've seen more passion from my clients than from some of the pros. Their desire tends to be very honest. 'I want to stand on top,' they say. That's pure mountaineering to me."

Cory showed us some photos on his camera that he had taken of their proposed route and told us a bit more about what they might do on the upper part of the mountain if they managed to get past the "event horizon." At 27,000 feet, their line would intersect the standard route. If they could make it this far via terra incognita, they had no intention of clipping into the fixed lines and joining the circus for the final 2,000 feet. On the viewfinder of his camera, Cory zoomed in on an image and pointed out the small catwalk just below the Second Step that might allow them to stay off the main route and avoid the crux of the Northeast Ridge. This was the traverse, some have speculated, that Mallory and Irvine could have taken to reach the summit in 1924.

"How do you compare what you're trying to do to what Mallory and Irvine were attempting?" asked Renan.

"In a lot of ways, it's quite similar," said Cory. "Two people launching into unknown terrain on the highest mountain in the world. It's calling back to those early days of exploration. And that's exactly the point. We want it to be exploratory, to be unknown, because that's the driving force behind human innovation. How far can we go?"

"Can you keep an eye out for Irvine when you're on that traverse?" I asked.

Cory chuckled. "That would be funny, wouldn't it, if we ended up being the ones to find him?"

BEFORE WE SET OFF UP the mountain, we needed to ask Chomolungma for permission and good luck with a Buddhist ceremony called a *puja*, which is a standard part of any Himalayan climbing expedition. Dawa and his team had built a square altar out of rocks in the center of our camp. It was waist high, draped in an ornate yellow tablecloth and covered in offerings, including incense, candles, little bells, fruit, a gold chalice, and a dozen or so beautiful statuettes called *tormas* that the cook staff had carved out of butter and flour. Scattered in and among the other items were several brightly colored *thangka* paintings depicting Buddhist deities. (Conspicuously, there was no image of the Dalai Lama, presumably because that would not have been acceptable to CTMA officials who were also attending the ceremony and sitting amongst us.)

Jamie told us that we could place items we wanted blessed onto the altar. Several of the climbing sherpas put their axes and crampons up there and Renan offered up a vintage VPK camera that he had bought on eBay before the expedition. (Unlike Holzel's, which I had brought with me, Renan's worked, and he actually had film for it. A few days before I departed, Holzel's VPK arrived in the mail wrapped in tinfoil, with a note saying I should bring it to China "as a decoy," in case we found "the genuine article.") Thom put up a picture of his two boys. I offered a photo of my own family. I also added a small stuffed giraffe, which was once attached to my two-year-old's pacifier. When I had unpacked my duffel in Base Camp, I found a manilla envelope that Hampton must have snuck in there before I left. Inside was a long letter from her, some family photos, and the giraffe. The note said that Tommy wanted me to have it because it was "the one with all the love in it."

There were probably forty or so people gathered in a circle around the altar, sitting on mattresses and sleeping pads. As I looked around, I saw many familiar faces, but there were some sherpas I hadn't met yet. Expedition Himalaya was outfitting three other expeditions that season besides ours, all of whom were American. There was a fifty-five-year-old guy named Frank Campanaro from Florida, who had hired two sherpas to guide him to the summit; a financial planner from Oregon named Jim in his late fifties, who was climbing with a veteran American guide named Scott Woolums; and a group of trekkers from Arizona who had a permit to climb to the North Col, but not above.

A Sherpa named Ngati (pronounced *naughty*), sitting cross-legged at the head of the altar with a prayer book open in front of him, began to chant, and soon all the other sherpas joined in. As the sweet smell of burning juniper filled the air around us, Dawa walked around the circle rubbing *tsampa*, a flour made of roasted barley, onto our cheeks. He also ladled uncooked rice into the palms of our hands, which we flung into the air three times (an auspicious number for Buddhists) while the sherpas called out *lha gyal lo*, which means "victory to the gods." Half an hour in, some of the sherpas walked up with a long wooden pole. The end was stuck into a plastic five-gallon bucket in the middle of the altar and chocked into place with rocks as it was raised and guyed out with lines of prayer flags that were fastened to various structures around the camp. A breeze coming down off the glacier filled the air with the sound of fluttering flags, which now mixed with the rhythmic chanting.

The different-colored flags, I had learned, are always arranged in the same order: blue represents the sky or space, white is air, red is fire, green is water, and yellow is earth. Together, the colors signify balance. Each one is printed with prayers and mantras, which are picked up and carried by the wind, not to the gods, as I had always thought, but across the world, where they spread goodwill and compassion to all living things.

Dawa came around again, this time to give us necklaces with small felt satchels that held prayers wrapped inside. We would now wear these for the duration of the expedition. It was all very solemn and reverential, the kind of experience that makes you think about things like *Why am I here?* I have never put much stock in the idea of mountain gods, per se, but it didn't really matter what I thought, because the puja wasn't exactly for me. It was to help the sherpas be at peace with the climb and, perhaps more important, with us—the people for whom they would be risking their lives.

Just when it started to feel a bit heavy, a guy named Karma walked around the circle, handing out green cans of Lhasa beer. When he got to the end, he went around again, only now with a bottle of cheap Nepali rum, which he poured into the cap and offered to each of us in turn. Matt, who was sitting next to me, doesn't drink alcohol. He tried to turn Karma down, but Karma got a fierce look on his face and stood his ground. Matt did too, but after a minute or so, when it became clear that Karma wasn't taking no for an answer, Matt said, "Fuck it," and downed the shot. When Karma got to me, I tried to pour the shot into my mouth without having the cap touch my lips. I'd already seen numerous people put it right in their mouths. The combination of day drinking and swapping spit with three dozen people didn't seem wise. Getting sick is one of the most common ways you can derail an Everest expedition.

I'd been to puja ceremonies before, but never one like this. Karma just kept coming, and after his sixth time around the circle, Matt crawled off behind the dining tent, vomited, and passed out. At one point, I watched as Ngati, who apparently didn't drink, tried to insist that he was going to abstain. Several of the sherpas bodily held him down while one sloppily tried to pour the rotgut down his throat.

And they were just getting warmed up. Later, after I'd snuck away from the festivities, I decided to go look in on the sherpa dining tent, which had been transformed into a rum and beer-soaked disco dance party. Karma and a dozen other sherpas were bouncing off each other drunkenly like college kids on spring break, bottles of booze in their hands, cigarettes dangling from their lips. Jim, the financial planner from Oregon, was in there with them, and the last thing I saw before scurrying away was one of the sherpas sending him flying with a well-timed hip check.

THOM AND I set off for Interim Camp, halfway between Base Camp and ABC, late in the morning of April 26, our fifth day since arriving at Mount Everest. Renan and his crew were still packing and messing around with their camera gear and would catch up with us later in the day. We followed a flat sandy trail along the lateral moraine on the east edge of the Rongbuk Glacier. Most of the weather in this region comes out of the southwest, so the south sides of the Himalayan range get the bulk of the precipitation, while the north sides lie largely within the mountains' rain shadow. The glaciers on the Chinese side of Everest are consequently much smaller and easier to negotiate than those in the Khumbu Valley on the Nepal side. This is the main reason the north side of Everest is considered a bit safer than the south, even though it presents greater technical difficulty high up on the route.

To climb Everest via the South Col, every climber must pass through the notorious Khumbu Icefall, which spills over a bedrock incline along the Khumbu Glacier between 17,800 and 19,500 feet like a slow-motion Niagara Falls. The glacier in the steepest part of this section flows downhill at the rate of three or four feet per day, which is fast for a river of ice. Crevasses can open up right under your feet, and ice towers, called seracs, collapse without warning. Altitude sickness and its associated maladies claim more lives higher on the route, but you're far more likely to be randomly killed by the mountain itself in the icefall. In fact, its location just outside of Base Camp means it must be negotiated multiple times, at least twice in both directions by each member and in some cases more than a dozen times by the sherpas. Every season the route through the icefall is constructed by a team of sherpas called the "Icefall Doctors" with fixed ropes and aluminum ladders that bridge crevasses and surmount seracs. Sometimes multiple ladders are lashed together to achieve the needed span or height.

On April 18, 2014, a massive serac calved off the hanging glaciers on Everest's West Shoulder, sending thousands of tons of ice across the upper icefall in a section called the Popcorn Field. Dozens of sherpas ferrying loads to Camp I were in the area at the time. Sixteen of them died. Three of the bodies were buried so deep in the bowels of the glacier they couldn't be recovered. At the time, it was the single deadliest day in Everest's history. The disaster laid bare the practice of outsourcing Everest's inherent danger to sherpa workers, who, in addition to building the route, have the job of stocking the clients' camps with chairs, espresso, generators, and pallet loads of oxygen.

After the 2014 tragedy, Adrian Ballinger moved Alpenglow's Everest operation to the north side. He no longer felt he could justify the risk of traveling through the Khumbu Icefall. "It's like playing Russian roulette," he says. Ballinger was on the north side a year later in April 2015 when Nepal was rocked by the biggest earthquake in 100 years. Seventeen people were killed in an avalanche, triggered by the quake, that tore through Base Camp on the south side—setting a new fatality record. At the time, a team of Chinese rope fixers were approaching the North Col. They felt the tremors, but the slope on which they were perched didn't slide and nothing happened to them. All the various camps on the north side were spared as well.

A FEW MILES out of Base Camp, we reached the junction with the East Rongbuk Glacier, where the route hangs a left and continues up this smaller tributary of the main glacier to ABC. The temperature was comfortably pleasant, so we sat down to wait for the rest of the team.

In 1921, Mallory famously walked past the East Rongbuk junction while he and Guy Bullock were attempting to reconnoiter a route to the North Col. They explored the Main and West Rongbuk Glaciers and from a saddle on the ridge between Lingtren and Pumori, Mallory looked down into Nepal and saw the spectacular basin through which the Khumbu runs. He would name it the Western Cwm, a common Welsh term for a valley.

They didn't find a feasible way to reach the North Col from this, the west side, of it. The enormous crevasses at the head of the main Rongbuk appeared impassible, as did the wall that rose up to the North Col. The pair backtracked down the glacier, once again overlooking the minor side valley to the east that was the key to their objective. They would find a way to the North Col via a roundabout route well to the east, but the unnecessary detour cost the expedition nearly a month. Eventually, a teammate would discover the East Rongbuk route, which has been used by all expeditions on the north side ever since.

AS OUR TEAM neared Interim Camp partway up the East Rongbuk, I noticed that Nick had fallen well behind. We waited for him just outside camp, which was perched on a crumbling morainal ridge on the right side of the glacier at 19,000 feet. He eventually labored up to us, his chest heaving under a massive pack filled with camera equipment. He looked at me with glassy eyes, gasping for breath.

"I don't know what's wrong with me, but I'm having a hard time getting my wind," he finally managed to sputter. I didn't think much of it at the time, considering the load he was schlepping; no wonder he was struggling. But thin air has a way of dulling your perceptions. My mind went to what a Sisyphean task it is to make a film on an 8,000-meter peak, rather than concern for Nick's well-being. Just as Mallory had missed the direct route to the North Col, I was failing to discern signs that we had a developing situation on our hands.

I WAS SLUMPED in a chair in the Interim Camp dining tent, pressing my fingers into pressure points on the back of my skull, which was throbbing with the beginnings of a severe high-altitude headache, when the door unzipped and in stepped two Indians. Parth and Kuntal, who spoke perfect English with lilting accents, introduced themselves as members of an expedition that was sharing this camp with us, a mixed nationality team that included two Russians, three Ukrainians, and a French woman. Parth Upadhyana, twenty-three, was slight and clean-shaven, with a boyish face and perfectly coiffed hair. He was from Mumbai and had studied aeronautical engineering but was currently working as a trekking guide. This was his first Everest expedition. Kuntal Joisher, a thirty-nine-year-old software engineer, was more stout, with a broad, slightly crooked nose and a thick black beard. Joisher shared that he held the distinction of being the first vegan to climb Everest, which he had done in 2016. He was back because he wanted to experience the north side of the mountain, which he believed was the more challenging of the two main routes. He also had unfinished vegan business with Everest because he had used a down suit in 2016. This year, he explained, he was working with a company called Save the Duck. It had sewn him a custom high-altitude suit made entirely from synthetic materials. As far as I knew, Joisher was the only person on the entire mountain whose suit was not insulated with goose down. Despite decades of research in material science by companies like the North Face and Polartec, no material has yet been invented that can provide a better insulation-to-weight ratio than down.

As unlikely as it may seem that we still haven't improved on nature in this respect, it's even more remarkable that such an effective means of keeping warm wasn't employed more during the 1920s expeditions. I would have thought that, after both poles had been successfully reached, explorers of the day would have figured out that quilted down was far superior to wool or fur. It was, in fact, an enterprising member of the 1922 Everest expedition named George Finch who invented the down coat. Before the trip, he contracted with a clothing company to stitch him a knee-length jacket insulated with the soft feathers from the breast of the female eider duck. Finch was quite enamored of his new garment, but the rest of the team teased him about it. Finch, however, got the last laugh, for that year, he and Geoffrey Bruce set a new altitude record of 27,300 feet. "Everyone now envies my eiderdown coat," Finch wrote in his diary. But despite the evident benefit of down clothing high on the mountain, the 1924 team showed up on Everest without a stitch of it. Finch had been excluded from this trip for various political reasons, his opinionated and outspoken nature chief among them. And so, Mallory and Irvine ventured forth on their fateful climb wearing the traditional tweed and gabardine outfits that had been de rigueur for gentlemen mountaineers in the Alps since the Victorian era.

JOISHER ALSO HAD a permit for the south side. If all went according to plan, after summiting here, he would hightail it to Nepal in hopes of achieving an Everest vegan doubleheader.

"Yeah, people are nuts about Everest in India these days," said Joisher. "It's full-on Everest mania. This year, we're the number one nationality on the mountain."

Alan Arnette's preview of the upcoming season had correctly predicted that there would be a lot of Chinese and Indian mountaineers on Everest. According to the Himalayan Database, Indians and Chinese have become the two most prevalent nationalities on the mountain. The reason, in Arnette's view, is that both countries have an emerging middle class with disposable income, which the younger generation is using to pursue sports like mountaineering. What's also interesting is that Chinese climbers die at a low rate on Everest, whereas Indians perish at the highest rate of any nationality—a trend that only seems to be increasing.

Of course, the number of Chinese fatalities has to be taken with a grain of salt because it's well known that Beijing censors bad news. It's likely that the number of reported Chinese deaths on the north side—only ten to date—has been purposefully deflated as yet another way to bolster the superiority of the Chinese communist system. But Chinese climbers do by and large have more experience and mountain sense than their Indian counterparts because the government requires its citizens to have summited an 8,000-meter peak before attempting to climb Everest, at least from the north.

The collectivist culture in China bestows no great honor upon Everest conquerors, but in India, on the other hand, successful Everest climbers are celebrated as champion athletes. Furthermore, Joisher told me that many Indians who manage to scrap their way to the summit of Everest achieve not just fame and glory but often wealth and financial security. He thinks the phenomena may have started in 2010 when a woman named Mamta Sodha, from the northern Indian state of Haryana, was made a deputy superintendent of police, a lucrative government job that is typically a lifetime appointment, solely because she climbed Everest. She had no other relevant experience or connections. A few years later, another person from Haryana repeated Sodha's feat and petitioned the state to also be made a deputy superintendent of the police. The authorities said no, but the courts stepped in. A precedent had been set. You climb Everest, you get a government job.

Then there's the story of Malavath Poorna, the thirteen-year-old Indian schoolgirl who was hand-picked by the state government of Telangana to attempt Everest in 2014. Poorna summited, becoming the youngest female ever to climb Everest (a record that still holds). Poorna had made history, and she returned home to a hero's welcome. She and a young Indian boy, who also made the summit, were each awarded five acres of land and approximately $30,000 in cash, a life-changing windfall for a young girl whose parents were farm workers with an annual income of $600 a year. According to the *Financial Express*, Poorna thanked the government ministers for being the "messiahs of poor children in the state."

Poorna stuck with climbing and has gone on to complete six of the Seven Summits. In 2017, after the release of a Bollywood biopic about her life, titled *Poorna*, she told the Firstpost, an Indian news website, that the reason she climbed Everest was "to prove girls can achieve anything."

Poorna's mentor and coach, Shekhar Babu Bachinepally, a former police officer who himself climbed Everest in 2007, also received a cash reward. In the years since, he has continued to guide Indian underprivileged youth up Mount Everest through his company,

Transcend Adventures, and he was in Base Camp on the north side of the mountain this season to personally look after the latest batch of recruits. I later interviewed him and learned how he prepares these students for their trip into the Death Zone. He told me that the key to his program lies in the stringent selection process. He starts by touring schools, where he gets recommendations from teachers and coaches and personally meets with the students. The selection for the 2019 expedition began the year before with an initial batch of five hundred kids. He whittled the recruits down through a six-month process that involved a basic fitness assessment, mental training, various courses in rock climbing, mountaineering, and rope craft, culminating in a twenty-five-day mountaineering course in Ladakh during which they summited a 19,300-foot peak (5,885 meters) called Lhako Khagsay.

Vamini Sethi, a thirty-four-year-old businesswoman from Mumbai who was also part of the Transcend Adventures team (Bachinepally also guides regular paying clients, mostly from India), would later tell me that when a child was selected, the parents were told two things: best-case scenario, your child summits, they get fame, a cash reward, and a good job; worst-case scenario, they don't come home.

"The intention is in the right place," says Joisher. "They're trying to send a message to these underprivileged, underresourced kids that everything is possible, that we are here to support you. And look, I love my country, but the truth is that the entire Everest culture in India is broken and needs to be fixed."

There's no denying that Indians like Poorna, Mamta Sodha, Joisher, Bachinepally, and so many others have provided inspiration to millions of their fellow countrymen, many of whom dream of following in their footsteps. Alan Arnette told me that he is contacted by Indians at least once a week looking for advice on how they can climb "the Everest" even though many of them have no climbing experience or money. Some of these people manage to figure it out, via a combination of sponsorship, crowd-source funding, or their family taking out a second mortgage. For a lot of Indian families, stretching their finances to the limit is worth the risk because if the favored son or daughter can somehow succeed in clawing their way to the top of the world, the entire family may reap the rewards—possibly for generations to come if they manage their windfall well. In a country with a rigid caste system and limited opportunities, Everest offers a unique chance for upward mobility.

THE FINAL SIX MILES of the approach up the East Rongbuk Glacier to Advanced Base Camp follows a geologic oddity known as the Miracle Highway. The glacier here is covered in penitentes, high-altitude ice formations that look like giant shark teeth. Penitentes are found all over the Andes, where they were first described by Charles Darwin in 1839. In South America, they rarely exceed the height of a man, but on Everest, where everything seems to be on a different scale, some of these land icebergs stand more than 100 feet tall.

The "miracle" is not the ice towers themselves but the fact that there's a ridge of dirt and rock, known as a medial moraine, running right down the middle of the glacier, offering a straightforward walking path through a phantasmagorical wilderness of ice that would otherwise be all but impassable.

We shared this path with an endless procession of yaks. These short-legged "hairy cattle" are the engine that runs the north side of Everest. They look like a cross between a bison and an ox and they live across China, Central Asia, Mongolia, and Nepal at elevations between 13,000 and 20,000 feet. Descended from the wild yak, which evolved to live on the Tibetan Plateau, they don't fare well at lower elevations, where they fall prey to bovine diseases like foot-and-mouth.

Our expedition had approximately two tons of food and equipment that needed to be moved up to ABC. Broken down, this translated into about forty yak loads. Multiply this by a dozen expeditions and you start to get a picture of how much yak traffic there is on the East Rongbuk Glacier. For guides and outfitters like Jamie and Adrian Ballinger, hiring yaks adds slightly to the logistics, but that's more than offset by the relative ease and efficiency with which all the necessary supplies are ferried to 21,000 feet. On the south side, this kit has always been carried up through the Khumbu Icefall from Base Camp to Camp I on the backs of sherpas. (In 2019, for the first time, the Nepali government allowed equipment to be ferried to Camp I by helicopter.) On the north side, the hike from Base Camp to ABC is longer for the amount of elevation gained, but here sherpas don't have to carry heavy loads and the route is completely safe.

In the 1920s, the East Rongbuk Glacier was larger and more complex than it is today, so the British were able to use yaks only for transport as far as Base Camp. On May 10, 1924, a terrible storm hit while the team and its porters, known then as "coolies" (a term once used throughout the British empire for native servants), were ferrying loads up this section to their third camp located near present-day ABC. Most of the porters didn't have tents and had to huddle inside rock enclosures wrapped in thin blankets in subzero temperatures, with nothing to eat but some raw barley. Irvine, who was in Camp III during the blizzard, wrote in his journal: "Had a terrible night with wind and snow. I don't know how the tent stood it. Very little sleep and about 2" of snow over everything in the tent. Had a lot of rheumatism in the night and an awful headache this morning." After the storm, climbers and porters alike retreated back to Base Camp, leaving the loads of food and equipment strewn haphazardly all over the glacier. The expedition's supply chain was in complete disarray and two of the porters would later die as a result of trauma suffered during the storm, one from frostbite, the other from what may have been an aneurysm or a stroke.

"THAT'S A CATEGORY four cyclone," said Jamie. He was pointing at a giant white swirl that covered most of the Bay of Bengal on the satellite image he had open on his computer. Our team was sitting around a folding table in our dining tent, which was perched on a stone platform on the lower edge of ABC. The sun was blazing and there was hardly a breath of wind. The doors of the tent were tied open. Some Tibetans were hacking ice from a nearby serac for meltwater. The air was filled with the thunking of pickaxes and the tinkling bells of the yak trains that were shuffling endlessly up and down the valley. We were surrounded by another small tent city, occupied by hundreds of people, most of whom, like us, were preparing to move higher up the mountain. Out the back of the tent, I had a perfect view of Everest's Northeast Face and the couloir that Cory and Topo (who were somewhere nearby) were hoping to climb. A plume of snow, like the tail of a white dragon, trailed off the summit for miles to the east.

It was May 1, twenty years to the day since George Mallory's body was discovered a little more than a mile above us, on a snow terrace that I could almost see from where I sat. The incoming cyclone, now officially named Fani, currently had winds of 150 miles per hour and was being called the strongest storm to hit India in decades. It was predicted to make landfall in the next forty-eight hours. At that moment, millions of people living in Fani's path on the coast of India and Bangladesh were evacuating to higher ground. The center of the storm was more than nine hundred miles away, but the cyclone's counterclockwise rotation was predicted to pump moisture and high winds into the Everest region as it transited the Indian subcontinent over the next few days.

The latest forecast from Michael Fagin was for ten inches of snow on Friday, May 3, and another ten inches on Saturday. He predicted winds of 40 miles per hour at 23,000 feet over the next several days. We were discussing whether we should risk it and head up the next day to the North Col. Jamie was taking this forecast with a grain of salt and doing his own extrapolation with some of the same raw weather data that he said Fagin was using.

"If it [Fani] swings left," said Jamie, "it could bring high winds and dump a meter of snow on us in the next few days. But if it swings to the right, we could have great weather."

We all knew that we needed to get to the North Col as part of our acclimatization plan, but we were also eager to test the drones and maybe even have a first look at the search zone. After weeks of failed attempts to hack the Mavic Pro, Renan had finally given up and thrown his last Hail Mary pass: an email to a contact at DJI that begged for the code that would allow the drone to fly free. These codes are notoriously difficult to obtain, and no one thought we had a chance, which was why Renan had tried every other option first. In the meantime, there had been some interesting developments behind the scenes. Since we had arrived at the mountain, the Walt Disney company, which had acquired National Geographic and its parent company, 21st Century Fox, back in March, had completed the transition. Executives at Disney were briefed on our expedition and they had begun asking tough questions about the details pertaining to our film and drone permits. We were told that they went to the highest levels of the Chinese government to make sure we had the right permissions in place, and apparently their efforts on our behalf were successful. Not long after, CTMA officials in Base Camp informed us that we now had official permission to fly drones on the north side of Everest—the first time this had ever been granted.

Within a day of this news coming through, I heard Renan whooping in the dining tent. DJI had sent him the code. Why, exactly, we never found out. Renan immediately punched it in, stepped outside, and launched the drone. Two minutes later, it was 7,000 feet above our heads. My hope that we could conduct a meaningful search while also making a proper summit bid had just been given new life.

Above ABC, we hiked up a footpath on a lateral moraine until it disappeared into a basin of smooth blue ice that formed the head of the East Rongbuk Glacier, a spot climbers call Crampon Point. Here, we slipped on our harnesses, clipped crampons to our high-altitude boots, and headed across the final section of glacier to the base of the mountain.

Where a glacier ends and the mountain face begins, there is typically a gaping crevasse called a bergschrund. But on the east side of the North Col, the ice simply tilts up, and it was here that we found the tail end of a skinny blue-and-purple rope that would serve as our "yellow brick road," as some climbers call it, up Mount Everest. We clamped onto the rope with a device called an ascender that extended from our harness with a two-foot-long nylon tether. An ascender has a cam with small angled teeth. It slides up a rope, but clamps on when weighted and won't slide down. Provided you use it correctly, it will catch on the rope if you fall and keep you from tumbling off the mountain.

A lot of other people had decided to gamble on the weather. Several platoons of climbers were already working their way up the 45-degree snow and ice slope. I had gone only about 100 feet when I hit my first snag, a knot of climbers whom I deemed to be moving too slowly. Disregarding the fact that I was on Mount Everest at 22,000 feet, and not Mount Washington in New Hampshire, I unclipped from the line and punched up the slope to get past them all. As I passed them, I went completely anaerobic. When I reached the next anchor, I collapsed. As I lay there gasping for breath, all the people I had just passed slowly shuffled by me. One guy, who looked Russian, sniggered condescendingly, as if to say, "Well done, jackass."

Climbing steeply uphill at high elevation when you're not acclimatized is about as demoralizing as anything I've ever experienced, like being forced to do hard manual labor while seasick and hungover. Almost immediately, Nick fell behind. I was closer to the front of our group, so I couldn't talk with him or see exactly how he was faring.

I was two-thirds of the way up the slope when I heard a cheery "Hey, dude, how goes it?" I looked up to see Cory about twenty feet above me in a bright red outfit and a pair of white mirrored glacier glasses. Everyone else was hating life, but Cory, striking a jaunty pose, looked like he had just walked on set for a *GQ* photo shoot. And he was not clipped to the fixed line. Apparently, he had left from ABC early that morning and had blitzed up to 25,500 feet. It took me a few moments to catch my breath enough to muster a grudging reply.

"It's going."

"It gets easier, buddy. Hang in there." With that, he scooted past, nimbly skipping over the snow like one of Santa's elves.

A FEW HOURS LATER, I was crammed into a tent with Renan and Nick at the North Col camp. Renan had been anxious to fly the drones and commence our search for Irvine, so during a brief lull, he had launched one of the Mavics, a decision he was now regretting. He held the controller up so that Nick and I could see it.

"Check it out. I'm giving it full throttle down and it's still going up. This may be the last time we ever see this thing."

The mini flying machine was a couple thousand feet above us. Its camera was pointing straight down, revealing a bird's-eye perspective of the camp. About three dozen tents were scattered on various tiers of the North Col, a narrow snow saddle connecting the North Face of Everest to a subpeak known as Changtse.

Nick propped himself up on his elbow to see what was happening. He had eventually made it to the Col an hour after the rest of us, and he seemed to be hanging in there relative to how we all felt, which was rather miserable. He looked at me through slit-eyes and then fell back onto his sleeping bag as if someone had just shot him in the forehead. It may have been the orange glow from the tent fabric, but his face looked jaundiced.

"I'm trying to bring it back," said Renan. "But the wind must be stronger than forty miles an hour. It's not responding." He kept fighting the wind and in lulls between the gusts, he managed to slowly work his bird back over the next ten minutes. With seconds to spare before the battery died, he put it down hard in the snow just outside the tent. We hadn't been able to get a meaningful look at the North Face. I hoped that tomorrow conditions would be more favorable.

While Renan went to retrieve the drone, I moved to the adjacent tent that I was sharing with Matt and Jim. Jamie was in his own tent up the hill, and a few of our sherpas, who had carried up all the supplies and set up this camp, were holed up above and below us. Thom, who had awoken that morning with a crushing headache, had decided to stay back in ABC. He figured that it wouldn't unduly set back his acclimatization, but I wasn't so sure that he wouldn't later regret missing out on this rotation. Jim was curled up on his sleeping pad with his eyes closed, and Matt stared at me vacantly from his sleeping bag, looking morose.

As for me, my headache had grown steadily worse; it was now throbbing across the entire back of my skull. But I felt I should address Nick's situation. Something about the look in his eyes just then made me think he was a lot more checked out than the rest of us. I mentioned my concerns to Matt, who had been climbing just above Nick when we started up the fixed ropes.

"Oh, Nick was fucked today" was all he said.

I decided to make sure and check on Nick in the morning. There wasn't much to be done now except to make sure we were all as well hydrated as possible, so I positioned myself next to the vestibule and fired up the stove. One of the sherpas had spent a couple hours chopping chunks of ice off a serac wall behind us and had left a rice bag filled with ice chips outside the tent door. I slowly fed them into the pot, brought the meltwater to a boil, and stirred in a couple ramen soup packets. The three of us shared this meager meal and it was about all we could do to force it down. Extreme altitude makes eating and drinking a nauseating chore, the result of which is that the effects of low oxygen are compounded by low blood sugar and dehydration.

After dinner, I shoved myself into my sleeping bag. I had never climbed high enough before to warrant using a one-piece down suit, and I was discouraged to find that I could barely fit in my sleeping bag with it on. Jammed into the nylon cocoon like a foot in a sock that was too small, I tossed and turned, trying to find a position that would relieve the pressure in my skull. But there was no escape from it.

Along with my headache, the wind raged into the night. The tent fabric snapped violently in my face, but there was also another more ominous sound building high above us, not unlike rolling thunder, that I felt as much as heard.

The jet stream was announcing its arrival.

CHAPTER EIGHT

Fani

As I SURVEYED the carnage that had befallen our camp overnight, an empty tent still cartwheeling in the wind high above me, a single thought circled inside my head:

What the hell am I doing here?

Up the hill, I noticed four climbers, clipped to a fixed rope, shuffling down through camp about 100 feet away. Past them, toward the summit, I saw a dark, swirling cloud that engulfed the entire upper section of the mountain. At that moment, another blast hit us. I dropped to the snow and clutched the thin guy lines of our tent, trying not to get blown off the col. The fixed line was just out of reach, whipsawing through the air. When the gust passed, I stood up, and the air filled with shouting. The people I had seen a moment ago now dangled over the edge of an ice cliff. Jim, who had been groaning in his sleeping bag just a few minutes earlier, charged up the hill. The aluminum picket anchoring the near end of the climbers' rope was pulling out of the snow. He dove onto the picket and hammered it back into place with his ice axe. A group of sherpas used a second line to pull the hapless climbers back up onto the ridge.

A few minutes later, the foursome passed by us as they continued down. Jim told me that he had been watching them when the gust hit. It had picked one of them up in the air—a woman, he thought—and bodily flung her over the side of the cliff. When she came tight on the line, the tension ripped the other three off their feet.

"Let's get the hell out of here," I shouted.

We quickly shoveled snow onto our collapsed tent to keep it in place, clipped into the fixed line, and started down the hill, back to the relative safety of ABC.

WE STRAGGLED INTO Base Camp a day and a half later, having spent one night at ABC. Nick was the last to arrive. He walked straight to his tent, crawled inside, and collapsed. That morning, he'd told us that he didn't have the energy to make the twelve-mile hike down to Base Camp, but Jamie had insisted. With support from Jamie and the rest of the production team, Nick forced himself to trudge down the mountain. I spoke with him briefly when he got to camp, and he told me that the hike had been one of the hardest things he had ever done. But he'd toughed it out, which I took as a good sign.

In the morning, we checked in on him. He could barely prop himself up on one elbow. His chest hurt and breathing was difficult.

"On a scale of one to ten, how bad is the pain?" I asked.

"Nine," he said.

"When did this start?"

"I actually first noticed it the day before we set off for Interim Camp, when we were sorting loads for the yaks," he said. "I felt like I was getting the flu, but figured I was just feeling the altitude and it would pass. But it just kept getting worse."

Renan didn't say anything, but he gave me a look that said we should have done better by Nick. He never should have come up to the North Col with us.

The Transcend Adventures team had a doctor, so we took Nick over to the Indians' camp. A few of the teenage climbers sat outside the main tent. We said hello and asked where we could find their doc. They stared at us with hollow faces and pointed at a light blue tent. They looked shell-shocked. I learned soon after that they were the ones who had been blown off the ridge.

The doctor was a middle-aged Indian woman with a kind, pleasant face and a warm bedside manner. She took Nick's vital signs, all of which were within normal ranges. When he described his symptoms—severe chest pain, difficulty breathing, malaise—she asked if he had fallen. "Is there any chance this could be a pulmonary embolism?" I asked. My mother-in-law had one right before I left on the trip, and her symptoms seemed similar to Nick's. The doctor asked if he had any leg pain, presumably because pulmonary emboli are typically caused by blood clots that start in the calf. Nick said no. She wasn't sure what to tell us, but her best guess was that he had a chest or kidney infection. She gave him some antibiotics and said that if he wasn't better in a day or two, we should think about getting him to a hospital.

The next morning, I unzipped Nick's tent and crawled inside, where I was accosted by a rank smell, like an overripe locker room. Nick was propped up, lying with his back against his sleeping bag. He was bathed in sweat and his skin had a gray pallor. He obviously hadn't improved, but I tried to sound cheerful and encouraging.

"How you doing, buddy? How's your chest this morning?"

"It's a ten now," he rasped. "I can't even lie down because it hurts too much."

By his side stood a clear plastic bottle filled with a cloudy liquid that looked like a mix of orange juice and milk.

"Is that piss?"

"Yeah," he said, "I must have a kidney infection or something."

Jamie had slid in beside me. He asked Nick to describe how he felt, and Nick said that in addition to his chest, he now had pain in his calf.

"It feels a lot like it did when I got a blood clot in my leg on the Lhotse expedition."

"What? You had a blood clot on Lhotse?" said Jamie.

"Yeah."

"Did you get it treated?"

"They said it wasn't that bad and so I kind of blew it off."

Jamie looked at me with an annoyed expression on his face, like *Why are we only hearing about this now?* He motioned for me to follow him out.

"That's it," he said, "we're getting him the hell out of here."

If we had been in Base Camp on the south side, it would have been a simple matter of calling in a chopper, but since the Chinese military prohibits helicopters in Tibet, Jamie set about organizing an evacuation by vehicle. I crawled back into the tent and told Nick that we were getting him out to a hospital. He nodded his head as tears welled in his eyes. His expedition was over.

An hour later, with Nick now on oxygen, we loaded him and Jamie into a minivan. The two of them would spend the night back in Jilong, and the next morning, from the Nepal side of the border, Nick would catch a helicopter to CIWEC Hospital, one of the main hospitals in Kathmandu. Jamie said he would be back as soon as he could make sure Nick was safe.

At dinner the next night, my phone dinged. It was a text from Peter Hackett, who had been advising us on the situation with Nick. Hackett had been in touch with Nick's doctor at CIWEC and had taken it upon himself, even though he didn't know Nick, to make sure he was getting the best care possible. Nick was in intensive care and had been diagnosed with "bilateral pulmonary emboli"—one in the lower lobe of his right lung, and two in the upper lobe of the left, with a probable infection as well. He was in stable condition and expected to make a full recovery, but he would be in the hospital for at least another week. According to Hackett, had we waited another day to evacuate him, or if his condition had become critical higher on the mountain, Nick could well have died. "You can thank God he wasn't at Camp Three," he said.

FIVE DAYS LATER, we were back on the North Col. Renan sat cross-legged in the door of his tent, wearing a baseball cap with a black wool hat stretched over the top. Every few minutes, a pair of boots would crunch by as another climber arrived in camp.

I was on my knees, looking over Renan's shoulder at the controller in his lap. The viewfinder showed a section of the Yellow Band, maybe half an acre in size: A live feed from the Mavic Pro that was hovering some 4,500 feet above us.

"Where to, left or right?" he asked.

"I'm kind of guessing, but I think straight in," I said.

Renan thumbed the joystick, bringing the drone in closer to the face of the mountain. A wall of rock, maybe ten to fifteen feet tall, sandwiched between snow ledges, came into sharper focus. The limestone was striated, with a white, serpentine layer running horizontally through its middle. I squinted at a vertical gash, almost black in color, with reddish-tinged rock on either side. *Was that Holzel's spot?*

Renan was taking still photos with the drone about 100 feet out from the wall when it started beeping frantically. "Oh shit," he exclaimed. "It's crashing!" A sudden downdraft had taken hold of the little flying machine. The beeping was the drone's infrared collision avoidance system warning that it was about to smack into the side of the mountain. The drone, like a self-driving car, was designed to take control away from the pilot when a crash was imminent. But the wind must have been stronger than the drone's top speed, because it was now acting as if it were on a suicide mission.

And then, the beeping stopped. For a moment, it wasn't clear what had happened.

"Is it still in the air?" I asked.

"Yeah," said Renan, exhaling loudly. "That was close."

"Okay, then, bring it home."

When the drone plopped into the snow outside the tent a few minutes later, Renan dropped the controller onto his sleeping bag and stared absently at the floor of the tent. I squeezed his shoulders and said, "Congratulations. You just made history." On one of the flights, Renan had flown the drone to near the height of the summit. As far as we knew, no one had ever flown a recreational drone this high.

I WAS MUCH BETTER acclimated for this second rotation up to the North Col and managed to sleep several hours that night. In the morning, I awoke to the sound of a drone taking off outside the tent. There wasn't a breath of wind. The sherpas had fixed the broken poles, and the tent was now more or less intact. I gently nudged Thom to make sure he was okay. He grunted but didn't move. Storm Surf had predicted that the jet stream would finally dip to the south of Everest, and that forecast appeared to be panning out. When I scrambled out of the tent, Jamie walked up, holding a steaming pot.

"Coffee?" he asked.

For the next several hours, Renan and I worked together on a systematic aerial search for Sandy Irvine with a photo of the North Face of Everest pinned to the floor of the tent in front of us for orientation. On it, I had used a red marker to note key locations, including

Holzel's spot, the 1933 ice axe position, and Mallory's gravesite on the snow terrace at 26,770 feet (8,160 meters). Our goal was to blanket the search zone with overlapping aerial photos that we could study later on our laptops in Base Camp.

Most of the flights that morning lasted about twenty minutes. Like Bartek Bargiel had done on K2, Renan had hacked the security settings on the battery. Without this modification, the drone would have automatically flown itself back to base when the battery level reached 40 percent. Because the search zone was so far above us, it was critical that Renan use every last minute of battery.

Renan had also hacked the parameter controlling the speed at which the drone could descend, which was supposed to max out at 6 or 7 miles per hour. But at this slow speed, he'd never be able to fly all the way to the search zone and back before running out of battery.

Sending the drone up time after time, Renan shot hundreds of high-resolution photos of the search zone. During the half-dozen flights, we focused primarily on the area around Holzel's spot, but we also shot above it, to the sides of it, and below it, especially down the fall lines, where Irvine's body might have hung up on various ledges if it had been knocked off at some point by an avalanche or perhaps tossed by the Chinese. We also spent a fair amount of time documenting the snow terrace where Mallory had been discovered in 1999. Curiously, we never did locate his gravesite, where, according to Thom, we should have seen an unburied leg protruding from a pile of rocks.

On one flight, Renan flew the drone a mile up and off to the west, away from the mountain. He pressed a button on the controller and the gimballed camera attached to the underside of the drone began to rotate in a circle, taking a total of twenty-six wide-angle photos as it passed through 360 degrees.

In the afternoon, as it got warmer, we moved outside, and Renan flew a couple more scenic flights. The sun pulsed high overhead in a cerulean sky, and off to the east, across the East Rongbuk Glacier, I had a perfect view of the Lhakpa La, the pass that Mallory had used to approach the North Col in 1921 after missing the shortcut up the Miracle Highway. It was practically T-shirt temperature, and camp was bustling with sherpas who were packing up for a carry to high camp at 27,200 feet that night. The word circulating amongst the sherpas was that teams on the Nepal side of the mountain were already summiting.

Outside his tent, Lhakpa Tenje Sherpa, our head climbing sherpa, had built a corral with bamboo stakes into which he was stacking oxygen bottles like cord wood. As he dropped each one in, it made a clangy, metallic sound, which reminded me of the 1924 oxygen gong at the Alpine Club in London. The pile contained a mix of different bottles, and while I didn't realize it at the time, Lhakpa was separating them into stacks for members and support. The members would be using a state-of-the-art oxygen system from a British company called Summit Oxygen. These stainless steel bottles were reinforced with dark gray mylar that made the tanks look like they were made of graphite. The sherpas, on the other hand, would be using an older Russian system called Poisk. Poisk has been ubiquitous on the mountain since the 1980s. These bottles were a bit squatter and orange in color, with blue writing on the side. Most were dinged up and missing paint around the valves. Poisk is not necessarily inferior to the Summit Oxygen system, and Jamie told me that many of the sherpas prefer it because it's what they're used to. But the fact that, as clients, we were using a more modern oxygen system struck me as unfair.

Both types of bottles are about as big around as a two-liter soda bottle, but twice as long, and hold 1,200 liters of oxygen pressurized to 300 bar (or 4,350 psi—approximately the pressure of the liquid fuel used in rockets). Jamie told us that the Summit bottles were designed with pressure relief valves, whereas the Poisk bottles didn't have this safety feature. He recounted the story of a time he was sitting in ABC when someone dropped a Poisk bottle up at Camp III, two miles away. The explosion shook his tent.

I was interested to learn that, nowadays, most of the oxygen used on Everest is rented, and a hefty deposit is put down for each bottle. According to Jamie, many of the Everest outfitters got together in 2006 and agreed to pay sherpas a $100 bonus for every bottle brought down the mountain at the end of an expedition. That quickly solved the problem of oxygen bottles littering the mountain.

Unfortunately, because oxygen bottles, especially full ones, are valuable—and even more so the higher they are on the mountain—there's a disturbing trend of bottles being stolen from caches like the one that Lhakpa had built outside his tent. Jamie said he'd had oxygen stolen on numerous expeditions, and it was actually uncommon for it *not* to happen. Russell Brice, a Kiwi who has been running Everest expeditions through his company Himalayan Experience (aka Himex) since 1996, was having so much oxygen stolen from the South Col, that he had begun padlocking the bottles. Alan Arnette says the problem has been around since the 1990s but has gotten especially bad over the past five years, coinciding with the explosion of low-cost Nepali and Indian-owned guide services. "They purposefully don't take enough oxygen," says Arnette, "because they know they can steal bottles when they get on the mountain. They do it to save money, but they're putting people's lives in danger."

Two days earlier at ABC, Jamie had given us a refresher on the oxygen systems that we would soon rely on for our survival. Jamie handed us mesh bags that contained regulators and masks and told us to put a piece of tape on them with our names. He slipped on a pair of gloves, grabbed a bottle, stood it between his legs, and started screwing on a regulator. When he got to the last few turns, the bottle hissed loudly as if he had jabbed a knife into a car tire. The gloves were necessary because the rapidly expanding gas becomes supercooled as it is released from intense pressure and can freeze bare skin like liquid nitrogen.

When the regulator was firmly attached, the gauge showed a pressure of around 290 bar (4,200 psi). The dial on the regulator went from one to four, but there were also half settings, giving eight different flow rates. It is a simple system: On 1, you get one liter per minute; 2, two liters per minute, and so on. The lower the flow rate, the less oxygen you get, but the longer the bottle lasts. At one liter per minute, a bottle will last for 1,200 minutes, or twenty hours. At four liters per minute, a bottle will last five hours.

Jamie handed me a bottle. I put on my gloves, lined up the threads, and starting twisting on the regulator. I hadn't anticipated how much resistance there would be when the needle punctured the diaphragm in the bottle. Taken aback by the deafening hiss, I lost the plot for a few seconds as air blasted out of the tank like a fire hose. "That's why we practice down here," said Jamie, once I finally got the job done. "Imagine how much harder that's going to be at twenty-eight thousand feet." It was important that we knew how to operate and debug our oxygen sets, but up high, we were each supposed to have a climbing sherpa to guide us, and it was customary for them to change the bottles for the clients. "These guys have done it many, many times," said Jamie, "so just let them do it for you."

I connected the mask to a nipple on the regulator with a length of red rubber surgical tubing. The tube had a small clear plastic "flow indicator" with what looked like a spring inside. When the oxygen is flowing, the spring jiggles—a feature I would later come to greatly appreciate. The mask had a hard-plastic exoskeleton, but the part that went over my face was soft black rubber. Breathing through the mask felt similar to scuba diving. The noise, a rhythmic whooshing, sounded exactly like Darth Vader.

I slipped the bottle into my pack, ran the tube over my shoulder, and stood up to see how it felt. I was only at 21,000 feet, and I wasn't doing anything other than standing inside a tent, but still, I was relieved at how light the apparatus felt on my back. The bottle itself weighed about five pounds, the compressed oxygen another three and a half. All told, the entire system weighed only slightly more than a gallon of milk. What could the British have accomplished, I wondered, if they'd had the benefit of this system?

I've never seen a complete 1924 oxygen set. None exist, to my knowledge. The one Mallory is believed to have been wearing on summit day wasn't with him when he was found in 1999. It's presumed that he had run out of oxygen and ditched it before he fell. What we do know for sure is that the 1924 bottles (one of which I had seen at the Alpine Club) held 535 liters of oxygen at approximately 120 bar—less than half the capacity of today's bottles. The original 1924 oxygen sets, which were designed to hold three bottles, weighed thirty-three pounds. After his various modifications, Irvine managed to shave that down to twenty-eight pounds with three bottles, or twenty pounds with two (there is some debate about how many bottles they carried on summit day).

We had each been allotted five bottles total for the expedition, which Jamie said was fairly standard. We would start our first bottle when we set off from the North Col for Camp II (25,200 feet). We'd go at a low flow rate of .5 or 1, and we'd use that same bottle (at the same rate) to sleep on. The next morning, we'd tap into our second bottle for the climb to Camp III at 27,200 feet. Again, we'd go at a low flow rate, and we'd sleep on whatever was left. In a perfect world, this would leave us three bottles each to use above high camp.

Back in Kathmandu, Jamie had told us that the main reason we couldn't conduct a proper search and also go for the summit was because you typically only get one night at high camp. I did some quick math in my head. With three bottles to use above high camp, I'd have sixty hours at a liter per minute, thirty hours at two liters per minute, or twenty hours at three liters per minute. No matter how you sliced it, this wasn't a lot of time.

THE HIGHER THE PRICE TAG for an Everest expedition, the more bottled oxygen you'll likely be breathing. The Alpenglow Expeditions website states that climbers on its Rapid Ascent Everest trips, which have a price tag of $85,000, get nine bottles each. This allows them to sleep on two liters per minute in the camps above the North Col and use four liters per minute on their summit day. The higher flow rates, at least twice what we planned to use, give Alpenglow clients an edge over other people on the mountain, "maximizing safety and success," according to the website.

Jim Gile, a software engineer, mathematician, and avid ski mountaineer from Aspen, Colorado, created an often-cited graph correlating the perceived altitude at different elevations on Mount Everest with oxygen flow rates. According to his calculations, while breathing heavily with a flow rate of two liters per minute, the effective altitude at the summit feels like 22,500 feet. At four liters per minute, the perceived altitude drops to 19,000 feet—10,000 feet less than the actual elevation.

Mount Everest poses challenges and risks beyond just the lack of oxygen, of course, namely extreme cold and the potential for vicious weather. So summiting Everest on four liters per minute isn't comparable to climbing Mount Kilimanjaro in Africa (19,341 feet) or even Denali in Alaska (20,310 feet), but it's certainly less physically taxing than using a lower flow rate. And whether you summit on two liters per minute or four, you aren't even close to being in the same league as climbers using none at all.

As I sat in the dining tent in ABC, happily sucking down supplemental oxygen, I thought of my younger self, the guy who had pumped his fist in the air and yelled out a "Fuck yeah!" while reading Messner's essay, "The Murder of the Impossible." As recently as 2015, I had written an article in which I decried the growing trend of climbers using oxygen and excessive amounts of equipment on Mount Everest. I echoed Messner's sentiments that we should rise up to meet the mountain on its own terms and climb it "by fair means or none at all," as he boldly claimed he would prior to his 1978 ascent. "Is this form of fully catered climbing," I wrote, "enabled by a small army of Sherpas and other mountain workers who are exposed to enormous risk, really climbing at all?"

So what happened in the intervening four years? When I first started thinking seriously of climbing Everest, I dismissed the idea of going oxygenless right away. I guess it's easy to be dogmatic when you're not putting your own life on the line.

This debate about whether oxygen should be employed on the world's highest mountains has been going on for a long time. When I was digging through Noel Odell's papers at the Alpine Club, I found an undated, handwritten letter to the journal *Nature*, the subject of which was what Odell called the "Oxygen Debate." The letter concluded with the following: "Both engineer and physiologist may be reminded that among many mountaineers the opinion prevails that if Mount Everest, and other high Himalayan peaks, are worth climbing at all they should be ascended without such artificial aids as may reduce a sport to a mere laboratory experiment."

And yet Odell took on the job of head oxygen officer in 1924.

With the help of his young protégé, Sandy Irvine, who had been recruited specifically because of his engineering expertise, Odell worked to make sure the oxygen was ready to flow if it was needed. What's easy to lose sight of today is that in the 1920s, the oxygen debate was concerned primarily with the question of whether it was physiologically possible for any human, no matter how fit and genetically gifted, to climb to 29,000 feet without supplemental oxygen. They had no direct evidence, and scant theoretical knowledge, indicating one way or the other. Their best source of insight into the matter came from an eccentric and reclusive Scottish chemistry professor named Alexander Kellas, who made eight exploratory expeditions to the Himalaya between 1907 and 1921.

In 1910, Kellas made the first ascents of nine 6,000-meter peaks along the border between Sikkim and Tibet in the eastern Himalaya. A year later, in the same range, he stood on the summit of Pauhunri (23,385 feet). Though no one knew it at the time, it was the highest mountain that had ever been climbed—a record that would stand until 1930.

Kellas typically undertook his expeditions alone, accompanied only by a handful of Nepali Sherpas. He has long been credited with being the first Himalayan explorer to recognize the Sherpas' unique abilities to perform at high altitude, but he got the idea of using them, not just as porters but also as climbers and guides, from a Norwegian Himalayan explorer named C. W. Rubenson, who spoke at the Alpine Club in 1908. "The natives whom we found most plucky were Nepali Tibetans, the so-called Sherpahs [sic]," said Rubenson in his speech. "If they are properly taught the use of ice axe and rope I believe they will prove more of use out there than European guides, as they are guides and coolies in one, and don't require any special attention. My opinion is that if they get attached to you they will do anything for you."

It was Kellas, however, who instituted the use of Sherpas in Himalayan mountaineering, and some of the men he trained would later take part in the first British Everest expeditions. "Really, they are the most splendid fellows," he wrote. "They are strong, good-natured if fairly treated and since they are Buddhists, there is no difficulty about special food for them—a point surely in their favor at high altitudes."

Most explorers of the day treated the natives like servants, and made little or no mention of them in written accounts. Kellas, on the other hand, wrote glowingly of his favorite Sherpas and in his many letters and articles their personalities come to life. Tuny, for instance, was particularly adept at ice climbing, whereas Sona, who was also skilled with an ice axe, was more cautious. Native workers during the golden age of the British Raj were often treated as expendable, with the justification being that various Asian nationalities valued life less than Europeans did. But Kellas outright rejected this racist notion. In 1912, he wrote: "Coolies have a very keen sense of the value of their lives, and dislike being taken into places even approximately dangerous." In particular, he noted that the Sherpas didn't like climbing roped together when one person's slip might pull the rest of the team members to their deaths.

Kellas took a keen interest in high-altitude physiology in the years leading up to the 1921 Everest Reconnaissance expedition, eventually authoring a paper entitled "A Consideration of the Possibility of Ascending Mt. Everest." With data obtained from both his laboratory in London and the experiments he conducted on himself and his Sherpa companions in the Himalaya, Kellas analyzed oxygen partial pressures and saturation levels in the lungs and arteries at different elevations and barometric pressures. He made calculations for how much oxygen a climber might consume on a summit push, and from this he extrapolated what might be reasonable to expect for a rate of ascent both with and without the use of supplemental oxygen. In what turned out to be a remarkably prescient assessment, he concluded that "Mt. Everest could be ascended by a man of excellent physical and mental constitution in first rate training, without adventitious aids if the physical difficulties of the mountain are not too great."

In the fall of 1920, Kellas set off once again for the Himalaya. His plan was to attempt two peaks, Kabru (24,078 feet) and Kamet (25,442 feet). On the latter, he tested a new supplemental oxygen system, the first of its kind, adapted from equipment used by pilots during World War One. Kellas and his Sherpas reached 23,600 feet on Kamet breathing "English Air," as the Sherpas called it. He would later report to Arthur Hinks that the benefit of breathing supplemental oxygen wasn't great enough to warrant the bulk and weight of the apparatus.

Kellas spent that winter in Darjeeling in anticipation of a rematch with Kamet in the spring, and hopefully, an invitation to join the 1921 expedition. That invitation arrived in January, not long after it was announced in the London papers that the Dalai Lama had finally given the British permission to approach Mount Everest from Tibet.

Four months later, the members of the Everest Reconnaissance expedition were seated at a formal dinner at the residence of Lord Ronaldshay, the governor of Bengal. Mallory was instantly charmed by the scrappy, fifty-three-year-old Himalayan veteran and explorer, who would now be joining the climbing team. A week later, in a letter to Ruth, Mallory wrote:

"Kellas I love already. He is beyond description Scotch and uncouth in his speech—altogether uncouth. He arrived at a great dinner party ten minutes after we had sat down, and very disheveled, having walked in from Grom, a little place four miles away. His appearance would form an admirable model to the stage for a farcical representation of an alchemist. He is very slight in build, short, thin, stooping, and narrow chested; his head . . . made grotesque by veritable gig-lamps of spectacles and a long pointed mustache."

The team set off in two waves a week later, on May 18 and 19, heading north through enchanting forests of evergreen oaks and towering tree ferns. They entered Tibet via the Jelep La pass on May 24, riding their ponies down into the Chumbi Valley. By the time the team arrived in Phari, a grim, windswept hamlet that Mallory described as "the most incredibly dirty warren that can be imagined," many of the men were suffering from dysentery. Kellas, who had never recovered from a previous bout he had suffered during his spring expedition to Kamet, was now barely able to eat and was so weak he could no longer walk. From here on out, he would be carried in a makeshift litter.

No one was with Kellas, besides his trusty Sherpa companions who were carrying his litter, when he died from a massive heart attack while crossing a 17,000-foot pass. Unfortunately, neither Mallory nor Charles Howard-Bury, the expedition leader, recorded the names of the Sherpas, but we know that four of them had been handpicked and trained by Kellas. Perhaps his old friends Tuny and Sona were at his side when he died.

Mount Everest's first casualty was buried the next day on a stony hillside outside the village of Kampa Dzong. As Howard-Bury read a passage from I Corinthians, the small funeral party gazed out over the barren plains of the Tibetan Plateau toward the Himalaya, where Everest lay off to the west, obscured in clouds.

Somewhere in the team's baggage train lay the oxygen equipment, which only Kellas had the expertise to operate. It would never be used. The man who had predicted what Reinhold Messner and Peter Habeler would prove possible fifty-seven years later—had died within a day of getting his first view of Mount Everest.

As THE SUN BEGAN to set and the temperature on the North Col plummeted, I shuffled over in my down booties to check in with Prakash Kemchay, who was sitting outside his tent in an orange-and-blue down suit, with a stove purring between his legs. A warm smile spread across his face when he looked up and saw me approaching.

"Hello, Mark," he said, in a deep, baritone voice that belied his small stature. "How are you feeling?"

"I'm okay. How about you?"

Prakash said he was well, and he looked it. His brown eyes sparkled. A thin mustache covered his upper lip, and a similar patch of scraggle grew from the underside of his chin. He spoke almost perfect English and had told me earlier that he was studying to become an internationally certified mountain guide. Unlike all the other climbing sherpas on our team, Prakash was a technical rock and ice climber, and he had taken numerous courses in rope rigging and rescue techniques. His first Everest expedition had been the season before on the south side, but he hadn't summited. Jamie could have stacked our team with veterans, but a climbing sherpa has to get his start somewhere and, as with any other trade, the up-and-comers like Prakash and Dawa's son Sonam, both twenty-seven years old, were here to be mentored by more experienced sherpas like Lhakpa. Prakash was hoping that this would be his year to prove himself by reaching the summit.

Prakash, who grew up in a small village outside Pokhara, in central Nepal, in the foothills of the Annapurna Massif, is Gurung, one of the 126 ethnicities that make up the population of Nepal. While our support staff were mostly ethnic Sherpas, we also had guys on our team who were Gurung, Tamang, and Tibetan; and among the other expeditions, there were also Rai, Kulung, Bengalis, Indians, and Han Chinese. There are a host of jobs on Mount Everest, and many of these other ethnicities and nationalities work lower on the mountain as camp staff, whereas the vast majority of the high-altitude guides and porters tend to be ethnic Sherpas.

Prakash told me that he came from a long line of Gurkha soldiers, the famed Nepali warriors who formed part of the British army in the days of the Raj. Their motto is "Better to die than be a coward," and it is said that once they drew their traditional weapon—a powerful, curved knife called a kukri—it can't be sheathed again until it had tasted blood. Prakash had tried twice to follow the family calling, but the Gurkhas turned him down because his teeth weren't strong enough and he failed to complete one of the recruitment tests—a mile-long run in under 5 minutes and 30 seconds.

His pack was already loaded and sitting in the snow a few feet away. It was a beast, bulging at the seams, and I shuddered at the thought of even lifting it off the ground, let alone carrying it that night to 27,000 feet. It contained, among other things, seven oxygen bottles. Including his water, food, and other accessories for the overnight carry, it probably weighed close to seventy pounds.

The summit pyramid was ablaze with the last rays of the setting sun as Prakash shouldered his load, strapped on his oxygen mask, and joined the line of climbing sherpas heading out of camp. There was still no wind, but the Col had gone into the shade, dropping the temperature by a good thirty or forty degrees. I waved to Prakash and crawled into my tent.

I was bunking alone because Thom had gone back down to ABC earlier that day. Since he hadn't been feeling well enough to make the first trip to the col, the night before had been his first at 23,000 feet, and he had suffered just as I and the rest of our team had twelve days earlier. By morning he had a throbbing headache. Around midday he decided to descend rather than spend a second night on the col with the rest of us. I was beginning to wonder about his chances of making the summit. Almost every morning, Jamie passed around a pulse oximeter, an electronic device that slips over the forefinger and measures heart rate and blood oxygen saturation. Jim Hurst and I routinely scored the highest. Thom usually had the lowest, although Renan was often scoring in a similar range. (Renan's low oxygen saturation may be related to the fact that he severed one of his vertebral arteries in his 2011 ski accident.) Jamie told us that in his experience, these numbers were predictive of how his clients would fare on the mountain.

It was lonely in the tent without Thom. Throughout the expedition, his presence had been calming. Down in Base Camp, he had sprinkled a bunch of bird seed outside his tent. At any given time, there were so many birds milling about that I sometimes had to wear earplugs because of all the cooing and chirping, some of which came from Thom himself, who'd sit among his feathered friends in a camp chair and babble to them in baby talk. He had been the same way with every mangy stray mutt we'd met on the approach—although he didn't go as far as he did on an expedition to the south side of Everest in 2014, when he became so attached to a flea-bitten stray cur that he invited it into his sleeping bag with him. I'd always liked Thom, but here, in such a harsh and unforgiving environment, his big-hearted, gentle spirit made for especially good companionship.

I dozed off quickly, awaking a couple hours later with a painfully overfull bladder. To help with my acclimatization, I had chugged a liter of water before bedding down. I unzipped the back door of the tent, and while relieving myself into the snow, I watched a string of twinkling lights inching its way up the fin of snow they call the North Ridge. I couldn't see the moon, but I knew it was up somewhere behind Changtse because patches of ice in the Norton Couloir were gleaming and the entire North Face of the mountain was illuminated as if lit from within. The last light in the chain was green. I wondered if that was Lhakpa. He had been the final one out of camp, having stayed back to help Sonam, who had been struggling to get ready.

IT'S IMPOSSIBLE TO appreciate the prowess of the Sherpas without experiencing it firsthand and in direct contrast to your own feebleness. We had all started in Kathmandu (4,600 feet) at the same time, and we had more or less spent the same nights at the same elevations ever since. Hypothetically, our acclimatization should have been similar. Up until now, our support team had been acting more or less like regular guys. Some of them were still recovering from the party after the puja, and in Base Camp our cases of Budweiser continued to disappear, replaced a day or two later with Lhasa beer, the local, watery equivalent. My own acclimatization was progressing right on schedule and so far, I'd avoided getting sick or suffering any serious setbacks. And I'd set off on this expedition in close to the best shape of my life.

But none of that had made the second climb to the North Col any easier. My headache was gone, but it still felt like my boots were full of lead, and not a single step came easy. The wind, which had been our nemesis on our last climb to the Col, was nonexistent. Everest is the same latitude as Tampa, Florida, and we were only a month from the summer solstice, so the sun was high in the sky and beating down on us mercilessly. And, of course, high altitude makes the sun's radiant heat all the more intense. Expecting temperatures as cold as what we had encountered the last time, I had worn my down suit. Once I was buckled into my harness and clipped to the ropes on the steep wall of ice and snow, there was no taking it off. The best I could do was drop the top and tie it around my waist, which hardly helped. The combination of overheating and not getting enough oxygen made me feel like I was suffocating. It took a force of will I wasn't expecting I'd have to muster to keep from collapsing with despair.

Mallory had suffered something similar on the approach to the Lhakpa La in 1921. In a letter to Ruth on August 22, he wrote, "It is no use pretending that this was an agreeable way of passing time . . . we were enveloped for the most part in a thin mist which obscured the view and made one world of snow and sky—a scorching mist, if you can imagine such a thing, more burning than bright sunshine and indescribably breathless."

I made a concerted effort that day to mimic what Mallory called his secret breathing technique, which he described in detail in the official account of the 1921 Everest Reconnaissance expedition. The key, he wrote, was to "time the breathing regularly to fit the step, and to use not merely the upper part of the lungs, but the full capacity of the breathing apparatus, expanding and contracting not the chest only, but also the diaphragm." Mallory commented that it was easy to will oneself to breathe in this fashion. But to maintain this practice required a presence of mind that was easy to lose in the drudgery and pain of putting one foot in front of the other. "The moment attention to their performance was relaxed, the lungs too would begin to relax their efforts, and often I woke from some day-dream with a feeling of undue fatigue, to find the cause of my lassitude only in the lungs' laziness. The best chance of keeping them up to their work, I found, was to impose a rhythm primarily upon the lungs and swing the legs in time with it."

Hackett had explained to me why Mallory's breathing technique works, and that the climbing sherpas all use it to great effect. Whenever one of them blew past me on the trail, I noticed he was breathing at a significantly faster tempo than I was. Paradoxically, Hackett said that this deep rapid breathing technique partly explains why high-level athletes tend to perform poorly on Mount Everest. Hackett says strong endurance athletes often don't do well at altitude because they tend to be "lazy" breathers. The reason these people perform so well at sea level is because they don't get short of breath. They can sustain a high level of output while maintaining a comfortable breathing cadence, which is what they tend to do on Everest. And because they are accustomed to kicking ass in their chosen sport, they also tend to push harder than those who might be less confident in their abilities. Thinking they've got the mountain by the tail can quickly get them in trouble at high elevation. "It's extraordinary to see these sedentary slob attorneys from Chicago go up Everest with a fair amount of oxygen and do fine," says Hackett, "while marathon runners and triathletes fall by the wayside. This is why we call altitude the great equalizer."

When I finally straggled into camp after that hellish climb to the North Col, I went straight to my tent, where I collapsed and didn't move for an hour. If someone had put a gun to my head, I suppose I could have hiked a bit farther, but definitely not with a seventy-pound pack. And that's what accompanied each of the headlamps I was now watching—with a mixture of awe and chagrin—steadily marching up the Northeast Ridge.

HACKETT AND OTHERS have been studying Sherpas for decades in the hopes that if science can crack the code that allows these Himalayan natives to perform so well in low-oxygen environments, this knowledge could possibly be used to develop drugs and other therapies that could benefit critical-care patients suffering from hypoxia. Because Sherpas have lived at elevations between 10,000 and 15,000 feet for thousands of years, they have evolved specific adaptations that allow them to perform better at altitude than the rest of us. (While the Sherpa are the most well known of the region's ethnic groups that live at high altitude, most of the other Himalayan cultures—Tibetans, Gurung, Tamang, to name a few—share some degree of the genetic adaptations that give the Sherpa their extraordinary ability to live, work, and flourish at high elevation.) But these genetic changes, it turns out, are different from those found in other populations that also live at high altitude, in other parts of the world. In the Andean highlands of Peru, the indigenous people who live at elevations up to 17,000 feet have adapted to the thin air by increasing red-blood-cell production. There are distinct downsides to this adaptation, however. High red-blood-cell count thickens the blood and can lead to a host of maladies like high blood pressure, clots, strokes, and heart disease, all of which the Andean highlanders suffer from disproportionately.

Sherpas, on the other hand, have evolved to have *less* hemoglobin—the protein that carries oxygen in red blood cells. As a result, heart disease and related health problems are virtually unknown in these populations. According to Hackett, one of the best ways to measure a community's health and adaptation to their environment is by looking at fertility and birth weights, both of which are relatively low in the Andes and also low among Han Chinese who have been moving out onto the Tibetan Plateau over the past fifty or so years. Sherpa fertility and birth weights at altitude, on the other hand, are significantly higher.

About ten years ago, a geneticist at UC Berkeley named Rasmus Nielsen made a remarkable discovery about Sherpas. Nielsen had been studying "the Tibetan question"—that is, what is the genetic basis of the superpowers of Tibetans and Sherpas at altitude—when he discovered a variant of a gene called EPAS1 that is common in Tibetan genomes. EPAS1, the so-called "super-athlete" gene, provides instructions for making a protein called hypoxia-inducible factor 2-alpha (HIF-2α). This protein, like HIF-1 (which I mentioned in chapter five), is a part of a larger complex that plays a critical role in the body's ability to adapt to changing oxygen levels. Nielsen, who studies the molecular basis of evolutionary adaptation, was curious about how Tibetans had ended up with this gene variant, so he checked it against the 1000 Genomes Project—the same database your own genes are compared to if you have a DNA test by 23andMe or Ancestry.com. When the results came back, Nielsen was surprised to discover that this unique fragment of DNA didn't match with a single other human genome. So he began searching more obscure genomic databases until he finally found it in the genome of an archaic human called the Denisovan. Denisovans lived in Asia during the Paleolithic era, and were first identified in 2010 from mitochondrial DNA extracted from a fossilized pinky bone found in a cave in Siberia. The gene that helps Sherpas to be the most prolific high-altitude mountaineers in the world came from an extinct branch of the human tree that died out some 10,000 years ago.

According to Nielsen, 80 percent of Tibetans have the gene, and 7 or 8 percent of Han Chinese also have it (it is also found in Melanesians and aboriginal Australians). He thinks it was probably inherited by Tibetans' ancestors somewhere between 25,000 and 40,000 years ago. Tibetans and Han Chinese, who are closely related, diverged from each other somewhere between 2,750 and 5,000 years ago. In the years since, the Han Chinese lost most of their Denisovan DNA, including the EPAS1 gene, because it offered no benefit in the lowlands of eastern China. But for people living on the Tibetan

Plateau, EPAS1 offered a strong competitive advantage, and as such, it was naturally selected for and passed down over the generations. What's also interesting is that it's not just people who have benefited from this gene. The Tibetan mastiff also inherited a variant of EPAS1 from wolves; and domestic yaks, which descend from wild yaks that roamed the Tibetan Plateau during the Pleistocene, also carry variants of EPAS1.

Further research on Sherpas during several Everest expeditions, in which their physiology was studied and specifically compared to lowlanders, has revealed that when Sherpas go to altitude, their cells adjust to make do with less oxygen. It is a remarkable adaptation; each oxygen molecule in the bloodstream goes further, produces more energy than it would at lower elevations. Their cells essentially become more efficient at using oxygen and they are able to carry on as if they were at a much lower elevation. The rest of us can only respond by increasing our red-blood-cell count—a less effective remedy since the availability of oxygen in the air for our blood to transport is greatly diminished. According to Andrew Murray, a physiologist from the University of Cambridge, Sherpas function at high altitudes like highly efficient hybrid vehicles that get many miles per gallon, whereas the rest of us are gas-guzzling SUVs.

"The reason they are so special is because they have multiple adaptations, not just one," says Murray.

It's worth noting, however, that while EPAS1 is called the "superathlete" gene, these genetic adaptations confer no advantage at lower elevations. This stands them in stark contrast with athletes hailing from other high-elevation regions, who are famous for their strength and endurance when they come down to compete at sea level. Peruvian and Colombian cyclists have a long history of contending for the King-of-the-Mountains jersey in the Tour de France. And, of course, Kenyans and Ethiopians have completely dominated long-distance running competitions for decades. But you are unlikely to see a Sherpa winning the Boston Marathon or raising his arms in triumph atop the Alpe d'Huez.

One of the first climbing sherpas to arrive back in camp on the North Col the next morning was Pasang Gomba. He walked past me, smiling wearily, and then plopped down outside his tent, which was right below mine. Gomba was working as a private guide for Frank Campanaro, the guy from Florida. Campanaro, Gomba, and another sherpa named Dawa Dendi mostly operated independently from us, but we were often in the same camps at the same time and sometimes we ate meals together. Campanaro, who is a former Special Forces operator and national security contractor (and probably a spy) turned businessman, kept us entertained with stories of halo jumps into the Caspian Sea, big wave surfing in Maui, and hunting down rhino poachers in the Congo. If even half the stories he told us are true, he is hands-down the most interesting guy I've ever met.

As far as I could tell, Campanaro had set himself up with one of the best climbing sherpas on the mountain. Gomba was fifty years old, with 100 Himalayan summits to his credit, 32 of them 8,000-meter peaks. He'd been to the top of Everest eight times. He told Campanaro that he thought he could keep guiding Everest for another five or six years. Gomba spends most of the year in Kathmandu, where his kids are getting a first-class education with the money he makes working as a high-altitude guide. In the summer, after the Everest guiding season, he typically goes back to his home village, a tiny place called Kurima, located south of the Khumbu Valley, a two-day hike from the nearest road. I had noticed that Gomba didn't speak a lot, but when he did, everyone stopped what they were doing to hear what he had to say.

Gomba pulled off his boots. His feet steamed in the sun as he rubbed his left knee.

"How'd it go up there?" I asked.

Gomba looked up at me. He'd gotten so much sun that his face was darkened by two or three shades, except the pale skin around his eyes protected by his glacier glasses.

"Good," he said, clearing his throat. "But the conditions are very dry. There's not much snow between Camp Two and Three. It's tough on the feet."

This was our assessment of conditions during our drone flights, but it was good to hear an Everest veteran confirm that there was less snow than usual. The windstorm that had so terrified me had indeed swept the mountain clean. If we were going to find anything, this was the year to do it.

Chatting with Gomba, I learned that all the sherpas had made it to high camp, where they had stashed dozens of oxygen bottles, fuel canisters, stoves, and tents in tightly bound nylon rice bags. The Chinese rope-fixing team had made it to Camp III* the day before, and they had already descended. They were now going all the way down and out to Shigatse for some R&R, which meant it would be several days before they returned to push the ropes to the summit.

Two days later, as I was walking back into Base Camp, I felt a vibration in my pocket. I fished out my phone and saw the name Tom Holzel on the caller ID. I had just been wondering what Tom would

* Today, unlike in the 1920s, we don't begin numbering camps until the North Col. Thus our Camps II and III, at 25,250 feet and 27,200 feet respectively, approximately correspond to the British Camps V and VI.

think if he could see the high-res images of the search zone that we had captured over the past few days.

"Hey, Tom," I said.

"Mark, is that you? Where are you?"

"I'm walking into Base Camp."

"Really? The connection is so good. It sounds like you're in New Hampshire."

I proceeded to fill Tom in on what had been happening, how we'd captured four hundred images of the search zone, how he was going to be blown away when he saw the level of detail, shot from the drones' state-of-the-art cameras (capable of producing images with 12 million pixels per frame) fifty feet away from the Holzel spot. The harebrained scheme we had hatched at his house over that bottle of woodruff-infused wine was coming together.

"Send me as many images as you can," he said, "and I promise, if there is anything there, I will find it." The last thing he said before signing off was "This is a thrilling business." Something about this phrase rang a bell, but I wasn't sure why. A few days later, I was in my sawed-off chair in my tent, warming my feet by the electric heater I had "borrowed" from the dining tent, and rereading David Robertson's biography of George Mallory. I was leafing through the pages, looking for Mallory's account of his initial exploration of the Rongbuk Glacier, when I came across a letter he had written to Ruth on June 28, 1921. It ended with the following: "My darling, this is a thrilling business altogether. I can't tell you how it possesses me, and what a prospect it is. And the beauty of it all."

I had just walked into the dining tent when I heard Jamie reading a headline from the BBC website on his computer. "One dead, one missing on the south side."

The first official fatality of the Everest season was a twenty-eight-year-old Indian man named Ravi Thakar, who had summited the afternoon before. Thakar had made it back to Camp IV at 26,000 feet on the South Col but that morning was found dead in his tent. The cause of death was unknown, but it was likely that he died of what Hackett had categorized as "sudden death," probably a heart attack or stroke brought on by a combination of altitude sickness, dehydration, and utter exhaustion. A Bulgarian had also died that day descending Lhotse, a sister peak to Everest and the world's fourth tallest. In addition, an Indian soldier had died on Makalu, the world's fifth-highest mountain, which lies twelve miles to the southeast of Everest. Two days earlier, on Kangchenjunga, two more Indians had died near the summit, and a Chilean climber was missing and presumed dead (his body would never be found). All told, the first summit window of the spring 2019 season in the Himalaya had resulted in seven deaths on four 8,000-meter peaks.

Another climber was also missing on Everest, a thirty-nine-year-old computer science professor from Dublin named Seamus Lawless. He had summited the day before as part of a four-person team that included a South African woman, an Irish woman, and a veteran Irish guide named Noel Hanna. I'd later speak with Hanna, and he told me the story of what happened.

With hundreds of people all vying for the summit on the south side, Hanna had decided to get an early start. When the first summit window opened in mid-May, his team was already fully acclimatized. They set off from Base Camp on May 12, summiting four days later at 9 A.M. on May 16, in perfect conditions. Lawless, in particular, was in top form, moving quite a bit faster than the two women on the team, who were tiring and struggling with foggy goggles. When they arrived back down at the Balcony, a spacious ledge at 27,500 feet where climbers typically rest and swap out oxygen bottles, Lawless asked Hanna if he could keep moving with his climbing sherpa named Pemba. He and Pemba could get a head start on the brewing and have hot drinks waiting for the rest of the team when they arrived at the South Col. Hanna agreed, so Lawless and Pemba headed down.

"I'll see you at the col," Lawless said.

When Hanna and the women arrived at camp, Pemba met them outside their tents and solemnly shared the news that Lawless was gone. An hour earlier, on the final ice slope above camp, Lawless had clipped off the rope. He said he needed to relieve himself, then walked off to the west toward the Lhotse Face. The wind had been picking up, and they were beginning to get hit by stronger gusts. Pemba had looked away to give Lawless some privacy, then he heard a yelp. When he looked up, his client was sliding down a 40-degree slope of blue ice. Seconds later, Lawless disappeared over the edge of a 4,000-foot wall of 50-degree ice and snow. Pemba called his name over and over, but there was no answer, and there was nothing he could do except go back to camp and organize a rescue.

Hanna, Pemba, and some of the other sherpas went out to search for Lawless. They called for him and searched as far as they could, but the wind was now getting dangerous, and they had no ropes to protect them as they fanned out across acres of hard blue ice perched above the Lhotse Face. During the night, Hanna went out several times to see if he could spot any lights in the area where Lawless had fallen, but he saw nothing.

One of the news websites reported that Lawless had texted his wife from the summit to say that he had made the top and was "coming home." But Hanna says he didn't send the message from the summit, he sent it via a satellite texter called inReach that pinned his location at the exact spot from where he fell. He must have hit send right before he lost his footing.

Later, back in Kathmandu, a photograph surfaced that someone had taken the afternoon Lawless disappeared, looking up the Lhotse

Face from below. At the top, just below the col is a person, standing upright, apparently climbing through some rocks toward Camp IV. "We don't know that it was Seamus," says Hanna, "but there was no one else who would have been in that area." According to Hanna, these rocks are only about 500 feet below camp. Not that far, except that Lawless had lost his rucksack with his oxygen (they later found it at the base of the Lhotse Face) and he was probably hypoxic, injured, and rapidly succumbing to the cold. He never made it back to camp.

Hanna spoke admiringly of Lawless. "You couldn't imagine a nicer guy, he was full of joy and full of life." Lawless had kept his teammates entertained with his singing and stories throughout the expedition. It had been his dream to climb Mount Everest before his fortieth birthday. According to the *Irish Sun*, before departing for the climb, he had told his four-year-old daughter, Emma, "Don't go growing up on me. Keep staying the way you are until I come back."

I SPENT THE REST of the day and night in the dining tent studying the drone photos. Matt had given me his laptop with all the images. I took my time, clicking through and carefully scanning each one, as I sipped on cold Chinese ersatz Budweiser. This real-life game of Where's Waldo? was far from tedious because there was a tantalizing chance that, any moment, I could make an electrifying discovery.

I eventually homed in on one particular image. I turned to Renan.

"This photo right here. Look at that, a slot oriented at forty-five degrees." Exactly what Xu Jing had described—and in the right vicinity too.

Renan, Thom, and Jamie crowded in around me as I pointed to a dark vertical gash in the rock and hit the + on the keyboard. "I think this is the Holzel spot," I said. The photo did eventually pixelate, so I zoomed back out a couple clicks until I had the ideal framing. The detail was impressive. I could see individual striations in the rock and there was very little snow cover. It was clear that if a body had been lying out there somewhere in the frame, we'd see it. The one place we couldn't see was inside the slot. It looked to be a few feet wide and appeared to cut into the wall at an oblique angle. It was the only spot in the area big enough to hide a body.

I panned to the left, back toward the climbing route, when something caught my eye on the edge of the frame. I zoomed in.

"There's something there," said Renan.

"It's a dead body," said Jamie. "Not an *old* dead body, though."

"That black part, is that his leg?" asked Thom.

"Yep," said Renan.

We had just spotted our first dead body since this project began. "Jesus, man, that's so raw," I said.

Jamie said he knew who it was. A Japanese man named Shinichi Ishii. Jamie had passed him without realizing it in the middle of the night on his summit day in 2007. Ishii had tried to summit the day before and gotten benighted on the route. He may well have still been alive when Jamie's team passed him by. When they did see him, on their way down in the daylight, he was dead.

I looked closely at the body. His head hung over the lip of a small cliff. His suit, which was probably red at one point, was faded almost to white. But more than anything, what struck me was how big the body was. I would have expected it to be much smaller. It gave some much-needed scale to the terrain, and I realized that the slot wasn't nearly as big as I had imagined. The photos were even more finely detailed than I'd thought.

Ishii appeared to lie exactly in the spot where I'd want to leave the established route to investigate Holzel's spot. I could use his body as a guidepost.

I HAD NEVER QUITE gotten over the cough I had developed during the windstorm on the North Col. And then, even though I felt better on the second trip to the Col, it got significantly worse. Now I was hacking so hard that I'd started using an asthma inhaler to control it, an item that Peter Hackett had advised me to include in my first aid kit. On the south side, they call it the "Khumbu Cough," and I'd been warned to avoid it at all costs, because it can easily end your expedition if it gets bad enough. The inhaler worked well, but it increased my heart rate, which made it hard to sleep.

So, I was feeling less than chipper when I walked into the dining tent the next morning. I was greeted by a coughing Matt, who was also suffering with an ear infection. For the past several days, green gunk had been leaking out of his ear. He hadn't slept much either and seemed to be in a particularly foul mood. Apparently, he and Jamie were having a spat over a lack of sherpa support given to the film team as it moved around the mountain getting footage.

Jamie came in next, and now he too looked and sounded terrible. His eyes were glowing red and his face was flushed. His Kiwi accent had been replaced by a phlegmy, nasally voice that did not inspire confidence. He said he'd been fighting something since the day before. Whatever it was, probably some kind of bronchial infection, had won. He had started a round of antibiotics that morning. My cough sounded worse than Jamie's, but I wasn't feeling sick. I had just frozen my lungs. Jamie, on the other hand, was hacking up nasty green and yellow gunk, which he would spit into tissues that were quickly accumulating on the table in front of him.

While we wallowed in what seemed like a vibe of general malaise, the rest of the teams were staging for their summit bids. The day before, on our way down, we had passed Alex Abramov and his Seven

Summits Club, the Alpenglow Rapid Ascent team, as well as many other expeditions, all heading up to ABC. Michael Fagin and some of the other Everest weather forecasters, including a guy out of Belgium named Marc de Keyser, seemed to have settled on a brief weather window on May 23. The Chinese rope-fixing team was now on its way back up to try and get the ropes set to the summit, and the word circulating around camp was that every other team on the mountain, a total of about a dozen expeditions, was planning to follow them up.

"This is a very dodgy situation," said Jamie, "because the weather models are not showing a perfect window." The forecast was predicting only one or two days of low winds. This meant that people would have to fight their way to high camp in bad weather, summit during the brief lull, and then get the hell out of there before the jet stream moved back in. "The temperature levels on the summit are staying the same while everything else is warming up," added Jamie, "which is creating a massive instability. And since so many other teams are going for this first summit window, it's going to be crowded with tons of people and uncertainty."

In one way, it was good news that everyone was going to bunch up during this first weather window, because it would clear out the mountain, and if the weather gods smiled on us, we could go up after everyone else was gone. This was something Jamie said he had planned from the start, because he didn't think we'd be able to wander off the established route to search for Irvine if we didn't have the mountain to ourselves. Otherwise, the Chinese would be watching our every move, and we'd be stuck in a thick crush of other climbers.

"The bottom line," he said, "is that we need to avoid the big groups. And we need to stay the hell away from the Indians." Then he reminded us of a sobering statistic: About 1 percent of climbers die on their Everest summit day. Only five days hence, approximately two hundred people were planning to go for the top from our side of the mountain.

"Who wants to place a bet on how many of them will die?" he said.

Fani, by now, had stalked off to the north, beating itself out over Bangladesh. But the jet stream was still very much in play, licking at the summit as it flicked in and out of range.

CHAPTER NINE

The Day Everest Broke

FIVE DAYS LATER, I stepped outside the dining tent in Advanced Base Camp with my coffee, shaking off the haze from our first night back up at 21,000 feet. The sun was low in the sky above the Lhakpa La, but I could already feel its strength on my nose and cheeks. A string of prayer flags attached to a nearby boulder hung limp in the still air. High above, up in the troposphere, the heavens were eerily quiet. Michael Fagin had been right. The jet stream had dipped to the south and released the summit of Mount Everest from its grip. I looked around camp, and apart from a few yaks munching on some hay, there was no one around. Every other expedition on the mountain was now up in the Death Zone vying for the summit.

Several sherpas stood nearby, passing around a pair of binoculars and chatting excitedly. After a few minutes, someone handed them to me. I slowly traced the Northeast Ridge, past the three famous steps to the final pyramidal snow slope above which the summit thrust into a cobalt sky.

Thom hovered by my side like a fidgety kid waiting for his turn to play with a new toy. "What do you see?" he said.

A few wispy clouds obscured the First and Second Steps, but the mountain's upper pyramid was gleaming in the sun. A string of tiny black dots, like little ants, inched their way up the final snow slope below the summit. I handed the binoculars to Thom.

"Look at that conga line!" he said.

Indeed, there were more climbers attempting to summit Everest that day than ever before in history. When I later looked it up in the Himalayan Database, I found the names of 158 people, including both paying clients and support staff, who attempted to summit that morning on the north side alone. That number was less than half the swarm on the south side.

We didn't know it yet, but the photograph of the traffic jam that would come to define the spring 2019 Everest season was already going viral. It was taken the morning before, May 22, at approximately 9:30 A.M. on the Nepali side, a few hundred feet below the summit, by a Gurkha soldier named Nirmal Purja, whom everyone calls Nims. It shows a rainbow-colored line of people, all sharing the same fixed rope, crammed together precariously on a skinny ridge of rock and snow. It looks like a crowded line you would expect to see at Disneyland—if you swapped the down suits and oxygen masks for T-shirts and flip-flops.

The photo illustrates the commonly held opinion that Everest has turned into nothing less than an overrun, soulless tourist attraction. The media response to the photo was swift and damning, along the lines of "*What the hell is wrong with these people? What a bunch of fools.*" The headlines that ran alongside the image lamented the crowds, the environmental degradation, and the fly-by-night outfitters willing to take any warm body that was able to pony up the cash. The *New York Times* would call the scene "reminiscent of *Lord of the Flies*—at 29,000 feet."

ONE OF THE PEOPLE in that traffic jam was a fifty-four-year-old Utahan named Donald Cash, who summited at 8:10 A.M. According to witnesses, Cash fainted after dancing a jig to celebrate his completion of the Seven Summits (he had retired from his job as a software salesman five months earlier to climb the last two peaks: Mount Vinson in Antarctica, and Everest). His sherpa guide responded quickly by providing CPR and turning up his oxygen. He regained consciousness and was able to stand up and begin his descent. He passed out a second time while waiting in line at the Hillary Step, a notorious bottleneck at 28,770 feet. This time, his sherpa was unable to revive him. His body was too high on the mountain to be recoverable, so he was left where he fell.

Later that same day, a fifty-four-year-old Indian woman named Anjali Kulkarni, climbing alongside her husband, dropped dead not far above the South Col, also on her way down from the summit. The Indian trekking agency that organized her climb said that she had died from "energy loss" and "heavy traffic." Kulkarni had climbed several easier peaks, including Mount Elbrus and Kilimanjaro, but had never been higher than 21,500 feet before. Her guide, Gyaljen Sherpa, told the *Himalayan Times* that she had refused to turn back because she had invested a decade's worth of earnings to achieve the summit that season.

Amidst the media frenzy decrying the crowds and the trail of dead climbers, a data scientist named Teresa Kubacka became intrigued with the question: Who exactly is summiting Mount Everest these days? She later published her findings in an article entitled "Mount Mid-Life-Crisis." In it, she confirmed what many of us already knew anecdotally: The record crowds on Mount Everest are being driven by large increases in the fifty-plus-year-old male demographic. Women do make up a sizable proportion of Everest aspirants today, but males still outnumber females four to one. In the 1980s, before the birth of Everest guiding, expeditions were exploratory, not commercial. Teams were comprised of experienced mountaineers who were typically between the ages of twenty-five and thirty-five. Kubacka describes this demographic as the "sweet spot between the physical capacity of the human body and having enough experience, maturity and mental power to tackle mountaineering challenges." What's interesting is that the number of thirty-year-olds attempting Everest today is roughly similar to what it was in the 1980s—indicating that all the growth in numbers has come from people in their forties, fifties, and sixties. One obvious explanation is that a lot of people can afford an Everest expedition only after they have reached their maximum earning potential, usually in middle age.

Kubacka's analysis also reveals that the vast majority of people who attempt Everest these days get to the top. Below the age of fifty, four out of five climbers make the summit—the same odds as for those below age thirty-five. Climbers over age fifty have better than even odds of topping out. Compare this to 1981 when Peter Hackett was the 110th person to summit Mount Everest. That year, the odds of summiting were in the single digits and they stayed below 10 percent throughout the 1980s; by the 1990s, one's chances of summiting had risen only to about 20 percent. Ever since, the overall odds of summiting have been steadily increasing.

Various Western guide services including Himalayan Experience, International Mountain Guides, and Adventure Consultants, figured out how to maximize the likelihood of success for their clients. The two tactics that have had the greatest effect are securing the two standard routes with fixed ropes from top to bottom and offering a one-to-one ratio of climbing sherpa to client. Technology has also helped.

Modern mountaineering gear and clothing is state-of-the-art, the oxygen systems deliver a steady and reliable supply of "English Air," and weather forecasting is approaching precision accuracy. Professional meteorologists beam in daily—sometimes hourly—forecasts via LTE and satellite Wi-Fi. It all adds up to a relatively sure thing, even for inexperienced mountaineers with underqualified guides.

THAT MORNING, sitting in camp while everyone else was moments away from realizing their dream, I felt like a teenager sitting at home while the cool kids were off partying. Everyone up there had gambled with the weather, and their gamble was paying off. At that moment, many of this season's Everest suitors were standing on the highest point on Earth—or would be soon. By not going, we had gambled too. What if this was it? What if there was no second window this season? Earlier that morning, Dawa, our base camp manager, had grumbled about our decision to wait. Everest is a business, and businesses live and die by their balance sheets. Every extra day we were on the mountain cost Dawa money in fees, wages, food, and other expenses. By passing on this weather window, we had cost Expedition Himalaya thousands of dollars. And, of course, the CTMA couldn't leave either until we were done, and it had its own expenses and concerns. No doubt the Chinese CTMA officials were also anxious to get home to their families. The big question at this point was how much longer the Chinese would allow us to stay on the mountain.

At breakfast we had reviewed the long-range forecast with Jamie. It wasn't good. Both Fagin and Marc de Keyser, who runs what everyone refers to as the "Euro" Everest forecast, were in agreement that the current window was closing. High winds were now forecast for the next several days. They gave it a fifty-fifty chance of our getting another summit window. After everything we had been through, it now came down to a coin toss whether the North Col would be the high point of our expedition.

EARLIER THAT MORNING, in the wee hours, before any hint of daylight appeared, Reinhard Grubhofer, a forty-five-year-old Austrian businessman, hauled himself up and over a section of bare rock at the top of the First Step. Standing atop this famous feature at 28,100 feet, Grubhofer sucked hungrily on his oxygen mask and took a minute to get his bearings. It was snowing gently. The wind was light. According to the forecast, the ambient air temperature was supposed to be around –35°F. When he looked ahead, the ridge was lit up as if festooned with a string of Christmas lights. He reckoned he could see eighty headlamps, but in fact, there were almost twice as many strung out along the upper section of the Northeast Ridge. He wasn't sure why, but his team had been one of the last groups out of high camp, not setting off until 11 P.M.

Off to the south, he could see a similar string of lights in Nepal on the Southeast Ridge. It was a magical sight, hundreds of tiny fireflies slowly advancing toward the highest point on the planet. But Grubhofer felt no joy in what he saw. Instead, it made him deeply uneasy. When preparing for Everest, he'd had a recurring nightmare in which he was caught in a traffic jam high on the mountain, unable to move up or down. Now it might be coming true.

He thought about the promise he had made to his wife, Angelika, and their four-year-old daughter, Nora, whose nickname was Mouse. He had joked with them that he was like a boomerang that always flew back home safe and healthy after his adventures. He'd told his wife that he understood his body and knew his limits, and that when and if he got to the point where it was prudent to turn back, he would not hesitate to do so. This had sounded perfectly rational and reasonable in the comfort of their living room in Vienna, but now, on the crest of the Northeast Ridge, he realized that this high in the Death Zone, there is no black and white, only overlapping shades of gray.

His outfitter, a legendary Swiss guide named Kari Kobler, had told the team that in a perfect world, they would summit at sunrise, which would give them more than twelve hours of daylight in which to descend. But there was some wiggle room, and he had set their turnaround time as 10 A.M. Wherever you happened to be at that time, even if it was only 100 feet from the summit, you would turn around and head down, no questions asked. Eleven hours should have been more than enough time to get to the summit, but the crowding was slowing everything down to a crawl. Grubhofer had waited for almost half an hour at the base of the First Step. With 800 vertical feet still to go, summiting by first light was out of the question, and now it was even looking dicey as to whether he could make the top before the turnaround time. *Can I do it?* he asked himself. One moment, he'd look up and be filled with hope. *Okay, this is going to work. Stay focused, Reinhard. You're doing well. Let's move on and reach the bloody summit.* But then a different voice would say to him, *What are you doing? It's taking too long. You should turn around now.*

Hearing the sound of crampons scraping on rock, he turned around to see his tentmate, a fellow Austrian named Ernst Landgraf, hauling himself onto the ledge. Landgraf, sixty-four, lived in a small town in Styria, a bucolic state in southeast Austria known for its farming and mountains. Landgraf's dialect of German was particularly rough, so much so that Grubhofer, who lived only a few hours away in the capital, sometimes had trouble understanding him. Landgraf, a husband and the father of two grown children, was an experienced mountaineer and backcountry skier. He had climbed six of the Seven Summits and had retired two weeks before setting off for Everest after a long and successful career in the construction industry. Like a lot of people who aspire to join the Seven Summits Club, Landgraf had purposefully saved the most difficult mountain for last.

As Landgraf sidled up, Grubhofer considered it rather remarkable that his compatriot had even made it this far. Right from the start of the expedition, Landgraf had been suffering from headaches so severe that Kobler had him sleeping on supplemental oxygen in Base Camp. When they began their acclimatization rotations on the mountain, Landgraf was always off the back. In the dining tent, he spoke openly about his struggles with acclimatization and mentioned, on more than one occasion, that he was thinking about dropping out.

Grubhofer liked Landgraf, and because they were both Austrians, Kobler had paired them up in the hotels they stayed in on the approach. They were friendly with each other and there hadn't been any disagreements or tension between them, but it did slightly rub Grubhofer the wrong way that Landgraf didn't seem to have trained very hard for the expedition. Landgraf said that he had been ski touring in the Alps that winter and spring but hadn't strictly followed the training regime Kobler had laid out for all his clients. So Landgraf was not only the oldest member of the team, he was also the least fit. Considering that a mountaineering team is only as strong as its weakest link, it was hard not to be a bit annoyed that Landgraf hadn't prepared more thoroughly.

But then something strange happened. When it was time for the summit push, Landgraf suddenly found his stride. The day before, the pair had set off on the climb from Camp II (25,200 feet) to Camp III (27,200) at approximately the same time. Everest guides have learned over the years that this day is make-or-break for most climbers. Those who perform well have a good chance of summiting. Those who don't will probably be heading down instead of up the next day. Grubhofer had a tough day, perhaps in part because his oxygen mask didn't fit well over the angular features of his face. It kept slipping down onto his chin, and he never felt like he was getting a good seal. Early on, Landgraf moved out ahead and then he continued to put distance between them over the course of the day. Here he was again, on summit day, looking strong. Seeing his friend moving determinedly toward his goal was just the motivation Grubhofer needed. He turned toward the summit, promising himself that he would reevaluate when he got to the Second Step.

One of the lights Grubhofer had seen up ahead was that of Kuntal Joisher, the Indian vegan mountaineer, who was having his own moment of doubt at the base of the Second Step. Joisher had been among the first to set off for the summit from high camp that night. He and his climbing sherpa, Mingma Tenzi, were part of a bigger team, but they had gotten out ahead of the others, deeming it better to be closer to the front of the queue than the back. The two men had been climbing together for years. One of the things they had learned was that slower parties are more likely to let you pass if you're an individual or a team of two rather than a posse of six or eight. Since passing people efficiently was a necessary part of successfully climbing popular 8,000-meter peaks, they had developed a system where Mingma would turn up Joisher's oxygen flow to four as they approached the slower climbers. This would allow Joisher to close on them quickly, showing that he was moving well, and most people were happy to let them by. The pass entailed unclipping from the line temporarily, so it was important to time these moves so they happened in places where the terrain wasn't too severe. Once they got past and were safely clipped back into the line, Mingma would turn Joisher's flow rate back down. (Mingma's flow rate, like that of most climbing sherpas, was set to 1 and remained that way throughout the day.) They had employed this strategy to good effect several times that morning, but the one group they hadn't managed to get ahead of was Transcend Adventures. And now, at the base of the most difficult section of the entire route, they found themselves stuck behind three Indian teenagers as they flailed on the ladders of the Second Step.

The Second Step isn't a continuous wall. Overall, it's about ninety feet high, but it's broken into two tiers, with a lower-angled snow patch in between. The bottom, which is basically a zigzagging ramp, isn't as steep as the top. But the ladders on this part rattle and shift when you try to climb them.

One of the Indian kids simply could not figure out how to get himself up this wobbly contraption. As Joisher and several others looked on, the kid would step up onto the bottom rung, the ladder would shift, his foot would slip off, and he'd drop onto the rope to which his ascender was connected. Another kid was a little bit above, and a third was waiting down below. Three sherpas were in the mix, and Joisher heard them berating the teenager. The kids, who are from tribal areas in southern India, speak a dialect called Marathi, but most of them can understand Hindi, India's main language, which the sherpas were using. At first, they were saying encouraging things like "Come on, you can do this, you've been climbing great the whole time." But as the kid continued to flail, tensions began to flare. One of the sherpas started yelling at him to get his ass in gear. By now, a small traffic jam was forming at the base of the Second Step. Mingma had turned Joisher's oxygen down to 1, to help make up for the delay, and everyone stamped their feet and swung their arms to maintain circulation.

Finally, after a half hour of this hopeless floundering, two sherpas got under the kid and started pushing him up from below while another above, hanging from the ladder with one hand, reached down, grabbed the kid by his pack strap, and like an airport baggage worker, hauled him up to the ledge.

When Joisher and Mingma got to the top of the Second Step, the Indian kids were sitting on a small ledge, their chests heaving in and out as they stared down at their feet. Mingma shared a few words with the Indians' sherpas, then they carefully clipped past them and continued on. After scaling the third and easiest of the three steps, a 20-foot-high cliff, Mingma and Joisher set off up the snow slope where we would later see all those people making their way toward the summit. Joisher looked up and saw a headlamp about 100 feet above. Someone was taking a rest at the start of the rocky traverse, where the route cuts right onto the North Face of the summit pyramid to avoid a steep fin of snow. Joisher's headlamp had died, but the snow scintillated from the light of a waning gibbous moon that hung in the sky off to the west, flitting in and out of the clouds. It snowed lightly, off and on, the flakes swirling in Joisher's face. Mingma was in front. Every few feet, he'd turn around to shine his headlamp onto the slope below him, so Joisher could see where to place his feet. When Joisher looked past Mingma, he noticed that the light above was not moving.

When they got to the top of the snowfield, they found a sherpa sitting on a small ledge where a tangled knot of ropes was fastened to some pitons that had been hammered into cracks in the rock. Mingma shined his light on the sherpa's face. It was a young man, perhaps in his early twenties. His eyelashes and eyebrows were covered in a glaze of ice.

"Hey, how are you doing?" said Mingma, in Nepali. The man kept staring down at his feet. Mingma put his hand on the man's shoulder and shook him a bit and said something like "Hey, you, wake up, are you okay?" After a while, the man stirred and slowly looked up. He tried to speak, but the words came out all garbled. Mingma looked at Kuntal and stated the obvious, "He's in trouble."

At this point, Mingma pulled off the man's mask and put it over his own mouth. Nothing. Next, he opened the man's pack and saw that it was full of oxygen bottles. He was a porter, carrying oxygen for one of the climbing teams. He must have fallen off the back and run out of oxygen himself.

Mingma hooked him up to a fresh bottle and turned the flow to full blast. "Let's give it a few minutes and see what happens," he said.

As Joisher would later learn, the stricken climbing sherpa worked for a company called Seven Summits Treks (SST), which is owned by four Sherpa brothers who grew up in a small village in the Khumbu Valley near Mount Makalu. In 2011, one of the brothers, Mingma Sherpa, became the first Nepali to scale all fourteen of the world's 8,000-meter peaks—a feat he accomplished without the use of supplemental oxygen. Leveraging Mingma's newfound celebrity, the brothers launched a trekking and expedition agency, which has since grown into the largest Everest outfitter in the business. In the spring of 2019, SST (not to be confused with Seven Summits Adventures or Seven Summits Club) had one hundred clients on Everest, split between the north and south sides, managed by a team of 100 climbing sherpas. Including the other 8,000-meter peaks the company was guiding that season, SST had about 250 clients, which the brothers claimed on Facebook represented 40 percent of the market. But if you own 40 percent of the clientele, you're also likely to own 40 percent of the bad outcomes. In the spring of 2019, SST had already lost six clients: two on Everest (Seamus Lawless and Ravi Thakar), one on

The infamous conga line that clogged the upper section of the Southeast Ridge on the Nepal side of the mountain during the "day Everest broke." What many people didn't realize was that the Northeast Ridge on the Tibet side was also overrun. © MARK BALLARD

Sandy Irvine and Marjory Summers in England during the summer of 1923. Sandy's affair with his best friend's stepmother led her husband to file for divorce not long after this photo was taken. © SANDY IRVINE ARCHIVE 24/98C BY PERMISSION OF THE WARDEN AND FELLOWS OF MERTON COLLEGE OXFORD

A portrait of George Mallory and his wife, Ruth, taken while Mallory was on leave during World War One. Mallory served in the 40th Siege Battery in the Battle of the Somme. © CLARE MALLORY MILLIKAN/TOM HOLZEL COLLECTION

The 1924 British Everest team in Base Camp. Standing, left to right: Sandy Irvine, George Mallory, Edward Norton, Noel Odell, and John MacDonald. Sitting, left to right: Edward Shebbeare, Geoffrey Bruce, Howard Somervell, and Bentley Beetham.
© J.B. NOEL/ROYAL GEOGRAPHICAL SOCIETY VIA GETTY IMAGES

Mallory and Irvine preparing to depart the North Col on the morning of June 6, 1924, two days before they disappeared after a final sighting by Noel Odell at 28,200 feet on the Northeast Ridge. © NOEL E. ODELL/ROYAL GEOGRAPHICAL SOCIETY VIA GETTY IMAGES

When Mallory's remains were discovered on May 1, 1999, most of his clothing had been torn away by the wind. His left leg was crossed over his broken right ankle, a sign interpreted by some that he probably survived the fall, at least briefly, that landed him in this place. © THOM POLLARD

Mallory's leather mountaineering boot, as seen when his body was discovered at 26,770 feet on the North Face of Mount Everest in May 1999. Note the V-shaped hobnails for purchase on snow and ice in lieu of crampons. © THOM POLLARD

Members of the 2019 Sandy Irvine Search Expedition. Back row, left to right: Jim Hurst, Renan Ozturk, Mark Synnott. Front row, left to right: Matt Irving, Thom Pollard, Jamie McGuinness. © THOM POLLARD

Tom Holzel, the Everest historian whose decades of dogged research led to a set of GPS coordinates where he believed the team would find the remains of Sandy Irvine. "He can't not be there," said Holzel. He holds a 1920s era Kodak VPK, similar to the one the team was searching for. © MARK SYNNOTT

The 2019 Sandy Irvine Search Expedition was inspired by Thom Pollard, a mountaineer and filmmaker who took part in the expedition that found George Mallory in 1999.
© RENAN OZTURK

Bire Tamang, top right, prepared meals daily in Base Camp for as many as three dozen people. Here he sits down to enjoy his own meal with Dawa Sherpa (back left), the team's Base Camp manager, as well as Pasang Gomba Sherpa, a guide, and Chhumbi, an assistant.

Cory Richards in Base Camp. Richards and his partner, Esteban "Topo" Mena, were on Everest in the spring of 2019 to attempt a new route on the Northeast Face.

The sherpa climbing team celebrating after the puja, a Buddhist ceremony during which the team asked Chomolungma (the Tibetan name for Everest) for good luck with their expedition.

Prakash Kemchay, a young member of the sherpa climbing team. Kemchay and the author formed a particularly strong bond during the expedition.
© RENAN OZTURK

Lhakpa Tenje Sherpa, a forty-nine-year-old father of four, was the leader of the team's sherpa support team. © RENAN OZTURK

The Miracle Highway on the East Rongbuk Glacier follows a medial moraine through a wilderness of high-altitude ice formations called penitentes. Interim Camp is visible in the middle distance. © RENAN OZTURK

Yaks, which live at elevations between 13,000 and 20,000 feet across Mongolia, Central Asia, Tibet, and Nepal, are the engine that runs the north side of Everest, moving an endless train of food and equipment up and down the East Rongbuk Glacier.
© RENAN OZTURK

A drone shot looking up the main Rongbuk Glacier toward the North Face of Mount Everest. The standard route up the East Rongbuk Glacier follows the S-shaped river that branches left. © RENAN OZTURK

(facing page)
The 1,000-foot wall of ice and snow leading to the North Col at 23,000 feet.
© RENAN OZTURK

Renan Ozturk surveys the urine-soaked snow from which the team will need to melt water at Camp Two, at 25,200 feet. © MARK SYNNOTT

Nick Kalisz on the North Col during the windstorm that crushed the team's tents and nearly blew four Indian climbers off the mountain. © RENAN OZTURK

AXIOS

Potentially catastrophic Cyclone Fani nears Indian coast as a Category 4 storm

Satellite image of powerful Cyclone Fani approaching the coast of India on May 2. Image: NOAA

Cyclone Fani intensified into a monstrous, high-end Category 4 storm in the western Bay of Bengal on Thursday as it wobbled closer to the Indian coastline. It is forecast to cross the Odisha coast as a Category 3 cyclone between Gopalpur and Chandbali, near Puri, on Friday, according to the India Meteorological Department (IMD).

Fani, a category four cyclone, pumped moisture and record-high winds into the Everest region as it transited the Indian subcontinent. It nearly ended the 2019 season before it had begun. © RENAN OZTURK

Kamaldeep Kaur, a British woman of Indian descent. She told friends before heading to Everest that "mountaineering saved her life."
© CAROLINE GLEICH

Rolfe Oostra, a veteran Australian guide, took this selfie moments after passing out below the Second Step. Later that day he would single-handedly perform a daring rescue high on the Northeast Ridge. © ROLFE OOSTRA

Kuntal Joisher, the first vegan to climb Mount Everest. "The entire Everest culture in India is broken and needs to be fixed," he told the author. © MINGMA TENZI SHERPA

Austrian Reinhard Grubhofer was one of the climbers caught in the deadly traffic jam atop the Second Step on May 23, 2019. As he crawled toward Camp III, fighting for his life, he chanted, "Boomerang, Prinzessin, Maus"—the nicknames for himself, his wife, and his four-year-old daughter. © REINHARD GRUBHOFER

Ernst Landgraf, sixty-four, at the summit on May 23, 2019. © REINHARD GRUBHOFER

Kaji Sherpa and Lakpa Sherpa, high on the Northeast Ridge at sunrise on May 30, 2019. The peak in the background is Makalu, the world's fifth tallest. © RENAN OZTURK

At 28,700 feet, the Northeast Ridge routes follow an unlikely rocky traverse around a corner onto the North Face proper. © JAMIE MCGUINNESS

Team members negotiate a tricky traverse below the Second Step, a 90-foot cliff on the Northeast Ridge, at 28,250 feet. Ever since the last sighting of Mallory and Irvine in this vicinity, Everest historians have wondered if they could have surmounted this formidable obstacle with their rudimentary equipment. The ladder installed by the Chinese in 1975 is just visible, as are the bodies of two deceased climbers.

Looking up the Second Step from about halfway up. The crack below the chockstone to the left of the ladder is presumed to be the route Mallory and Irvine would have followed in 1924. The body in the blue suit is a climber who perished a week earlier after getting stuck in a traffic jam atop the Second Step.

The author leaving the security of the fixed lines at approximately 27,700 feet and descending into the no-man's-land of the Yellow Band in search of Sandy Irvine and the fabled Kodak camera on May 30, 2019. © RENAN OZTURK

Gonbu, at right, was one of the three summiteers during the landmark 1960 Chinese expedition, which made the first ascent of Mount Everest from the north side. Four years later, in June 1964, Gonbu attended the Ninth National Congress of the Communist Youth League of China, where he was received by Chairman Mao Zedong.
BAIDU BAIKE

A portrait of the ravages of high-altitude climbing. The author in Base Camp at the end of the expedition.
© THOM POLLARD

Annapurna, and three on Makalu. And the main push on Everest had only just begun.

In recent years, the business of Everest guiding has shifted away from Western companies to Nepali-owned outfits. According to Alan Arnette, in 2010, the ratio of Western to Nepali Everest outfitters was four to one. Today, that ratio has been flipped. Nepali-owned companies like SST now dominate the industry.

It could be argued that the seeds of this reversal were first planted back in 1922 when seven local porters died in an avalanche on the North Col after George Mallory insisted that the team make one last bid for the summit, despite the mountain being buried in deep snow from a recent storm. In a pattern that seems to have repeated itself ever since, the porters, who were in the back of the line toiling under heavy loads, were the only ones who died. Howard Somervell, who had been swapping the lead with Mallory at the time of the avalanche, would be tormented by the recurring memory of digging the bodies out of the crevasse in which they had been buried. He would later write, "Only Sherpas and Bhotias killed—why, oh why could not one of us, Britishers, shared their fate? I would gladly at that moment have been lying there, dead in the snow. If only to give those fine chaps who had survived the feeling that we had shared their loss, as we had indeed shared the risk."

As much as the British claimed to admire their "coolies," the colonial mindset was so deeply baked into their worldview that they never fully acknowledged the extent to which they were exploiting these men. After the avalanche, Mallory would write to Ruth that "they were children where mountain dangers were concerned." The Mount Everest Committee would later award 250 rupees to each man's family. (Today, the death benefit paid by the Nepali government to the family of a climbing sherpa who dies on Mount Everest is $15,000. The Juniper Fund, a nonprofit, matches this amount, but spaces out the payments over five years.)

When the Everest guiding industry began to explode in the early 1990s, Western Everest guides like Guy Cotter, Russell Brice, Todd Burleson, and Eric Simonson began training Sherpas to be actual guides and not just load carriers. These Sherpas were well treated and well respected by their employers, and they were able to make as much as $5,000 for a two-month Everest season, which was pretty good in a country where the per capita annual income was $700. Most of the Sherpas were content with this arrangement. Some of them invested their earnings wisely and became rich men. So there was plenty of incentive for this first generation of Sherpa Everest guides to accept their lot and not make too many waves. But still, they knew the Western guide working alongside them was often making ten times as much for doing the same job—likely without working as hard or taking as much risk.

By 2010, a new generation was coming up through the ranks, many of whom were children of the Sherpas who pioneered the Everest guiding industry in the 1990s and 2000s. With the money their fathers earned working on Everest, many of these younger Sherpas had grown up in the bustling city of Kathmandu, not the villages. They attended private schools and were fluent in English. With ready access to television and the internet, they were keen studies of Western culture and consumerism. Many of them left Kathmandu to seek their fortunes in Europe or New York City, but others stayed and took up the Everest torch from their fathers and uncles. And with this more cosmopolitan, progressive, and ambitious worldview, the new generation became more willing to question why it was that white people from far away were the main profiteers of Everest Inc.

Then, on September 23, 2012, disaster struck on Manaslu, the world's eighth-tallest mountain. A little before 5 A.M., American extreme skier Glen Plake was in his tent at 23,000 feet preparing to set off for the summit. Plake's tentmate, a Frenchman named Greg Costa, heard it first: the faint but unmistakable thunder roll of an approaching avalanche. The menacing sound quickly crescendoed and moments later the entire camp, along with thirty other climbers, was swept clean off the mountain. When the dust settled, Plake found himself half-buried in a crevasse 1,000 feet below camp, still inside the tent. Costa was gone, as were ten other people.

Dozens of articles were written about the three professional skiers from the US and France who died that morning. At the time, very little mention was made of the other eight who perished—all Sherpas. But about a year later, Grayson Schaffer, in an article for *Outside* magazine entitled "The Disposable Man," wrote: "For more than a century, Western climbers have hired Nepal's Sherpas to do the most dangerous work on Mount Everest. It's a lucrative way of life in a poor region, but no service industry in the world so frequently kills and maims its workers for the benefit of paying clients. The dead are often forgotten, and their families left with nothing but ghosts." The piece fueled the Sherpa community's simmering sense of outrage. Sherpas were assuming most of the risk, while reaping little of the financial reward.

Then, when tragedy struck again in 2014, taking the lives of sixteen Sherpas in the Khumbu Icefall, their surviving brethren rebelled. For the first time in history, Sherpas refused to climb, out of respect for the dead, and the entire commercial season was canceled. It was time to take back their mountain.

Nepali-owned outfitters began to proliferate. By cutting out expensive Western guides, and reducing wages for climbing sherpas, Nepali outfitters were able to offer guided Mount Everest ascents at a significantly lower price point. The rate for a budget Everest expedition dipped as low as $20,000, which garnered these companies the majority of the market within a few years. By 2019, the discount rate had risen to between $35,000 and $40,000—roughly what we had paid per person for our package with Expedition Himalaya. Grubhofer, on the other hand, had paid Kobler & Partner $65,000. The Alpenglow Expeditions Rapid Ascent package was going for an impressive $85,000. For the higher price tag, you get experienced Western guides, better accommodations, higher-quality food, a more comfortable Base Camp, a lot more oxygen, and overall a better chance of success—and of coming home alive.

Perhaps the most critical difference between the low- and high-end expeditions, though, is that the latter do a much better job vetting their clients. If you want to climb Everest with Alpenglow or Kobler or IMG, you will need to have completed an ascent of an 8,000-meter peak as a prerequisite. Most of these companies sell Everest as a package deal with Cho Oyu. You climb Cho Oyu in the autumn and then return six months later for the big E. For many, the time, expense, and effort required to tackle a smaller 8,000-meter peak as a stepping-stone to Everest is a deal breaker. If you choose to go with a discount Everest outfitter, your partners on summit day are more likely to be climbing above 8,000 meters for the first time in their lives.

As the market for sherpa services has grown, the established one-to-one support-to-member ratio has caused the demand for quality climbing sherpas to outstrip the supply. According to Alan Arnette, some of the discount Nepali and Indian-owned outfitters have been hoovering up Sherpas, Tamang, Gurung, and others from villages in the Khumbu, Rowaling, Makalu, and other districts of Nepal. The Nepali government itself lacks any rules or standardization for mountain guiding, essentially qualifying every Nepali to be a mountain guide, regardless of whether they've had any training or not. Arnette, who has reported extensively on this subject, says that outfitters are offering inexperienced climbing sherpas only $1,000 to $2,000 for two months of work, and then throwing them straight into the deep end. Many accept these wages in the hopes that a successful summit will lead to better-paying work in the future.

But Mingma Sherpa, the chairman of SST, refutes the idea that his workers are underpaid. He told me that he employed five hundred climbing sherpas in 2019 and invested $100,000 in training the next generation of up-and-comers. "If I don't pay good money," he says, "why do so many sherpas work for me?"

One nonprofit that has been working tirelessly to make sure that climbing sherpas are properly trained in mountaineering skills and Leave No Trace ethics is the Khumbu Climbing Center (KCC) located in the village of Phortse. It was founded in 2003 by Jennifer Lowe-Anker, Conrad Anker, and Panuru Sherpa and is funded by the Alex Lowe Charitable Foundation. Every year, it trains dozens of Nepali climbers in climbing techniques they would otherwise have been forced to learn on the fly. To date, it has run hundreds of climbing sherpas through its multiweek curriculum. Its capacity is limited, though, and it isn't able to accommodate everyone who applies to take part in the program.

JOISHER AND MINGMA sat quietly on the snow ledge, observing the sherpa and hoping that the oxygen would bring him around. Joisher understood, of course, that his dream of a "proper" vegan ascent of Everest now hung in the balance. A climbing sherpa who gets in trouble high on Everest can't count on being rescued, because the only people who would have any real chance of effecting that rescue are other sherpas, and they usually already have their hands full with their own clients, whom they can't desert. But in this case, Joisher believed that if the man didn't recover, he and Mingma would abandon their climb to try to save him. They had not discussed it, but he had no doubt Mingma felt the same way. Joisher realized that the decision would be a relatively easy one because he had summited before. But what if he hadn't? What if he'd come across this nameless sherpa back in 2016?

Joisher had been dreaming about Everest since he was a child. He had grown up idolizing Tenzing Norgay. Norgay had moved to Darjeeling, India, shortly after making the first ascent of Mount Everest with Edmund Hillary, and Joisher had always thought that Norgay was Indian. So, in 2010, he contacted Alan Arnette, looking for advice on how to climb "the Everest." Arnette told Joisher that the key to Everest was coming up with enough money. At the time, Joisher was in charge of India operations for a California-based IT company called WebVisible. He was already a supervisor, making US wages in Mumbai. He had money, but the tradeoff was that he spent most of his waking hours behind a desk and he was fifty pounds overweight. So Joisher approached his boss and they worked out a deal. After training his successor, he shifted to working as an independent contractor, and every summer, he took off four months to train in the Indian Himalaya. He purchased mountains of gear, took multiweek-long mountaineering courses, trekked hundreds of miles, and climbed numerous 6,000-meter peaks. By 2013, the only hurdle left was to raise the funds for his Everest bid. Joisher's boss, who had witnessed firsthand his transformation from unhealthy couch potato to model of physical strength, agreed to underwrite the climb.

In the spring of 2014, Joisher arrived in Base Camp on the south side just before the massive avalanche in the Khumbu Icefall. The season was shut down and Joisher returned home empty-handed. But almost immediately, people began approaching him, offering what they could to keep his dream alive. By the time the next season rolled around, Joisher had managed to crowdfund $30,000 for another shot at the mountain. That spring, he was back on Everest when Nepal was rocked by the hundred-year earthquake. In addition to killing seventeen people in Base Camp, it injured seventy more. Joisher was lucky to come away unscathed, but once again, the Everest season was shut down and he was out another $30,000 (as a rule, refunds aren't given in such circumstances).

When he got home, his parents and other family members told him he had wasted too much money on a venture that had killed too many people—with nothing to show for it. It was time to let this go, they said. But he had been questing for Everest for five years now. It had given direction to his life and profoundly transformed him, not just physically but spiritually. He now had a calling, something to live for. So he cashed in the last of his saving bonds and took out a home equity loan. And on May 19, 2016, he achieved his dream of standing on top of the world.

As the sun began to break over the Tibetan Plateau, so too did the young sherpa begin to emerge from his delirium. One moment he was hunched over, staring at his feet, his chest heaving in and out, the next he was lifting his head, his eyes growing wide as he came back to his senses. Finally, he made eye contact with Mingma and Joisher.

"What happened?" he asked.

Mingma told him that he had run out of oxygen and they had found him in a catatonic state. The man shook his head. He said he didn't remember anything and wasn't even sure how he had ended up on this ledge. Under the circumstances, Mingma didn't want to be too harsh, but he did admonish the young man to be more careful. "Dhanyabad, dhanyabad, dhanyabad" (thank you, thank you, thank you), the sherpa kept saying over and over. After a few more minutes, he stood up, said thank you one last time, and set off across the rocky traverse as if nothing had happened.

ROLFE OOSTRA OPENED his eyes and saw his feet pointing at the sky. He was lying on his back, upside down, head hanging above the lip of a small cliff. *How the hell did I end up here?*

The sun had just peeked over the horizon, and the sky was leaden gray. But it was light enough for Oostra, a veteran Australian mountain guide, to see that he was not far below the base of the Second Step. He grabbed a hunk of stone with his hands and slid his legs around until he was upright in a sitting position. Now, looking down the North Face between his boots, he bolted wide-awake as he realized how close he had come to falling to his death. Had he tumbled another few feet, he would have flown off the cliff and tomahawked down the North Face, potentially all the way to its base, 7,000 feet below.

Oostra arched his back and used his hands to probe his body for injuries. Miraculously, he didn't seem to be seriously hurt. *But how did I come unclipped from the fixed line?* Then he remembered that his oxygen mask had been acting up. It must have stopped flowing as he was moving his tether from one rope to the next.

In the periphery of his tunneling vision he now saw flashing lights, as if he was on the highway getting pulled over by the police. As those lights grew brighter, he knew he needed to get back to the relative safety of the ropes before he passed out again. He clawed his way back up the slope and clipped in. Then he thought about what to do next. *How long was I out*? The last thing he remembered was meeting up with one of his clients, a British woman named Kamaldeep Kaur, who went by Kam. She had had fallen off the back from the rest of his group. He looked around and she was nowhere to be seen. She must have already climbed the Second Step. Right then, he was blinded by another flash of light, as if someone was shining a halogen spotlight in his face. But there was no one around him. It was coming from inside his head.

BY 9:30 A.M, Reinhard Grubhofer had pressed his way into the crowd of roughly two dozen people jostling for position on the summit, a mound of snow around which the mountain dropped away in every direction. Grubhofer had arrived at the top of the world, but rather than marveling at the mountain's pyramidal shadow or at the curvature of the Earth, he found himself staring at the fabric of some random stranger's down suit. More bodies were arriving by the minute from both sides of the mountain and elbowing their way into the scrum to get their obligatory selfie. It felt like he was jockeying for a seat on a crowded city bus, and he was shocked that some of the people were actually shoving him out of the way. *What is wrong with these assholes?* he thought to himself.

Landgraf, who had arrived a few minutes before him, was sitting on the north side of the summit. He gestured to Grubhofer and slid over a bit to make room for him to sit. Grubhofer took a minute to compose himself, then he shook hands with Landgraf, and they congratulated each other. Grubhofer's guide, Tashi, took a few photos. Grubhofer held up a banner for his employer in Austria, Big Bus Tours. FIRST STOP, ADVENTURE. ON TOP OF THE WORLD. Then he made his fingers into the shape of a heart. Before putting the camera away, Tashi took one more photo of Grubhofer and Landgraf sitting side by side. The front of Landgraf's suit was covered in a thick layer of ice. He had his goggles off, and he was squinting in the bright morning sun. When Grubhofer looked at him, he saw that Landgraf's eyes were red and puffy and deeply etched with crow's-feet. He looked profoundly fatigued. But that was to be expected. Grubhofer assumed that he looked equally ravaged himself.

When an opening finally appeared in front of him, Grubhofer was able to look north and west, where thick clouds were beginning to envelop Lingtren and Pumori. A radio fastened to the lapel of one of their guides, an Austrian named Andreas Neuschmid, crackled. Grubhofer recognized the voice of Kari Kobler, who was in Advanced Base Camp and had been monitoring his team's progress with a spotting scope.

"The weather is turning bad at lunchtime," said Kobler. "Get down."

Grubhofer was keenly aware of the old mountaineering adage that the summit is only the halfway point, and that 70 percent of those who die on Everest do so on the descent. Now a storm was brewing. He thought about the promise he had made to Angelika and Mouse. The boomerang had reached its apex. It was time to fly back home.

As Grubhofer hauled himself onto his feet, he turned to Landgraf. "Hey, be careful," he said. Landgraf stared back at him vacantly. He didn't say anything, but eventually he nodded in return. Minutes later, he stood up and followed his partner down the hill.

A FEW HOURS LATER, back in Advanced Base Camp, Cory Richards turned to me and said, "I have never had a longer night in the mountains. At one point I was shivering so uncontrollably that my teeth were chattering like a cartoon skeleton."

It was after lunch and five of us sat around a table in the Alpenglow Expeditions dining tent. Cory and Topo were slumped, side by side, in a couple of lawn chairs, sitting across from Renan, me, and Emily Turner, Alpenglow's Base Camp manager. For the past half hour, Cory and Topo had been recounting the ass-kicking they had just taken on their new route up the Northeast Face. Topo's nose looked like a piece of ham that had been left out to air dry in the sun. His face was covered in black stubble and his eyes had a faraway look. Cory's nose was burnt too, and his hair was sticking straight up. Whatever fire had been burning in them the last time we'd hung out had been snuffed out. The two men sitting before us appeared like burnt-out shells of their former selves.

At the end of the first day of climbing, they had found themselves at 24,300 feet on a 55-degree limestone slab covered in a foot of loose, unconsolidated snow. Wasted and with nowhere to set up their tent, they had been forced to sit out the night on a tiny ledge the width of a staircase tread, with their legs dangling over the edge. The anchor to which they were attached—two pitons driven upward under a loose flake of rock—was so dubious that neither of them dared to weight it. They had stuffed themselves into their three-season sleeping bags with their boots on, only to realize that they were perfectly positioned for spindrift sifting down the gully to pour directly into the opening around their necks. It didn't take long for their bags to fill with snow, and they found themselves packed in ice, like a couple of frozen tuna in the hold of a fishing vessel.

Earlier that morning, while organizing gear at their cache at the base of the Northeast Face, they realized they had forgotten their medical kit in Base Camp. This meant that they had only one or two oral doses of dexamethasone, a powerful steroid that is used to treat HAPE and HACE. They hoped and assumed they wouldn't need the medicine, but Cory couldn't help wondering if maybe this was the first mistake in a string of events that would lead to catastrophe. He flashed to the time several years earlier when he had almost died in a scuba diving accident. That fiasco had started with a similar, seemingly inconsequential event that cascaded into a situation in which he found himself 100 feet underwater without any air left in his tank.

Their kit included a small, single-wall tent, two 20-degree sleeping bags, six days of food (2,800 calories per man, per day), a stove, a few fuel canisters, a 260-foot-long, 6.5-millimeter rope, a small rack of rock climbing gear, and four ice screws. All told, the load, which they split between their two packs, weighed about seventy-five pounds. As the sky slowly turned from black to blue, they set off, climbing in tandem, but unroped, with Topo in the lead and Cory a few feet behind. Their only belay was through their ice axes, which were connected to their harnesses with short tethers called "umbilicals."

The ice apron was about 45-degrees at the start, but it slowly steepened as they picked their way toward a gully 2,000 feet above. Unfortunately for Cory and Topo, the slope was encased in a sheet of rock-hard ice covered in six to eight inches of snow—what Cory described as "dust on crust." If the surface had been more forgiving, they could have walked up it using the French technique, whereby mountaineers zigzag up a snow slope, rolling their ankles outward so the bottom points on the crampons are oriented at 90 degrees to the surface, while using their ice axe in the uphill hand as a cane. French technique is an efficient way to move quickly up steep slopes, but it is generally appropriate only on firm but more forgiving snow, where it is possible to drive in the pick of one's ice axe full depth as a means to self-arrest in the event of a foot slip. On the bulletproof ice that Cory and Topo encountered, the only safe way to climb was to face in, kicking the front points of their crampons into the ice while trying to gain purchase with just the tips of their axe picks. But the ancient ice was brittle and tended to fracture and exfoliate when struck with the pick. Every upward move required several swings of the axe before chipping away down to more solid ice. Since the slope was only about the steepness of a 12/12-pitch roof, the men had to hunch far over in order to swing, which put intense strain on their lower backs and calves. Cory had trained like a fiend, but he quickly realized that he should have spent less time building his aerobic base and more time specifically conditioning the muscles in his legs. His calves were soon burning with pain.

As the sun rose, and the ocean of ice on which they were clinging like two tiny insects turned the color of cotton candy, the enormity of what they were undertaking washed over them. Cory felt like they were riding a massive wave of earth that had been thrust into the sky. The pull of gravity on his heels manifested as a cold knot of fear in his gut, but at the same time he felt exhilarated. This was the moment upon which he had focused a year of his life.

The climbing remained tedious and unrelenting, with no way to relieve the strain on their calves, and it went on like this for hours. They finally reached the gully they had been aiming for all morning. Here the snow was deeper with a firm layer on top. They could now stand in the post holes created by punching their feet through the surface. But the snow beneath was rotten and feathery. They were climbing on what's called a "wind slab," a notoriously dangerous type of snow that can avalanche at any moment. This slab was so tenuous that it reverberated like the skin of a drum each time they took a step.

At the top of the slab, they encountered tendrils of vibrant blue icicles spilling down over steep rocks. In places, the ice runnels were vertical and barely two feet wide. It was exactly the kind of extreme terrain that Cory and Topo had been dreaming about since 2016, when they first envisioned this route. But now, face-to-face with the objective, Cory wasn't so sure. It looked daunting, and he knew from past experience that it would climb even harder than it appeared. If the ice was as brittle as what they had found lower down, it would be extremely strenuous and slow going. Cory could see that Topo was champing at the bit. He was hungry for it. Cory wasn't. They discussed it briefly, and Cory convinced Topo that they should skirt this section via a gully to the left and then cross over higher up.

By the time they had worked their way into the next gully over, it was midday and the sun was high overhead. There was no wind. They began to overheat in their down suits. The mountain was also coming alive as coal-black rocks melted out of the ice and began raining down from above. The small ones were the size of golf balls. They made a zipping sound as they hurtled past. The bigger ones, around grapefruit size, shrieked like incoming artillery.

They climbed all through the afternoon, taking their chances with the falling rock and following the path of least resistance. At 7 P.M. they found themselves on down-sloping slabs of dark rock covered in loose powder. With each step, their crampons skittered on the fragmented jigsaw puzzle of loose stone underfoot. There was now nowhere to secure their axes. If either man lost his footing, the next stop was the base of the Northeast Face some 3,000 feet below. Topo was in the lead, eagerly questing into the unknown. Cory struggled to keep pace, both physically and psychologically. Topo stopped at a narrow ledge to let Cory catch up to him.

"How are you feeling?" asked Topo.

"Not that great," replied Cory. "I'm not comfortable climbing this terrain in the dark. I think it's time to call it a day."

Topo nodded and didn't say much in return. Cory was pumping the brakes at the very moment it was time to hit the gas. Topo wanted to climb through the night, which was actually the smart thing to do, because there was nowhere to set up a proper bivouac. Stopping now would only sap their energy while wasting precious time. It was time to man up, to dig deep. But Cory had lost his nerve.

TWELVE HOURS LATER, as the two of them shivered in their ice cocoons, the sun slowly worked its way down the face toward their miserable bivouac. Cory had decided hours ago that the climb was over. In the middle of the night, he had said as much to Topo, who by then agreed. A night of nearly freezing to death had sucked the gusto out of him too. But when the sun finally hit, things didn't seem that bad. Topo fired up the stove and a few minutes later they were both sitting in the sun, sipping hot tea. Somewhat revived, they decided they weren't quite ready to abandon the climb. But four hours later, feeling the toll that the sleepless shivering night had taken on their bodies, they realized that they were only climbing themselves deeper into trouble. They turned around. After seven hours of tedious and treacherous down climbing, they staggered out onto the East Rongbuk Glacier and headed for camp.

NOW, TWENTY-FOUR HOURS LATER, drinking tea with us, they were licking their wounds and plotting their next move.

"I'm definitely not ready to give up on this season yet," said Cory.

"Me neither," said Topo.

The conversation shifted to what they had learned, and how they would adjust their tactics on their next attempt. They would trim down on gear to reduce the weight of their packs. They would climb only at night when it would be colder, so they wouldn't have to worry as much about rockfall. And they would stick to the center of the gully, where the footing would be more secure. But it all felt rather half-hearted. I sensed that they were done. And perhaps Cory and Topo sensed it too. Cory then added, "I hear the next good window might not be until June first."

It was my turn to feel deflated. "If that's the next opening, we're dead in the water," I said. "That's eight days from now. There's no way the Chinese will let us hold out for that long. And even if they did, we'll be wasted if we sit in ABC for another week. And if we bail down to Base Camp, that's it—the Chinese will never let us back up here."

Turner's radio had been squawking every few minutes with reports from Camp III, high above us. Alpenglow's Rapid Ascent team had been in position to go for the summit that day, having arrived at high camp the afternoon before. But their guides were worried about the crowds and decided to hold the team in place for an extra day. As they huddled in their tents, prepping to leave for the summit at 10 P.M. that night, a powerful storm was brewing. High winds were battering the upper mountain, it was snowing heavily, and visibility was low. Whenever anyone called Turner on the radio, you could hear the howling wind and the incessant flapping of tent fabric. It was beginning to look like the Rapid Ascent team had gambled on the weather and lost. At one point, I saw Cory and Topo share a knowing look. I assumed they were feeling thankful to be safe and secure in ABC and not somewhere up in the "event horizon" battling the maelstrom.

Turner's phone dinged with an incoming text. She picked it up off the table. The message was from Kari Kobler, whose team was attempting to make its way down from the summit.

"Oh no," she said. Then all the color drained out of her face.

IT WAS APPROXIMATELY 12:30 P.M. when Reinhard Grubhofer arrived at the top of the Second Step. A line had formed. Grubhofer estimated that there were about ten people ahead of him waiting for their turn to climb down the ladder. He hoped the delay wouldn't be too long because the weather was rapidly deteriorating. As he had worked his way down from the summit over the past two hours, clouds boiling in the valleys below had risen up and engulfed the top of Everest. Now it was snowing heavily, and the wind was blowing steady at about 35 mph and gusting higher. With the windchill, the temperature had plummeted to –20°F.

Grubhofer's biggest concern was that he couldn't see. On the way up, in the predawn darkness, his goggles had fogged and then frozen. There was no way to resurrect them, so he stuffed them into his pack. Now he was wearing his backups, a pair of Adidas wraparound sunglasses. They had worked well during the clear, sunny weather of the morning, but inside these frozen clouds that were swirling over the Northeast Ridge, the glasses were getting coated in rime ice every few minutes. The only way he could clear them was to remove his outer mitts and wipe them clean with his thin fleece liner gloves. After a few of these cleanings, his fingertips began to go numb. He realized that it was only a matter time before frostbite set in.

Distracted by his glasses, about fifteen minutes went by before Grubhofer thought to himself, *What's going on? Why is this line not moving?* That's when he realized that a Chinese woman at the front of the line was jamming everything up. He knew she was Chinese because she was wearing the same red suit as everyone else on the Chinese team. Two sherpas were yelling at her to step down onto the ladder, but she was frozen with fear, like a little kid on the high dive at the pool, and she refused to budge. There was only one way down and she was blocking it. No one could move until she got her act together.

Time slowed down as Grubhofer continued to fiddle with his glasses. Half an hour went by and nothing changed—the woman was still there. People were grumbling. Someone called out: "For god's sake, why is she not moving?" Grubhofer looked back. A queue of at least twenty people had now formed behind him. A few people back, he saw Landgraf standing there silently. He was staring at his feet and not moving. His blue suit was completely coated in rime ice.

Forty-five minutes had passed.

"Fuck! Move on!" yelled Grubhofer. Other people began screaming at her. The sherpas were pulling on the woman, but she refused their urgings. Grubhofer's mood was getting dark. This Chinese woman, who clearly had no business being on the mountain, was going to cost him his life. *I cannot keep my promise*, he thought. *I'm going to die here. This is just like 1996. Why should I freeze to death up here because of this idiot? She is going to kill us all. I should go down and kick her off. It's either her or me.*

And then, just as he felt the aggression starting to boil over, he saw the red suit disappear over the edge. It had taken an hour, but the woman had finally screwed up her courage and climbed down onto the ladder. It took another half hour before Grubhofer reached the front of the line. All told, he had been waiting in a blizzard at 28,200 feet for an hour and a half. By now, he could hardly feel his fingers and toes. He was so dehydrated his mouth felt like it was filled with crumpled paper.

Twenty minutes later, after stepping down off the bottom ladder, Grubhofer was making his way across the difficult traverse below the Second Step when he heard another commotion flare up behind him. People were yelling. One voice, a screaming woman, stood out above the others. Grubhofer had to keep moving or he would only further delay the people immediately behind him. He thought of Landgraf and how listless he had been on the summit. *Please, don't be Ernst,* he thought to himself. *PLEASE, don't be Ernst.*

AT THE TOP OF the Second Step, a twenty-seven-year-old woman from Jordan named Dolores Al Shelleh stood just behind Landgraf in line. After he climbed down two or three steps on the ladder, she saw him slip off. He was dangling from the fixed rope, upside down. His pack had pulled him over backward. Like a beetle stuck on its back, Landgraf was flailing his limbs, unable to right himself. *That's not normal*, she thought. *He can't even pull himself up*. "ALEX!" she screamed at the top of her lungs, trying to get the attention of her Russian guide, Alex Abramov, who was a couple people in line behind her. A few minutes earlier, Abramov had instructed a sherpa to short-rope Al Shelleh down the ladder. The sherpa had clipped a tether between their harnesses, and he now had Al Shelleh attached to him like a dog on a leash. But Al Shelleh wanted to be short-roped by a different sherpa whom she trusted more, so she started complaining. "It's okay, Dolores," said Abramov firmly. "Just go down." Everyone in the vicinity had witnessed this exchange, so when Al Shelleh began screaming, they all assumed it was because she was afraid to climb down the ladder—just like the Chinese woman. Some of these folks had now been waiting almost two hours. They were getting dangerously cold, running low on oxygen and completely out of patience. Tempers exploded. Someone yelled, "What the fuck is wrong with you?" Another bellowed, "Are you crazy? Get down the fucking ladder!"

By now, Landgraf's sherpa guide had moved down and he was pushing up on his client's pack from below, trying to help him get back on the ladder. All of a sudden, Landgraf, who had now been bent over backward for about ten minutes, stopped flopping. He looked up at Al Shelleh, then his eyes rolled back into his head and his body went limp.

Al Shelleh screamed again and then started crying. Abramov had now moved up past a couple people to where she was, and he was pissed. He still assumed her hysterics were about the earlier dispute. He was cursing at her in Russian when he looked down and saw

Landgraf lying at the bottom of the upper ladder. Now he understood. Landgraf was attached to the rope with a rappel device, which must be controlled with a brake hand on the rope below. He had been holding himself in place on the rope the whole time he was flailing about, trying to right himself. When he lost consciousness, his hand came off the rope, and he dropped about twenty feet to the bottom of the ladder. Abramov climbed down to him, joining Landgraf's sherpa. Landgraf was hanging upside down by his harness, his legs above his head. His mask had come off and his bottle had slipped out of his pack and fallen down the North Face. His eyes were closed. Abramov shook him and tried to wake him up. But Landgraf was unresponsive and he wasn't breathing. He was dead.

Abramov considered lowering the body down to the bottom of the Second Step to get it out of the way, but this would take at least another hour and would require the help of several sherpas, who were badly needed to take care of their ailing clients. It was now close to 3 P.M., and if they didn't get the line moving, more people were likely to suffer the same fate as Landgraf. So Abramov tied the body off, pushed it as far to the side as he could, and called up for Al Shelleh to come down. She tried, but for some reason the sherpa to whom she was clipped wouldn't move. When he saw that Al Shelleh was still not moving down, Abramov climbed back up the ladder. He grabbed her by the leg and started pulling, not realizing that she physically could not move. With the Russian pulling her from below, and the sherpa holding her tight from above, Al Shelleh started screaming again, causing even more hell to break loose up above, where no one knew that someone had just died. Finally, she reached up, unclipped herself from the sherpa, and began climbing down with no belay. At the bottom of the ladder she had to shoulder Landgraf to the side, her body sliding down along his blue suit as she pushed past.

MEANWHILE, GRUBHOFER, Tashi, and Neuschmid were working their way along the tricky traverse below the Second Step. It was obvious from the cacophony behind them that something terrible had happened. Grubhofer was directly behind Neuschmid, when the guide's radio crackled. It was Landgraf's sherpa. "Old man dead," he said. "Old man dead."

Grubhofer dropped to his knees. He leaned his head against the rock, thinking about his friend, and how he wasn't going home to his family. It all began to feel overwhelmingly depressing. A sense of resignation crept over him. But Grubhofer realized that he had to take this moment and turn it into something positive, something motivational. No matter what, he had to keep his promise to little Mouse. *Ich nicht*, he said to himself. *Ich nicht* (not me). And with this new mantra, he got up and began plodding down the mountain.

As he neared camp around 5 P.M., he finally ran out of oxygen and immediately found himself struggling to remain conscious. His eyes began to close involuntarily, then his legs gave out. As he crawled the remaining distance, fighting for his life, he chanted, over and over, "Boomerang, Prinzessin, Maus, Boomerang, Prinzessin, Maus."

PART THREE

BEYOND ALL

CHAPTER TEN

Kam

When Jamie had asked a week earlier who wanted to wager on how many people would die during the first summit window, I had thought it was a callous and flippant remark. These were people's lives—people just like us—he was talking about. On the afternoon of Thursday, May 23, as I hugged Emily Turner, who was choking back tears, I realized that Jamie had been through situations just like this on several occasions. Anyone who kept coming back to Everest year after year, engaging with death as they plied their trade, inevitably buffered themselves with some kind of psychological armor. Jamie was no different.

And now I had to find a way to keep pressing forward with our expedition despite the proximity of death to our team. I hadn't properly met Landgraf, but we had passed Kobler's team on the trail a few times, and when Turner described him, I could picture his face. I could further imagine him telling the story of his climb to the top of the world to his grandchildren for many years to come had he lived to enjoy his retirement. Now he was hanging dead on a rope at 28,200 feet. And the day wasn't done. There were further reports coming in over the radio of more climbers in desperate circumstances.

With these thoughts swirling in my head, we sat down a short while later with our sherpa support team to discuss logistics in case the weather cooperated, and we got our own chance to head up the mountain. We could see that the Death Zone was still engulfed in dark, menacing clouds, but down at 21,000 feet where we sat in a big group outside the cook tent, there was intermittent sunshine. We started with some introductions, since not all of us had attended an earlier team meeting down in Base Camp. Thom kicked things off by explaining that he had been a member of the expedition in 1999 that found the remains of George Mallory. He also shared that he had summited in 2016 on the south side. "I love the culture and the people," said Thom. "Summiting is beautiful, but the best part of these expeditions is becoming friends with you guys." It seemed like the sherpas might not have understood exactly what Thom was saying, or didn't care, because they sat there stone-faced, not reacting in any way. One of the younger sherpas had a rock in his hand and he was cracking it, over and over, on a boulder he was sitting next to.

Thom had mentioned to me several times that he felt a bit uneasy that we hadn't formed stronger bonds with our sherpa team. "It seems like some of them are consciously making a point to keep themselves at a distance," he said. "It's almost as if someone has spread doubts about us." He told me he'd made a point to connect with some of the more aloof guys. They'd have a conversation, trade contact info and Facebook accounts, and Thom would think, *Okay, I think we're good.* But then the next day he'd see them in camp, and they'd look right through him, like he was a total stranger. As it turned out, these were the climbing sherpas who had been assigned to us by the CTMA. At the time, we didn't realize how poisonous this situation would eventually become.

Renan now spoke to the guys in Nepali, and since no one was translating, I didn't know what he was saying, but it must have been funny because all the sherpas were laughing. Renan has been to Nepal close to twenty times since he'd spent a semester abroad in Kathmandu. In many ways, Nepal has been his home away from home, and his fluency with the language has opened many doors over the years. Several of Renan's trips to Nepal were for cinematography work he did on a film called *Sherpa*, a 2015 documentary about Phurba Tashi, a legendary Sherpa who climbed Everest twenty-one times. The film explored Tashi's spiritual relationship with the mountain, as well as the conflict he felt between making a living and the stress that his dangerous occupation put on his family. Unlike the Hollywood movie *Everest*, which told the story of the 1996 Everest disaster and was universally hated by the Sherpa community, *Sherpa* was well received in Nepal. When Renan mentioned that he had worked on the film, a murmur of approval went through the group.

"I came here this year with Mark to tell a different story about Everest," said Renan. "This story is not about the summit. Maybe Mark will tell you more."

I then made a few remarks about my climbing background, how I had traveled the world for most of my adult life looking for unclimbed big-wall rock climbs—not high-altitude peaks—but that now I finally had an opportunity to realize my childhood dream of climbing an 8,000-meter mountain. At this point, I turned to Jamie. "Are we at a point where we can lay it all bare?" I asked.

"I have already," said Jamie.

I took a deep breath and launched into an off-the-cuff account of how I had been drawn into one of the most enduring mysteries in the history of mountaineering. "When we go up high on the mountain, whenever that might be, we're not going straight for the summit, we're going to do some searching in the Yellow Band for Sandy Irvine, and we hope that you guys can support us and help us."

I looked from one sherpa to the next, but not a single one of them said anything. Someone coughed, then one of them straightened his leg and sent a rock clattering down the slope. A few of them were looking up toward the summit, where the drama was still unfolding.

Lhakpa turned to Jamie. "Not going to the summit?"

I was about to say that I hoped we could both search and go to the summit, but Lhakpa spoke first. "Big problem."

The moment these words came out of his mouth, pandemonium erupted. Lhakpa, who up until this moment had been the perfect model of equanimity, began speaking crazy fast in Nepali. Ngati, the sherpa who had led our puja, kept saying something over and over in his now raspy smoker's voice. The only pieces of it I could make out were "written rule" and "blacklist." Pemba Tenzing, a young sherpa who typically didn't even respond when I said hello to him in camp, was the most outspoken of anyone.

"This is not Nepal," he shouted in English. "This is China."

As the sherpas became more and more worked up, Lhakpa grabbed a radio and walked away from the circle. I was sure he was calling Dawa, which it turned out he was. He came back a few minutes later and unloaded an earful on Renan in Nepali.

"Okay, okay, everyone. I'm going to translate," said Renan. He explained the various problems the sherpas had with our plan. First, the CTMA had a "written rule" that stated no one was allowed to leave the ropes. The only exception was to relieve oneself. Second, the sherpas were keen to summit. Everest summits are like currency for climbing sherpas. The more you have on your résumé, the better. Some of our guys were rookies who had never been to the top before. Their desire to summit was the same as everyone else's—and if they pulled it off, it would directly impact how much pay they could command in subsequent years. Even the veterans like Lhakpa were here to climb the mountain—not to look for a dead body. Most if not all of our climbing sherpas were Buddhists and as such they had strong feelings against messing around with the dead. It's bad luck. If they had known from the start that this was our plan, maybe they wouldn't have signed up for this expedition. Third, the CTMA had pulled them aside recently and specifically dictated that we were allowed to spend only twelve hours in Camp III. Ngati, who was kneeling with his elbows on his knees and a buff covering his mouth, said, "If you spend more than twelve hours at eighty-three hundred meters, then it won't be good. That's very dangerous for everyone."

But the thing that gutted me the most was that Lhakpa and the others were clearly feeling let down that we hadn't told them the true plan from the start. "Different plan, makes our work very hard," said Lhakpa in English. We had put them in a tenuous position, asking them to do things that the CTMA had specifically forbidden, things that could drastically affect their ability to provide for their families. It was one thing for us to break the rules. Nobody wanted to get banned from climbing in China, but if we did, it wouldn't be the end of the world. There are plenty of other countries with big mountains to climb. But if these guys were blacklisted by the CTMA, it could mean the end of a lucrative career.

And that's how we found ourselves on the edge of a full-blown mutiny. After two grueling trips to the North Col, I certainly had no illusions that we could climb the rest of the mountain without these guys' support. If they walked away, our expedition would be over.

At this point, all eyes turned to Jamie. He had just told us that he had shared the search plan with the leadership of Expedition Himalaya and the climbing sherpas. Jamie and I had agreed before the expedition that our sherpa team had to know exactly what they were signing up for. And yet here they were, saying that they didn't.

Jamie had a black neck warmer pulled up over his nose. He slipped it down and evidently tried to speak; his mouth moved, but no words came out. He put his hand to his throat and pantomimed coughing to indicate that he had lost his voice.

"You're kidding," I said. "You've lost your voice right now? How convenient." Jamie shrugged and walked away. The situation was quickly spiraling out of control. Renan thanked the sherpas for sharing their concerns and apologized for the misunderstanding. He told them we would discuss and get back to them right away. As we headed for the dining tent, I watched as they crowded together into a tight knot. The voice of Pemba Tenzing rose above all the others. He was speaking in Nepali or Sherpa, so I don't know what he was saying, but he pointed toward the summit. The cloud enshrouding the summit had grown darker still.

Back in the dining tent, I confronted Jamie. "What gives? I thought you told them about the search."

Jamie, speaking in a barely audible whisper, said that he had indeed told Dawa and some of the others, but maybe not Lhakpa. But what he was most concerned about now was the time limit the CTMA had put on how long we could stay in Camp III. In all his years working on Everest, he had never heard of such a thing. Had the CTMA known all along about the search? One thing was sure: If it didn't already know, it would soon. Pemba Tenzing was probably on the radio to the CTMA at that very moment.

"So, what are we going to do?" I said.

"I'm worried that we're fucking with their livelihoods," said Jim. "That's not right."

"It seems like the summit just went from being the second priority to now being the first," said Thom. "What if we were to go for the summit and then do the search on the way down?" Thom had voiced exactly what I was thinking.

"The single most important thing at this point with respect to the search is to get to the Holzel spot and to have a look in that crevice," I said. "I see it as a fairly minor variation off the route. If we give the sherpas what they want, and go to the summit, I could veer off to hit the Holzel spot on either the way up or down."

"On the way down. It's better," whispered Jamie. Holzel would have agreed. He always thought it was important to approach the search area from above, so that the terrain would appear the same as it did to Xu Jing back in 1960. Besides, if we left for the summit at the normal time, it would be dark on the way up.

"I'm worried about what's going to happen when Mark has his sherpa next to him on the descent and he unclips from the rope and starts descending into the search zone," said Renan.

"If that's the plan, I'll be super careful," I said. Then I added, "Is this between us?" Everyone knew what I meant.

"Let's do it like that," said Jamie.

We called Lhakpa into the dining tent to tell him the new plan. Renan took the lead, speaking to Lhakpa in Nepali, and then saying the same thing in English so we could follow along. "We are going to follow the most simple plan possible," he said. "Going to the summit, following the rules, filming along the way . . . We want to work with all your guys and not create any problems for the government, for your future climbs, so we're going to go for the summit, come down safe. What do you think, *thik chha*? [OK?]"

Lhakpa nodded "Thik chha, thik chha."

"Simple plan is the best plan right now," said Renan, "because we just want to have a good expedition. And for all of us, this is work and we want to work in the mountains more and we know it's hard with the government." At this, Renan looked around the table inquiringly, then added, "I don't want to be the only one to talk here."

"We thought, by not talking about our plan, we were actually protecting you guys," said Thom. "We didn't want to get anybody in trouble with the CTMA."

"Yeah, yeah," said Lhakpa.

"Let's go get the summit, make a great movie, come home, and have a great big party," said Thom.

"Hear, hear," said everyone. Lhakpa was now chuckling and smiling warmly. Inwardly, I did a little fist pump. The sherpas had resolved the dilemma that had been nagging at me ever since arriving in Base Camp more than a month earlier—whether we would prioritize the search and forgo the summit. That the decision was now made for me was a kind of relief.

No one had mentioned the possibility that I might go rogue on the descent. Lhakpa, for his part, hadn't asked any tough questions, and it seemed like what had been left unsaid was that we had found a reasonable compromise, and that if there was ever a time when it was better to beg for forgiveness than ask for permission, this was certainly it.

AROUND THE TIME that Grubhofer and Landgraf were summiting that morning, Rolfe Oostra, the Australian guide, straggled back down into Camp III. He might not have made it had he not caught up with a Chinese woman and a sherpa below the First Step. They too had run out of oxygen, but they quickly determined that each party had what the other needed. Oostra had full bottles but lacked a working regulator. They had working regulators but empty bottles. Hooking one of their regulators to one of his bottles, they passed around the mask, sharing hits of the life-sustaining gas. After a few minutes, Oostra felt better and decided he had recovered enough to make a dash for camp, leaving his bottles with the two strangers.

The first thing he did when he got to camp was to crawl into the tent where the spare oxygen bottles were stored. He was on his knees, with a bottle in his hands, when he felt the mountain shift underneath him. The wall of rocks propping up the downhill side of the tent was collapsing. The tent ripped loose from its stakes and Oostra cartwheeled down the mountain—for the second time that day. *What a ridiculous way to end it all*, he thought, as oxygen bottles spilled out the open door. After rolling about 100 feet, the tent caught on a boulder. He could hear the bottles clanking and exploding as they ping-ponged down the North Face. Oostra checked himself out. He was banged up and bruised, again, but not seriously hurt.

He scrambled back up the hill, found another tent, and managed to get himself hooked up to a fresh bottle of oxygen. Around midday, the wind picked up and it began to snow. By 3 P.M., it was gusting to 40 miles per hour and Oostra could hear nearby unoccupied tents ripping loose and hurtling down the mountain. He kept checking in via radio with his climbing sherpas to see how his team was making out. Everyone, apparently, was now on their way down, even the slow-moving Kam. Kam, he was told, had been the last person to summit that day from the north side. The sherpas said they were having a tough go of it but coping. They would do what was needed.

Other teams straggled into camp. Oostra heard people moaning and crying in English, Russian, Hindi, Chinese, and Sherpa. One woman in particular was ranting hysterically. Then someone else yelled at her. "If you don't shut the fuck up, I'm going to slap you." The woman quieted.

Oostra pulled out a satellite texter and sent his wife a message. "It's 96 all over again." Around 4 P.M., his first client straggled into camp. Jamie Ironmonger, a police officer from the UK, had not summited. Worried about the crowds and the possibility that he might run out of oxygen on the descent, he had turned back shortly after surmounting the Second Step. According to Ironmonger's account of his summit day, he had sat on a rock to take in the view of the Himalaya before heading down. Just then, Kam appeared, moving very slowly. Ironmonger wasn't sure of the time but it was probably around 9 A.M.

"I think you should come back down with me," he said. "The storm is coming and there is going to be another window tomorrow, so we can have another go." Ironmonger knew that no one goes back up for another try the next day, but he thought it might be a way to convince Kam to turn around with him.

According to Ironmonger, Kam replied something to the effect, "No, I'm fine, I'll be fine, I'm carrying on." And with that, she plodded on toward the Third Step.

Chris Dare, an officer with the Canadian Armed Forces, was next to arrive in high camp. He had summited around 10 A.M. and was now covered in ice and unable to speak. His sherpa guide tried to say something to Oostra, but his speech was slurred and incoherent. Oostra shoved them into an unoccupied tent and helped them to get a brew on.

Next came Arthur Prestige, a cabinetmaker from the UK, and Sheena West, both fifty-three years old. They had summited at around 11 A.M. Prestige was barely able to walk. His sherpa was crying. But West, the only one who appeared to have come through relatively unscathed, gave Oostra a huge hug and said, "That was brilliant, I am so happy."

Darkness fell and there was still no sign of Kam or her sherpa, Bir. Finally, at around 8 P.M., Bir appeared out of the gloom. When he arrived outside Oostra's tent, his legs buckled, and he collapsed onto the ground. Oostra kneeled by his side and put his hands on his shoulders. "Hey, are you okay? Where's Kam?" But Bir was totally done in and unable to speak or even make eye contact. With some help from the other sherpas, Oostra dragged him into a tent, gave him oxygen, and forced him to drink some warm liquid. After about twenty minutes, he came around.

"Where's Kam?" Oostra now asked again. "WHERE—IS—KAM?"

Bir looked up slowly. "I don't know."

GOING, GOING, GONE. That was the thought that went through Kam's mind as she watched Bir clamber across the ridge ahead of her. There was something about the way he was moving that told her he was leaving her behind. She pulled her mask off and screamed, "Hey, don't leave me." Bir stopped. To Kam, it felt like she was watching a movie in slow motion. Bir turned. He looked back at her but didn't say anything. Then he turned around and kept moving down.

Kam plopped down onto a ledge as a cold fear gripped her chest. It was probably around 5 P.M., maybe a little later, and she was somewhere on the ridge between the First and Second Steps. She had summited around 11:15 A.M. In the intervening hours, she had managed to descend only about 500 vertical feet. The sun was close to setting now, and she couldn't feel her fingers or toes. She had been moving more or less nonstop in the Death Zone for twenty hours. She knew that she was nearing her limit, both physically and mentally. *I can't do this on my own,* she thought. Yet she had no choice. She was the last one. Every other person on the mountain was somewhere below. No one was coming back for her.

Not far above, a body in a blue suit dangled from a rope on the Second Step. Between high camp and the summit, the trail was littered with about a dozen bodies. But this one hadn't been there on the way up, and it wasn't even fully frozen yet. On the way down the ladder, she had pushed it out of the way to get by. *Is this what's going to happen to me?* she had wondered.

The storm was abating. Mist swirled and it was still snowing lightly, but the wind had eased up. The clouds billowing up over the ridge from the Kangshung Face struck Kam as serenely beautiful in the late-afternoon light. For a moment, it all felt rather pleasant. But she knew she was slowly dying.

Kam snapped out of her revelry. *Stay in the present, stay focused. Keep moving.* She couldn't let her guard down; the end would come all too easily.

KAMALDEEP KAUR WAS BORN IN London in 1983. Her father, a native of India, had immigrated to England when he was seventeen years old. For decades, he supported the family as a bus driver. In the mid-1970s, he married a teacher from Lahore through an arranged marriage and brought her to the UK. Kam was the baby of the family. Her two brothers were five and seven years older. They lived in a small house in a town called Walsall, eight miles outside of Birmingham. Money was tight. For several years, the three children shared the same room. Their neighborhood was a rough place, rife with gangs, crime, and drugs. Racism was rampant.

As a young girl, Kam was the shy type who followed her mother everywhere, holding her skirt. When she got older, she played a bit of hockey and netball, and tried to keep up with her big brothers, whom she idolized. But unlike them, she was never a natural athlete. By age ten or eleven, she began to struggle with her body image and self-esteem. Sometimes, she would hide behind the couch, waiting to see if anyone would notice that she was missing.

Kam had never been a great student. By age twelve, she had given up on academics. She fell in with the delinquents, skipped school, and started using drugs and alcohol.

When Kam was fourteen, she was abducted by a group of men who brought her to a home not far from where she lived and gang-raped her for a week. They eventually dropped her in the street, and she walked home. In Indian culture, a woman who has been so violated is tainted for life. It brings shame to the family, and she is unmarriable. Kam knew that it would gut her family to know what had happened to her, so she told them that she had run away. She never reported the men, even though, to this day, she knows where it happened, and she remembers some of their faces.

She had long suffered from insomnia, but now she couldn't sleep at all.

The only escape she could find was to drink until she blacked out. One day she woke up in the hospital with alcohol poisoning. When she got home, her mother, Yashpal, asked her what had happened to her when she went missing. Kam kept silent. Not knowing how else to break her daughter free from this self-destructive downward spiral, Yashpal took Kam to India. Kam's father later joined them.

One day, the three of them visited a holy site called the Golden Temple in the city of Amritsar. After a long day in the hot sun, they found themselves on a crowded, rickety bus, heading back to their accommodations. Kam noticed that her mom looked a bit peaked. When Kam asked her mom if she was feeling okay, Yashpal mumbled something that sounded like goodbye, then she swooned, closed her eyes, and collapsed in Kam's arms. Kam and her father dragged her off the bus, flagged down a taxi, and brought her to the nearest hospital. Yashpal was still breathing, but the hospital said they couldn't treat her because she wasn't a resident of the city. They would need to try a different hospital. On the way to that one, Kam was in the back of a van giving her mother CPR as her body turned blue.

When they got to the emergency room, they loaded her on a gurney, but it was too late. Yashpal was dead.

The hospital said it couldn't take the body, so Kam stayed with her mom while her dad went to get ice. They wrapped Yashpal in a sheet, then laid her onto the frozen blocks in the back of the van. On the long drive through the night back to New Delhi, as the vehicle slowly filled with the smell of death, Kam watched as her mother's body became stiff and cold.

It was an image, like the faces of the men who held her down and raped her repeatedly, that she would never get out of her head.

After the funeral in New Delhi, where they cremated the body, Kam and her father headed back to England. All Kam wanted to do was sleep so she could escape the "chattering monkey" inside her head, the dark secrets she was still hiding. But her insomnia was resistant to all but the most potent cocktails of drugs and alcohol. When she did pass out, which was never for more than a few hours at a time, she was haunted by nightmares. In her search for an escape, she overdosed twice. The first time after taking a mouthful of her mom's prescription antidepressants, which caused her to hallucinate for a week. It was around this time that she started cutting herself with any sharp implement she could find.

By seventeen, she was on the dole and had moved out of the family home. By the time most people were having their first cup of coffee, Kam was typically deep into a bottle of whisky. One day, while lost in a desolate wilderness of despair, she heard her mother's voice saying, "Kam, don't go over the cliff. You need help." Kam looked in the yellow pages and found the name of a psychotherapist—Dr. Trent. She found Dr. Trent's office in Birmingham and knocked on his door. As luck would have it, he wasn't with a patient. "I need your help," said Kam. Dr. Trent said he was a private doctor. He was very busy. His rates were high. Kam would need to apply through the

NHS and get on a waiting list. "I'll be dead by then," she said. Dr. Trent asked her what she could afford, and they made a deal: eight sessions at £10 (approximately $12) per session, once every two weeks. Dr. Trent thought it was important that Kam pay for the appointments, even if it was at a fraction of his normal rate.

Over the next four months, Kam told Dr. Trent her story. Little by little, he taught her that her self-loathing wasn't being forced on her by anyone else; it was coming from inside her. If she wanted it to be different, she was the one who had to change it.

The memories didn't go away, but they did fade a bit over the next several years, as Kam learned to take better control of her emotions and to not blame herself for the bad things that had happened in her life. But she still had her demons, and she continued to abuse drugs and alcohol. She eventually moved to Buckinghamshire and ended up in an abusive relationship with an alcoholic who taught her to keep her mouth shut if she didn't want to get smacked. She learned not to talk, to be seen but not heard, because her opinions didn't matter, because, as she remembers it, she was a woman and was supposed to do what she was told. Kam knew that she should leave the man, but she didn't.

When it got ugly, she would leave their flat and go for walks. One day, she's not sure why, she started running. She liked it. Soon, she was running ten miles a day, five days a week. Kam had found what she calls a different type of self-destruction, one that was actually good for her physical and mental well-being. Her runs eventually led her into the green spaces all around Buckinghamshire, where she found a sense of freedom and release that she had never felt before.

Through running, she found work in sports retail and became involved with fitness culture. People started asking her to compete in races and to take part in charity events. Kam was never competitive with anyone but herself. She did learn, though, that when the going got tough on the racecourse, she possessed a rare ability to detach emotionally from the pain, a handy skill for a long-distance runner—or a mountaineer in the making. In 2011, she completed the UK Three Peaks Challenge, climbing the highest mountains in England, Scotland, and Wales in twenty-four hours. She also ran the Jungfrau Marathon in the Swiss Alps.

She was beginning to make a name for herself as an athlete, which led to an invitation to participate in a climb of Mount Kilimanjaro that was raising money for the local firefighters' association. Without knowing anything about the mountain, Kam said yes, and that summer she headed to Tanzania. On summit day, just below the 19,340-foot peak, Kam saw her first mountain sunrise. "Oh—my—god!" she gasped. "Is this real?"

One of the guides on that trip was Rolfe Oostra, whose company, 360 Expeditions, specializes in guiding the Seven Summits, including Kilimanjaro, the highest mountain in Africa. A few months later, Kam joined Oostra's expedition to Aconcagua (22,841 feet), the tallest peak in South America. Showing the same grit that she had displayed in her running and also on Kilimanjaro, Kam summited. Without having ever really thought about the Seven Summits, she now had two of them, including one of the hardest, in the bag. But more important, she had found a calling. Mountain climbing gave her a sense of control she had never experienced before. Whether she climbed a mountain or not was no one's decision but her own, and mountains had no expectations of her. Finally, Kam had found the orientation and purpose her life had always lacked. She told her friends that mountain climbing had saved her life. And perhaps for this reason, she found that when she was in the mountains, for the first time in as long as she could remember, she was able to sleep.

When she came home from South America, she left her abusive boyfriend and poured herself into her climbing. She worked three jobs, retail during the day, then waitressing and bartending at night. When she got home, she worked out and did yoga into the wee hours of the morning. On a good night, she'd nap four hours, then get up at 5 or 6 A.M. and do it all over again. Too obsessive-compulsive to take rest days, she followed this pattern day in and day out. Kam still had her demons, and she hadn't yet gotten her addictions under control. She continued to drink, take drugs, and cut herself. And yet, even as she gnashed her teeth in the depths of clinical depression, she systematically ticked off one mountaineering classic after another.

Oostra had been her guide on every climb so far, and yet it wasn't until they climbed Mera Peak in the Nepal Himalaya that they formed an actual friendship. Oostra liked Kam. She was tough and scrappy. He knew her background and appreciated her grit and the idea of using mountaineering as therapy. In the coming years, they climbed more peaks together: Mount Elbrus in the Caucusus, the tallest peak in Europe; Gran Paradiso in the Italian Alps; Denali, the tallest peak in North America; and Cho Oyu in Tibet, her first 8,000-meter peak. Kam didn't have any sponsors, but she was good at saving money. And despite her low self-esteem, she was always able to project a certain charm and presence when she applied for jobs. She came across as authentic. People liked her. If she ever came up short when saving for an expedition, she'd sell her jewelry or paintings. It was just stuff, after all.

By 2018, she had ticked off four of the Seven Summits, but Everest wasn't yet on her horizon. Instead, her dream was to climb Makalu, the world's fifth-tallest mountain. The first time she saw a photo of this peak, she had butterflies in her chest. She didn't know why exactly, but she felt a spiritual connection to the mountain, that somehow Makalu had an important lesson to teach her.

As a stepping-stone on her path to Makalu, Kam set off in the fall of 2018 for Ama Dablam, a highly technical, 22,349-foot peak in the

Khumbu known as the Matterhorn of the Himalaya. Until now, she had stood on the summit of every mountain she had attempted.

But on Ama Dablam, things didn't go according to plan. Kam developed a nasty gastrointestinal illness, which required three courses of antibiotics. By the time she set off for the summit, she was a shell of her former self, and with nothing in the tank, she hated every step of the climb. She turned back, several hundred feet from the summit, utterly defeated. A few days later she was back in Kathmandu.

Before the expedition, she had quit all her jobs and committed herself to making a living as an athlete, guide, and yoga instructor. This climb was important, and she had worked so hard to get to this point. How could she give up now? After a few days of rest and recovery in Kathmandu, she felt better, so she headed back into the mountains. A week after she had turned back the first time, she stepped onto the most important summit of her life. She had climbed bigger mountains, but she had never dug so deep.

Things started happening. The climbing sherpas wouldn't take a tip from her. They told her to keep the money and use it to go for Everest. Word began to spread of the remarkable young British woman of Indian descent who came from a hard-knocks background but had found salvation and redemption through mountaineering. Companies in both India and the UK reached out to her. They told her she was an inspiration to young Asian women. They wanted to invest in her and get her to Mount Everest.

Six months later, Kam set off with Oostra on the biggest climb of her life.

It was dark by the time Kam arrived at the top of the First Step, but she wasn't sure when that had happened. The sunset must have been beautiful, but she had no recollection of it. It was still lightly snowing. Every once in a while, the mist would clear, and she could see stars twinkling in the sky above the Tibetan Plateau. Looking down, she could clearly see Camp III, where a dozen tents glowed on the ridge. *If I can just get there*, she said to herself.

A rope was anchored right in front of her, but she knew that her fingers were too frozen to rig a rappel. She couldn't feel them at all anymore. They were like blocks of wood, as if they belonged to someone else. She would have to down climb the First Step, as Mallory and Irvine would have in 1924. Kam managed to clip her tether to the fixed line with her wooden hands, then she wrapped the rope around her arm a few times, and sitting on her bottom, facing out like a kid on a playground slide, she slid over the lip of the sixty-foot-high almost vertical wall.

Hanging from the rope by one arm and clawing at anything she could get her hand on with the other, Kam lay back, hoping the friction of her body against the rock would slow her down. As she scraped down the spiny limestone, she could hear her suit tearing apart as down feathers filled the air all around her and danced in the dimming beam of her headlamp. Looking down, she saw that there was a small ledge about a body length below. She let the rope slip through her hand and before she knew what was happening, it slipped off her arm and she felt herself going weightless. She barely had time to register that she was falling and that her next stop would be the base of the step where she would land with a leg-breaking crunch, when suddenly she jerked to an abrupt stop. Her rucksack had snagged on a sharp point of rock.

Kam hung there like a marionette waiting for the adrenaline to dissipate. *Come on, Kam*, she said to herself. *You've made it this far. You can't die now. Whatever it takes to get down. Do it.* The bottom part of the wall was plastered with snow, which she dug into with her crampons, managing to push herself up off the spike. Sliding and clawing at whatever features she could, she arrived at the base of the step in one piece.

Looking out across the section of ridge that still lay between her and camp, she saw a light that was surprisingly close. *Oh my god*, she thought, *I've actually managed to catch up with someone*. It was a man in a red suit. She pulled off her mask and yelled, "Hey! I need help. Wait for me." She thought he might have looked back and waved, but the boundary between real and imaginary was getting fuzzy. Kam staggered, bumped, crawled, and slid down to where the man was sitting. "Oh, thank god you're here," she said. "I need you." The man turned his head and Kam saw his face. He was middle-aged with brown skin and round eyes. He looked like he might be Indian. He showed no expression, and she realized that he was in dire straits himself. Kam sat down behind him and leaned against his back, desperate for body heat. By now she was shivering uncontrollably, and she knew she was freezing to death. She had to keep moving. But she was too tired to move any more. She let her face sink into the back of the man's down suit and allowed her eyes to close. *Just for a few seconds*, she told herself.

If that's Kam, she's fucked, thought Oostra. He was standing outside Camp III in the pitch-dark. Several hundred vertical feet above, he saw a flickering light. *There is no way I can get that high*. He had almost died himself that day—twice—and now, at 9 P.M., having not slept for at least forty-eight hours, the thought of climbing back up the Northeast Ridge filled him with despair. But he knew the light he was seeing up there had to be Kam. Everyone else had been accounted for.

There were other teams now gearing up for a second round of

summit bids, but Oostra, an old hand in the game of Himalayan guiding, knew he couldn't rely on any of them to save Kam. Sure, there was a chance they would abandon their dreams to rescue a random stranger, but Kam's life hung in the balance, and he knew he couldn't leave it to chance. By morning, she'd be dead.

Oostra turned his own headlamp toward the light and flashed it three times, the universal signal for SOS. After a little while, the light above flashed back three times.

IT WASN'T KAM who was signaling, though. It was the mystery man against whose back Kam was currently resting. Kam opened her eyes, and she saw the flashing light down below. *Could it be Rolfe? Was he coming to get her?*

A few minutes later, the man in the red suit hauled himself onto his feet and staggered away. He never looked back. Kam realized that he hadn't uttered a single word to her.

AS OOSTRA STRUGGLED back up the route for the second time that day, he found himself growing angry. If Kam had listened to the people who tried to turn her back, neither of them would be in this precarious position. Early that morning, not long before he had nearly fallen off the mountain, he had caught up with Bir and Kam at Mushroom Rock, a famous landmark at 28,100 feet on the ridge between the First and Second Steps. The pair had fallen behind the rest of the group, and Bir had pulled Oostra aside to tell him that he was worried about their slow pace and was thinking about turning Kam around. The sun was rising, and high above, other climbers who had made better time, including Joisher and Mingma Tenzi, were already summiting.

Like every other climbing sherpa, Bir knew that a fit mountaineer should be able to make it from high camp to the summit in about eight hours, perhaps a little longer with delays due to crowding. He and Kam had already been going for that long, and yet they had made it only to a little over 28,000 feet, not much more than halfway from Camp III to the summit. At this pace, they would run out of oxygen before they made it back to high camp. Oostra said something to the effect that he trusted Bir's judgment and would support whatever he decided to do. At any rate, Kam had already moved on, so Bir put a final decision off for the time being.

Bir was in his early thirties and had been guiding 8,000-meter peaks since 2010. He had summited Everest five times, and had also been to the top of Annapurna, Lhotse, Dhaulagiri, and Cho Oyu. After the Everest season, he had plans to guide K2. Bir would later claim he had tried to turn Kam around on three occasions, but each time, she had insisted they continue on toward the summit. Eventually, after running out of oxygen himself late in the afternoon, he realized there was nothing more he could do for Kam. He had a wife and children, and like everyone else on the mountain with a family, he had promised them he would make good decisions and come back home, no matter what.

Whether Kam should have turned around would later be argued over bitterly. As far as Oostra was now concerned, her inability to make it back to camp before nightfall spoke for itself: She had behaved recklessly and selfishly and now he was risking his own life to go save her from her own folly.

As he slowly toiled upward, Oostra kept checking to see how far he was from the light. For half an hour or so, it continued to flash, and he could tell that it wasn't moving downward. And that pissed him off even more. *If you're able to operate your goddamn light, why can't you keep moving down?* When the light stopped flashing, he stopped and yelled up into the darkness, "Kam, is that you?" Silence. He yelled again, louder. And then a third time. There was a long pause, then he heard a weak, "Yes, I'm here."

A few minutes later, Oostra came upon a man, who must have been Kam's silent companion, being lowered on a rope by a sherpa above. After he passed the incapacitated climber, Oostra heard someone above yelling, "Where is your team, where is your team?" Di Gilbert, a Scottish guide who was leading three clients on their way up to the summit, had just encountered someone lying prostrate, hanging off a rope at approximately 27,550 feet. As one of Gilbert's climbing sherpas moved forward to investigate what was going on, the body dropped about 10 feet onto the ledge where they were standing. When the person staggered upright momentarily, Gilbert was taken aback. "Oh shit," she exclaimed, "it's Kam."

She had met Kam in Base Camp, when Kam had come over to their camp to say she wasn't getting along with her own team. After that, she started spending a lot of time with the Adventure Peaks expedition members and she formed a bond with a woman named Kirsty, a doctor in the British army who had done multiple tours in Afghanistan. When Kirsty realized that it was her friend standing in front of them on the ledge, she unclipped from the rope and moved to Kam's side. Kam was panicky and one of her hands was bare—she had lost a glove. Kirsty and Gilbert looked around for it, but it was nowhere to be seen. Kam seemed confused and wasn't making sense, but they eventually figured out that she was saying she was out of oxygen and had been abandoned by her sherpa. Gilbert noticed a single light coming up from below. She called down. Oostra yelled up. *At least one person was coming to Kam's aid.*

Gilbert now faced a choice: Abandon her clients' summit bid to help get Kam down to high camp or carry on and hope that Oostra could somehow manage it on his own. Kam seemed to still be functioning mentally, but she was clearly done in physically. She would need to be manhandled down the remaining 500 vertical feet to Camp III, a herculean task for one person at this altitude. Nevertheless, as Oostra had earlier assumed the ascending teams would do, Gilbert decided to carry on with the climb. She felt her primary responsibility was to her clients, who had hired her to get them to the summit. "Fight for your life," she said to Kam, as she motioned to the sherpas that they should move on. "Fight for your life—and keep moving," echoed Kirsty.

Kam shuffled a few feet across the ledge to the next anchor point, where one of Gilbert's sherpas set up a rappel for her. As the Adventure Peaks team headed up the next rope, she looked down and saw Oostra's light shining in her direction. Then her eyes closed.

Every Everest climber knows—or should know—that on summit day they might roll up on some wretched soul, frostbitten, disoriented, and unable to move under their own power. I think most, however, don't prepare themselves for the moral dilemma they actually have a fairly high likelihood of encountering. Some, I suspect, even assiduously avoid contemplating it. So, when it happens, there's no predetermined decision matrix. It comes down to whether a climber feels compelled to give up the summit to help the anonymous victim. Most often, what the climber clearly wants, in return for all the time, effort, and money they've invested, is to stand on the summit. The consolation prize of having done a good deed isn't worth the many tens of thousands of dollars, months of training, and untold hours spent daydreaming about this moment. The supporting rationalizations follow: *They're too far gone, there's nothing much I can do for them anyway, it's their own stupid fault they didn't turn back when they should have.*

And what makes it such a damned conundrum—at least for the casual observer, if not for the climbers themselves in the moment—is that these rationalizations aren't by any means unsound. The average Everest climber is not a mountain rescue professional, and they're likely to be operating right at their own physical limit. It's entirely understandable that they would be wary of getting entangled in someone else's mess—especially one that was likely caused by that person making some seriously poor decisions.

There is also the simple fact that no one is in their right mind when they're climbing at these elevations. Oxygen deprivation puts every climber into a cognitive haze, inducing a state of tunnel vision that is only compounded by the goggles, hood, oxygen mask, and darkness. When questing for the summit in the middle of the night, most climbers don't see or notice much outside the narrow beam cast by their headlamps, and it's all they can do to just put one foot in front of the other. As Thom Pollard says, "You're not the same person in the Death Zone as you are at sea level."

This every-man-for-himself attitude is a big part of why there are so many Everest haters, which is understandable. But it's also true that most of the people who find themselves facing this moral dilemma will have nothing in their life experience to call upon as a model for making the right decision. Where else but on Everest would a person find themselves faced with the choice of paying $40,000, $60,000, or even $80,000 in order to possibly—not definitely, mind you—save the life of someone they've never met? It sounds like the plot of a twisted reality TV show. The fact is, we know that most people end up rationalizing the decision to carry on and preserve the sizable investment they've made in a project that has deep personal meaning to them. The fact that, time and again, people have walked right up on this very quandary, said to themselves "There but for the grace of God go I" or some such incantation, and carried on toward the summit, seems to give a clear indication of where our moral factory settings lie. On Everest, where the number of climbers attempting the mountain increases in inverse proportion to the general level of competence, it's become so common as to be almost unremarkable.

Nevertheless, certain instances do stand out, including the tragic story of David Sharp, a thirty-four-year-old British engineer who lost his life on the Northeast Ridge on May 15, 2006. Sharp's story is particularly dismaying because during the many hours it took him to die in the vicinity of Green Boots Cave, below the First Step, he was passed by dozens of climbers on their way both to and from the summit. Even a climber moving quite fast would take eight hours to go from Sharp's location up to the summit and back, more than enough time for a couple of relatively strong clients and their sherpa guides to have assisted Sharp back down to Camp III, or even lower.

Sharp was climbing alone, without teammates, sherpa support, or a radio. He carried a limited amount of oxygen. Adopting the same style Noel Odell had advocated, he hoped to summit without resorting to bottled oxygen, but he prudently carried a couple of cylinders in case he came to grief and needed them. We don't know exactly what happened to him, but he somehow lost the plot on the way down from his summit bid.

Every climber who passed him by as they headed up the next day, it seems, had a plausible story. Some said they didn't see him at all, even though the cave is basically adjacent to the trail. Others said they saw him but thought he was fine and was just taking a rest. Still others said they thought he was already dead. One of the teams that passed Sharp that night was filming for a popular Discovery Channel reality TV show called *Everest: Beyond the Limit*. The summit party that night included Mark Inglis, a Kiwi who was attempting to become the first double amputee to climb Everest. The team's guide,

Mark Woodward, saw Sharp sitting by the side of the trail. Sharp was alive but unresponsive and apparently in a hypothermic coma. "The poor guy's stuffed," thought Woodward. The team continued on.

Many hours later, on their way down, one of the team's sherpas captured footage of Sharp with a helmet-mounted camera. He was shivering uncontrollably but was coherent enough to state his name and that he was with Asian Trekking. Sharp's expedition was not a traditional commercial venture. He had paid $7,000 to be part of a loose conglomeration of climbers who shared a Base Camp and Advanced Base Camp but operated independently, without guides or climbing sherpas. Now he was paying the price for not having any support. It had been a particularly cold day, and Sharp had been above 27,000 feet without oxygen for more than thirty-six hours. His feet were frostbitten stumps, and his hands were blackened to halfway up his forearms. His nose was black. Some of the sherpas worked on him for a while. They gave him oxygen, and they massaged his body, trying to create some blood flow. They yelled at him and hoisted him to his feet. He came around somewhat but was never able to support his own weight. It was too late. Not even the strongest sherpa can carry a fully incapacitated climber at this elevation, so they eventually left him. At some point later that night, he became the seventh Everest fatality of that season.

When word of this seemingly preventable tragedy reached Edmund Hillary, who at the time was eighty-seven years old and near the end of his own storied life, he told *New Zealand Herald* that "the whole attitude towards climbing Mount Everest has become rather horrifying. The people just want to get to the top. They don't give a damn for anybody else who may be in distress." Hillary said that on his expedition in 1953, it would have been absolutely unthinkable to leave someone "lying under a rock to die." Modern Everest climbers, he said, had completely lost sight of what was important. "If you have someone who is in great need and you are still strong and energetic, then you have a duty, really, to give all you can to get the man down and getting to the summit becomes very secondary."

The one person who notably didn't criticize the climbers who failed to save Sharp was his own mother. She told the *Sunday Times* that up in the Death Zone, "your responsibility is to save yourself—not to try to save anybody else."

TEN DAYS LATER, a similar situation unfolded a bit higher up on the Northeast Ridge. A veteran Australian mountaineer named Lincoln Hall, who had garnered some fame in 1985 as a member of the team that pioneered a direct route up Everest's North Face called White Limbo, began to suffer hallucinations while returning from the summit. Jamie was in Advanced Base Camp at the time, carefully monitoring radio transmissions, and he says that somewhere around 28,500 feet, just below the Third Step, Hall became combative with his climbing sherpas and began raving like a lunatic about three women, lying in wait for him lower on the mountain, who were going to "cut him up." Jamie speculates that Hall's psychotic break with reality could have been caused by a combination of oxygen deprivation and HACE.

Several sherpas spent hours trying to rescue him. During this time, they were in close contact with their expedition leader, Alex Abramov, as well as Jamie, who was helping out because of his Nepali language skills. Jamie says that as night fell, Hall became unresponsive. He was still breathing but appeared to be in some kind of coma. The sherpas were running low on oxygen, but they resolutely refused to leave Hall, knowing that if they did, they were signing his death warrant. At one point the sherpas, thinking they too might not survive, asked Jamie to relay messages to their wives and children.

"No," said Jamie, taking command even though it wasn't his team, "you've done everything you could. Save yourselves. It's one life or four lives." Reluctantly, the sherpas agreed. According to Jamie, one of them, Dawa Sherpa, was sobbing.

The next morning, a team of four men led by an American guide named Dan Mazur was on its way to the summit when they encountered Hall. They had heard of his plight on the radio the day before and were expecting to come across his frozen body. Instead, they found him sitting cross-legged with the top of his down suit pulled down. His head was bare, as were his hands, and he wasn't wearing an oxygen mask. Hall was lucky (or, as he later titled his book, "dead lucky"). Not only had he regained his lucidity, but it had been a mild night, which had probably saved him from freezing to death. "I imagine you are surprised to see me here," he croaked, in his Aussie accent. Mazur and his two clients, Canadian Andrew Brash and Brit Myles Osborne, along with Jangbu Sherpa, promptly abandoned their summit attempt and began organizing a rescue. Abramov sent up a dozen sherpas and Mazur's team gave Hall a fresh oxygen bottle and administered some drugs. With the help of the arriving sherpas, they spent the next twenty-four hours getting Hall down the mountain. By the time Hall reached ABC, he was walking under his own power. Jamie took a photo of him as he strolled into camp. The night before, a message had been relayed to Hall's family that he had perished high on the mountain. Jamie promptly emailed the photo to the family with the news of subsequent developments. Thanks to the efforts of Mazur and his team, Lincoln Hall would end up escaping from his ordeal on Everest with only the loss of some fingertips and a toe due to frostbite.

Later, when asked why he had abandoned the summit in perfect conditions, only a few hundred feet from the top, Mazur said, "The summit is still there and we can go back. Lincoln only has one life."

Thom Pollard has his own story about encountering ailing and dying climbers on Everest. It happened in 2016 during his third expedition to the mountain. In 1999, he forwent the summit to search for Irvine and the camera. In 2014, like Kuntal Joisher, he never set foot on the route as a result of the avalanche that killed sixteen Sherpas in the Khumbu Icefall. Thom had been actively dreaming about climbing Mount Everest since he was a child. Now, at fifty-four years old, he had his first shot at making the summit. The stars had finally aligned. When he and his climbing sherpa, Lhakpa Pinasa, exited their tent on the South Col at 8 p.m., the sky was clear, the moon was full, and there was no one ahead of them on the route. The perfect summit day was unfolding before them. An hour later, Thom and Lhakpa were firing on all cylinders when they looked up and saw a headlamp shining down from above. *That's odd*, thought Thom, who was quite sure they had been the first team out of camp. A few minutes later they encountered a young, shell-shocked climbing sherpa on his way down the hill. He told them that he had just left his Indian client, who had died not far above. Thom and Lhakpa gave the sherpa some hot water from their thermos and continued on.

At approximately 27,300 feet, not far below the prominent ledge known as the Balcony, Thom and Lhakpa rolled up on a body in a yellow down suit. It was lying sideways across the slope on its right side, hanging from a rope. The man's arms were frozen stiff, sticking out from his waist as if he was reaching to catch a ball. His gloves were off. His hands, frozen into blocks of ice, were clenched. Thom shined his headlamp into the dead man's face, which was glazed in ice. His eyes were closed.

THE MAN, Thom later learned, was a fifty-year-old police officer from Kolkata, India, named Goutam Ghosh. This was Ghosh's third attempt in as many years to climb "the Everest," a dream for which he had saved up for the past ten years. He was part of a four-person team that included three other Indians from West Bengal. Twelve hours earlier, near this same spot, Ghosh's Nepali guide, Bishnu Gurung, had tried to turn the entire team around. It was midmorning, and they were still only at 27,700 feet. Other climbers who had already summited would soon be passing by on their way down. If they kept going, they would surely run out of oxygen. Ghosh wept when he realized that his dream was slipping away. Then one of his teammates, Subhas Paul, a forty-four-year-old truck driver who had cashed in his father's pension to pay for the expedition, pushed past Bishnu and continued plodding toward the summit. Paul's sherpa, Lakpa, initially didn't follow. He was trying to call Paul's bluff, hoping the man would turn back. Instead, Paul called Lakpa's bluff and never looked back. "Sherpas can't use force or hit him in that situation," Lakpa later told John Branch, who wrote a lengthy article about the Indian climbers for the *New York Times*. "They are our guest. All we could do is convince. As he wasn't convinced, I followed him." Bishnu also followed, as did Ghosh, Sunita Hazra, a forty-two-year-old nurse, and the other supporting sherpas. Only Paresh Nath, a fifty-eight-year-old one-handed tailor was convinced to turn around.

Details as to what happened next and whether any of them reached the summit are sketchy, but by all accounts, Ghosh, Paul, and Hazra pushed themselves to the brink. (A video later surfaced of Ghosh on the South Summit, 300 feet below the actual summit. His bloodshot eyes stare vacantly into the camera.) What's known is that the Indians were dangerously behind schedule. Everyone eventually ran out of oxygen. At this point, the sherpas, now fighting for their own lives, abandoned their clients.

"Is HE ALIVE?" asked Thom. At that exact moment, almost as if Ghosh had been listening, the body twitched, and Thom nearly jumped out of his skin. He would later describe the scene of watching what he thought was a dead man come to life as something straight out of a horror movie. Apparently, Ghosh was not actually dead—not completely, not yet.

"Should I give him my spare mittens? Should we try and drag him down to camp?" Thom asked.

"No," said Lhakpa, "he's gone. Let's go." As Lhakpa moved on, Thom unclipped his tether from the rope and stepped over Ghosh's legs. They hadn't gone far when they arrived at essentially the same scene. A body in a yellow suit lying sideways across the trail. This was Sunita Hazra. Her gloves were off, and she was holding her hands out. She wasn't moving. As far as Thom could tell, she was dead. For the second time in about fifteen minutes, Thom stepped over another body and continued on.

Thom and Lhakpa made excellent time. They summited well ahead of schedule at 2:30 A.M., after less than seven hours on the move. In this same amount of time the day before, the Indians had ascended only about one-third as far.

The sun was rising when they arrived back at the spot where they had seen the dead woman. Thom had told himself he wasn't going to look closely at her, but when he got to the spot, the body was gone. In its place, there was a track in the snow, as if someone had dragged her away or she had slid down herself. Thom and Lhakpa looked at each other, realizing that the woman may still have been alive when they stepped over her.

IN FACT, two or three hours after they had passed Hazra, a British soldier named Leslie John Binns, who had served in Bosnia, Iraq, and Afghanistan, and lost an eye to an IED, came upon her and determined that she was still alive. He immediately abandoned his own summit attempt and tried to save her. Seeing that she was out of oxygen, he gave her his own spare bottle, clipped her to his harness and began dragging her down the hill, creating the track that Thom and Lhakpa had seen in the snow.

Thom and Lhakpa encountered Ghosh right where they had left him. As they got close, Lhakpa accidentally dislodged a chunk of snow that rolled down the hill and collided with the man's head. He didn't move or react in any way. Lhakpa unclipped and moved in close, putting his face right in front of Ghosh's, to see if he was breathing. Lhakpa didn't look at Thom or say anything, he simply clipped back into the rope and kept going.

As they approached camp on the South Col, they saw a man sitting on the slope above the Lhotse Face, hundreds of feet off the route. He wasn't wearing a pack and was holding his arm up, as if drinking a cup of tea. The slope between them and the man was rock-hard blue ice and riddled in crevasses. Thom called and whistled, but there was no response. A few minutes later, the person toppled over sideways. Thom later learned that this was probably Paresh Nath, the one-armed tailor.

They continued on and just outside camp they saw yet another distressed climber, sitting on the ground not far from the trail, with someone in attendance. This area was safe, so they unclipped from the fixed line and began moving toward the pair, when the one who was standing began calling and gesturing that they shouldn't come over. They weren't sure why, maybe the person was dead, or a rescue team was already on its way. In any event, their help evidently wasn't needed and they'd had a big day, so they continued on to camp. Soon after, the person was dragged into camp. It was Subhas Paul, the one who had trudged on in defiance of the guide's plea to turn around and whom the others had followed like the Pied Piper. (Paul would later set off down the Lhotse Face, heading for Camp II, but he succumbed to exhaustion along the way and never made it.)

Thom crawled into his tent and sat for a moment with his legs sticking out the door, his crampons still attached to his boots. Then he started sobbing.

Later in the day, the one-armed tailor somehow straggled into camp, but that was as far as he would get. The only member of the Indian team to survive was Sunita Hazra, whom Thom and Lhakpa had given the least scrutiny, cursorily deciding that she was already dead. Later, in an Indian TV interview, she said, "I owe my life to him [Leslie John Binns]. I could return home to see my child. What else can I say?"

THE DAY EVEREST broke was still far from over when Oostra found Kam lying on a ledge at approximately 10:30 P.M. "Hey, Kam, are you okay?" At first, there was no response. He grabbed her shoulder and shook her. She stirred. He helped her to sit up. It took her a minute to realize that her old friend was standing there in front of her. "I can't move my hands, babe," she said. Oostra checked her oxygen. It was empty, so he took the bottle out of her pack and stashed it on the ledge. He decided against giving her what he had left in his own bottle because he wasn't sure he could get her down without it.

Regardless, he would soon run out himself. Before setting off on the rescue, Oostra had been unable to locate a single spare oxygen bottle to bring to Kam. Several of the backup cylinders they had stashed in Camp III had been lost when Oostra tumbled down the hill, and the few remaining were being used by the other team members.

Oostra realized that if he was going to get her down, he'd have to drag her. The ground immediately below them was steep, so he rigged a tandem rappel. After clipping Kam to his own rappel device, he held the brake end of the rope with one hand and used the other to grab Kam by the waist belt on her harness and drag her off the ledge. When they were both over the edge, he carefully let the rope through his hand, while straddling Kam and using his legs to keep her upright. In this position, they rappelled 150 feet down a sloping rock wall to a gravelly terrace where the bottom of the rope was anchored. The next section angled downward on rubble-covered ledges.

"Kam, I need you to stand up," said Oostra firmly.

Kam tried to get up onto her feet, but her legs gave out. Her body simply didn't work anymore.

"STAND UP!" screamed Rolfe.

Kam tried again but couldn't muster the strength. She was crying now. "I'm so sorry. I'm so, so sorry. I'm trying my hardest."

Oostra grabbed her under the arms and helped her onto her feet. She leaned against him, with an arm around his waist. After two wobbly steps, her legs buckled, and she plopped down onto her backside. "Can you crawl?" asked Oostra, now trying a gentler tone. Kam crawled for a bit, with Oostra holding the waist belt of her harness, helping her along. It was brutally strenuous for Oostra, and they were barely moving. Kam collapsed again. Oostra tried to drag her, gouging a trough through the gravel. "I need you to do something," screamed Oostra, "or you are going to die." Kam struggled to her feet. With Oostra holding her up, they took a few more faltering steps. Then she fell again. Oostra yelled, he screamed, he cajoled, he sweet-talked. Whatever it took to keep her moving.

They were about 250 feet outside of camp when they came across the mystery man in the red suit. He was lying by the side of the trail on his side, not moving. The sherpa who had been helping him earlier was nowhere to be seen. Kam looked to the side as they shuffled past.

Sometime after midnight, they arrived at a 30-degree snow slope just above camp. Oostra rigged up another tandem rappel and walked down the hill, using the rope and his legs as leverage to angle Kam over the snow toward the tents. Camp was spread out over a wide area and since everyone was asleep, there were no lights to guide them in. By now, Oostra had reached the end of his own tether. His oxygen had run out shortly after he got to Kam. In his addled state, he couldn't find any of his team's tents. Finally, he yelled as loud as he could, "ARTHUR!" A light came on, and Arthur, the cabinet-maker, popped his head out of a nearby tent. "Please, can you take Kam?" Oostra implored.

Kam had been on the move continuously above 27,000 feet for twenty-eight hours, many of those without oxygen. It was now early in the morning of Friday, May 24. Thanks to Oostra, Kam had survived. But she wasn't out of danger yet.

CHAPTER ELEVEN

English Air

On May 24, 1924, Sandy Irvine was convalescing in Camp II on the East Rongbuk Glacier. The evening before, Edward Norton had asked him to assist in the retrieval of four porters marooned on the North Col, but Irvine had been suffering from a stubborn case of diarrhea and awoke feeling so "seedy," he told Norton he would be more a hindrance than a help. He had previously hoped to be setting off up the mountain, around this time, for a summit attempt with Mallory. Instead, young Sandy retreated downward, his prospects of having a proper go at the mountain evaporating.

Nothing, it seemed, had been going according to plan. Since the storm of May 9 and 10, which had left the expedition's supply chain in complete disarray, a deep low-pressure system had stalled to the west of the Himalaya. It had been pumping out heavy snowfall, blistering cold, and high winds for weeks. Many of the loads that had been abandoned all along the East Rongbuk Glacier still lay where they had been dropped.

By this point in the season two years before, a bubbling stream had coursed through Camp III (near today's ABC location), and the men had lounged in the sun in their shirtsleeves. Now, that same camp was a frozen wasteland. On May 22, the team recorded a temperature of –24°F—the coldest of the entire expedition. Irvine's feet had gone numb in his sleeping bag that night, forcing him to get up multiple times and do jumping jacks to get his blood flowing.

Two days later, on May 26, after the porters on the North Col had been rescued, the team convened on a grassy bench at Camp I, not far above the spot where the East Rongbuk Glacier meets the main glacier. Norton, a highly decorated career military man who had fought in most of the major campaigns of World War One, including the Battle of the Somme, called a "council of war" that afternoon. His primary concern was the health of the team. The day before, one of the porters, a cobbler named Manbahadur, had died from complications arising from the severe frostbite he suffered on his feet and legs during the May 10 storm. Of the fifty-five porters still on the mountain, only fifteen were deemed fit enough to continue with their work. Camp IV on the North Col had barely been established with a few tents and sleeping bags. Much of the food and equipment needed for the higher camps, rather than being neatly stocked on the North Col, was strewn so haphazardly across the East Rongbuk Glacier that no one knew for sure where it all was. Now, without the manpower to move all this material up the mountain, and with many of the climbing team members suffering from various ailments, Norton had no choice but to restructure the plan of attack.

The biggest variable was the weather, which had begun to resemble the early stages of the summer monsoon. It had been snowing heavily, with fronts riding in on telltale southwesterlies, which Norton recorded in his diary as the preliminary "monsoon current." The expedition was running out of time.

The war council lasted through the evening, but no decisions were made. In the morning, Norton sent a note to Camp II asking for Odell, E. O. Shebbeare, and John Noel, the team photographer and filmmaker (and the one who had purchased the VPK cameras for the team) to come down to join the discussion. No one recorded the exact details of the deliberations that took place over these many hours, but we do know, from various accounts, that one of the central questions was whether or not to include the use of the supplemental oxygen in the plan. It was Geoffrey Bruce, more than any other, who now championed the no-oxygen ascent, which is interesting, considering that in 1922, Bruce had climbed to 27,300 feet—the standing altitude record at the time—with George Finch, using a prototype oxygen apparatus.

On that attempt, the men were pinned down in a terrible storm for two nights at 25,500 feet. Finch later wrote movingly of the experience. "A dead numbing cold was creeping up my limbs . . . Something had to be done. Like an inspiration came the thought of trying the effect of oxygen . . . A few minutes after the first deep breath, I felt a tingling sensation of returning life and warmth to my limbs. We connected up the apparatus in such a way that we could breathe a small quantity of oxygen throughout the night. The result was marvellous. We slept well and warmly. Whenever the tube delivering the gas fell out of Bruce's mouth as he slept, I could see him stir uneasily in the uric, greenish light of the moon as it filtered through the canvas. Then half unconsciously replacing the tube, he would fall once more into a peaceful slumber. There is little doubt that it was the use of oxygen which saved our lives during this second night in our high camp."

The next day, Finch and Bruce, using oxygen, climbed to their record high point in just two hours, a rate of ascent equal to 900 feet an hour. An attempt the day before, led by Mallory, had covered some of the same ground without oxygen, averaging only 330 feet an hour. Those in favor of using oxygen this time around pointed to this attempt as strong evidence in its favor.

The oxygen apparatus represented the one piece of kit that was well organized and ready to go, thanks to the work of the team's young engineer. At that moment, six oxygen sets were sitting in Camp III, ready to be moved up the mountain. But Bruce argued strongly that they would be better off to ditch the oxygen in exchange for more stoves, tents, sleeping bags, food, and fuel. With their limited resources, it was hard to argue against his logic, and later that day the team voted unanimously to "scrap the oxygen altogether," as Norton put it.

The new plan called for establishing two camps above the North Col, one at 25,500 feet and another at approximately 27,000 feet on the North Ridge, to the east of Bruce and Finch's 1922 high point. The latter would be more a bivouac than a proper camp. Mallory lobbied for this high camp, perhaps recalling the advice of Alexander Kellas, who had predicted that this was the lowest anyone could hope to camp and still make it up to the summit and back during daylight. It turns out Kellas and Mallory were, if anything, optimistic in this regard; while today's high camp is normally situated almost exactly where the British hoped to set theirs in 1924, climbers typically set off well before midnight and do much of the ascent in the dark in order to have enough daylight to get down.

All that was left then was to determine who would comprise the two summit teams. It was decided that one team would consist of Mallory's two trusted lieutenants from the 1922 expedition, who had accompanied him to his high point of 26,985 feet, Norton and Somervell. Both were highly experienced mountaineers and currently performing well.

It was left for Mallory to choose his partner for the second team. Irvine was up against Geoffrey Bruce, the man whom the expedition doctor, Richard Hingston, had deemed the strongest of them all. Bruce was also a much more experienced mountaineer. As the use of the Mark V oxygen apparatus was no longer part of the plan, Mallory gave the spot to Bruce.

This must have been a bitter moment for Irvine, who desperately wanted his own shot at the summit. But as was his wont, he accepted his new assignment as a member of the support team, alongside Noel Odell, with a stiff upper lip. That night, he didn't even mention it in his diary. "Geoff's plan was voted for unanimously, as it required so few porters up to the North Col," he wrote. "Went to have a look at the ice caves in the side of the glacier snout this afternoon. Have three letters [to send], but no envelopes. So have missed the mail."

At this critical juncture, Mallory was less than sanguine about the expedition's prospects. He concluded the last letter he would ever write to Ruth: "Darling, I wish you the best I can—that your anxiety will be at an end before you get this, with the best news, which will also be the quickest. It is 50 to 1 against us, but we'll have a whack yet, and do ourselves proud. Great love to you."

BY MAY 24, 2019, the day after Everest broke, Nims's photo of the traffic jam high on the Southeast Ridge was front-page news on every major media outlet, and as a result, my phone was blowing up. For a while, it felt like a part-time job simply telling people that the photo was from the south side of the mountain and I was on the north, and that our team had deliberately held back to avoid the crowds.

And there was developing news of yet more casualties from the slow-motion summit stampede. That morning, with our shaky satellite Wi-Fi signal, Jamie had pulled up the story online of two more people who had died the day before on the south side. Nihal Bagwan, twenty-seven, from Pune, a city in western India, had summited late that day. It was his second attempt, having made it to approximately 27,700 feet in 2017. His outfitter, a Nepali company called Peak Promotion, told the *Hindustan Times* that Bagwan died of "dehydration, exhaustion and tiredness after being caught in the jam of climbers."

Kalpana Das, fifty, a lawyer from India, had previously summited Everest in 2008, back when very few Indian women had climbed the mountain. She had played her cards well and managed to leverage her Everest summit into minor fame and fortune in Odisha, a city on the east coast of India on the Bay of Bengal. Now, eleven years later, Das was back to lead the Three Women Expedition. Her partners hailed from Nepal and China. The three summited around 12:55 P.M. On the descent, Das began to complain of leg pain and breathlessness. She died late that afternoon just above the Balcony at approximately 27,700 feet. Naveen Patnaik, the chief minister of Odisha, said in a statement, "Her legacy in mountaineering will inspire generations of young women in the state." According to reports, Patnaik made arrangements with Nepal's ministry of tourism to have her body brought down the mountain so it could be returned to India to be properly laid to rest.

Later that afternoon, a thirty-two-year-old Nepali mountain guide named Dhruba Bista, a father to a baby girl and a friend of Prakash Kemchay, would collapse outside Camp III—halfway up the Lhotse Face on the South Col route. He was airlifted by helicopter (in favorable conditions, rescue helicopters can now fly as high as 26,000 feet on Everest) to Base Camp but died later that day. On Makalu, Nima Tenji Sherpa died outside Camp II on his way down from the summit. The cause of death was unknown. By day's end, the 2019 death toll on Everest would stand at nine, while the same number had perished on other 8,000-meter peaks.

SOBERED BY ALL the bad news but knowing that successful summiteers were now trickling into camp, I set off after lunch to see if I could find any. Twenty-four hours earlier, with everyone lined up at the summit, this place had been a ghost town. Now it was buzzing as conquering heroes staggered into ABC. Many had spent the previous night at Camp I on the North Col, on their way from the summit. Support staff now worked feverishly to dismantle camp and send it all back down the mountain. An endless train of yaks—a veritable Himalayan cattle drive—ambled in and out of camp, their bells tinkling like running water. As I scanned the sea of yellow nylon domes scattered across camp, I saw down suits draped over the tops of tents. These multicolored garments, steaming in the sun, were like flags that proclaimed: Herein lies an Everest veteran.

Trails spiderwebbed before me, leading into the various enclaves, but I stuck to the main thoroughfare. A few yards to my left I saw a frazzled-looking, middle-aged man in long johns, sitting cross-legged on a foam pad in front of his tent, holding his feet in his hands. His face was covered in several days' worth of thick stubble. Greasy hair stuck every which way. He was staring absently in my direction, so I stopped and hailed him. "Hey, how did it go? Did you summit?"

"Yes," he replied wearily, in a clipped German accent.

"Congratulations," I called back. Smiling now, he mouthed *Thank you* and pressed his two hands together, his fingers pointing toward the sky.

Continuing on, I passed more tents covered in suits and sleeping bags. Then I came upon a tent perched on a landscaped rock pedestal a few feet to the side of the trail. A pair of boots, with the liners pulled out of them, was sitting outside the door, wreathed in a cloud of vapor. Nearby, in a pile of rocks, lay an orange harness, a rappel device still clipped to the belay loop. A blue ascender hung at the end of a well-worn tether. The tent door was right at eye level, so I snuck a quick peak inside as I moseyed past. A pair of bare feet framed the doorway, past which lay a man on his back, chest slowly heaving in and out.

Ahead, a climber clopped down the trail in his clunky, high-altitude boots, and we soon found ourselves standing face-to-face next to a muddy puddle where a yak was tethered to a wooden stake. I wore sneakers, nylon trekking pants, a light puffy coat, and a baseball cap. The man was still dressed in his Death Zone outfit. The front of his orange suit was zipped all the way down to his waist, where he still wore his harness, festooned with gear like a carpenter's belt, including a pair of crampons that dangled by a carabiner. The man stopped, no doubt a bit taken aback by my fresh-looking appearance. I reached out my hand and offered him a fist bump, which he obliged.

"How are you?" I asked.

"Tired," he replied in a thick eastern European accent. "Glad to be down." He was looking off to the right, where I assumed his camp was beckoning.

"Did you summit?"

"I did. What a day. Rough conditions. I'm okay, but it was touch and go on the descent. So cold and windy. It was blowing forty knots. I barely got any photos. What are you doing?"

I told him that we had held back and were now waiting for the next summit window. We hoped to be heading up in a few days' time. His climb was over. Mine had yet to begin.

"Big wind is coming," he said. Then he pursed his lips and cocked his head to the side, as if to say, *I think maybe you have made the wrong call.*

"Well done, my friend, well done," I said, clapping him on the shoulder as he staggered on toward his tent. Two climbing sherpas were close behind, wearing massive backpacks that towered over their heads, with multiple oxygen bottles T-boned on the top. They were walking more resolutely, so I stepped out of the way, but held out my fist. Both of them bumped me as they went by, nodding and smiling warmly.

Toward the top of ABC, the trail led straight through the middle of the Chinese camp, which sprawled across the crest of a small hillock. Several dark green army tents were set up on either side of the trail, and I could hear the hum of kerosene stoves and Chinese pop music that blared from a speaker inside one of the tents. A few guys were sitting around. I said hello but barely got a nod in return.

Earlier that morning, one of these guys had stopped by our camp to ask about our plan. In addition to rope fixing and guiding, the Chinese "climbing sherpas," all of whom were actually Tibetan, were also responsible for search and rescue on the mountain. Every climber here had paid an additional fee to the CTMA, an insurance policy of sorts, to cover the hassle and hazard in case we got into trouble and needed to be rescued. Jamie said the CTMA told these guys they couldn't leave until we were off the mountain. So, owing to us, they might be stuck here another week, at least.

But would we get a chance to go higher on the mountain? According to the latest forecasts, the jet stream had split and was now shifting in both altitude and latitude. The current weather window was closing. The wind at the summit was supposed to crank up to 70 or 80 mph for the next few days. There was a chance of a brief respite on the twenty-eighth and then possibly again on the thirtieth. But these windows were short, only twenty-four hours or less, which meant that we'd have to climb up to high camp in strong winds.

The two small teams attached to our permit had also held back, one being the former Special Forces operator, Frank Campanaro, "the most interesting man in the world" as we had dubbed him, and the other the veteran guide Scott Woolums and his client. It wasn't clear to me whether they had arrived at that decision independently, or, since we were all on the same permit, if there was some value placed on all of us going up together. My guess was that their sherpas, who were all friends with ours, preferred to set off as one group rather than as smaller independent units. Campanaro, Woolums, and their lead sherpas had sat in on our weather briefing that morning. If we wanted to catch the short window of lighter winds on the twenty-eighth, we'd need to leave the next day for the North Col. But this would mean battling our way to high camp in sixty-knot winds. Gomba, the veteran climbing sherpa whose goggle tan was now even more pronounced, flatly said no and walked out. This left the thirtieth as our last remaining possible summit day, but only if the weather window expanded. "The wind has to be in range on the days we climb to Camp II and III," said Scott. "If it's blowing sixty, we're out."

"Where do you put our odds at this point?" I asked.

"I hate to say it, but I think we're down to about fifty-fifty," he said.

A DAY LATER, on the morning of Saturday, May 25, Thom and I were sitting in the dining tent, drinking tea and observing all the hubbub through the doorway, which was tied open. Camp continued to slowly disappear before our eyes. An endless stream of members, support, and heavily loaded yaks had been heading down the hill all day.

"Hey, what's that?" said Thom. He was pointing at a yak with something unusual strapped to its side. "Oh no, I think that's a body."

We got up from our chairs and stepped outside so we could pay our respects. The body was burrito-wrapped in a blue tarp and tied to the right side of the yak with an old piece of rope. Some duffels, to counterbalance it, were hanging on the other side of the wooden harness.

The word circulating around camp at this point was that three or four people had died on the north side, but details were sketchy. We'd heard that Ernst Landgraf was still dangling on the Second Step, and a fifty-six-year-old Irishman named Kevin Hynes had died the day before in his tent on the North Col. Another supposed dead was a British woman of Indian descent named Kam. And there were rumors that a Polish guy suffering from ataxia high up on the Northeast Ridge had also succumbed.

Jamie sidled up and told us that he'd heard that a team of six climbing sherpas had spent the past two days bringing Hynes's body down from the col. "This must be him," he said. I didn't know this at the time, but Hynes, a plasterer by trade, had spent part of the past eight years in Windham, Maine, to be near his son. Windham, a town where I had attended many youth soccer games over the years, is only an hour and a half from my home.

TWO DAYS PREVIOUSLY, on May 23, Kevin Hynes had set off with the rest of the 360 Expeditions team—Rolfe Oostra's outfit—from high camp at approximately 10 P.M., but he made it only about 100 yards up the hill before he decided to tap out. He wasn't sure why, but he had no energy and was barely able to put one foot in front of the other. A year earlier on the south side, he had no such issues, and he managed to snag an 8,000-meter doubleheader, ascending both Everest and Lhotse back-to-back. A few years before that, he had climbed Broad Peak in Pakistan (26,414 feet), the world's twelfth highest. Hynes was a good friend of Oostra's, and he was also, by far, the most experienced and solid member of his team. When they saw the mountain for the first time from the Tibetan Plateau, Hynes had turned to Oostra and said, "We struck gold here boyo."

Oostra escorted Hynes back to Camp III and left him in the care of two experienced sherpas. He told them to rest until daybreak and then head down, hopefully all the way to ABC. According to the sherpas who brought him down, Hynes was moving slowly, but he was cracking jokes and acting like his normal, cheerful self. When the storm hit in early afternoon, they crawled into a tent in Camp II and rested for five or six hours before carrying on down the mountain. The sun had set by the time they reached the North Col. Hynes, who had been on oxygen throughout, was exhausted but seemed okay otherwise. The sherpas served him more hot drinks and a warm meal. They made sure he had oxygen for the night and then put him to bed.

In the morning, at around 7 A.M., one of the sherpas went to Hynes's tent. He heard snoring and decided he'd let him sleep another half hour. When he returned at 7:30, the tent was quiet. The sherpa zipped it open and Hynes was lying motionless in his sleeping bag. The autopsy that would later be performed in Kathmandu concluded that Hynes died of so-called natural causes—not altitude sickness. It was another classic case of sudden death.

NO ONE SLEPT much the night of May 25. As forecasted, the jet stream had shifted back over the mountain and dropped in elevation. That night it hit the top of Everest with unmitigated fury. In ABC, conditions weren't as bad, by any means, as they had been during the cyclone Fani windstorm on the North Col, but one of the gusts was strong enough to break the tent pole in my vestibule. For the rest of the night, the front of my tent flapped like a flogging genoa on a sailboat. Instead of sleeping, I spent hours coughing. And the more I coughed, the more irritated my lungs became until, eventually, I was hacking more or less continuously. The endless shaking in my chest transmitted up into my head, and before long, I was also suffering from a severe headache. Around 4 A.M., I unzipped the door of the tent and kneeled outside the crumpled vestibule to hack up a wad of phlegm. It was a clear night, illuminated by a waning yellow moon, and the summit pyramid was silhouetted against a backdrop of the Milky Way. A plume of jet-stream-driven snow trailed off to the east like a silken scarf. It was beautiful, but it testified to the ferocity of the winds up there. And in my ailing state, I was in no mood to appreciate it.

BY MIDMORNING ON SUNDAY, buoyed by several cups of coffee, I was strolling through ABC when I looked up and saw an Indian woman with long brown hair walking awkwardly down the trail. I was surprised to see her; camp was now deserted. I'd thought everyone had left. She was hobbling on her heels, arms held out in front of her like Frankenstein, her hands wrapped in bandages. We shared a brief exchange. She said she had summited on the twenty-third but had a harrowing descent. Her hands and feet were badly frostbitten. She was waiting for a yak that would transport her to Base Camp. She looked at me impassively, as if wrung dry of all emotion. Then she told me her name: Kam. If I startled or showed my surprise, she didn't seem to notice. Or perhaps she was just too drained to care. In any case, I didn't mention that she was rumored to have died and, instead, wished her luck as she lumbered off down the trail.

WHEN ARTHUR, the cabinetmaker, heard Oostra shout his name late on the night of May 23, he poked his head out of his tent and saw his guide dragging Kam through the camp. But there wasn't much that he and Sheena could do to help because they were barely holding on themselves. The stone platform supporting their tent floor had collapsed and they had been lying precariously, sharing a single sleeping bag. Earlier that night, after they crawled into the tent, Arthur had refused to zip shut the door of the tent. He was sitting in the opening, staring intently at something and saying over and over, "Have you seen the shit going on in that tent over there?"

"Close the bloody tent," spat Sheena.

"Can you see the baby with the big head?" he said. "And there is a face coming out of that giant mirror. Can you see it? Look, look."

Sheena crawled out and she and Oostra dragged Kam into another partially collapsed tent, the door of which wouldn't close. Once situated, Kam and Sheena shared a single sleeping bag and one oxygen bottle. Kam was complaining about her hands and feet, so Sheena unzipped her down suit and Kam put her frozen hands between Sheena's thighs.

In the morning, Kam's hands and feet were throbbing painfully, and she was so dehydrated she could barely swallow. Oostra had managed to borrow some oxygen cylinders from Alpenglow and at 8 A.M., Bir came by the tent and hooked her up to a fresh bottle. Shortly thereafter, they set off down the mountain.

The descent from high camp to ABC—6,000 vertical feet—took fourteen hours, from 9 A.M. to 11 P.M. Every single step on her frostbitten feet was excruciating. The rope, which she wrapped around her arm, constantly rubbed against her frozen fingers, jolting her with stabbing pain that brought tears to her eyes. But she was helped along and attended to at every step of the way by Bir and Chris Dare, the Canadian soldier, who refused to let her give up. Approaching ABC, she collapsed several times, but Bir and Dare kept picking her up and she eventually staggered into camp.

A sherpa helped her to pull off her boots and soon her blue and swollen fingers and toes were warming in bowls of lukewarm water. As blood began to flow back into the frozen tissue, big, fluid-filled blisters began to form. The pain was unbearable. In a hospital, frostbite patients are administered powerful painkillers like morphine. Kam went through it with nothing. After about thirty to forty-five minutes of warming, her frozen digits, the worst of which were the big toe on her right foot and her left pinky, had turned from blue to purple. Broken and destroyed, Kam turned to the sherpas and asked them to carry her to her tent. Two of them lifted her up by her arms, while a third held her legs. Once situated in her sleeping bag, still wearing her high-altitude down suit, she passed out.

I HAD JUST CRAWLED OUT of my tent, when I heard Thom say to Jamie: "I've never experienced anything like that before." They were standing a few feet away outside their respective tents. It was the evening of May 26, about twelve hours from our scheduled departure for the summit.

"Hey," I called over to them. "Is everything okay?"

Throughout the trip, Thom had never failed to greet me with anything less than a boisterous "What's up, dawg?," if not something more off color, like the time he texted me an audio clip of him farting in his tent. Now he just stood there looking despondent.

A couple hours ago, he explained, he had been wandering around, taking photos of the abandoned camp when, all of a sudden, he felt an intense tingling in his face. He said that it started in the fatty part of his cheeks and radiated up into his eyes as far as his temples and then down into his mouth and lips. "It sounds weird to say this," he said, "but I would almost describe it as a pleasant feeling. It's worn off now, but for about fifteen minutes, I couldn't really move my lips."

"Were you able to speak?" asked Jamie.

"I'm not sure," said Thom. "I was kind of freaked out, so I just crawled into my tent and lay there for a while. I didn't talk to anyone."

The first thing I thought of was a story Jamie had told us early on in the expedition about a neurologic incident he had suffered on Broad Peak in 2008. After becoming the first Kiwi ever to summit the mountain, he was hiking down a gargantuan load when he experienced symptoms similar to what Thom had just described. Jamie's facial paralysis had lasted for two days. He told us that he never fully recovered, and still had trouble pronouncing certain words. He said that it was called a TIA, which stands for transient ischemic attack. (According to Peter Hackett, it is more likely that Jamie had a mini-stroke, because the effects of a TIA, by definition, do not last longer than twenty-four hours.) Increased hematocrit levels make the blood of high-altitude climbers more viscous and greatly elevates the likelihood of blood clots, which usually manifest in the legs but can also occur in the brain, causing a stroke. A TIA is considered an early warning sign of a full-blown stroke.

While Thom explained to the rest of the team what happened, I texted his symptoms to Peter Hackett. Jamie called in Sonam, Dawa's son, who was studying to be an emergency medical technician. Sonam took Thom's blood pressure (180/100) and his oxygen saturation (high 60s). Blood pressure is normally elevated at altitude, but Hackett said that 180/100 was higher than what he'd expect to see. And Thom's oxygen saturation was dangerously low. I had taken mine earlier that day and it was in the low 80s, which was more like what you would hope to see in an acclimatized climber at 21,000 feet.

Hackett texted me back right away, explaining that facial numbness or tingling could occur from taking Diamox, but that paralysis needed to be taken seriously as a possible TIA.

"You definitely had trouble moving your lips?" I asked Thom.

"Yeah," he said quietly, shaking his head. "Definitely."

I read aloud the rest of Hackett's text, which cautioned Thom to play it safe and not go farther up the mountain. He promised to speak with some colleagues and get back to us with a confirmation of this recommendation.

All eyes turned to Thom. He had pulled his buff up over his mouth, and he was holding his right hand over his eyes.

"Hey, it's okay, man," I said. "There's no need to make a decision right now. Let's sleep on it and see how you feel in the morning."

Thom looked up at me and nodded but didn't say anything. There were tears in his eyes.

Later that night, when reading about Mallory and Irvine, I was reminded that something similar had happened in 1924. On May 12, in the aftermath of the storm that had caught the team spread out across the East Rongbuk Glacier, a man named Shamsher, a lance corporal in the 6th Queen Elizabeth's Own Gurkha Rifles, suffered symptoms not unlike Thom's. "Another porter sick—paralysis—probably due to a clot on the brain from frost-bitten fingers," wrote Irvine in his diary. Shamsher died the next day about a half mile outside of Base Camp.

SATURDAY, MAY 27, dawned bright and still. I walked into the dining tent around 7 A.M. The rest of the gang were all in there.

"What's up, brother, how'd you sleep?" asked Thom.

He looked at me over his reading glasses, which were perched on his nose. He had his legs crossed and held a steaming mug of coffee between his two bare hands. His diary was open on the table in front of him. Even for Thom, he was remarkably bright-eyed and bushy-tailed at such an early hour. I understood immediately that he had decided not to let a little twitch in his face stop him. I looked around the table. No one else said anything. *Well, if his mind is made up, then I guess he's going up with us,* I thought. And so it seemed the team had reached a unanimous tacit agreement to just forget what had happened to him.

I spent the next hour exchanging a flurry of texts with Hampton. I'd heard that my phone might work up high, but no one seemed to know for sure. It was possible I'd be out of communication until we got back down.

Anxious to get going, Thom was the first out of camp at about 9 A.M. I wanted to hike with him, so I quickly filled my water bottle from a thermos of hot water in the dining tent, took one last sip of coffee, and bid farewell to Bir, who ran the kitchen in ABC. As I walked past the communications tent, realizing I was about to lose my Wi-Fi signal, I fished my phone out of my pocket. Sure enough, there was one last message from Hampton wishing me well and sending her love. Then I noticed that there was another message—from Peter Hackett. For a second, I thought about turning off my phone and pretending I hadn't seen it.

Hackett wrote that responses to his queries were mixed on whether Thom should abandon the climb, but his personal opinion was that it was too risky to go higher without a proper medical assessment. I called up the trail after Thom, but he ignored me and kept walking.

"THOM!" I yelled again, louder. Now he stopped and turned.

"Yo, what's up?" he answered. I waved for him to come back.

A few minutes later, I read the latest text out loud to the team in the dining tent. Thom's head hung low, and he held his hand over his eyes. He was wearing the baseball cap that he had custom-made for the trip. It was black, with a yellow logo that Thom calls the "Sundog"—a spiral that morphs into a cartoonish dog, Thom's totem animal, apparently. His brother, who committed suicide in 2005, made the logo for him thirty years ago. Thom had repurposed it for our expedition. Underneath, also in yellow, it said 29035.ONLINE—the URL for Thom's website.

No one said anything. I turned to Thom. "It's your call, dude."

"It's just a chunk of rock," Jamie now said, "and we're probably not going to find anything." As he said this, Jamie was bending a piece of wire back and forth in his hands. In 1933, the British had strung twelve miles of this stuff up the East Rongbuk to use for telegraphing messages back and forth between camps. If you poked around, you could still find pieces of it here and there by the side of the trail.

"You've got kids," I said. "Is it worth it for them?"

"Do you want me to make this decision for you?" asked Jim.

Thom was crying now. He looked at Jim and nodded his head.

"Don't go," said Jim.

"It's not worth it," said Matt.

That was it. Thom's climb was over. And the rest of us didn't have time to sit around and commiserate with him. Our packs were sitting outside the door. Two minutes later, we were outside the tent, taking turns giving him hugs. Thom promised to "keep it coming" at us on the radio. He started to say something about not second-guessing the decision, but his voice cracked before he could finish. He gestured toward the summit, grimacing and shaking his head. "Fuck, it's right there. It's right there."

Moments later, we were on our way up the trail, having lost the guy most responsible for making this expedition a reality—and the heart of our team.

THE MORNING OF June 2, 1924, found Sandy Irvine on the North Col, busily preparing breakfast for Norton and Somervell, who were packing up for their summit attempt. The day before, Irvine and Odell had performed the same task for Mallory and Bruce, waking at 4:30 A.M. for the job of coaxing the primus stove to life with frozen fingers and a box of wooden matches. Now, twenty-four hours later, Mallory and Bruce were 2,000 feet above, in Camp V, getting ready for their push to Camp VI.

To go from being Mallory's partner to the camp "scullion," as

Norton described it, must have been demoralizing for Irvine, yet by all accounts, he put on his best face and did the thankless job uncomplainingly. He and Odell cooked, served meals, filled thermoses, and provided roped escorts across the crevasses above the North Col. Their teammates passed through camp with a tip of the hat as they headed up into the fray. Norton would later write that "Odell and Irvine gave such an exhibition on how it should be done that those of us who once passed through their hands are now spoilt for life . . . In a year when to a conspicuous degree, all played for the side, none did so more conscientiously or with less thought of self than these two."

The closest Irvine came to an actual complaint was a typically terse entry in his diary on June 1. "Very cold and disagreeable job. Thank God my profession is not to be a cook!"

Sometime between 9 and 10 A.M., a bedraggled porter named Dorjee Pasang, a member of Mallory's party, staggered down into camp. Five of Mallory and Bruce's porters had failed to reach Camp V the day before, dropping their loads a few hundred feet shy at 25,000 feet and retreating back to the col. While Mallory hacked tent platforms out of the ice, Bruce and the strongest porter, Lobsang, had made two carries each to get the four additional loads up to camp.

Pasang now reported that the others—Mallory, Bruce, and two remaining porters—were pressing on. But at 11 A.M., Irvine looked up the North Ridge and saw to his surprise that the four men were on their way down. He lit two stoves, filling the pots with chunks of ice chipped from a nearby serac, grabbed a rope, and set off up the hill to meet them on the edge of the crevasse field. When Mallory arrived, he told Irvine that they had endured a withering wind the day before on their climb up the North Ridge to Camp V. That night, he and Bruce shared one tent; the remaining three porters crammed into the other. It had been a particularly cold and windy night, and in the morning, the porters resolutely refused to go any higher. Without their support, the game was up. Mallory could have continued up with Bruce to establish Camp VI for Norton and Somervell, who were on their way up from the North Col at that very moment, but instead, he chose to retreat. His gaze was still fixed on the summit—not on providing a supporting role for Norton and Somervell. By this point, it seems, he had lost faith in the non-oxygen attempt strategy, because no sooner had Mallory arrived back in Camp IV on the North Col than he pulled Irvine aside and divulged his intention to make one more attempt with the oxygen sets, with Sandy as his partner. Minutes later, Mallory, Bruce, and Irvine were on their way down to Camp III.

Once there, Mallory went to work scraping together a support team of porters, while Irvine focused on preparing the oxygen sets—cobbling together the best parts, testing the valves and various connections—until he was confident he had two sets on which they could rely. Irvine must have felt conflicted, though, because as much as he wanted to have his own crack at the summit, and as diligently as he had worked on the oxygen system, he had always felt misgivings about using it. "I really hate the thought of oxygen," he wrote in a letter to a friend. "I think I'd sooner get to the foot of the final pyramid without oxygen than to the top with it."

And the pain of using oxygen was more than just an ethical one. The two days Irvine had spent at 23,000 feet on the North Col had significantly worsened the situation with his face, and as he tested the oxygen masks, he realized that they seated exactly in the places where his skin was most tender around his mouth and across the bridge of his nose. That day he wrote in his diary, "A most unpleasant night when everything on earth seemed to rub against my face, and each time it was touched bits of burnt and dry skin came off, which made me nearly scream with pain."

On June 4, as Norton and Somervell were making for the summit, Mallory and Irvine put the oxygen sets to the test on their climb back to the North Col. At a flow rate of 1.5 liters per minute, they made great time, and Irvine noted in his diary that the oxygen helped reduce his respiratory rate to a third of what it had been on previous climbs to the col. Odell had been glassing the upper mountain with binoculars all day but hadn't seen any sign of Norton and Somervell. Mallory, though, thought he saw tracks in the snow at 28,300 feet. At 8 P.M., just as the sun was setting, Norton and Somervell were spotted on the snow slope above the North Col. While Mallory and Odell set off to meet them, Irvine fired up the stoves and began preparing tea and a hot meal.

THE MORNING BEFORE, in Camp V, Norton and Somervell had faced the same situation with their own porters as Mallory and Bruce had. But rather than berating the men, as Bruce had done, Norton appealed to their honor and vanity. "If you put us up a camp at 27,000 feet and we reach the top," Norton said, "your names shall appear in letters of gold in the book that will be written to describe the achievement." The tactic worked, and Norton was able to convince three of the four to continue on.

Somervell struggled that day on account of his raw throat and lungs, which continually doubled him over with the same racking cough that had been plaguing him for weeks. But the weather was holding, and Norton was cheered by the idea that they would soon be camping higher than anyone had ever climbed without oxygen. They had hoped to establish Camp VI on the broad terrace at 27,200 feet that Finch and Bruce had reached using oxygen two years earlier. But by 1:30 P.M., still at only 26,700 feet, they realized that one of their porters was done in, so they set about scraping out a platform for their single tent. An hour later, the porters were sent down with a note praising their performance and instructing Noel and Hazard that the men were to be "fed on the fat of the land," and ushered all the way down to Base Camp for a well-earned rest.

Norton and Somervell spent the afternoon melting snow, forcing themselves to eat, and resting as best they could. That night, they slept with their boots and thermoses in the bottom of their sleeping bags. Norton slept soundly, recording in his diary that he had "the best night since I left Camp I," although he woke to discover that the cork had fallen out of his thermos overnight, and the tea had soaked the bottom of his bag. Somervell didn't fare as well, though, being kept awake most of the night by his persistent cough.

June 4 dawned fine and windless. Despite the bitter cold, it offered near perfect conditions for their summit bid. They were on the move by 6:40 A.M.

Daunted by the steep rock steps on the skyline, they decided to bypass the Northeast Ridge altogether, and instead set off on a diagonal traverse that soon brought them to the bottom edge of the Yellow Band. They slowly worked their way along a series of horizontal ledges leading them west toward a snow gully they had dubbed the Great Couloir. Both men were dressed in leather boots with hobnails and thick wool socks. Norton's base layers were wool, above which he wore a thick flannel shirt, two sweaters, and a "lightish knickerbocker suit of windproof gabardine the knickers of which were lined with light flannel." In place of snow gaiters, which nowadays are built integral into the uppers of high-altitude boots, Norton wore cashmere puttees, almost like soft elastic scarves, which he tightly wrapped around his calves. His outer wear consisted of a Burberry windproof suit made of gabardine, the same style used by Ernest Shackleton in the Antarctic. On his hands he wore two pairs of wool mittens, a lighter inner pair, and a thicker outer with a long cuff that came partway up his forearm to keep out snow. His head was covered with a rabbit-fur-lined leather motorcycle helmet and a pair of metal-rimmed goggles with green lenses and an integrated leather patch that covered his nose and cheeks. Around his neck he wrapped a thick woolen scarf.

This outfit, which was considered state-of-the-art in mountaineering clothing (notwithstanding George Finch's Himalayan debut two years earlier of the quilted down jacket), was woefully inadequate. Even with the exertion of moving steeply uphill, both men found themselves shivering uncontrollably. At one point, Norton's body was shaking so violently that he thought he might be having a malarial attack. Norton had been taking his goggles off whenever he was on rock; the sun's glare seeming to be tolerable without them. But as they neared 27,500 feet, his eyes began to tear and he started seeing double.

By now, Norton and Somervell were higher than all the adjacent mountains, which had a strange way of flattening and rounding off the edges of the surrounding tableau. Norton would later write that "much of the beauty of outline was lost. To the north, over the great plateau of Tibet, the eye travelled over range upon range of minor hills until all sense of distance was lost, only to be sharply regained on picking up a row of snow-peaks just appearing over the horizon like tiny teeth. The day was a remarkably clear one in a country of the clearest atmosphere in the world, and the imagination was fired by the sight of these infinitely distant peaks tucked away over the curve of the horizon."

By noon, as the pair approached 28,000 feet, Somervell's throat had become so raw he struggled to breathe. He sat down beneath a rock directly below the Second Step, not far from the edge of the Great Couloir. He told Norton to go on without him. To get into the gully, Norton had to climb across a buttress of rock that he likened to traversing on the tiles of a slate roof. He knew that if he faltered, his next stop would likely be the bottom of the North Face.

Norton had hoped for easier going in the gully, but instead, he found it nearly impossible to gain any purchase in the waist-deep, loose and powdery snow. After an hour of wallowing in the gully, he had gained only 100 vertical feet. He had another 200 feet to go before he would emerge onto the summit pyramid, where he assumed the snow would be wind-blasted, providing for better footing. It was 1 P.M. and there was still 900 vertical feet between where he stood and the summit. If he pushed hard, there was a chance he could make the top before dark, but then what? Exhausted, frozen, oxygen-deprived, and suffering from the early stages of what would turn out to be a severe case of snow blindness, he was in no condition to survive an open bivouac. Prudently, he turned back.

In hindsight, Norton would wonder why he had not felt more disappointment at that moment. "Twice now I have had thus to turn back on a day when success had appeared possible, yet on neither occasion did I feel the sensations appropriate for the moment," he later wrote. "This I think is a psychological effect of great altitudes; the better qualities of ambition and will to conquer seem dulled to nothing, and one turns downhill with but little feelings other than relief that the strain and effort of climbing are finished."

Norton retraced his steps back to Somervell. What Somervell would have done if Norton had continued on was never discussed, but, of course, he too could not have survived had he been forced to bivouac without shelter while waiting for Norton. The pair had proceeded only a short distance when Somervell's ice axe slipped from his hand. The axe bounced a few times and then plummeted down the face, never to be seen again. They stopped briefly at their high camp, where Somervell grabbed a section of tent pole to use in lieu of an axe. They reached Camp V at sunset. At this point, Norton decided to glissade the North Ridge snow arête leading down to the North Col. He got far ahead of Somervell, and when he realized that his companion had fallen behind, Norton sat down in the snow to wait. He thought his friend might be sketching the beautiful panorama of peaks to the west that were bathed in alpenglow.

In fact, Somervell was sitting in the snow hundreds of feet above, unable to breathe. Whatever had been constricting his throat had now completely plugged his esophagus. Panicking, he squeezed in on his chest as hard he could with both hands, while making, "one last almighty push." With a loud retching sound, he blew out a bloody wad onto the snow. He didn't know it at the time, but he had just coughed up the mucous membrane that had formerly lined his larynx.

When they arrived at the North Col at 9:30 P.M., Irvine was ready with hot soup, tea, and some warm food. Norton and Somervell drank greedily but had little in the way of appetite. At high altitude, "one eats from a sense of duty," wrote Norton, "and it is impossible to force oneself to take enough food even to begin to make good the day's wastage of tissue."

That night, Norton shared a tent with Mallory. As Norton slowly went blind, Mallory told him about his plan to make one last attempt, this time with oxygen, with young Irvine as his partner. Norton wholeheartedly supported one last bid for the summit and was "full of admiration" for Mallory's "indomitable spirit." But he did not agree with Mallory's assessment that Irvine was the right man for the job. To Norton's mind, Odell was the obvious choice. Odell was one of the most experienced climbers in the world, and while he had acclimatized slowly, and thus had appeared for many weeks to be one of the weaker members of the team, in recent days he had come into his own and was, at that very moment, probably the strongest.

Mallory didn't question Odell's strength or experience, and he was, after all, the head oxygen officer of the expedition. But there was a critical difference between Irvine and Odell. While both disfavored using oxygen, Irvine's reservations were a matter of style. He truly believed in the efficacy of the system he had designed and the advantage it would lend to a summit attempt. Odell, on the other hand, still thought the weight and clumsiness of the apparatus outweighed its practical benefit, and thus, unlike Irvine, he hadn't taken much interest in perfecting it. Mallory, who by now had made several summit attempts without oxygen, no longer believed that it was possible for anyone to get up Mount Everest without it. The thought of going for the summit on an oxygen attempt with a naysayer seemed the wrong tack to Mallory. If supplemental oxygen was the key to finally solving the Everest enigma, who better than the youthful Mr. Fix-It, who had designed and largely built the system, to make sure that the precious "English Air" would flow freely into their lungs?

We will never know exactly what Mallory was thinking in those final days, but the explanation as to why he chose Irvine may be even more elemental than anything to do with his protégé's mechanical aptitude or opinion on the practicality of bottled oxygen. In his final letter to Ruth, Mallory had written that he had little faith in the other team members that were at his disposal—Bentley Beetham, John Hazard, and Noel Odell. "None of these three has any real guts," he wrote. The decision may well have come down to Mallory concluding that only the young Irvine had the gumption to follow him to the top of the world—even if it was doomed to be a one-way trip.

CHAPTER TWELVE

Above the Brink

THE SUN HIT my tent on the North Col at around 6 A.M. on Tuesday, May 28. I'd been in my sleeping bag for a solid twelve hours, so I was anxious to get moving up the hill. It had been a fitful night, but I hoped that all the hours on my back were equivalent to a few hours of actual sleep. The third climb to the col had not been any easier than the previous two. Jamie said it was because we had spent five nights in ABC at 21,000 feet. Our peak of acclimatization had passed. We were no longer getting stronger. Instead, we were wasting away.

I could hear Jamie's voice outside, so I pulled on my boots and crawled out of the tent. The air was perfectly still, the sky a deep blue. When I stood up, I noticed that I had no tightness in my lower back or soreness in my right knee. Despite hardly sleeping, I felt reasonably good.

But just as my psyche for the day's climb was ramping up, the CTMA Base Camp manager came over the radio.

"Dechen for Jamie. Dechen for Jamie."

"Jamie here."

"Jamie, very strong wind coming. Chinese forecast bad weather.

Very bad. Big wind is coming." I didn't catch all of what he was saying, but the gist was that, according to official Chinese forecasts, which varied markedly from our own, tomorrow and the next day would see 100 knots of wind on the summit. From what I understood, Dechen was insisting we were all going to die if we kept going. "Everybody has to come down. Repeat, come down."

The CTMA was bent on scuttling our climb. Frustration and anger replaced my excitement. Jamie remained calm.

"Thank you. We have our own forecast, and it is very good," he said. "Wind is in range for the next two days, twenty miles per hour or less. With your permission, we would like to proceed to 7,700 [meters] and assess the weather from there."

Between our team and those of Scott Woolums and Frank Campanaro, there were a total of fifteen climbing sherpas on the North Col that morning. Every single one of them, it seemed, got on the radio at the same time. Our Base Camp manager, Dawa, was talking to Dechen and another, even higher-ranking CTMA official named Pemba. Radios were squawking all over camp like a flock of seagulls. Some of the talk was in English, but most of it was in Nepali. After about fifteen minutes of nonstop chatter, Jamie got on the radio with Mingma Sherpa, the managing director of Climbalaya, a Kathmandu-based Everest outfitter. We'd had a few interactions so far with Mingma, and during one of them we had learned that, technically, we were climbing on his permit. Jamie now asked him point-blank if we could proceed to Camp II at 7,700 meters and make a decision from there. Jamie said that if the weather was good the next morning, we would keep going, and if it wasn't, we would come down.

There was a long pause, then Mingma said, "Yes, seven thousand seven hundred, no problem."

"Okay, then," said Jamie. "My decision is to go."

Disaster, it seemed, was averted. But then the radios came to life once again. This time, the back-and-forth with Base Camp went on for two hours. According to Jamie, the Chinese wanted us off the mountain, but since they couldn't order us to come down, their tactic was to backdoor us with the climbing sherpas, whom they threatened to blacklist if they helped us to go higher.

What followed was the equivalent of a Himalayan political caucus. While Jamie went from sherpa to sherpa, trying to win them to our cause, Mingma, Dawa, and the CTMA were on the radio trying to talk the sherpas into pulling the plug on our climb. Jamie was having some success with our guys, but Karma, Scott Woolum's head sherpa, was iffy, and Pemba Tenzing, one of the sherpas the CTMA had imbedded in our team, who seemed to have been against us from the start, was now lying down with his arms behind his head and a smug look on his face. I heard him saying that it was all or nothing. Either everyone had to go up, or everyone had to go down. And no matter what, he was not going to help us get one foot higher up the mountain.

I eventually learned that Pemba Tenzing and others were leveraging a monetary incentive to convince our sherpas to abandon us. Expedition Himalaya owned the Poisk oxygen bottles the sherpas were using, but they had rented the Summit Oxygen cylinders intended for the members and paid a hefty deposit on each bottle. At one point, I heard Ngati say it was $450 per bottle, which sounded right, considering they retail for $560 apiece. With thirty-four of these bottles previously stashed at high camp, the outfitter had $15,000 sitting up on the mountain, which the sherpas fully intended to recover, knowing that if they didn't, the loss would be deducted from their pay. If the Chinese forecast was correct, the sherpas needed to hightail it up to 8,300 meters today in order to collect the bottles before the supposedly imminent hurricane-force winds ended the climbing season for good. By supporting us and climbing only to Camp II today, each sherpa potentially jeopardized $1,000 of his pay. We had built bonuses into all of their pay, regardless of the outcome of our climb, but the oxygen bottle deposit was a separate item between them and Expedition Himalaya.

When we realized that this was part of the problem, our only choice was to throw in more money. Renan went straight to Lhakpa and told him that his production would cover the cost of the abandoned bottles if we didn't make it to Camp III. Lhakpa nodded. Karma did too. But for Pemba Tenzing, the oxygen wasn't really the issue. He was reporting directly to the CTMA, not to Jamie, and seemed particularly intent on thwarting our climb. He could see that the tide was now going against him, so he went to work on the other sherpas, trying to talk them out of going up with whatever arguments he could think of.

"Okay, let's go, let's go to the summit," said Jamie. Lhakpa's guys began getting their loads ready, but Pemba Tenzing was haranguing anyone who would listen, saying that it was all or nothing. If he didn't go, no one could.

"Hey, Jamie," I said, pointing at Pemba Tenzing. "This guy is a bad apple. He needs to be dismissed."

"I agree," said Jamie. "But there's nothing I can do. He doesn't answer to me."

While I was getting my pack ready to head out, Jim came up to me. "Hey, man," he said. "I'm out."

"What? Why, what's wrong?"

Jim said he had hit a wall. He didn't know what was wrong with him, but he barely had the energy to stand, let alone go any higher on the mountain. The North Col would be his high point. I gave him a hug, told him to be safe, and that was it. As I shouldered my load, I saw that Pemba Tenzing was doing the same. Apparently, he was coming too.

On my two previous visits to the North Col, I hadn't ventured more than about thirty feet from my tent, so it was with a feeling of anxious anticipation that I clipped my ascender to the fixed line and set off toward the ridgeline at the top of the col. Matt was a few feet ahead of me. When we breached its crest a few minutes later and stepped out of the lee for the first time, we were hit with a strong wind that nipped at the patches of exposed skin above my oxygen mask and below my sunglasses. A few feet ahead of us was the sheer drop down the other side of the col to the head of the main Rongbuk Glacier, 1,500 feet below. Out of the maw of black, bottomless crevasses—some of the biggest I've ever seen—the North Face of Mount Everest rose in a clean icy sweep for 8,000 vertical feet. It was a view at once terrifying and irresistible.

The ropes now led us up an elegant fin of snow. Matt and I soon settled into a rhythm, as we got used to breathing through our oxygen masks. I reminded myself about Mallory's deep-breathing technique and focused on drawing the English air as far down into my lungs as I could. Cory had described this as the most hateful and monotonous section of the entire route, but I was thrilled to be climbing higher up the mountain at long last, breaking my personal altitude record with each step, and gazing in awe at the dizzying sweep of the North Face to my right. Helped in no small measure by the extra oxygen, I hardly minded the toil.

It was late afternoon when Matt and I arrived at Camp II. My first day of breathing supplemental oxygen had gone remarkably well. I had felt better on this stage than I had on any of my three trips up to the North Col. The camp was set up on a series of horizontal shelves scattered across a buttress of shattered rock. Up until this point, the camps had all been remarkably clean and tidy, but we had now arrived at the point, on the verge of the Death Zone, where all environmentally conscious pretense went out the window. Camp II was a dump. The ground was covered in old matted tent fabric, bits of rope, broken tent poles, empty fuel canisters, and other unidentifiable junk from decades of expeditions.

Kaji, a veteran climbing sherpa and one of our strongest guides, handed Matt and me a tent and pointed to the terrace below the one on which he was setting up his own. We clambered down a small vertical wall of snow, which was festooned with urine stains. It looked like an army troop had used this ledge as its latrine, and I retched a little, thinking that somewhere around here we'd have to find some snow to melt for drinks and meals.

Before crawling into the tent to relax and make dinner, I took a minute to look around and appreciate the fact that I was about to bivouac somewhere in the general vicinity of where Mallory and Irvine had spent the night of June 6, 1924. The campsite was a trash heap, but the view probably hadn't changed that much in the past ninety-five years. To the west, I stared across the North Face of Everest, past the West Shoulder out over the Khumbu Valley and the foothills of the Himalaya. An azure sky was framed by gauzy cirrus clouds up high and a churning sea of cumulonimbus below. Most of the peaks were cloaked in this colorless shroud, but a few poked their heads into the firmament like islands rising from a foggy ocean. Closer in, the glacial valleys surrounding Everest were wreathed in mist, which rose up the sides of the mountain like steam from a boiling kettle. Renan was taking it in too, through the lens of his camera. He stood a few feet in front of me, shutter clicking away, his bright yellow suit shining like a beacon against this ethereal backdrop.

An hour later, Matt and I were forcing down a bowl of freeze-dried curry I had whipped up with what I hoped was noncontaminated snow, as we listened to yet more drama on the radio. Once again, most of the conversations were in Nepali. I figured it was just as well, since there was nothing I could do about it anyway.

When I pulled out my phone and took it off airplane mode, I saw that I had a good signal. The first thing I did was send a quick message to Thom to let him know we had arrived safely at Camp II. Within seconds, my phone lit up with a string of messages.

Thom reported that Base Camp was a "hornet's nest" of CTMA activity. "If you hear me in any transmission saying that they cancelled," he wrote, "it's no joke. They're looking for one of Matt's farts to give a reason to cancel."

I had switched my oxygen mask for a nasal cannula, a clear plastic tube with little nozzles that stuck into my nostrils. It didn't give as much oxygen as the mask, but I could talk and eat with it, and I figured it would make sleeping a lot more comfortable. I was trying to force down a few more bites of gruel when I heard Pemba, the CTMA official, on the radio. Thom had texted me that he was spending a lot of time with Pemba, who was Dechen's boss. Pemba now said that the Chinese forecast showed a "deadly storm" approaching, with 100-knot winds—the equivalent of a Category Three hurricane. We had to come down in the morning. Period. He was also upset with Jamie for leaving Jim alone on the North Col. Sonam was currently the low man on the totem pole and would benefit most from an Everest summit. Jim had seemed okay when we left him, so rather than assign Sonam to escort him down to ABC, Jamie allowed Sonam to tag along with us. But as it turned out, Jim wasn't quite as okay as we thought, so Jamie now said he would send down not one but two sherpas right away. In a way, it was a blessing in disguise because he chose Pemba Tenzing, the troublemaker, as the other one.

But Jamie wasn't willing to turn us back. The forecasts from Michael Fagin and Marc de Keyser were still predicting low winds on the thirtieth, our scheduled summit day. Different forecasts often do vary from one another, but in this case the Chinese one was radically different. It was hard not to think that they were using it as a pretense to end our expedition. Jamie suspected this as well, and he wasn't going to let them run us off the rails without a fight.

Eventually, Pemba threw out his final offer. "Jamie, if you come down, we can give you a five-thousand-dollar discount off your permit next year," he said, "for you and your clients. We will welcome you next year. Many different conditions now. I hope everyone can be safe and next year we can try again. Of course, the mountain will always be there. So, Jamie, what do you think?"

"This group is not coming back," replied Jamie. "Either we go now, or we go down. And if we go down, in the National Geographic film and article, it will say exactly what happened. We don't write wrong things. We only write the truth."

There was a long pause, then Pemba said, "Ah, please repeat. I can't hear very well."

Jamie took his time responding, and apparently, he decided not to repeat his threat. I wondered if this was something he had learned in negotiating with the Chinese. "Conditions are good now," he said. "Why not let's see tomorrow morning? But this group is not coming back next year. Not possible."

"Okay, okay," said Pemba. "Of course, I really worry about you. I know you are an experienced mountain guide, but it is not only you. There are clients and Sherpa."

"In more than twenty-five expeditions, we have never had a problem, and this time we won't have a problem either. I'm sorry for the worry we are causing you."

"Okay," said Pemba. "Thank you."

Now Dawa jumped in. He wanted to pick up where Pemba let off, to have his own crack at talking us out of going for the summit. But Jamie cut him off. "Let it go, Dawa," he said. "If you guys don't stop stirring the pot, we're never going to get any sleep. Good night. Over and out."

I turned the radio off, and Matt and I looked at each other with relief. Whatever the CTMA guys were up to, they evidently couldn't flat-out order us off the mountain. Jamie had held his ground. We were going up tomorrow.

I burrowed down into my sleeping bag and willed myself to stop coughing. But the itch in my lungs had a mind of its own. Matt's lungs were irritated too, so throughout a long, cold night, one of us was coughing at any given moment. Our inflatable sleeping pads jiggled in sync with each other's coughing fits and neither of us got much sleep.

At 6:30 A.M., I sat up groggily to fire up the stove. I was exhausted, and my lungs were fried, but I didn't have a headache, and the wind was only slightly rustling the fabric of the tent. As I brewed up some hot water for coffee, I pulled my phone out of the inside pocket of my suit and saw that I had a message from Hampton. Before lying down for the night, I had sent her a long text with a picture of the sun setting over the Khumbu Valley.

"Wow, that pic is insane," she wrote back. "I'll keep my fingers crossed for you and it is amazing we can communicate and wonderful. We just did a bunch of errands today—got the tires switched out and getting the house ready for your return! Keep keeping me posted. It's so comforting and exciting getting your messages."

A few minutes later, I turned on the radio. Dawa and Mingma were back at it, trying to talk Jamie into turning around. Scott Woolums came on. He was camped a bit higher and the wind was cranking where he was. He said the forecast was for it to blow 25–30 knots until 3 P.M., then the wind was supposed to lie down. Tomorrow, May 30, the wind was supposed to be 20 knots or less, which was in range for a summit attempt.

Now Jamie came on. "Get your stuff together," he said. "We leave in an hour."

AS I TOOK my first few steps uphill, I realized that I felt nothing like I had the day before. My legs were filled with lead, and I was immediately out of breath. I had bonked before I even got out of camp. *Was this how Jim felt yesterday? Will I even make it to Camp III?* Today was the day that supposedly indicated whether I had the fitness to make the summit. I couldn't have started worse. Maybe the nasal cannula had been the wrong call. Or perhaps it was the lack of calories. That morning, I had tried to eat an energy bar, but it tasted like sawdust, and I almost vomited up the first bite. My morale was low.

The wind was probably blowing 25 knots and even though it was early, clouds were already boiling up from below. The terrain ahead was mostly bare rock and gravel. The fixed line led the way through the gloom, but it offered little in the way of security because it was entangled in piles of loose rock. Weighting the rope risked pulling a rock down onto my head. I hoped the others above and below me recognized this hazard because I was too out of breath to say anything. As high as the death toll is on Everest, I marveled nonetheless at the fact that so many inexperienced climbers manage to get up and down this route without incident. I couldn't imagine putting myself in a situation where I would be on this rope with a bunch of teenagers climbing above 8,000 meters for the first time. I had to hand it to Jamie for holding us back and betting on a second weather window.

The route wove between little crags of rock, occasionally requiring us to search out handholds in order to surmount small ledges or blocky sections. One of the knocks against Everest, which I sanctimoniously parroted in my younger days, is that it's not a technical mountain and requires no skill to climb. I can now attest that the north side at least, while not beyond the ability of the dilettante mountaineer, is certainly no walk up, or slog, as we used to say. Much of the route, I was discovering, demands a high level of concentration and agility.

We had been climbing for about an hour when I looked up and saw three people standing on a ledge about 100 feet above. As I got closer, I could see that it was Woolums, Karma, and their client Jim. Their packs were off. It was snowing now, and the wind was picking up. It was too soon to be taking a full break and too cold to sit around chatting, so what were they doing?

By the time we caught up to Woolums, a fog bank had rolled in, completely engulfing the North Face. It felt like we were inside a ping-pong ball. Our exchange was brief. He didn't like the weather. The way the wind was building, he was afraid they wouldn't be able to get tents erected at high camp. They were pulling the plug. To me, the decision didn't make sense. Yes, the weather was looking grim at the moment, but he himself had said on the radio that morning that conditions were supposed to improve this afternoon. So why turn around now? For all we knew, it was going to be beautiful later on. Woolums is one of the most experienced guides in the business, so it wasn't my place to try and talk him out of his decision, but his abandonment of the climb raised a problem for us. Our team of sherpas was already on the verge of deserting. When they saw Woolums and Karma coming down the hill, it would probably snap the last filament of morale holding our team together.

Sure enough, Jamie came over the radio a few minutes later. The gist of it was that he wanted us to hold and not climb any higher. There happened to be an abandoned, half-crumpled tent sitting on the ledge where we had met Woolums, so Matt and I, along with Renan, who had caught up to us, climbed inside. I propped my pack against the back wall, took my oxygen mask off, laid back, and pecked out a message to Hampton, thinking now that our climb was probably over.

Jamie called about ten minutes later. A bunch of the sherpas, including Ngati, who had led our puja, were bailing. "There are too many things working against us," he said. "I'm sorry, but I'm afraid this is it. I need you guys to come down." Renan was sitting up, next to me, wearing a wolf fur hat with giant earflaps. Matt was kneeling in the doorway, filming.

I had an idea. I grabbed my radio. "Mark to Frank, Mark to Frank."

"Frank here, go ahead."

"Hey, Frank, how's it going up there?" I asked.

Frank Campanaro, Pasang Gomba, and Dawa Dendi were the only ones ahead of us at this point, somewhere up in the gloom. Campanaro would later tell me that when I called, they were traversing a narrow ledge called the Sidewalk at around 8,000 meters. It was squalling, visibility was nil, and it was blowing hard, just like it was where we were. He knew exactly what was going on because Jamie hadn't just ordered my team down, he had ordered everyone down, including Campanaro. Technically, Jamie was Campanaro's guide too, even though Campanaro was more or less operating independently. But Gomba wasn't going to be ordered off the mountain. The night before, when things were getting ugly on the radio, Gomba had simply turned it off. He was okay with the weather. Campanaro had hired him to get him to the summit, and that's what he intended to do. He didn't care what Jamie or anyone else thought. They were carrying on.

"It's sunny up here and there's no wind," Campanaro lied. "We're above that blizzard you guys are in. For us, it's safer and easier at this point to carry on. Over and out." Campanaro handed the radio back to Gomba, who then turned it off.

"Do you think we could pull this off on our own, without any sherpas?" I asked, turning to Matt. It was a contingency we had been discussing since the mutiny on the North Col. There were thirty-four oxygen bottles at high camp. If we could scrounge up a few additional items, maybe we could spend the night at high camp and at least try to get to the Holzel spot. Matt said if it came to that, he was in. But Renan was iffy. What if the Chinese were right? What if we got hit by hurricane-force winds at high camp? Both Fagin and de Keyser agreed with the Chinese that the jet stream was indeed ripping the sky apart directly over Mount Everest. But it wasn't predicted to drop below 30,000 feet. What if they were wrong and it dipped down to 29,000 feet, or even lower? We had already experienced hurricane-force winds on the North Col. No one wanted to find out what that would be like in the Death Zone.

Jamie came back on the radio. "Okay," he said. "I've got six sherpas who are willing to continue. Let's do this." Renan, Matt, and I looked at each other in disbelief. This explained why Jamie was lagging behind the three of us. He was rallying the troops. A little while later, a rock pinged off the tent. We crawled out and Jamie was standing there under a massive load. He was now carrying a bunch of the gear that he had picked up from sherpas who had turned around. With him were Prakash, Bal, Kusang, Kaji, Lhakpa, and Temba.

By midday on Wednesday, May 29, the ten of us were spread out across the Sidewalk. For me, the earlier drama may well have been a blessing in disguise, because we'd been able to lie down and rest for a solid forty-five minutes without freezing our asses off. After Jamie revived our climb and I got a pep talk via text from Hampton, I felt better. My resolve to at least make it to high camp was strong. At the end of the Sidewalk, the rock band beneath which we had been traversing turned a corner, and I realized that I was in the vicinity of the place where Odell had made his famous last sighting of Mallory and Irvine. Coincidentally, it was almost the exact same time of day.

And, as if on cue, the sky began to brighten. One minute, I was worrying about how much snow was pooling inside my collar, the next, the sun was burning through the fog. In a scene that seemed remarkably reminiscent of what happened to Odell, I watched as the Northeast Ridge and its three famous steps were slowly revealed. I pulled my camera out of the inside pocket of my suit, where I had it tied in with a thin piece of cord, and I snapped a few frames. I was surprised how easy it was to identify the First, Second, and Third Steps and how distinctively they stood out from one another.

In the foreground, the First Step appeared the largest of the three, a rounded hump with a distinct crescent of snow rimming its skyline in the shape of a frowny face. The Second Step, although I knew it to be taller, looked smaller, and had a shape more like a tooth, above which stretched a bench that was almost perfectly horizontal. The Third Step, the smallest of the three, had a blocky look, with a wind-fluted dollop of snow on its top. I decided, without too much thought, that if someone were up there at that moment climbing any of these features, it would not have been difficult to see them with the naked eye—or to discern one step from the other.

Odell set off from Camp IV with his porter, Nema, on the morning of June 7, 1924, a day behind Mallory and Irvine. He had wanted to accompany his friends, which would have allowed him to cook and care for them, but due to the porterage issues, neither of the higher camps had enough tents to accommodate him. So Odell staggered his supporting-role climb by a day. He might still provide assistance on the descent should it be needed. Odell climbed without an oxygen set. He knew that one had been stashed on the route to Camp V, and he intended to pick it up along the way. But when he got there, he discovered that it was missing its mouthpiece. Irvine had probably scavenged it on the way up. Odell grabbed the set nonetheless and brought it up with him, in case there was a spare mouthpiece in Camp V. As it turned out, there wasn't, but Odell paid no mind. At this point, he was well acclimatized and had little difficulty breathing. He would later write that he was better off "without the bulky inconvenience of the whole apparatus," confirming his bias against using oxygen.

Shortly after Odell and Nema arrived in Camp V, they heard the clatter of rockfall and looked up to see four of Mallory and Irvine's porters on their way down the mountain. They carried with them two notes, one for Odell and the other for John Noel. The note to Odell was written in pencil on a small piece of paper with a jagged righthand edge where it had been torn from Mallory's pocket notebook. "Dear Odell," it read. "We're awfully sorry to have left things in such a mess—our Unna Cooker rolled down the slope at the last moment. Be sure of getting back to IV to-morrow in time to evacuate before dark, as I hope to. In the tent I must have left a compass—for the Lord's sake rescue it; we are without. To here on 90 atmospheres for the two days—so we'll probably go on two cylinders, but it's a bloody load for climbing. Perfect weather for the job! Yours ever, G Mallory."

Nema was suffering from the altitude, so Odell sent him down with the others and settled in for a quiet night alone. Without a stove, he sipped judiciously off his thermos and ate some cold macaroni with canned tomatoes. Looking out the door of the tent, as so many other alpinists have in years since, Odell marveled at the view.

To the northwest, a "savagely wild jumble of peaks" dominated by Cho Oyu and Gyachung Kang were "bathed in pinks and yellows of the most exquisite tints." To the south rose "the gaunt cliffs of Everest's North Peak . . . its dark bulk the more exaggerate the brilliant opalescence of the far northern horizon of Central Tibet, above which sharp-cut crests of distant peaks thrust their purple fangs, one in particular rising supreme among them."

Odell may have been alone at Camp V, but in spirit, he was connected through the otherworldly beauty of the sunset that night with the climbers 2,000 feet above, who were surely taking it in too, with what he imagined were "hopeful feelings and exultant cheer."

With two sleeping bags for warmth and no one else cramped into the tent, Odell was able to stretch out, and he slept well. By 8 A.M., he was on the move. He left the oxygen set behind and carried only a small rucksack filled with provisions for Mallory and Irvine, with whom he hoped to rendezvous at the end of the day on their return from the first ascent of Mount Everest.

Odell ranged off the route, out onto the North Face, in a hunt for fossils and other clues about the geologic history of the mountain. In an interview with Tom Holzel six decades later, Odell would tell him that he never regretted not being chosen for the summit parties because he saw his purpose on Everest as studying the mountain's geology—not standing on its summit. Some of the rock specimens Odell collected that day contained fossilized crinoids, a type of sea lily related to starfish and urchins. These fossils offered the first proof that the rocks comprising the upper reaches of Mount Everest are marine limestones that once formed the bed of the Tethys Sea, which separated the Indian continent from mainland Asia, some 225 million years ago.

The day had dawned clear, but mist soon began to sweep up the face as the sun burned off the fog that had settled overnight in the surrounding valleys. The wind was light, though, and Odell believed, by the radiance of the murk above him, that the clouds around him were a local phenomenon and not the portent of a brewing storm. These "rolling banks of mist," as Odell called them, were part of a familiar pattern, one that Mallory seemed to have anticipated in the note he had written to John Noel the day before. "We'll probably start early tomorrow (8th) in order to have clear weather," Mallory wrote. "It won't be too early to start looking out for us either crossing the rock band under the pyramid or going up the skyline at 8.0 p.m." The time being noted as P.M. rather than A.M. has always been interpreted as a mistake and typical of Mallory's absentminded nature. Odell would have been hopeful that while he rambled unhurriedly in the direction of Camp VI, his two friends might already be closing in on the top of the world.

At 26,000 feet, Odell encountered a 100-foot-high crag that he easily could have skirted by means of a gully to the side of it. It was a tempting challenge, however, the type of terrain he regularly sought out and happily scrambled, back in Wales. So he decided to tackle it head-on as a test of his fitness. He climbed it without incident, and as he pulled over the top, he saw that the veil that had enshrouded the upper reaches of the mountain all morning was lifting. High on the Northeast Ridge, at a spot he would record a few days later in his diary as "nearing the base of the final pyramid," Odell spotted two tiny objects moving up one of the rock steps protruding from the ridge. The objects, of course, could be none other than his intrepid friends.

In an official dispatch that Odell posted from Base Camp less than a week later, on June 13 or 14, which would later be published in the *Alpine Journal*, he wrote, "There was a sudden clearing of the atmosphere, and the entire summit ridge and final peak of Everest were unveiled. My eyes became fixed on one tiny black spot silhouetted on a small snow crest beneath a rock step in the ridge; the black spot moved. Another black spot became apparent and moved up the snow to join the other on the crest. The first then approached the great rock step and shortly emerged on top; the second did likewise. Then the whole fascinating vision vanished, enveloped in cloud once more."

It seems Odell believed that it was the Second Step atop which he saw Mallory and Irvine. And if that was the case, and they had indeed passed the crux of the route, there would have been no major difficulties left between them and the summit. But, months later, Odell doubted himself. Maybe it was the First Step. He couldn't be sure.

AS ODELL WORKED his way toward Mallory and Irvine's final camp, the clouds that had obscured the view of his teammates dropped even lower and the wind began to build. If anyone was checking the barometer in Base Camp at that moment, they likely would have noted that the pressure was dropping precipitously, the result of an upper-level trough colliding with a surface low. Modern-day meteorologists who have studied the barometric record of the 1924 expedition have determined that the storm that afternoon was likely a common pre-monsoon weather phenomenon called a "western disturbance." An extratropical storm that had originated in the Mediterranean was now engulfing Everest.

Odell, not to mention Mallory and Irvine, would have known none of this, only that a powerful snow squall had engulfed the upper reaches of the mountain, and the wind was building to gale force. By the time Odell reached Mallory and Irvine's tent at 26,700 feet, an hour after he sighted them, the wind was howling and visibility had dropped to a few feet. He crawled inside, seeking shelter and hoping to find a note with some indication as to what might have caused them to be running so grievously late. Mallory had said in his note to look for them on the summit ridge at 8 A.M. (we presume) and yet by 1 P.M., they were still only partway across the ridge. But a quick survey of the tent revealed nothing. On the floor lay two eiderdown sleeping bags, some bits of food, clothing, oxygen cylinders, and scattered bits and pieces of an oxygen apparatus. A less-trained eye might have assumed that it was a problem with the oxygen sets that had caused the delay, but Odell, knowing his young friend's propensity for tinkering, would have been surprised had the tent not been strewn with various parts. "Nothing would have amused him [Irvine] more," Odell would later write, ". . . than to have spent the previous evening on a job of work of some kind or other in connection with the oxygen apparatus, or to have invented some problem to be solved even if it never really had turned up! He loved to dwell amongst, nay, reveled in, pieces of apparatus and a litter of tools, and was never happier than when up against some mechanical difficulty." Odell's heart sank when he saw Mallory's flashlight sitting on the floor of the tent. It was just like Mallory to have forgotten such an important piece of equipment.

Worried that Mallory and Irvine might be struggling to find the tent in the whiteout conditions, Odell continued farther up the mountain, whistling and yodeling as he climbed. Nothing but the shriek of the wind answered his call. After climbing 200 feet in a whiteout in which he could hardly see more than a few yards, Odell huddled in the lee of a rock, where he carefully examined the stones near his head in case there might be more fossils to add to his collection. After an hour, he decided that he was on a fool's errand, so he headed back down the hill.

By the time he arrived back at the tent, the clouds were parting again. Shortly, the entire upper part of the North Face was suffused with warm sunshine. For several minutes, Odell scanned the slopes of the Yellow Band, the Northeast Ridge, and the summit pyramid, but his two friends were nowhere to be seen. He crawled into the tent, made sure the provisions he had carried up were carefully stowed, and then placed Mallory's compass in the corner.

At approximately 4:30 P.M., Odell crawled back outside and closed up the tent. He scanned the terrain above one more time, then turned his gaze toward the North Col and started down.

IT WAS 5 P.M. when I finally staggered into Camp III at 27,200 feet. Spread across a broad terrace below the Dijon-mustard-colored strata of the Yellow Band was the most depressing scene I've ever encountered in the mountains. The garbage heap laid out before me looked more like a Third World landfill than the staging point below the most glorious summit in the world. There was so much trash strewn across the camp, I could barely see the ground underneath. The remains of crushed and battered yellow nylon tents were everywhere. Sixteen or so, according to my quick tally, were still partially upright. These were the tents from some of the expeditions that had cashed in on the first summit window a week earlier. To be fair, not every team had walked away from their camps without dismantling them. Alpenglow and Kobler, for example, practice diligent Leave No Trace ethics on Mount Everest. They had carried down everything they brought up. But not everyone is so conscientious.

The tents were mostly cheap knockoffs of the classic North Face VE 25, and some outfitters see it as cost effective to just walk away from the tents and buy new ones the following year. During a typical expedition to the north side of Everest, climbing sherpas will make multiple carries to get high camp stocked for the summit bid. But when everyone returns from the summit, many teams will do only one carry down. Unless an expedition is willing to send the sherpas all the way back up to high camp for a second load, much of the gear is simply abandoned. On some of the tent platforms, I could see multiple years' worth of destroyed tents that were serving as ground sheets for the current occupant, which would soon be broken, shredded, and beat down by the weather into yet another layer on the pile.

When half our sherpas bailed on us earlier that day, one of the reasons we were able to continue was that Jamie knew there would be more than enough abandoned tents at Camp III for our slimmed-down team. He reshuffled some of the loads and sent the others down with our own tents as well as other gear he assumed we could scavenge.

Renan bent over and picked up a pair of brand-new socks, identical to what you'd pull off the rack at REI, remarking on how he could use a fresh pair. As I staggered up the hill, looking for an empty tent that wasn't completely shredded, I grabbed an unopened pack of ramen and a Snickers bar. Along the way, I saw piles of unused fuel canisters, a sleeping bag, a pair of goggles, and various other clothing items, including a perfectly good pair of mittens. No need to go to the gear shop when you can equip yourself for your summit day right here.

The one item I didn't see (apart from our own stash, which was carefully packed into white nylon rice bags) was oxygen bottles. The deposit Summit Oxygen requires is an economic incentive that works.

Matt and I found a tent and crawled inside. The sun had pleasantly warmed the interior and an odor, like a dirty laundry bin, hit me straight off. Two foam sleeping pads were already laid out. I could see the imprint from whoever had last slept here. In the corner, there was a pair of dirty socks and a stove with several unused fuel canisters. Various other items were stashed in the mesh pockets, including a red cotton T-shirt. I could tell by the way it was folded that it was freshly washed and hadn't been worn. Why anyone would bring a cotton T-shirt to high camp on Mount Everest was beyond me.

Matt and I spent the next five hours in that tent, resting and trying to marshal our resources for the summit push. Most of that time is a blur, but when I later compared notes with Matt, he said that Lhakpa brought us a bowl of soup at one point. I have no recollection of consuming any of it. I know from a text I sent Hampton that I blasted my oxygen for a while before turning it back down. This time I used the mask, fearing that the inefficient nasal cannula I'd used the night before was probably part of why I'd had such a tough day. I do remember Lhakpa asking for our water bottles early on. My system was to carry two pint-size plastic bottles in the mesh, inside pockets of my suit so they wouldn't freeze. When Lhakpa brought them back filled with hot water, he also handed me an additional liter and told me to drink it before we left. But not only did I have no appetite, I also had no thirst, despite being badly dehydrated. I kept telling myself I would drink the water later.

Jamie came by at 10:30 p.m. and told us it was time to go. I hadn't managed to sleep at all, but I had lain very still in my sleeping bag, and I felt much better than when we arrived. I went through my pack, stripping it down to make it as light as possible. I checked the pockets of my down suit, taking a long look at my lucky talismans—a crumpled family photo and Tommy's stuffed giraffe. I put fresh batteries in my headlamp, and double-checked that the lids of my water bottles were screwed on tight. Then I forced down one solid glug of the extra water Lhakpa had given me and stashed the rest in my sleeping bag to drink when I got back. The wind was light, and it didn't seem to be too cold, so I wore only one pair of long johns under the suit. On top, I wore two shirts, one made of bamboo fiber, the other polypropylene, and a navy blue cashmere sweater that Hampton had given me for Christmas. My neck was protected by a thin blue buff and a heavier fleece neck warmer. I covered my head with a lightweight ski hat. On my hands, I opted for a pair of warm ski gloves into which I had stuck two hand warmers. I would carry a warmer pair of down mittens in my pack as backup.

I managed to force down a couple small pieces of beef jerky and a handful of cashews. Between this meager snack and the curry I had eaten at Camp II, I had ingested only about 300 or 400 calories since leaving the North Col. And in the sixty hours since I had left ABC, I had slept only a few hours. The last thing Matt and I did before leaving the tent was to hook ourselves up to fresh bottles of oxygen. We set the flow rate to two liters per minute and slipped on our masks.

My concerns about whether I still had anything left in the tank were somewhat alleviated when we started grinding up the hill at 11 P.M. I noticed right off that I felt better than I had the day before. Perhaps, knowing that this was our summit day, my body somehow willed itself to make one final effort. It was pitch-black with no moon, so I put my head down, focused on the ground illuminated by the beam of my headlamp, and concentrated on moving as smoothly and efficiently as possible.

It was too daunting to think about how much terrain there was to cover on the route to the summit, so I decided to do something that had worked for me on other big climbs in the past. I broke the climb down into sections and allowed myself to think only as far as the next milestone. For now, the goal was the crest of the Northeast Ridge at 28,000 feet. I told myself that this was an important landmark, because even though it was a long way from there to the summit, much of the terrain thereafter was a lower-angle traverse to the summit pyramid.

A couple hours later, I was shuffling along the ridge behind Jamie, now focused on the next goal, the First Step, when I coughed a little, trying to clear my throat. Suddenly, I couldn't breathe. Panicking, I ripped off my mask and tried to hack up whatever was clogging my throat. But this only plugged it up tighter. For a moment, I thought I would choke to death. Then I was racked by a violent gag reflex and a globule of thick mucus shot out of my throat onto the slope in front of me. This was followed shortly by my vomiting up the cashews and jerky paste. Panting and fighting down the nausea, I looked ahead. Jamie was moving toward the base of the First Step and hadn't noticed my convulsions. Whoever was behind me was also unaware. After a couple minutes, the nausea passed. I slipped my mask back over my face and continued plodding along.

Soon I arrived at the base of a daunting rock outcrop, a jumble of large boulders plastered with nearly vertical, wind-blasted snow. The fixed rope led straight up it. Two climbers were on the rope ahead of me, each scaling the wall with an ice axe in one hand and an ascender attached to the rope in the other. I'd always heard that the First Step was rather inconsequential, so this couldn't be it. Was I already at the Second Step? Did I pass the First Step without knowing? I had climbed over a few rocks so far. Maybe one of them was it. Lhakpa came up behind me.

"Is this the Second Step?" I asked him.

"No, First Step."

Getting up the wall was strenuous work. When I clawed my way over the last boulder, my heart was pounding. The First Step had nearly taxed me to my limit. I would have to dig deep to get up this mountain. As I recovered from the effort, I surveyed the route ahead. There were thirteen of us going for the summit that night. Our team consisted of Jamie, Matt, Renan, and me, plus six climbing sherpas. Frank, Gomba, and Dawa Dendi, who had left camp about an hour before of us, were up ahead. I was somewhere in the middle of the line. When I looked up the ridge, I could see three lights a few hundred feet ahead, plus a few more, closer in. It was hard to see much outside the beam of my headlamp, but I did notice that the sky above was filled with stars. The wind was light, somewhere between 5 and 10 knots, I guessed. With the hand warmers in my gloves, my fingers were quite toasty, and my toes were warm too.

The section between the First and Second Steps has a reputation for being sketchy. I'd been warned that it's wildly exposed and even though climbing at night prevents you from taking in the full depth of the void, you sense the bottomless maw of the North Face all too well by the angle of the terrain in your immediate vicinity. But I figured with my background as a big-wall climber, surely I wouldn't find it difficult or be daunted by the position.

As I balanced precariously along the narrow catwalk like a chimney sweep walking the ridge of a roof, I couldn't help but marvel again that people with no mountaineering experience somehow manage to get themselves up and down this route.

In places, the catwalk was mere inches wide and my crampons skated on the tightly grained limestone with a nerve-jangling sound like fingernails on a chalkboard. On the most difficult section, I used handholds in the wall overhead while working out tricky sequences with my feet just like I would on a technical rock climb. The rope to which I was clipped, usually with others directly on either side of me, was strung loosely enough that if any of us fell, we'd pull the others off too. We'd all end up dangling in a bunch below the route—that is, if the anchors held. The anchor points were spaced anywhere from 50 to 200 feet apart and usually consisted of pitons hammered into cracks in the limestone. At the end of one particularly daunting section, I inspected the anchor. Holding the rope to the mountain was a single "bird beak," the smallest-size piton that embeds only about an inch into the rock.

We eventually came upon a bulbous pinnacle of shattered limestone around which someone had tied several strands of rope—one of the only anchors so far that I could have some measure of faith in. On the far side of this famous spire, which is known as Mushroom Rock, there was a perfectly shaped stone bench that seemed to be hewn from the mountain with the express purpose of providing a seat for a weary climber. By now, we had passed several dead bodies by the side of the trail, and here was yet another. This person, wearing a faded yellow suit, must have died after stopping to rest here. Prakash would later tell me that the man was a relative of Ngati's. He was lying on his side, with his back facing us. I sat down next to him. At first, I hunched forward, not wanting to lean against a dead man, which seemed not just creepy but disrespectful. But as tired as I was, I eventually gave up on any show of decorum and made full use of the available backrest. Renan came along and sat down next to me, then Lhakpa arrived and told us that it was time to change our oxygen bottles.

There's a decent ledge at the base of the Second Step, and it was here, while waiting for one of our group to clear the first ladder, that I got my first look at this famous landmark. As I panned my headlamp beam, the first thing I noticed was the body of Ernst Landgraf hanging from a rope on the snowfield that separated the upper and lower tiers. It was oriented facedown in the snow, one arm outstretched below the head. Every dead body we had seen so far shared one thing in common: Its down suit was heavily faded from years of exposure to ultraviolet radiation. But this one shone bright blue.

There are other ways to get to the summit pyramid besides scaling the Second Step, as Norton and Somervell demonstrated in 1924, even if the pair didn't quite get there. In his book, *Through Tibet to Everest*, John Noel wrote that Mallory discussed two options for reaching the summit pyramid. One was Norton's route, a lower traverse that veered off the Northeast Ridge well below the First Step and linked up with the Great Couloir (aka the Norton Couloir). The other was a higher traverse that detoured around the Second Step before angling back to the Northeast Ridge in the area of the Third Step. Norton wrote in *The Fight for Everest 1924* that Mallory favored sticking as close to the ridge as possible.

We know that Mallory and Irvine ultimately did choose the ridge because the 1999 Mallory and Irvine Research Expedition found one of their oxygen bottles stashed in some rocks just below the First Step. Hemmleb definitively identified it as bottle #9, one of the cylinders that Mallory had noted on the envelope of the letter from Stella that was found in his pocket. And, of course, there was also the testimony of Noel Odell.

But the question remains: Was Mallory capable of scrapping his way up the formidable Second Step?

The Chinese spent upward of three hours scaling this feature in 1960, and while they were not highly skilled climbers, they did have pitons, carabiners, and nylon ropes, which were indispensable to their eventual success. In 1924, Mallory and Irvine had nothing but their hobnailed boots, their ice axes, and a flimsy, 100-foot length of seven-millimeter-thick flax rope. Is it possible that they could have ascended this near-vertical cliff at 28,600 feet in fifteen minutes, as described by Odell?

It was exactly this question that Conrad Anker set out to answer on May 17, 1999, two and half weeks after he found Mallory's body. Anker would later tell me that he had been recruited for Simonson's team shortly before the expedition set off specifically because of his skill as a technical climber. His main job wasn't to search but to see if he could free climb the Second Step, that is, scale it without the aid of the in situ ladders or fixed ropes. The idea was that if the team didn't find either of the bodies, it could still advance the narrative by ascertaining whether a skilled climber—and Mallory was the best in his day—could have gotten up the Second Step.

That morning, Anker, Dave Hahn, Jake Norton, Tap Richards, and two sherpas set off from high camp for the summit. Anker was carrying a climbing rope and a small rack of camming devices and chocks to use as protection points in the rock. When the team reached Mushroom Rock, Norton and Richards turned back. One of the sherpas went down with them. The other sherpa accompanied Anker and Hahn to the base of their objective, then he turned back too. Hahn ascended the ladder up the first tier, while Anker free-climbed the zigzagging ramp system, using his ascender on the fixed rope as a belay.

Regrouping on the snow ledge midway up the step, Hahn put Anker on belay. First, Anker checked out a crack on the right side of the ladder. It looked to be the easiest way up, but the rock was shattered and loose, which made it impossible to protect. So he moved to the left-hand option, a fifteen-foot-high, six-inch-wide crack that terminated below an overhanging nose of rock. Anker decided against using a shoulder stand like the Chinese had in 1960. It's a technique that was once popular but has since gone out of fashion. Plus, Anker wasn't going to remove his crampons (let alone his boots, as Qu Yinhua, the Chinese lumberjack, had done in 1960), as modern climbers typically prefer crampons to stiff boot soles when conditions are too cold or snowy for more supple rock shoes. Instead, he shoved his left elbow into the crack and flexed his arm to create a type of hold that climbers call a "chicken wing," while sliding his left knee up the crack. There were a few niches in the right-hand wall where he was able to find purchase with his right hand and foot. When the crack narrowed two body lengths up, he was able to get a solid hand jam and place a three-inch-wide camming device to which he could clip his rope. But he deliberately didn't rest his weight on the anchor—that would have defeated his purpose. It was there only as a fail-safe to prevent him from hitting the ledge in the event he fell.

By this point, though, Anker was gassed. Before setting off, he had taken off his pack and oxygen set to give himself more unrestricted movement. He was now panting, and his arms were rapidly "pumping out." But he fought on, knowing all that remained was to move out from under the overhang and scramble up over the lip of the cliff. There was a perfect foothold out there to facilitate this move. However, the ladder obstructed it. He tried to get his foot onto it without touching the rungs, but it was impossible. With his arms giving out, he stepped on to the ladder, letting loose with a string of curses. If only the ladder hadn't been in the way, he was sure he could have done it. He plopped down at the top of the second tier and checked his watch. It had taken him five minutes to climb it.

Cameras were rolling in ABC when Anker radioed Simonson a few minutes later. It was a made-for-TV moment. "Could Mallory have scaled the headwall?" asked Simonson. Anker said yes, it was possible. He reckoned the second tier was a climb of intermediate difficulty by modern standards, a grade we know Mallory routinely climbed in his Peak District stomping ground. But Anker would later question his initial impression and revise his assessment, saying he thought the crux of the Second Step was probably beyond Mallory's ability.

But this did not settle it for Anker. In 2007, he returned to Everest to play George Mallory in reenactment scenes for a documentary film called *The Wildest Dream*. On summit day, some sherpas removed the ladder on the Second Step and in a remarkable bit of high-altitude technical climbing, Anker succeeded in making the first documented free ascent of the Northeast Ridge. This time he resolutely insisted that Mallory could not have done it.

It wasn't long after conceiving the Sandy Irvine Search Expedition that I started wondering whether I might have my own go at free-climbing the Second Step. I'd then go to the UK and try some of Mallory's hardest climbs, assessing them in direct comparison to the Second Step.

I had no interest in "leading" the crux section, that is, climbing with a belay from below, as Anker had done. I didn't want to bother with the hassle of bringing extra gear up the route, let alone take the associated risk. My hope was that the fixed rope on this section was close enough to the crack that I could keep my ascender clamped to it as my belay.

After going up the ladder on the first tier, I stood on the snow ledge, sizing up the situation on the second tier. The fixed ropes hung about five feet to the side of the crack. I saw that if I fell out of the crack, I would swing hard into the ladder. I was in no mood to take more risk than necessary at this point, so up the ladder I went. Near the top, I paused on the ladder to take a close look at the final moves, and I saw something that I'm not sure anyone else has ever noticed. The horizontal crack under that nose of rock, the same one, presumably, into which Qu Yinhua nailed that foot-long piton in 1960, appeared to be the perfect size to slot the handle of an ice axe into, especially a long-handled wooden axe like the one I had held in my hands at the Alpine Club. Jamming the shaft of an axe into a horizontal crack is a well-established technique, one that I have used many times over the years. On one particularly memorable climb, I actually swung my leg over the axe handle and sat down on it to rest.

Perhaps Mallory took a shoulder stand from Irvine—certainly his ever-faithful companion could be counted on to withstand a few hobnails to the clavicle (and besides, wool makes for much better padding than down)—and stretching out his full five-foot eleven-inch frame, he managed to slot his axe shaft into the crack. At that point, if the axe provided a solid anchor, he could have employed a number of creative techniques to get around the overhang and then scramble to the top of the step. It would have been a brilliant piece of mountaineering ingenuity—exactly what Mallory was known for and why he was the undisputed leader of the summit assault.

At the top of the ladder, I got a good stance on a small ledge and pulled out my camera to shoot a video of Renan coming up behind me in the dark. Twenty feet below, Landgraf's body hung from a yellow rope.

"This shit is horrifying," said Renan.

"Gnarly, huh?" I replied.

"Yeah, I just lost half my oxygen."

His regulator was sticking out of the top of his pack, and I could hear it hissing. It had smacked against a rock when he threw down his pack at the base of the step to fish out his camera. Renan topped the ladder and we moved ahead to a ledge to wait for Lhakpa. When he arrived about ten minutes later, he gave Renan a spare regulator that he had in his pack and a fresh bottle. What neither of us knew at the time was that the regulator was a Poisk, which has threads that are similar—but not identical—to those on the Summit Oxygen bottles. Unbeknownst to Renan, he had just traded one problem for another. Before setting off, I asked Lhakpa to check my bottle. He said it was reading around 200 bar—75 percent. Perfect.

We were now following a smooth, well-trodden trail, not unlike the type of single track I had grown up hiking in the White Mountains of New Hampshire. The shoulder from the top of the Second Step to the summit pyramid is so broad here that people call this section of the route "the plateau." I understood now why the standard route goes the way it does. With the ladders that the Chinese installed in 1975, the Second Step has become little more than an inconvenience (as long as climbers know what they're doing and don't turn it into a deadly choke point). Once you're beyond it, the route to the summit is both safe and without undue difficulty. One thing that most experts have always agreed on is that if Mallory and Irvine had somehow made it above the Second Step, nothing would have stopped them from carrying on to the summit. And indeed, I was heartened to see that the Third Step, some 300 feet ahead, was only about 20 feet high and split by a shallow cleft.

I was halfway across the plateau when I first noticed that a horizon was forming off to the east. It began as a barely perceptible thin white line that slowly thickened as the center of it turned faintly orange, then blue. As it bulged into the inky black sky above, the stars twinkled out one by one, and the contours of the surrounding mountains took shape. The summit snow slope where I had seen the conga line a week earlier was now directly above me. It was glowing pink. I could see Campanaro, Gomba, and Dawa Dendi nearing its apex. When the sun finally broke the horizon a few minutes later, the summit lit up like a lantern.

But closer in, the scene was decidedly less sublime. Directly in front of me, a frozen dead body was lying on the ground right next to the footpath. Including Landgraf, we had passed half a dozen corpses so far. I had made a point to acknowledge each one as I climbed past, reminding myself that they had once been living, breathing people like me who somehow pushed themselves incrementally too far. Like all the others, this one was upside down, with his head downhill. It seemed that it wasn't possible to die on Everest in any other position. His suit was probably bright red at one point but was now faded to light pink. His gloves were missing, and his bare hands were black and desiccated. It looked like he had been clawing at the snow when he died. About 100 feet farther on, there was another body just like it.

TSEWANG SMANLA AND Dorje Morup were police officers from the Ladakh region in northern India who were caught out high on the Northeast Ridge on May 10, 1996, during the infamous storm that would claim eight victims. The following day, two Japanese mountaineers, Eisuke Shigekawa and Hiroshi Hanada, with the storm still raging, battled their way to the summit. On the way down, the pair passed the Ladakhis. By now, Morup appeared to be dead. Smanla was still alive but tangled up in a rope. One of the Japanese team's sherpas helped to free him, but that was all they did for the man.

Richard Cowper, a journalist with the *Financial Times*, interviewed the Japanese climbers when they arrived back in Advanced Base Camp and asked why they didn't help the dying Indians. Hanada, apparently distressed, responded in faltering English, "We didn't know them. No, we didn't give them any water. We didn't talk to them. They had severe high-altitude sickness. They looked as if they were dangerous."

"We were too tired to help," said Shigekawa. "Above 8,000 meters is not a place where people can afford morality."

A third member of the Ladakhi team, Tsewang Paljor, had managed to fight his way down to a small cave below the First Step, where he too met his end. Until 2014, when someone finally moved his body off the trail, his bright green boots were a famous landmark on the Northeast Ridge.

"ARE YOU OKAY?" said Prakash, when he caught up with me below the Third Step.

I told him I was fine but asked if he would check my oxygen level.

"You're at sixty," he said.

"Sixty percent or sixty bar?"

"Sixty bar."

"Oh shit, that's like twenty percent. What the hell happened to all my oxygen?"

Prakash checked out my regulator. It was set on 2, as it had been for most of the climb. Yet somehow, I had used 80 percent of a bottle since Mushroom Rock. It made no sense.

"Do you have any spares?" I asked.

"I do," he said. "But let's get up the Third Step, and we'll change it at the top."

Prakash went first, and I shot a video panning across the Tibetan Plateau, past Makalu, which pokes up out of a cottony bed of clouds, and then into the gully, where Prakash, in his blue-and-orange suit stands a body length above me, poised on the steep rock. A green piece of duct tape covers a tear in the seat of his suit.

When I caught up to him, Prakash swapped my bottle and then held my pack to make sure I didn't drop it down the North Face as I slipped it back on. I looked at Prakash and held out my fist. Our gloves touched. We were 400 feet below the summit. Campanaro, Gomba, and Dawa Dendi passed us as they descended from the top, while Jamie, Matt, and Kaji worked their way up the triangular snow slope just above us, now gleaming in full morning sun. Renan and Lhakpa were below us. The others were out of sight somewhere above. The Chinese had been wrong about the weather. There was not even a breath of wind. The sun felt warm on my face.

An hour later, as I took my final steps to the summit, I made a conscious effort to savor the moment. I was having the type of summit day that all Everest aspirants dream about—but few actually get.

At 7:12 A.M., Jamie and Prakash congratulated me as I stepped onto a plot of wind-blasted snow as big as a king-size mattress. Kaji, Bal, Kusang, and Temba were busy taking photographs of each other. One of them was holding up a big red banner. No one seemed to notice—or care—that it was upside down. On the very highest point of snow sat a three-foot-tall golden statue wrapped in prayer flags that fluttered gently in a light riffle of wind. A kata scarf was tied to its neck, above which the statue's left hand, with index finger extended, pointed toward the sky.

To the east, the sun shimmered in a crystal-clear blue sky, hovering above the Tibetan Plateau. The horizon appeared slightly off-kilter, like the floor in a carnival fun house. In my addled state, I didn't realize that I was seeing the actual curvature of the Earth. To the south, I gazed down on the summits of Lhotse and Makalu, the world's fourth- and fifth-highest mountains, which looked like models in a diorama. Closer in, I looked down the Southeast Ridge into Nepal. A two-foot-deep trench was plowed into the snow where the conga line had been in that viral photo.

There wasn't a soul in it.

CHAPTER THIRTEEN

High Endeavors

SITTING NEXT TO the golden statue, I stared absently down the way I had come up. My oxygen-starved brain begged me to lie back and close my eyes, but some vestige of clarity and reason understood that if I did, I might never wake up. Renan was about fifty feet below, crawling up the final section of the Northeast Ridge on all fours. Lhakpa was one step behind him, silently urging his charge on to the finish line. The forty-nine-year-old father of four was about to summit Everest for the sixth time. Five feet below the top, Renan kneeled and put his hands together in a gesture of prayer. He would climb no higher. He later told me that he specifically didn't climb to the highest point because he didn't want to "stand on the head of the Sherpa's god."

After a few minutes, it occurred to me that I should take a photo to prove that I had made the summit. When I pulled my phone out and took it off airplane mode, I saw that I had a full LTE signal and a text from Hampton: "Thinking of You love You so much." I held my phone out at arm's length and a few seconds later a selfie was on its way through the ether to New Hampshire. With frozen fingers, I typed back, "A very quick note to let u know we topped out and r on our way down. All is well. I love u too." What I didn't know was that my kids and entire extended family were peppering Hampton with questions and requests for updates. They had all seen Nims's viral photo and heard the news that eleven people had already died on Everest that season. Hampton forwarded the selfie, letting them all know that I was on top of the world—but still a long way from home.

In the same inside pocket where I carried my phone was the Snickers bar I had found amongst the detritus in Camp III. I pulled it out and stared at it for a moment. It looked revolting, but I knew I could use the energy if I wanted to go off the ropes and get to the Holzel spot. I pulled down my mask, stuck the bar into my mouth, and bit off a frozen chunk. The instant the chocolate hit my palate, I started retching. The only thing that prevented me from vomiting onto Chomolungma's head was that there was absolutely nothing in my stomach. I managed to slowly chew the bite into a paste that I forced myself to swallow, but the rest of the candy bar went back into my pocket.

Then I noticed Renan lying down in the snow with his head on his pack.

"Are you okay?"

"No," he croaked. "There's something wrong with my oxygen. I don't think it's flowing."

"Let's get out of here," I said. "The sooner we can drop elevation the better."

As soon as I started down the ridge, I realized that descending required almost no energy compared to going up. Gravity would now do a lot of the work for me, and as long as I could maintain enough focus to avoid tripping over my crampons, I was confident I could get myself down the mountain. But going off the ropes was another matter. It would require an entirely different level of both physical and mental capability. Would I have the focus, the precision, and the agility to clamber around unroped in the Yellow Band? Now that I had reached the summit, the Holzel spot became my raison d'être. Could I get there? Would I kill myself trying?

The next two hours passed in a hazy blur. I only vaguely recall rappelling the Third and Second Steps. What I do remember are the feelings of unease and dread as I approached the decision point, and how much I would rather have just been able to bask in the accomplishment of climbing Mount Everest as I put one foot in front of the other, securely clipped to the ropes. I arrived at the dead man's bench next to Mushroom Rock and decided to sit down and wait for Renan. Once again, I leaned against the body, only this time with no compunctions. After a few minutes, Renan came along, moving with more confidence. Lhakpa had been fiddling with Renan's oxygen system since the summit and had finally gotten a good seal with the regulator. Now, Renan said, for the first time in hours, he felt like he could actually breathe.

I looked down at the GPS device in my hand. We still had to cross the difficult traverse and get down the First Step before looking for Xu Jing's more direct route down through the Yellow Band, but I wanted to make sure the GPS was working. Squinting at the tiny screen, I saw that it had indeed locked onto the waypoint for Holzel's spot. It indicated I was now within 900 feet. The arrow on the compass screen pointed north-northeast.

More than fatigue, my biggest concern was my roiling stomach. Every few minutes, bile would rise up my throat, and I'd have to fight back the urge to vomit. Shortly before, while working across a tricky section below the Second Step, it had boiled over, and my one bite of Snickers came up. As the brownish-yellow liquid splattered the wall in front of me and dripped onto the front of my suit, I thought, *That's it. I'm out.* But now, as I rested on dead man's bench, the burning sensation in my throat subsided and my stomach felt more settled. The bright sun was high overhead and there wasn't the slightest wisp of wind. Conditions were downright pleasant. The curiosity about whether Sandy Irvine might just be holed up in that crevice came back, and my feelings of foreboding began to dissipate. I realized I was ready to go off the ropes. *I've come too far to give up now*, I told myself. *I'm going to find Sandy Irvine and the camera and solve this damn mystery once and for all.*

Matt was filming Renan and me as we sat there. When he put the camera away, he said to Lhakpa that he was almost out of oxygen. Lhakpa gestured that we needed to keep moving. Matt set off first, followed by me, Renan, and Lhakpa. We had gone about fifty feet past Mushroom Rock when Matt's head bobbed like someone falling asleep at the wheel. He fell into the mountain against the rock on our right. Had he gone left, he'd have pulled us all off the narrow catwalk.

"I'm—out—of—oxygen," he gasped.

Lhakpa leapfrogged past Renan and me, grabbed Matt's empty bottle out of his pack, and swapped it with his own. I realized then that he didn't have any more spare bottles. Once he was back on the gas, Matt was able to pick himself up and carry on. Lhakpa resumed his position as sweep and drove us on, seemingly unfazed by having given up his own oxygen. It didn't even occur to me to question what Lhakpa had done. It's a common practice, and I had heard that many sherpas had done the same this year when traffic jams had caused some parties to spend upward of twenty hours on their summit pushes.

At the bottom of the First Step, I checked the GPS again: 600 feet. Moving more slowly now, I carefully scanned the terrain below the ridge, putting myself in the shoes of Xu Jing and asking whether any of the gullies dropping from the ridge crest looked like logical shortcuts to the 8,200-meter snow terrace where high camp was situated.

I was behind Renan and directly in front of Lhakpa. The GPS

hung from a cord around my neck. Several times I stopped to reference it and lingered for longer than was reasonable, hoping that Lhakpa would get impatient and pass me, leaving me in the back where I could veer off into the no-man's-land of the Yellow Band unimpeded. But he would just stand there, eyeing me impassively. I assumed he knew exactly what was going on, that I was looking for the Holzel spot, which I had described to him in detail a week earlier.

When I got within 200 feet of the waypoint, I noticed that the numbers on the GPS were toggling up and down between 200 and 175 feet, which could mean only one thing: I was traversing above the Holzel spot. Ten minutes later, we were working our way down a shallow gully when about 30 feet below, I saw the remains of the Japanese climber we had spotted with the drone. I had missed this detail when we had ascended this section in the dark. His down suit was light pink, like the petals of an evening primrose. He lay upside down, his head hanging over the lip of a small cliff. One of his hands, missing its glove, was blackened and frozen in midair, as if he had been reaching for something when he died. This was my signpost indicating it was time to venture off the ropes.

Jamie was sitting on a rock a few feet away, with Matt a short way below him. Renan was now a few body lengths above me. Lhakpa was bringing up the rear, along with Bal, who had materialized to join him as the caboose of our team. It was no coincidence that Jamie was sitting where he was. He knew this was the decision point. The veteran Kiwi mountaineer had slipped off his oxygen mask and removed his sunglasses. Several days of gray stubble covered his chin. His skin had a sallow, corpse-like pallor. He looked hard at me with sunken, bloodshot eyes, and said, "Don't do it, Mark. You're too tired. It's not worth it."

Puffy clouds boiled over the mountains that surrounded us, but the sky above was still clear. Wind whispered through the thin air.

Fourteen thousand feet below, the arid plain of the Tibetan Plateau shimmered like a mirage.

I looked at the GPS: 175 feet. The Holzel spot wasn't visible, but I knew it was tucked into one of the rock bands just below me. As I waited for Renan to catch up, I leaned back against a rock and took a moment to assess how I felt. My stomach had remained calm since Mushroom Rock. The air felt noticeably thicker down here at 27,700 feet. I knew it wouldn't last long, but I seemed to be getting a second wind. *You can do this*, I whispered to myself. The only thing holding me back at this point was Lhakpa. How was he going to react if I unclipped and went off the route?

Renan arrived and plopped down beside me. No one on our team was more sensitive about respecting the sherpas.

"What do you think?" I asked him.

His chest heaved in and out and he didn't reply right away. Finally, he caught his breath and I heard his muffled voice through his oxygen mask. "You should go for it."

I looked back up the hill toward Lhakpa. He was thirty feet above, looking right at me. Turning now to Renan, I said, "Yeah, can you grab my ice axe off my pack for me?" He unhooked it and handed it to me. I unclipped my tether from the rope.

"Be careful," said Renan.

Climbing down about six feet, I planted my right foot sideways in a patch of gravel and leaned my left knee into the slope.

"No, no, no, no!" Lhakpa yelled.

I turned to face him and pointed my axe toward the Holzel spot. "I just need to go right there."

"No, no, no, no."

I started jabbing the end of the axe into a thin patch of snow, the mountaineering equivalent of nervously tapping one's foot. The spike made a tinking sound as it repeatedly struck a rock under the snow. After everything I had been through to get to this point, it now came down to whether I was willing to openly subvert a command from our head climbing sherpa, whose job was to make sure we made it down safely—and followed the CTMA rules. I knew that if I fell or disappeared, Lhakpa would be obliged to go looking for me, risking his own life in the process. If I died, he would have to explain to the Chinese officials why I left the ropes after they had explicitly told him that his job was to prevent us from doing so. More important, by this point in the climb, I knew that Lhakpa genuinely cared about me. And the feeling was mutual.

I have always struggled with the concept that Everest, or any mountain, belongs to a government that can dictate where exactly a climber can or cannot go. In my view, the wildest and most mountainous regions of our world belong to no one and everyone. I can accept jumping through the bureaucratic hoops of permits, fees, and so forth in order to get here, but once up on the mountain, climbers should be free to roam like eighteenth-century explorers on the high seas—accepting, of course, that we must take full responsibility for our own decisions. I also knew that Lhakpa was just following orders. He didn't have a dog in this fight. As long as I made it back to the route safely, he would forgive my transgression.

When I set off across the sloping ledge, Lhakpa jumped onto the radio. Mine was switched off, but angry chatter filled the air around me. I assumed that Lhakpa was covering his ass and telling the CTMA that I had gone rogue. I might end up on a Chinese chain gang, but at least Lhakpa was off the hook, and that made me feel a little better about what I was doing. A few feet out, I stepped on a chunk of loose stone that slipped out from under my foot, and I wobbled.

"Very dangerous, very dangerous," yelled Lhakpa.

After traversing about a hundred feet, I looked down and saw a gully cutting through a steep band of rock to the next snow ledge below. I remembered this feature from the drone photos of the terrain. Could this be where Xu Jing had taken his shortcut down through the Yellow Band?

I turned to face the slope and jammed the pick of my ice axe into the snow. The steel blade squeaked as it punctured the wind-blasted surface. Looking down between my legs, I took in the dizzying void between me and the glacier, more than a mile below. I could see I was directly above the snow terrace where Mallory had been found. I checked the GPS once again. The arrow on the compass now pointed northwest. Fifty more feet.

I down climbed a few body lengths before my progress was interrupted by a small rock step about eight feet high and as steep as a playground slide. It would have been inconsequential almost anywhere else, but up here, in my depleted state, alone and without a rope, it was a daunting obstacle. I looked up the gully I had just come down and thought about retreating back up it and pulling the plug on this foolhardy venture. But I knew I could climb down this small cliff if I could just maintain my composure. With the pick of my axe still in the snow, I stepped down onto the rock. My crampons skittered but found enough purchase. Step after timid step, I made my way down.

At the bottom of the cliff, I stomped my foot into a panel of rock-hard snow, took a few deep breaths, and paused to take in my surroundings. Ten feet to my right was a small alcove hemmed by a rock wall a bit taller and steeper than the one I had just climbed down. The middle of the wall was striped with a vein of dark brown rock with a fissure in the middle. My eyes opened wide.

The GPS indicated that I had arrived at Holzel's spot.

As Odell worked his way down toward the North Col from Camp VI late on the afternoon of June 8, 1924, he kept stopping to look back, hoping to spot his two friends like he had earlier that afternoon. Nothing but rocks, snow, ice, and swirling clouds met his fervent backward glances. He made excellent time downhill, taking just over two hours to cover the same terrain that had taken two days on the way up. Odell later wrote that he found descending "little more fatiguing than at any other moderate altitudes." He reflected that it might be surprisingly easy for anyone coming down from on high. On the final snow arête below Camp V, Odell found the snow conditions suitable for a standing glissade, a boot-skiing technique that he employed with great care "to avoid the Scylla of the rocks on the one hand, and the Charybdis of the cornice edge on the other!"

John Hazard was waiting for him at Camp IV on the North Col with soup and tea. The two men spent the rest of a clear evening studying the upper mountain for any sign of their friends. The moon rose, bathing the upper mountain in a faint glow that they hoped might aid Mallory and Irvine in finding their way down to high camp.

In the morning, they were up again before dawn, straining to detect any movement on the upper mountain. As the sun rose, they carefully studied the tents at both Camp V and VI with binoculars. There was good reason to hope that Mallory and Irvine had slipped into camp late that night unseen. But as the hours wore on and there was no sign of movement anywhere up high, Odell and Hazard began to fear the worst.

The scene was equally tense down in Camp III, where Norton was still recovering from his bout of snow blindness. While porters arrived from below to start dismantling camp, all eyes were on the upper mountain. The longer they went without seeing any sign of

Mallory and Irvine, the more their anxiety grew. By 11:10 A.M., Norton had decided that the worst-case scenario had come to pass. He wrote in his diary, "It appears almost inevitable that disaster has overtaken poor gallant Mallory & Irvine—10 to 1 they have 'fallen off' high up." Norton sent a runner to the North Col with a note for Odell, saying that no one was to head higher up the mountain in search of the missing men unless it was certain they could return to Camp IV that same day. Everyone was to be off the mountain by 4 P.M. the next day, at the latest. The most important thing, wrote Norton, was "to risk no more lives in trying to retrieve the inevitable."

While the note was en route, Odell set off from Camp IV with two porters at 12 P.M. It was a cold and windy day, and the three men were buffeted by strong gusts along the way. Nonetheless, they made remarkably good time, arriving at Camp V by 3:30 in the afternoon. As night fell, the temperature plummeted and the wind grew, threatening to tear the tent from its perch.

In the morning, the porters wanted no part in going any higher, so Odell set off alone for Camp VI, this time using an oxygen set that had been stashed in Camp V. The weather was terrible, with a "boisterous and bitter" cross wind raking the North Ridge, forcing Odell to take shelter in the lee of rock outcroppings to restore circulation in his frozen fingers and toes. When he was an hour below Camp VI, he decided that the oxygen was doing nothing for him, even with the regulator set to its highest flow rate, so he switched it off.

Arriving at high camp and daring to hope that he might find his exhausted friends huddled together in the tiny tent, he pulled back the flap. Peering inside, he saw that apart from one broken pole, everything was exactly as he had left it. The thermos, Mallory's compass, the food, and all the other items sat right where he had left them two days earlier. He shoved the oxygen apparatus inside and immediately set off up the hill in search of his teammates. "This upper part of Everest must be indeed the remotest and least hospitable spot on earth," he later wrote, "but at no time more emphatically and impressively so than when a darkened atmosphere hides its features and a gale races over its cruel face. And how and when more cruel could it ever seem than when balking one's every step to find one's friends."

Odell searched for two hours before giving up and heading back to the tent. He grabbed the two sleeping bags in which his friends had slept two nights earlier and dragged them up the hill to the nearest snow patch. According to a predetermined code, he pegged them to the slope in the shape of a T. From the North Col, 4,000 feet below, Hazard saw the mark, which meant the worst: Odell had found no trace of Mallory and Irvine—all hope was lost. With the help of the two porters, Hazard then relayed his own signal down to Camp III by arranging wool blankets in the shape of a cross. John Noel, who had been watching the mountain for days with his telephoto lens, saw the sign and took a photo of it.

Back in the tent, Odell looked around for any items that might be worth retrieving. He grabbed Mallory's compass and the Mark V oxygen set that Irvine had been obsessing over ever since they had first engaged in the oxygen debate on the Spitsbergen expedition. Odell left everything else as it was, crawled back out of the tent, and sealed it up, just in case, by some miracle, Mallory and Irvine might yet find their way back.

Outside, Odell looked up toward the summit, which peeked in and out of the clouds. "It seemed to look down with cold indifference on me," he later wrote.

SOMETHING WASN'T RIGHT. As I hunched over my axe, with my chin on my chest, I sucked on my oxygen mask, trying to clear the clouds from my head. According to the GPS, I was at the Holzel spot. But where was the slot we had seen with the drone? I looked around, blinking in the midday sun. Then I looked more carefully at the dark vertical stripe in the rock wall before me. I hadn't noticed it for what it was at first, being so close to it and intent on finding the crevice I was sure would be here. But now I understood that what had appeared as a dark cleft on the image shot from the drone was in fact a black, basaltic intrusion in the limestone. There was a crack in the middle of it, but it was only about nine to twelve inches wide—far too narrow for a person to crawl inside. At its base, though, I spied a small niche, and while it offered nothing in the way of real shelter, it looked like a spot where someone could curl up and rest. It was about ten feet in front of me, and mostly devoid of snow.

There was nothing there. I looked around. No one could see me. I was all alone. High above, the summit of Chomolungma shimmered against a pale blue sky.

Any remaining curiosity that had driven me to go off the fixed lines and descend to this spot on the mountain evaporated in an instant. There was nothing to find, nothing more to search for. I suddenly felt naked, and all I wanted was to be back home safe with my family. My attention now turned entirely to finding my way back to the security of the fixed ropes. The tongue of snow on which I was balanced was about fifty degrees and peppered with bits of black gravel like a poppy seed cake. It ran diagonally across the face, only a few feet above a precipice, the bottom of which I could not see. Which way should I go? As a climber, I had learned long ago that the devil you know is better than the devil you don't. But to go back the way I had come meant climbing up the rock wall and the gully above. In my exhausted state, this was likely to be even more dangerous than descending into the unknown. I tried to remember the details of the drone photo. I was fairly certain that the snow ramp below my feet intersected about 200 feet farther down with a bigger horizontal ledge that I could follow back to the main route.

As I faced into the wall and began climbing down the snow ramp, I cursed myself for not borrowing a second axe from Renan or Matt. They certainly didn't need them where they were, and with two tools, my situation would have been far more secure. The surface was as firm as snow gets without being ice. On the one hand, this left little margin for error, but on the other, when my pick was embedded in the slope, I could trust it to hold. And yet, with only one tool, I couldn't have this assurance at all times. Each time I repositioned my feet a step below by kicking the front points of my crampons into the slope, I had to remove the axe and reposition it lower to set up for the next step down. Essentially, I was climbing down a ladder with one hand tied behind my back.

After I had descended about 150 feet, the snow petered out and I found myself standing on a narrow shelf. I was looking down onto a slab of bare rock that was perched directly above what I knew to be the sheerest rock face in the Yellow Band. A quick glance at the slab told me I wanted nothing to do with it. The gray rock was covered in bits of loose stone that would act like ball bearings under my crampons. But there was also no way I was climbing back up the way I had come.

Willing myself not to panic, I made sure my stance was secure. Gripping the head of the ice axe, I looked around for a way out. The shelf I was standing on extended out to the east in the direction I wanted to go, cutting horizontally through a steep band of rock above the slabs. It was down-sloping, like everything else on the North Face of Everest, but not so severely that it looked impassable.

Holstering my ice axe into the gear loop on the side of my harness, I took a deep breath and set forth across this ledge system. It started out the width of a doormat, with a place for my hands on a horizontal break in the rock. To get a better grip, I pulled my gloves off with my teeth, one at a time, and shoved them into the collar of my suit. The limestone was cold to the touch but grippy, with a texture like frosted glass. It reminded me of sea cliffs in Maine. After climbing sideways for about twenty feet, I arrived at the narrowest section. Here, the ledge was only about six inches wide. I turned my left foot sideways and tried to do the same with my right, but standing duckfooted threw me off-balance, so I turned my right boot perpendicular to the wall. The back end of my crampon now hung over the void.

After a few moves, the ledge widened. Shortly after that, I slid down a six-foot-high wall, plopping onto a gravelly bench, which I staggered across back to the fixed lines. Once I clipped in, I sat down to wait for the team. Matt, Renan, and Jamie arrived a few minutes later. I slipped off my oxygen mask.

"There was nothing there," I said.

The others nodded, as if to indicate that I had merely confirmed what they already knew.

Lhakpa was the last one down the hill. When he got to where I was sitting, he stopped. For a brief moment, he towered above me as we stared intently at each other. Neither of us said anything. I smiled wanly and shrugged, hoping he might return a similar gesture. I detected only the faintest eye roll as he turned away and started down ahead of me. He was done running sweep.

CHAPTER FOURTEEN

Home

IT TOOK EIGHT days for a runner to reach the nearest telegraph station with the terrible news that Mallory and Irvine were lost and presumed dead. On June 19, Arthur Hinks, the head of the Mount Everest Committee, received the telegram in his office at the Royal Geographical Society.

All the expedition's communiqués were sent in code, to prevent rival newspapers from scooping the story from the *Times*, which had helped underwrite the expedition in exchange for exclusive access to the latest breaking news.

The typc was on four separate lines, which had been cut out and glued onto the thin paper in the memo section. The first two lines read:

OBFERRAS LONDON ENGLAND
MALLORY IRVINE NOVE REMAINDER ALCEDO

Hinks's heart sank. According to the code, "Nove" meant "killed in last engagement." The expedition on which the British Empire had staked so much, the conquest that was to serve as redemption for having been beaten by the Americans and the Norwegians to the

North and South Poles, the improbable feat that would offer a ray of hope after the horrors of the Great War, had ended in disaster.

Hinks notified the *Times* but waited twenty-four hours before sending a note to Irvine's parents and Mallory's wife, Ruth. At Herschel House in Cambridge, the Mallory family home, Ruth read the telegram as she sat alone in her living room at dusk.

Ruth had already put the children, Clare, eight, Beridge, six, and John, three, to bed. She decided to let them sleep in peace for one last night. In the morning, she roused them early, gathered them in her bed, and told them their dad had been lost on Mount Everest and was never coming home. Holding each other tightly, they "all cried together."

WILLIE IRVINE WAS at home alone in Birkenhead on the evening of June 20 when the telegram from the Mount Everest Committee arrived. He called Lilian, who was vacationing at the family's cottage, Ffordd Ddwr, in Wales, with Sandy's two younger brothers. Then he called his eighty-nine-year-old father.

Willie was fifty-five years old at the time of his son's death. He had been raised in a strict Presbyterian household. He was "a deeply sensitive person," writes his great-granddaughter, Julie Summers, "but he had been brought up to suppress his feelings at all costs, something which he passed on to his children: giving in to emotion was, he believed, a sign of weakness." The next morning, with Lilian still away, Willie awoke early, dressed, and set off on foot from the house to go to work. On his way to the train station, he crossed paths with an acquaintance, and for a few minutes the men made small talk. Willie made no mention that he had just lost his son.

Lilian, for her part, showed similar resolve. "Her instinct led her to mould her children rather than to mother," writes Summers. "If one or the other of them took a tumble she would reach for the cotton wool and iodine, rather than for the child to comfort him . . . Lilian's doctrine was that you couldn't expect life to be fun all the time and being brought up correctly was a serious business."

Months later, when her oldest son, Hugh (the pilot in the Royal Air Force who had given young Sandy the tip about the need for the synchronization gear), became engaged, Lilian wrote to him that she hoped God would protect her children and that when Sandy had asked for his parents' permission to go to Everest, she and Willie had prayed before giving their consent. And while they never second-guessed the decision, having entrusted it to God, "It does not stop the hole in our hearts."

NOEL ODELL ARRIVED in London on September 13, the return journey from Everest having taken nearly three months. Odell had been away from his wife, Mona, and his young son, Alasdair, for half a year, but nonetheless, he spent only two nights at home before he set off for Birkenhead to pay his respects to Willie and Lilian. He certainly felt obliged to make the call, considering his concerted lobbying on behalf of the young Irvine to get him invited on the 1924 expedition. But if he felt apprehensive of a chilly reception in carrying out this somber errand, his concerns, according to Julie Summers, were alleviated the moment Willie and Lilian opened their door and welcomed him into their home.

Odell told them all about the expedition and, in so doing, was able to fill in many of the blanks for them. He surely would have told them about his last sighting of the two men, and his belief that they had surmounted the crux of the route, with no real difficulties left between them and the summit. Of all the members of the 1924 expedition, it was Odell, more than anyone else, who believed that

Mallory and Irvine, once above the Second Step, would not have turned back before standing on top. Willie, for his part, always believed that his son had summited.

Willie and Hugh eventually got around to unboxing the personal effects that had been shipped back to England with the rest of the team's kit. The suitcases had been packaged up by Odell, who had gone through both Mallory and Irvine's possessions in Base Camp and chosen which items would be sent back to their families. The rest were burned in a bonfire where all of the team's rubbish was incinerated. Amongst the items in the case was a pressure cooker, which Irvine had brought to Tibet from England to see if it would boil water more quickly (today, pressure cookers are ubiquitous on Himalayan expeditions). There was also an expedition patch (which Odell had removed from Irvine's rucksack before burning it), an address book, his passport, and his wallet.

Inside the wallet was a train ticket from Birkenhead to Oxford, a Merton College academic calendar, and a folded-up newspaper clipping. It told the story of a daring young motorcyclist who had ridden to the top of the 3,000-foot-high Foel Grach in Wales in the summer of 1919, where he startled Odell and his new bride when he pulled up on his beloved Clyno and asked, "Is this right for Llanfairfechan?"

AT THE CONCLUSION of our Everest expedition in June of 2019, Jamie set off guiding a series of treks in the Indian Himalaya that kept him in the mountains for several more months. By the time he returned to Kathmandu in late October, he had been climbing and trekking in the Himalaya for close to half a year. One of his local contacts, who would like to remain anonymous, told Jamie that he had heard directly from a CTMA official that the Chinese had beat us to the

Holzel spot and carried Irvine's body off the mountain and back to Lhasa, where it is kept under lock and key with other Mallory and Irvine artifacts, including the VPK.

This narrative echoed rumors that we had heard earlier in the expedition but were unable to confirm. In 2012, a Chinese liaison officer told Jamie that the body had been removed some time prior to 2008. Jamie had shared this information with Thom and me before the expedition, but at the time, it sounded like yet another unsubstantiated rumor. After hearing Jamie's more recent revelations, I started to wonder if there was something more to it. I shared these reports with Jochen Hemmleb, who revealed that he had heard the same thing from his own Chinese contacts. Interestingly, Mallory's body also seems to now be missing from the mountain. Conrad Anker returned to Mallory's gravesite in 2007 and couldn't find it, though he says it may have been buried under the snow. We searched the gravesite area extensively, flying to its exact GPS coordinates with the drone, and also came up empty.

This is all, of course, only more rumor, innuendo, and hearsay. But we now have multiple sources all saying essentially the same thing: The Chinese found Irvine, removed the body, and are jealously guarding this information from the rest of the world—all to protect the claim that the 1960 Chinese team was first to reach the summit of the Third Pole from the north.

AFTER OUR EXPEDITION, I made inquiries with the CTMA. Pemba, the CTMA director who had tried to get us to abandon our climb, agreed to meet with me in person and answer questions if I could get to Lhasa. Through an intermediary, I made a point to confirm that in addition to discussing the various problems Mount Everest is experiencing these days with overcrowding and environmental degradation, I also wanted to ask questions about Mallory and Irvine. I was told that it was all "no problem."

Around this same time, I also learned that Gonbu, the Tibetan army man who was part of the 1960 summit team, was still kicking at age eighty-seven and splitting his time between Lhasa and Chengdu. He was one of the last surviving members of the team, and the only summiteer who was still alive. He agreed to meet me in person in Chengdu. I had plane tickets and hotel reservations and a tour booked to see the pandas, when a novel coronavirus began spreading in Wuhan, China. My trip was canceled, and it was unclear when or if I would ever have a chance to conduct these interviews.

In the meantime, Jochen Hemmleb gave me a contact in Beijing, who in turn put me in touch with a Chinese journalist with expertise in the history of mountaineering in China. After I contacted him through a Chinese messaging app, he responded immediately. "Hi Mark. Do you remember me in YNP on year 2008?" Attached was a photo of us having dinner together in Yosemite. Turns out we had taken part in a cultural exchange eleven years earlier during which I had spent several days giving a group of Chinese climbers and journalists a tour of my favorite climbing area. I told this man that I was researching the 1960 Chinese ascent of the North Face. He said I was in luck. He had recently come into possession of an unpublished internal report from the 1960 Everest expedition that he'd found in the personal papers of a noted Chinese climber named Dayi Liu, who had passed away in 2017. Liu was a primary member of the 1960 expedition and was also a summiteer on the 1957 Chinese climb of Minya Konka (24,790 feet), which was used as a stepping-stone to Everest. He emailed me a copy of the document. It was written in Mandarin and approximately 60,000 characters—the equivalent of sixty-six single-spaced pages in English.

The report is entitled "Everest Work Summary," and in the corner of the title page it says TOP SECRET. It is dated June 12, 1962, and seems to have several authors. It appears that it was prepared for none other than Mao Zedong and other high-ranking Communist Party officials. It has five chapters, numerous detailed illustrations, and a long appendix. It was written to impress, with endless facts and figures, lists of species discovered, kilometers of road built, and scientific analyses of equipment, physiology, geology, hydrology, and meteorology.

Much of the report is infused with communist propaganda and hyperbole. As the team prepared to set off on the final assault of the summit, the climbers held a ceremony in Base Camp during which they swore a pledge to Chairman Mao and the Communist Party. As they faced the "Red Flag of the great Motherland, the team members raised their right fists, eyes brimming with tears, and fervently shouted an oath: 'We will not go back without setting foot on the summit of Qomolungma . . . If our right hands are frozen off, we'll use our left hands to help our comrades reach the summit." They called the summit team "commandos," each of whom carried his own small flag, and "they would reach the summit even if at the last breath of the last man."

The document has five appendices, and I found the last one, "Reactions of various countries towards our ascent of Qomolungma," the most interesting. This section indicated how the Chinese felt when the West, particularly the British climbing establishment, cast aspersions on the validity of the ascent. The first section of this appendix is titled "The achievement of Chinese Mountaineering is a triumph of the General Line of the Party and the Great Leap Forward," and it quotes media sources in various communist countries, including North Korea, Indonesia, and the Eastern Bloc, all of whom celebrated the ascent as a boost to communist ideology—and a stick in the eye to the British imperialists.

The document goes on to declare the Chinese conquest of Everest a severe blow to Indian prestige. Tensions had been rising between China and India throughout the 1950s, especially after the latter gave refuge to the Dalai Lama in 1959, but the major bone of contention was a disputed border running along the crest of the Himalayan mountain chain both east and west of Everest. The Indians also attempted to climb Everest in 1960, via the South Col. They were on the mountain at the same time as the Chinese but failed to reach the summit. A contact in China with knowledge of the expedition told me that the Chinese summit party carried a pistol in the event it had a hostile encounter with the Indians at the top of the world. Within two years, this rivalry would erupt into the Sino-Indian War.

The report acknowledges "a few attempts of vicious attack and alienation" due to a lack of photographic proof. "Because our publicity and reporting work was insufficiently rigorous, and we were unable to clarify important details of the mountain climbing process in a timely manner and with a unified tone, unnecessary errors and contradictions appeared in many reports which had a definite effect on publicity outcomes." Early on, before the Communist Party was able to harmonize the story, various members of the 200-person team gave reports to a myriad of Chinese publications. *China Youth* magazine caused an international incident by writing that the Chinese planted "the five-star red flag on the highest peak in our country," prompting Nepal's foreign minister to remind China that it did not have sole sovereignty over Mount Everest.

There is also reference to a Xinhua News Agency report stating that the team found the remains of a British explorer and that the Chinese performed a proper burial on the mountain. The official account, which was widely reported in the international media at the time, was that this body was found "below the North Col," which would have meant that it had to be Maurice Wilson, the British mystic who disappeared on Everest in 1934. But the original Xinhua News Agency story, as quoted in the internal report, states the location as "below the summit." This section also references a story in a now defunct Chinese publication called *Traveller* that reported that the Chinese climbers "smashed the skull of the dead British expedition member with ice picks."

Toward the end, the report tallies up all the reasons the British failed, including their "lack of courage to persist to the end . . . After tasting all manner of defeat, these foreign explorers were finally compelled to sadly acknowledge that it was impossible to ascend this summit, which even birds could not cross, from the north ridge with its multitude of natural barriers. [The British] even referred to Everest's north ridge as an 'unscalable' death route."

The section ends with a proposition that the 1953 first ascent of the mountain by Edmund Hillary and Tenzing Norgay was a hoax perpetrated by the British, who were intent on bringing about a new Elizabethan age.

The *Everest Work Summary* was not shared with the outside world. The Chinese were well aware of their detractors, but none of the climbers themselves ever publicly acknowledged the controversy. It is likely that the party line was to diminish these "vicious attacks" by not deigning to acknowledge them. For the Chinese Communist Party (CCP), it was vitally important that the first ascent of the North Face of Everest be held up as a symbol of communism's triumph over British and American imperialism because the Great Leap Forward, which was supposed to modernize and revive China, allowing it to surpass Great Britain within ten years and the United States in fifteen, had proven an unmitigated disaster. The Chinese climbers returned from Everest to both a cultural revolution and a famine that would claim 20 to 30 million lives over the next two years.

I NEVER MANAGED to meet Gonbu in person, but I was eventually able to interview him remotely through a translator. I learned that he had grown up herding sheep on the Tibetan Plateau before he joined the Chinese army in 1956. His life after Everest was relatively comfortable, but he enjoyed little of the celebrity or fortune Edmund Hillary and Tenzing Norgay experienced in their post-Everest years. He and the other Chinese heroes were flown to Beijing, where they were congratulated personally by Mao Zedong, feted by the leaders of the CCP, and labeled "Brave Peak Conquerors." But the emphasis was always on the collectivist spirit and not the individual accomplishment. After the ceremony in Beijing, Gonbu was flown back to Lhasa, where he took a job as a trainer at the Tibet Mountaineering Training Camp. Keeping his head low so as to assure he would get fed and avoid persecution, he eventually rose to become the vice chairman of the Tibet Mountaineering Association. Before his retirement in 1996, he established a forty-bed hospital in Gucuo, the town where he grew up, to support local farmers and herdsmen.

Gonbu confirmed that he was the one who carried the plaster bust of Chairman Mao to the summit. He says this was important for the Chinese because there was a bronze statue of Lenin on Lenin Peak in Tajikistan. He stashed it, along with a wool glove in which they stuck a note with their three names, in the rock cracks under the snow slope on the north side. "On behalf of the 600 million Chinese people," says Gonbu, "I climbed to the top of the world and showed the world [the] five-star red flag. The development and progress of society makes the challenge of peaks not difficult for mankind, but the spirit of climbing the peak is not only meaningful for mountaineering. For young people, this spirit is also needed. Isn't there such a sentence? We must not only climb the peak, but also create the peak."

NOEL ODELL SHIPPED OFF to Harvard University in 1927. Two years later, he made his famous lead of Odell's Gully on Mount Washington, a route that set a new standard for ice climbing in the United States. That same winter, Odell received a letter from Arthur Hinks reprimanding him for making statements about a forthcoming British expedition to Mount Everest. It seems that Odell had gotten himself on the wrong side of Hinks and the Mount Everest Committee, which Holzel believes was because the British climbing establishment was pressuring Odell to change his story. It would be easier to raise funds for the next attempt, whenever that might be, if the summit was still considered to be inviolate.

When the British did remount an expedition in 1933, Odell was passed over for inclusion on the team, despite the fact that he was far more qualified than many of the other members. Afterward, the leader, Hugh Ruttledge, openly challenged Odell's famous sighting, stating that all he had seen were two rocks, or perhaps some birds. Odell was incensed. "I am absolutely certain that they were climbers," he said. "They were moving actually, moving figures."

Odell was spurned again by Ruttledge in 1935 and 1936. As a consolation, he went to Nanda Devi (25,643 feet) in the Indian Himalaya in 1936 with the Harvard Mountaineering Club, who had nicknamed him "Noah." Odell and another British climbing legend, Bill Tilman, succeeded in making the mountain's first ascent. Nanda Devi is the world's twenty-third-tallest mountain and an extremely difficult climb. At the time, it was the highest and likely the most difficult peak that had ever been summited—a record that would stand until the French climbed Annapurna in 1950. Tilman was given leadership of the 1938 Everest expedition, and this time Odell was invited. Having finally gotten back to Mount Everest after fourteen years, he was intent, not on summiting, but on finishing his geologic research. At age forty-eight, he climbed circles around many of the other climbers, some of whom were young enough to be his children. None of these 1930s expeditions, though, managed to best the efforts of the 1924 team.

IN THE MID-1980S, Holzel visited Odell at this home in Cambridge. Holzel, like so many historians before him, had been dissecting the wording of Odell's various accounts. He lost the notes from this meeting but recalls that Odell was fed up with being pressured into changing his story.

"After being snubbed so many times by the Mount Everest Committee and the British climbing establishment," says Holzel, "he was done playing politics about what he had seen."

As a follow-up to this in-person meeting, Holzel sent Odell a copy of a German-Austrian topographical map of Mount Everest. He asked Odell to mark the map with the route he had taken to Camp VI on June 8, 1924, and also to note where he had seen Mallory and Irvine on the ridge. When Thom and I visited Holzel at his home before our expedition, this map was proudly hanging on the wall in his office, Odell's penciled-in markings still clearly visible. He had drawn a squiggly line up the North Ridge and placed an X at the location where he made his famous sighting. From there he drew a straight line with an arrow at its end pointing to a spot on the crest of the Northeast Ridge. Pasted on top of the map was the letter from Odell that accompanied it. Holzel must have left it hanging for many years in the direct sun, because the ink had faded to the point that Odell's letter was completely illegible. But Holzel is sure that in what was likely his final testimony on the subject, Odell was steadfast in his belief that it was indeed the Second Step where he had seen Mallory and Irvine that fateful day.

Odell would die a few years later, in 1987, at age ninety-six, still believing in his heart that there was "a strong probability that Mallory and Irvine succeeded," as he had written back in 1925 for the official expedition account.

Of course, we have to keep in mind that Odell had a personal stake in whether Mallory and Irvine made the summit. Clearly, he felt great responsibility for the death of his young friend. If Irvine had left his footprints on the summit late that day, it was no small consolation for his loss. Contrary to other teammates' belief that the climbers must have fallen off the ridge, Odell always clung to the idea that they had been benighted on the descent after making the summit. Succumbing to the cold would have been decidedly less horrific than falling off the mountain and dying battered and broken on some ledge. Like all climbers who have lost a close friend in the mountains, Odell would have imagined the end. He would have wondered, as many of us have, what young Sandy was thinking when he realized that all his wonderful potential as a human being would never be realized.

As I SIT HERE at home in New Hampshire's White Mountains, I can see Mount Washington out my office window, towering above Pinkham Notch. The green forests are starting to show their fall colors. Huntington Ravine is in clear view, though I can't quite make out Odell's Gully, which is tucked away in a craggy fold. I'm wearing old sweatpants and that same cashmere sweater that Hampton gave me for Christmas. Through the ceiling above, I can hear Tommy squealing with delight as he plays with Lilla in the living room. On the windowsill in front of me sits a crumpled photo of my family, permanently creased from the many weeks it rested inside my pocket on Mount Everest. Looking at it now, I'm struck by the thought that our greatest endeavors are less about what we set out to do than what we bring back.

I returned from Everest without finding Sandy Irvine or the camera. And yet for me, the project was a success, not just for the obvious reason that I joined the club of 5,000-plus other aspirants who have succeeded in standing at the highest point on Earth, but for the human stories I gathered in the process. A friend and old climbing buddy asked me shortly after I got home whether Everest had whet my appetite for other 8,000-meter peaks. Did I have any interest in attempting, say, K2, which many call a true "climber's mountain"? Interestingly, I hadn't considered that question, which I realized meant no. I've spent a good part of the summer of 2020 sailing the coast of Maine with my family, and I'd be content to never quest into the Death Zone again.

I did ask myself this summer, as I sat at the helm enjoying a broad reach on a fresh southwesterly, whether I'd feel the same way had I not summited. What if that second perfect weather window had never materialized, and my high point on the mountain was only the North Col? Would I still be able to enjoy a moment like this, with my family, to its fullest? Or would I feel the nagging, magnetic tug of the Third Pole—halfway around the world, yet ever present in my psyche?

I can't know the answer to this question, but I can say with certainty that orienting one's life around a peak like Mount Everest is a perilous proposition, not only because the mountain will likely kill you eventually, but because it may also consume your soul in the process. Renan's refusal to stand on the very top of Chomolungma was an act of humility, a way of symbolically guarding the most important part of himself and not giving it over to ambition. I'd like to think that, had we not succeeded in reaching the summit, I could live today with a similar humility and let Everest go, enjoy what I have, value the experience and memories I brought home from the expedition, regardless of its outcome. But I know all too well the pull of that summit pyramid and how deeply it resonates with our humanity—as passionate and beautifully flawed as that is.

When I last spoke with Cory Richards, he was training full-time for a rematch with Everest's Northeast Face. This time, he said, he's putting more focus on building up the strength in his legs. Both sides of the mountain were closed to climbing during the spring and fall of 2020 due to COVID-19, but if the north side is open again come spring 2021, Cory and Topo will be back, intent on pushing their new route to the top—in alpine style and without oxygen, of course. They hope to bring a third partner, to split the load and help with the trail breaking. Last I heard, they hadn't yet found any takers.

I've also been in touch with Kam. In the days following her harrowing ordeal, her big toe and pinky turned black from severe frostbite. Years ago, doctors almost certainly would have amputated them, but Kam had been advised by Kari Kobler not to have surgery until the digits became gangrenous. It turns out this was sound advice. Many months later, when a doctor peeled off the dead, blackened skin, they found that her big toe was still alive, as was half of her pinky. Now that she has mostly recovered, Kam is back training too. Not long ago, she sent me a copy of a sponsorship proposal, detailing her aim to become the only Indian woman to scale all the 8,000-meter peaks *and* the Seven Summits. As soon as the Himalaya reopens to climbing, she wants to have a crack at Kangchenjunga, the world's third-tallest mountain.

Out of everyone in this story, it may be Thom Pollard who is having the hardest time getting Everest out of his system. With one successful summit already under his belt, I had assumed the climb this time around wasn't make-or-break for him, so I was surprised when I learned in the months after our expedition how devastated he was by not having made the summit from the north. I suppose it's understandable that he still yearns to have a more pure experience than he did in 2016. Over martinis at his cabin one summer evening, he turned to me and said, "Not an hour goes by when it [Everest] isn't on my mind."

So, I GUESS I'm fortunate that my own Everest journey has come to an end, that my infatuation with the top of the world lasted less than a year, that I'm not haunted by a sense of unfinished business. But there is one idea that I cannot shake: the possibility that someone, likely a high-ranking Chinese official, might know the answer to the mystery. Perhaps their curiosity got the better of them and they developed the film on the VPK before destroying it and erasing the evidence forever. Or, maybe, those photos still exist, locked away in some vault in Lhasa or Beijing. Of course, given the present trajectory of geopolitics, the VPK might as well have gone down one of those gaping crevasses at the bottom of the North Face, so slim is the likelihood that the Chinese government would reveal to the world what's on that film.

And so, like Odell, I am left with only my imagination and the vision of those two intrepid souls, still "going strong" for the summit—despite the late hour of the day, and the odds stacked terribly against them.

POSTSCRIPT FOR THE PAPERBACK EDITION

IN EARLY MAY of 2021, less than a month after the publication of this book, I received an email with a subject line that read: "Book or article idea." Intrigued, I opened it to find the following:

> Dear Mr. Synnott,
> My name is Wayne Wilcox. I'm a former Marine officer, former US State Department Regional Security Officer, and retired corporate security director, now living in England with my wife and two boys. . . . My wife works for the British Foreign Office. Since 2008 I've been sitting on some information that I think would make a good story. With your new book out, I feel that you are the logical person to tell it. I'm not a real writer, I don't have the time or resources to research and write it, and I don't have the clout to get it published, but it's a story that I think should be told.

Wilcox went on to explain that his source, a high-ranking official in the British Embassy, had direct knowledge that the Chinese found the remains of a foreign climber at 8,200 meters during their 1975 expedition to the North Face of Mount Everest. And on that person, they had recovered the long-lost Kodak VPK and brought it back to Beijing. Wilcox also wrote: "They screwed up the development of the film and ruined it. Rather than admit they made a mistake, they erased all evidence that they had found the camera or the body." I immediately sent Wilcox a copy of this book, which he had not read, and we arranged to speak over the phone. On that call, I learned that in 2008, Wilcox and his wife, Juliette, were stationed in China. As a diplomat with the British Foreign Service, Juliette was invited to attend the opening ceremony of the summer Olympics at the Beijing National Stadium. The event lasted over four hours and included more than 15,000 performers. By all accounts, it was an opening ceremony par excellence. Toward the end, the Olympic flag was carried in by eight Chinese national heroes, one of whom was a petite Tibetan woman in her late sixties.

After the ceremony, Juliette met up with a seasoned British diplomat who told her that he recognized the Tibetan woman. "That was Pan Duo," he said. "She was the first Chinese woman to climb Mount Everest." This man, whom I will call "the diplomat," noted that when the other flag bearers waved to acknowledge the Chinese leaders, Pan Duo had conspicuously abstained. This small detail had caught his attention, because years ago he had interviewed Pan Duo, and she had told him an interesting story.

IT TOOK MONTHS, but I eventually made contact with this diplomat. He agreed to share his story with me on the condition that I not reveal his identity. The information wasn't classified, it was just that he was now retired and didn't want to be hounded to the end of his days by journalists (like me).

The diplomat's interview with Pan Duo had taken place in 1984 at the headquarters of the Chinese Mountaineering Association

(CMA; later to become the CTMA) in Beijing. The meeting had been arranged at the behest of Sir George Bishop, who at the time was the president of the Royal Geographical Society (RGS). Bishop was a former British civil servant and businessman who served from 1972 to 1979 as chairman of Booker McConnell, the food wholesaler that founded the Man Booker Prize for literature. Bishop was also a skilled photographer and mountaineer who took part in eighteen expeditions to the Himalayas. The diplomat couldn't recall why Bishop was in Beijing, but China had recently opened up to foreigners and the RGS may have been seeking a mountaineering permit.

There were two Chinese representatives of the CMA at the meeting, Pan Duo and Wang Fuzhou—the same Fuzhou who summited Everest on the 1960 Chinese expedition. At the time of the meeting, he was the president of the CMA. Pan Duo was the second woman of any nationality to climb Mount Everest (missing out on being the first to Junko Tabei of Japan by eleven days) and the first to do so via the North Face. She grew up in western Tibet, and her father died when she was a toddler. By age six, barefoot and shabbily clothed, she was working in the fields, subsisting on a single barley cake per day and sleeping with yaks. In 1959, she was twenty years old and working on a state-owned farm when her physical strength and work ethic caught the attention of recruiters looking for trainees to join the fledgling Chinese mountaineering program. Later that same year, Pan Duo summited Mustagh Ata, a 24,636-foot mountain in Xinjiang. At the time, it was the highest elevation ever attained by a woman. On the descent, Pan Duo survived an avalanche that killed five of her comrades.

The British diplomat is the only person still alive who attended this meeting at the CMA (Pan Duo passed away in 2014, Fuzhou in 2015). Many of the details have since faded from his memory. When we spoke over the phone in October of 2021, he told me that he couldn't remember a single thing about Fuzhou; Pan Duo, on the other hand, had made an impression. He remembered her as being "tiny" and having a beautiful, high voice. "I thought, 'How amazing that this was the woman who climbed Mount Everest,'" he said. One detail that did lodge firmly in his mind, and which he never forgot, is that Pan Dou and Fuzhou told him and Sir George that on the 1975 Chinese expedition to the North Face of Everest, the team had found the Kodak VPK and brought it home. Later, Chinese technicians attempted to develop the film but were unable to recover any images. Wilcox had taken this to mean that the Chinese had botched the development process, but, of course, it could be that the film was not salvageable, or perhaps, Mallory and Irvine never shot any photos.

As all members of the British Foreign Service are trained to do, the diplomat took thorough notes at the meeting. He later wrote a memo, which he sent to Sir George Bishop and possibly the Foreign Office as well. The obvious place for this document to have ended up was the archives at the RGS, but according to Jan Turner, the librarian who helped me during my visit to the Foyle Reading Room in 2019, the RGS doesn't have it. If the memo had been shared with the British Foreign Office at the time, it would now be part of the UK National Archives. On my urging, the diplomat spent two days poring through these files in person, but this too proved to be a dead end. I have also been in touch with Sir George's relatives, who told me that upon his death his widow burned all of his papers. As of this writing, the document remains unconfirmed.

I have, however, obtained a transcript of an email that the diplomat wrote to the British Ambassador to China, Sir Anthony Galsworthy, on May 6, 1999. At the time, the story of Conrad Anker's discovery of the remains of George Mallory at 26,700 feet on the

North Face of Everest was spreading like wildfire across the globe. With all the speculation that was floating around about the missing camera, the diplomat wondered why Sir George wasn't coming forward with the information the two men had learned back in 1984. It wasn't until much later that he learned that Bishop had passed away on April 6, 1999, three weeks before the discovery of Mallory's remains.

The subject line of the email to Ambassador Galsworthy reads: "Did Mallory climb Everest?"

"I DON'T HAVE the answer to this question," writes the diplomat, "but just possibly I know how to find it [the camera] or to prove that it can never be found." The email goes on to explain how Wang Fuzhou and Pan Duo told the diplomat and Bishop that the 1975 Everest team had recovered the camera. "We asked whether it had been possible to develop the film. I seem to recall that we were told there had been nothing on it (which could of course mean that an attempt to develop it had been made and something had gone wrong). I also recall that we were told that the camera was in the Mountaineering Association's museum. Wang said that from the position in which it had been found, he thought Mallory/Irvine could not have reached the summit, but he gave no explanation for this hypothesis. I wrote a letter of this exchange at the time and sent it to the chairman of Booker McConnell. I suggested at the time that he might want to send it to the Royal Geographical Society, but I never heard anything further. Someone should speak with the Chinese Mountaineering Association. This was all a long time ago and I could have got it wrong, although I don't think so. And that meeting has always stuck in my memory. If the film really was mucked up, I imagine it is quite possible that the association [CMA] would deny that the camera had ever been found."

WHEN WAYNE WILCOX was chasing this story back in 2008, he arranged for the editor of *The Economist*'s China desk to interview Pan Duo. That interview took place through an intermediary shortly after the conclusion of the Beijing Olympics. Wilcox never published it because he was planning to use it in his own telling of this story, which never came to fruition. The following is a shortened transcription that has been edited for length and clarity.

ECONOMIST: Roughly where on Everest did you discover the body?
PAN DUO: Probably at around 8,200 meters.
ECONOMIST: What was the condition of the body at that time?
PAN DUO: It was a foreigner, and he had a yellow *zhangfeng* [tent] with nothing else inside. The things had probably already been carried away.
ECONOMIST: When you saw the body, did you judge he had slipped on his way down from the summit, or did he die in some other way?
PAN DUO: He probably froze to death.
ECONOMIST: What about the camera?
PAN DUO: I don't remember the details of this. . . . We buried him under a pile of stones: it wasn't bad. We stood there freezing. The body lay on the floor, when we went to pull him, maybe spleen or whatever, all would have been damaged. We considered it and then put small stones on his body, to show our grief/mark the grave.
ECONOMIST: And what about the camera?

PAN DUO: After we came down, we didn't see anything. Maybe others discovered it. I don't know.

Like most other clues in this mystery, this interview offers more questions than answers, but we do have Pan Duo admitting that the team found and partially buried the body of a foreigner in 1975 at around 8,200 meters. She doesn't admit to finding the camera, but it's likely she may not have been speaking as freely as she did with the diplomat back in 1984. As previously noted, by 2008 the Chinese were no longer acknowledging that they had found any bodies high on Everest during the 1960 and 1975 expeditions.

How certain can we be that Pan Duo and her team found Sandy Irvine in 1975? Could she be referring to the discovery of Mallory by Wang Hongbao, who found the old "English, English" dead when he wandered out of Camp VI in 1975 on the North Ridge looking for a missing teammate named Wu Zongyue? Or had she possibly come across Wu himself, who had fallen to his death and whose battered remains were later found at 8,100 meters? It is possible, of course, that Pan Duo had mistaken Wu's body for that of a "foreigner," but this cannot explain away why Pan Duo and Fuzhou would have told the diplomat and Bishop in 1984 that they found the camera. (And, of course, one has to wonder why they would make all this up, only to later deny it.) It also doesn't add up that the body could have been Mallory, because we know from Jochen Hemmleb's research that Hongbao was well off the route the Chinese were following that year when he found Mallory's remains. We know that in 1975 the Chinese hewed closely to the route they had followed in 1960, and it's fair to assume they would have known about Xu Jing's purported sighting of Irvine. Pan Duo said the body was wrapped in a "yellow tent." Xu Jing testified to Hemmleb and Eric Simonson that the body was in a sleeping bag, which might be taken for a tent, or vice versa.

If Pan Duo's memory and account of this incident are accurate, then it seems most likely that the body she came across was indeed that of Sandy Irvine.

ABOUT A MONTH after I spoke with the diplomat, I managed to track down Dechen Ngodrup, the CTMA official who had been on the mountain with us in 2019. Via a Chinese messaging app, I told him about the recent revelation regarding the camera and asked him if he knew anything about it. He said he didn't, but that he knew Pan Duo personally. "She is an amazing lady in China," he wrote. After her Everest climb, which cost her three of her toes, Pan Duo told a reporter, "Chinese women have a strong will; difficulties can't stop us. We climbed the highest peak in the world; we really hold up half the sky." She went on to be elected five times as a deputy to the National People's Congress. In 1981, she moved from Tibet to eastern China, where, as the vice director of the Wuxi Sports Administration, she trained the next generation of aspiring Chinese mountaineers, one of whom was Dechen. In 1986, she told the *Beijing Review* that she missed her home in Tibet terribly and was still struggling to adjust to the climate and the food in Wuxi. "Compared to Han cuisine," she said, "mountaineering is simple."

Dechen told me that Pan Duo had never mentioned the camera to him, and he did not know of it being in a museum in China. But he promised me that he would ask the surviving members of the 1975 expedition. I have not heard back.

If the camera was found in 1975, one possible place for it to reside is the Tsering Chey Nga Snow Mountain Museum in Lhasa. I don't know of anyone who has been to it, but I did find a program online from Chinese state TV that offered a guided tour of sorts. Jochen Hemmleb reviewed some of the historical items that are shown in this program and concluded that the Chinese hold artifacts that have not previously been reported.

Of course, I'd like to be able to visit this museum and ask its director point blank about the VPK. But as I write this from my desk in northern New Hampshire, COVID-19 continues to restrict travel to China. The mystery of Mallory and Irvine endures.

Mark Synnott

Jackson, New Hampshire

November 4, 2021

NOTES ON SOURCES

After Thom Pollard's Everest lecture in October of 2017, the first two books I read on the mystery of Mallory and Irvine were *Into the Silence: The Great War, Mallory, and the Conquest of Everest* by Wade Davis and *Fearless on Everest: The Quest for Sandy Irvine* by Julie Summers. It is fair to say these powerfully written, richly researched books inspired me to write this one. *Into the Silence* and *Fearless on Everest* also served as important sources of information on the historical narrative that is woven throughout *The Third Pole*. For anyone looking for a deeper dive into the character of these two men and the times in which they lived, I cannot recommend these titles enough.

Other important sources for this book include the three George Mallory biographies: *George Leigh Mallory: A Memoir* by David Pye, *George Mallory* by David Robertson, and *The Wildest Dream: The Biography of George Mallory* by Peter and Leni Gillman. I also spent a lot of time with *The Irvine Diaries* by Herbert Carr (the original diaries on which this book is based are housed at Merton College, Oxford). Another important diary I referenced frequently was that of Edward Norton, the leader of the 1924 expedition. Thanks to his grandson Christopher Norton, this material can be found in *Everest*

Revealed: The Private Diaries and Sketches of Edward Norton, 1922–24. To learn more about the early Everest expeditions, I read *Mount Everest: The Reconnaissance, 1921* by C. K. Howard-Bury, George Mallory, and A. F. R. Wollaston; *The Assault on Mount Everest, 1922* by C. G. Bruce; and *The Fight for Everest 1924* by E. F. Norton. In the latter, chapters five, six, and seven served as primary sources of information on the events that took place on Mount Everest during the final days of the 1924 expedition.

Additional reading on the early Everest expeditions also included Howard Somervell's biography, *After Everest: The Experiences of a Mountaineer and Medical Missionary*; *Climbing Everest: The Complete Writings of George Mallory*; *Everest: The Mountaineering History* by Walt Unsworth; and *The Mystery of Mallory and Irvine* by Tom Holzel and Audrey Salkeld.

In *The Third Pole*'s historical narrative, if something appears in quotations, it has been quoted from a letter, diary, journal, book, or other published source. Wherever possible, I tried to quote from the most primary source. Some of this material, like the two notes that Mallory wrote from high camp on June 7, 1924, I saw in its original form during my research visit to the UK. All these quotations are cited in the following notes, except in a few cases where there are multiple quotes on a single page that all come from the same section in a quoted source. In this case, to keep these endnotes concise, I cited the source once rather than repeating the same one several times. For this same reason I have not included sources for facts that are widely known and easily referenced, or in cases where I quote directly from personal interviews, conversations, and interactions.

Details and dialogue in my first-person narrative were sourced from my note-taking and the photos and video shot during the course of the expedition, as well as extensive interviews conducted both during and after the expedition. A critically important source for my reporting was the many hours of audio that Jim Hurst recorded throughout the expedition and later shared with me. We had hoped to create a podcast from this story, but so far, that has not come to fruition. Much of the dialogue that appears between quotation marks is quoted verbatim from transcriptions of these recordings. Other dialogue for which I did not have a recording was sourced from reviewing film footage and also from notes that I took during the course of the expedition. Often, I was able to take notes in real time, but when I was prevented from doing so because I was climbing or otherwise unable to write, I took notes at the next available opportunity. All the principal characters in my first-person narrative had a chance to review the manuscript and to offer corrections before the book went to publication.

PROLOGUE

xvii teammate spotted them "going strong": Christopher Norton, *Everest Revealed: The Private Diaries and Sketches of Edward Norton, 1922–24* (Cheltenham, UK: History Press, 2014), 112.

CHAPTER ONE: AMONG THE DEAD

Sources for chapter one include *Ghosts of Everest: The Search for Mallory and Irvine* by Jochen Hemmleb, Larry Johnston, and Eric Simonson; *Detectives on Everest: The 2001 Mallory and Irvine Research Expedition* by Jochen Hemmleb and Eric Simonson; and *The Lost Explorer: Finding Mallory on Mount Everest* by Conrad Anker and David Roberts. I also conducted interviews with several members of the 1999 expedition, including Thom Pollard, Conrad Anker, Jochen Hemmleb, Eric Simonson, Jake Norton, Andy Politz, and Graham Hoyland. Anker, Pollard, and Hemmleb also fact-checked the manuscript. The dialogue between the searchers on May 1, 1999, was sourced from the BBC film *Lost on Everest*, which can be found on YouTube and also from the Nova Everest website, which contains a treasure trove of information on the expedition, including transcripts of the teams' radio transmissions.

5 "I think posers . . .": Mark Twight, "Justification for an Elitist Attitude," *Climbing* magazine 199 (December 2000).

6 first commercial client on Everest: Bill Stall, "Conquers Mt. Everest to Fulfill Dream: Millionaire First to Climb Summits of All Continents," *LA Times*, May 2, 1985, https://www.latimes.com/archives/la-xpm-1985-05-02-mn-20109

-story.html. See also: Dick Bass and Frank Wells, with Rick Ridgeway, *Seven Summits* (New York: Grand Central, 1986).

7 **"It is almost unthinkable . . .":** Transcribed with permission of the Master and Fellows of Magdalene College, Cambridge, Magdalene College Archives F/GM/III/4, GM to Ruth April 24, 1924.

7 **silhouettes "moving expeditiously":** E. F. Norton, *The Fight for Everest 1924* (London: Edward Arnold, 1925), 103.

7 **"My eyes became fixed . . .":** "The Mount Everest Dispatches," *Geographical Journal* 64, no. 2 (August 1924): 164.

8 **"It has always seemed . . .":** The letter from Lord Curzon to Douglas Freshfield is undated but was written in the spring of 1905. A.C. Committee: Minutes, January 13, 1903–November 21, 1911, Alpine Club Library. Reference: AC2S-9.

8 **"dry as dust":** T. S. Blakeney, "The First Steps toward Mount Everest," *Alpine Journal* (1971): 43.

9 **"Our forefathers were terrified . . .":** "Sir F. Younghusband and the Alpine Spirit," *Englishman*, Calcutta (December 21, 1920): Alpine Club Archive, Press Cutting volume December 1920 to September 1921.

10 **The precedent set in 1875:** John B. West, *High Life: A History of High-Altitude Physiology and Medicine* (New York: Oxford University Press, 1998), 55–58.

12 **Howard Somervell reported loaning:** From a BBC interview with Howard Somervell in 1970. Jochen Hemmleb shared a video copy of the interview with me. Somervell's direct quote was: "When Mallory set off on his expedition, he borrowed my camera—and of course it never came back. If ever Mallory's body was found, I wonder if the camera would still be in his pocket. And if we'd develop the film, preserved in ice for perhaps a hundred or 200 years, would it be capable of producing any pictures? If so, we may find out whether or not he reached the top."

13 **most important pieces of evidence:** Wang Hongbao's account of finding the old "English, English" dead was unearthed by Tom Holzel in 1980 after he wrote to the Japanese Alpine Club, asking if they would keep an eye out for Mallory and Irvine on their upcoming expedition to the north side of Everest. The Japanese expedition was the first non-Chinese group to attempt the north side of Everest since the British in 1938. Hiroyuki Suzuki wrote back that on their reconnaissance expedition the year before, Wang Hongbao, who was working for the Japanese as a porter, told one of their expedition members that he had found an old dead body at 8,100 meters during the 1975 Chinese expedition. The day after he dropped this bombshell, Hongbao died in an avalanche on the slope below the North Col. This clue remained little more than an unsubstantiated rumor until 1986, when Holzel tracked down Hongbao's tentmate in Beijing (then Peking), a man named Zhang Yun Yan. Holzel asked the man if he remembered Hongbao leaving the tent. "Yes, he

went out for a twenty-minute walk," said Zhang. Did he find anything? "Yes, he told me had found the body of a foreign mountaineer." This clue would eventually lead to the discovery of Mallory's body in 1999. For more on this story, see: Tom Holzel and Audrey Salkeld, *The Mystery of Mallory and Irvine* (London: Pimlico, 1986), 1–44, 326–27.

13 "accidentally dropped when a slip . . .": Hugh Ruttledge, *Everest 1933* (London: Hodder and Stoughton, 1938), 137, 145.

16 "this is George Mallory!": BBC documentary, *Lost on Everest—The Search for Mallory and Irvine* (2000), https://www.youtube.com/watch?v=Z7KyVKop3sc.

17 other items included a sewing kit: Conrad Anker and David Roberts, *The Lost Explorer: Finding Mallory on Mount Everest* (New York: Simon & Schuster, 1999), 35.

17 According to Mallory's family: Peter and Leni Gilman, *The Wildest Dream: The Biography of George Mallory* (Seattle: Mountaineers, 2000), 269.

19 "Thanks, Jochen": From transcripts of the radio transmissions on May 1, 1999, https://www.pbs.org/wgbh/nova/everest/lost/search/day.html.

19 "Hey, congratulations": This conversation was re-created from Thom Pollard's memory and his journal entry from that day.

20 Mountain Zone's site logged: Peter Potterfield, "The Mountain Zone—A Look Back," MountainZone.com, https://www.mountainzone.com/mountaineering/mountainzone-looking-back/.

21 "heartfelt thanks": From Thom Pollard's journal.

21 "Frankly, it makes me bloody angry": Ed Douglas, "Everest Row over Photo Profits from Body of Pioneer Mallory," *Guardian*, May 8, 1999, https://www.theguardian.com/uk/1999/may/09/theobserver.uknews.

25 "the mystery of Botticelli . . .": Paul Levy, ed., *The Letters of Lytton Strachey* (New York: Farrar, Straus and Giroux, 2005), 178. Letter from Strachey to Vanessa and Clive Bell, undated, spring 1909.

CHAPTER TWO: MOSCOW RULES

28 "Isn't Everest 29,035 feet high?": Since 1999, the official "American" height for Everest has been 29,035 feet, a figure based on a GPS survey by Bradford Washburn and the National Geographic Society. On December 8, 2020, Nepal and China jointly announced a new height for Everest of 29,031.69 feet, measured via satellite, theodolite, and ground-penetrating radar (to estimate the height of snow above the highest rock). As of this writing, National Geographic, pending analysis of the Chinese and Nepalese data, has yet to verify the new height. Nepal's official previous height for the mountain was 29,029 feet and China's was 29,017 feet.

28 Geologists aren't in perfect agreement: This figure is debated, and obviously it is extremely difficult to measure the height of Mount Everest to within millimeters. I fact-checked this number with David Mencin, a research scientist with the University of Colorado, Boulder; Alex Tait, National Geographic's geographer; and David Lageson, a geology professor at Montana State University. Mencin says that the broader range of the Himalaya is growing at approximately 1–2 centimeters per year. Tait said half a centimeter. Mencin, Tait, and Lageson all noted that the Himalaya actually subsides during large earthquakes, like the ones that hit Nepal in 1934 and 2015. Tait speculated that Mount Everest might actually be shorter today than it was in 1934. Lageson says, "As climbers stand on the summit of Qomolungma, they are literally standing on rocks formed from an ancient seafloor when India was thousands of miles to the south and the geography of Planet Earth was totally different—long, long before the dinosaurs! In my mind, this is what is sacred about Qomolungma—that great mountain is a storybook written in stone and ice of the evolution of one of the greatest mountain systems in the world . . . The mountains are a battleground between Earth's internal tectonic forces causing uplift, and erosion driven by external sources of energy . . . and the hydrologic cycle. Right now, tectonics is winning." See: Michael Jackson and Roger Bilham, "Constraints on Himalayan Deformation Inferred from Vertical Velocity Fields in Nepal and Tibet," *Journal of Geophysical Research* 99, no. B7 (July 10, 1994): 13,897–912, https://doi.org/10.1029/94JB00714.

29 "top secret" set of GPS coordinates: As it turned out, Holzel's coordinates were wrong, because the map datum on the 1984 Washburn map was off. With help from the cartography department at National Geographic and analysis on Google Earth, we later corrected the coordinates to 27°59.749N 86°55.898E.

33 controversial article he wrote: Tom Holzel, "The Mystery of Mallory and Irvine," *Mountain* 17 (September 1971): 30–35.

33 "Americans with an electronic thesaurus . . .": From a now defunct Mallory and Irvine online forum in the UK. Holzel copied it and shared it with me. The document is titled: "Phil's Lament."

36 "Absolutely, and if they discover . . .": From a transcript of an audio recording. All the dialogue in this chapter is verbatim from the transcripts of audio recordings.

36 "Years ago, the senior copyright lawyer . . .": Dave Green, "A Nest of Claims," February 7, 2010, excerpted from an unpublished article, "The Copyright That Almost Was," http://www.henotbusy.com/page4/page4.html.

37 One was a Sherpa named Chhiring Dorje: I made numerous unsuccessful attempts to interview Chhiring Dorje. At one point during our overland approach to Everest, Jamie called Chhiring and he picked up, but as soon as Jamie mentioned that he was calling about Irvine, the line went dead. Jamie speculates that Chhiring probably signed an NDA with the individual who funded his 2004 search expedition, and therefore he is not at liberty to discuss the subject. The secondhand accounts from Chhiring that I was able to collect had enough inconsistencies that I decided his account was not credible, which is why I don't discuss it in more detail in the book. A Mallory and Irvine researcher named Pete Poston shared an email exchange with me that he had with Kiyoshi Furuno, the leader of the 1995 Japanese expedition on which Chhiring purportedly saw the body. Furuno wrote: "I have not confirmed the body of Andrew Irvine, and I don't know if Sherpa have seen this body or not . . . If our Sherpa could see this body, other many sherpas and members of north-ridge route should find his body. I can not believe this sherpa's story." For more on Chhiring Dorje's account, see: https://people.wou.edu/~postonp/everest/index.html.

38 In August of 2001: Jochen Hemmleb and Eric R. Simonson, *Detectives on Everest: The 2001 Mallory and Irvine Research Expedition* (Seattle: Mountaineers, 2002), 181–88.

40 In 1965, the Russian Geographical: Tom Holzel, "Two Eyewitness Accounts of Spotting Irvine," originally published on Holzel's now defunct website, Velocity Press (September 2009). The article contains the bulletin from the *St. Petersburg Alpine Club Journal*, which Holzel had translated. Holzel supplied me with a written copy of his old website.

42 In 1955, the Chinese adopted: Zhou Zheng and Liu Zhenkai, *Footprints on the Peaks: Mountaineering in China* (Seattle: Cloudcap, 1995), 55–69.

42 According to the official expedition: Shih Chan-Chun, "The Conquest of Mount Everest by the Chinese Mountaineering Team," *Alpine Journal* 66 (1961): 28–35.

43 Liu had an idea: Zhou Zheng and Liu Zhenkai, *Footprints on the Peaks*, 75–84. All the quotes from the climb are from *Footprints*.

46 The news was initially celebrated in England: T. S. Blakeney, "Editor's Note," *Alpine Journal* 66 (1961): 36–41.

47 "One must never forget . . .": G. O. Dyhrenfurth, "Observations on the Chinese Everest Expedition 1960," *American Alpine Journal* (1962): 270.

47 ran a thirty-page special supplement: From Audrey Salkeld's notes of her research visit to China, November 1–15, 1998, care of Jochen Hemmleb. I reached out to Salkeld several times but was unable to make contact with her. The information re the special supplement came from Xu Jing.

49 "If the British had climbed . . .": From Audrey Salkeld's notes, care of Jochen Hemmleb.

52 no Mallory-Irvine searchers had: Holzel said that no Mallory-Irvine searchers had been to his "spot," but Jochen Hemmleb points out that Frank Smythe and Eric Shipton passed through this area in 1933 and Jake Norton was also in the vicinity during his search in 2004. In the spring of 2019, I asked Norton about his exact search route, but he was unsure if he had been to the Holzel spot.

CHAPTER THREE: *HAUT MONDE*

My sources for Mallory's war experience in the Battle of the Somme include all his correspondence with his wife, Ruth, from the fall of 1915 through November of 1917, transcribed with permission of the Master and Fellows of Magdalene College, Cambridge. Additional sources for this section include *Into the Silence* by Wade Davis, *George Mallory* by David Robertson, *The Wildest Dream* by Peter and Leni Gillman, and *George Leigh Mallory* by David Pye. For background on the Battle of the Somme, I read *The Somme: The Darkest Hour on the Western Front* by Peter Hart (New York: Pegasus, 2008). I also spent many hours digging through articles on the Newfoundland and Labrador Heritage website, a joint project of the Memorial University's Smallwood Centre for Newfoundland Studies and the C. R. Bronfman Foundation of Montreal.

My sources for Sandy Irvine's biography include *Fearless on Everest* by Julie Summers, *The Irvine Diaries* by Herbert Carr, and the Sandy Irvine Archive at Merton College, which includes his diaries and all the letters he sent on the 1924 expedition, among other items. The letters, diary entries, and documents from the Sandy Irvine Archive are quoted with the permission of the Warden and Fellows of Merton College, Oxford.

54 "It was very noisy . . .": Magdalene College Archives F/GM/II/2 GM to Ruth June 25, 1916.

55 "the rim of a seething cauldron": Magdalene College Archives F/GM/II/2 GM to Ruth July 1, 1916.

55 "It's too too wonderful . . .": Magdalene College Archives F/GM/IV/1 GM to Ruth July 1, 1916. The quote that begins "Firstly, what is religion?" is from the same letter.

55 "I wonder dear how much . . .": Magdalene College Archives F/GM/IV/2 Ruth to GM August 10, 1915. Also see: Peter and Leni Gillman, *The Wildest Dream: The Biography of George Mallory* (Seattle: Mountaineers, 2000), 128.

56 "The wire had been cut . . .": "Beaumont Hamel: July 1, 1916," Newfoundland and Labrador in the First World War, Newfoundland and Labrador Heritage website, https://www.heritage.nf.ca/first-world-war/articles/beaumont-hamel-en.php.

57 "I don't object to corpses . . .": Magdalene College Archives F/GM/II/3 GM to Ruth November 18, 1916.

57 "'Between you and me . . .'": Magdalene College Archives F/GM/II/3 GM to Ruth August 15, 1916. Also see: Wade Davis, *Into the Silence: The Great War, Mallory, and the Conquest of Everest* (New York: Knopf, 2011), 192.

57 "Life presents itself very much . . .": David Robertson, *George Mallory* (London: Faber and Faber, 1969), 123.

59 ". . . wafted over seas of amaranth . . .": Paul Levy, ed., *The Letters of Lytton Strachey* (New York: Farrar, Straus and Giroux, 2005), 179.

59 "The responsibility for upwards . . .": George Mallory, *Boswell the Biographer* (London: Smith, Elder, 1912), Preface.

60 "Now that the poles . . .": J. B. Noel, "A Journey to Tashirak in Southern Tibet, and the Eastern Approaches to Everest," *Geographical Journal* 53, no. 5 (May 1919): 289–308, https://www.jstor.org/stable/i303443. This paper was read to the membership of the RGS at a meeting at their headquarters in London, March 10, 1919. See also: John B. West, *High Life: A History of High-Altitude Physiology and Medicine* (New York: Oxford University Press, 1998), 166–67.

60 "It looks like Everest . . .": Robertson, *George Mallory*, 148.

60 "What a wonderful life . . .": Magdalene College Archives F/GM/VI/5 GM to Ruth November 12, 1918.

61 "important work in the field . . .": The dialogue in this chapter was recorded in notes I took at the time.

63 covered in gray paperboard boxes: Royal Geographical Society, the George Leigh Mallory Collection: Artefact D 14 (1), Conrol no. rgs230831.

63 V-shaped "boot nails": Anker, Pollard, and I refer to these in the text as "hobnails," a generic term used for any form of boot nail. Technically, the nails in Mallory's boots are "V-nails" and "Tricouni nails." Hobnails are a cruder form of boot nails, similar to a big tack that is hammered through a boot sole.

65 was made of flax: The supplier list of the 1924 expedition from the RGS/IBG archives includes three 100-foot "Flax Alpine ropes, ord. size." *Mountain Craft* by Geoffrey Winthrop Young (London: Methuen, 1920) stated that flax rope "in point of ultimate tensile strength and extension surpasses considerably any other rope." A table gives 1,900 pounds as the tensile strength.

68 A one-page obituary: Charles Houston, "Noel Ewart Odell 1890–1987," *American Alpine Journal* (1988): 320–22.

68 "As far as I know . . .": Odell folder, Alpine Club Archive, Noel Odell Papers B75.

73 model of a racing yacht: Herbert Carr, *Irvine Diaries* (Goring Reading, UK: Gastons-West Col, 1979), 28.

73–74 "We saw on the Clyde . . .": Carr, *Irvine Diaries*, 28.

74 manufacturing millions of rounds: Julie Summers, *Fearless on Everest: The Quest for Sandy Irvine* (Seattle: Mountaineers, 2000), 34.

75 "Kitch's great talent . . .": Summers, *Fearless on Everest*, 40.

75 Henley Royal *Peace* Regatta: Andrew Guerrin, "The King's Cup and the 1919 Henley Peace Regatta," *Row360*, March 7, 2019, https://row-360.com/the-kings-cup-and-the-1919-henley-peace-regatta/.

76 "It was the most awful . . .": Carr, *Irvine Diaries*, 31. See also: Summers, *Fearless on Everest*, 38.

78 "intrepid young motorcyclist": Summers, *Fearless on Everest*, 51.

78 "seemed at once to typify . . .": Summers, *Fearless on Everest*, 64.

79 "like a badger house": Summers, *Fearless on Everest*, 74.

83 "expected to have to . . .": Carr, *Irvine Diaries*, 18.

84 "Oxygen apparatus all day . . .": Carr, *Irvine Diaries*, 89.

84 "They made two fine gongs . . .": Carr, *Irvine Diaries*, 89.

85 "Grandfather will never own me . . .": Sandy Irvine Archive, Merton College, Oxford, letter from Sandy to Lilian Irvine, April 24, 1924.

85 ". . . After an early tiffin . . .": Sandy Irvine Archive, Merton College, Oxford, Everest Diary, entries from June 4–5, 1924.

CHAPTER FOUR: THE REDHEADED STEPCHILD OF PRODUCT TESTING

My primary source for the Rick Allen Broad Peak story is an interview I conducted in person with Bartek and Andrzej Bargiel at the Banff Centre Mountain Film Festival in November of 2019, and also the website www.PlanetMountain.com, which reported extensively on this story. Most of the dialogue from my visit to NTS comes from transcription of audio and video recordings. A small portion is from notes taken at the time. For background on drones, I interviewed Renan Ozturk and Rudy Lehfeldt-Ehlinger. I also read several articles on www.droneenthusiast.com and the Nevada Institute for Autonomous Systems, https://nias-uas.com/evolution-commercial-drone-technology/, among others.

91 footage became an instant sensation: https://www.youtube.com/watch?v=TiGkU_eXJa8&vl=en.

95 CIA used a Predator drone: Chris Woods, "The Story of America's Very First Drone Strike," *Atlantic*, May 30, 2015, https://www.theatlantic.com/international/archive/2015/05/america-first-drone-strike-afghanistan/394463/.

CHAPTER FIVE: DAMNABLE HERESY

The dialogue in chapter five was created from my notes. In places where I was unsure if I had recorded something correctly, I checked with Hampton and Cory. Cory read the entire manuscript before publication and gave me his blessing to include his story, including all the material in this chapter. The information about aerobic and anaerobic thresholds and Aerobic Deficiency Syndrome was sourced from an interview with Scott Johnston. Johnston also fact-checked this section. See also: Steve House and Scott Johnston, *Training for the New Alpinism: A Manual for the Climber as Athlete* (Ventura, CA: Patagonia, 2014).

107 Ballinger says he first heard: Jeff Chapman, "Interview: Adrian Ballinger on His Lightning-Fast Ascents of Cho Oyu and Everest," *Climbing* magazine, May

25, 2018, https://www.climbing.com/news/interview-adrian-ballinger-on-his-lightning-fast-ascents-of-cho-oyu-and-everest/.

108 summit Everest in fourteen days: In May of 2019, Lydia Bradey of Alpenglow Expeditions guided Roxanne Vogel, a thirty-three-year-old sports nutritionist, to the summit of Everest in fourteen days, door to door, from her home in Berkeley, California.

110 According to Dr. Joe Vigil: Mike Touzeau, "Joe Vigil: The 'Dean of Distance Running,'" *Green Valley News*, April 16, 2008.

110 World Anti-Doping Agency: Randall L. Wilber, "Application of Altitude/Hypoxic Training by Elite Athletes," *Medicine & Science in Sports & Exercise* 39, no. 9 (September 2007): 1610–24.

112 "they were the most unresponsive . . .": Magdalene College Archives F/GM/III/3 GM to Ruth January 26, 1923.

112 the audience went away "fizzing": Magdalene College Archives F/GM/III/3 GM to Ruth February 9, 1923.

112 SAYS BRANDY AIDED MT. EVEREST: "Says Brandy Aided Mt. Everest Party," *New York Times*, February 5, 1923, 4.

113 "Why did you want to climb . . .": "Climbing Mount Everest Is Work for Supermen," *New York Times*, March 18, 1923, 11.

114 ". . . sounds more like war than sport . . .": David Pye, *George Leigh Mallory: A Memoir* (Bangkok: Orchid Press, 1927), 131.

115 "Your affectionate Stella": Peter and Leni Gillman, *The Wildest Dream: The Biography of George Mallory* (Seattle: Mountaineers, 2000), 270.

115 woman named Eleanor Marjorie Holmes: Abbie Garrington, "'Write Me a Little Letter': The George Mallory/Marjorie Holmes Correspondence," *Alpine Journal* 120 (2016): 123–33.

115 ". . . Shall we see it blaze . . .": Ian Johnston, "George Mallory: Man Who Died Climbing Everest Sent Secret Love Letters to Woman He Never Met," *Independent*, October 2015, https://www.independent.co.uk/news/people/george-mallory-man-who-died-climbing-everest-sent-secret-love-letters-woman-he-never-met-a6712846.html.

115 "I fear I don't make . . .": Magdalene College Archives F/GM/III/4 GM to Ruth March 8, 1924.

116 ". . . I have rather often been cross . . .": Gillman, *The Wildest Dream*, 236.

116 There is a story: Wade Davis, *Into the Silence: The Great War, Mallory, and the Conquest of Everest* (New York: Knopf, 2011), 485.

117 "Effects of Age and Gender . . .": Raymond B. Huey et al., "Effects of Age and Gender on Success and Death of Mountaineers on Mount Everest," *Biology Letters* 3, no. 5 (2007): 498–500.

118 According to the database: The Himalayan Database: The Expedition Archives of Elizabeth Hawley, https://www.himalayandatabase.com/. Alan

Arnette, an expert at analyzing the database, helped me with many of my inquiries related to its data.

118 hoping to identify a gene: Michael Grocott, Daniel Martin, Denny Levett, et al., "Arterial Blood Gases and Oxygen Content in Climbers on Mount Everest," *New England Journal of Medicine* 360, no. 2 (January 8, 2009): 140–49.

119 Another paper cataloged the various: Paul G. Firth et al., "Mortality on Everest, 1921–2006: Descriptive Study," *BMJ* (2008): 337:a2654.

121 The image landed on the cover: The film *Cold* can be accessed here: https://www.youtube.com/watch?v=ZUBjJVL9NNM&has_verified=1.

122 "were as big as dinner plates": Devon O'Neil, "To Get to the Summit, Cory Richards Had to Lose It All," *Outside,* August 24, 2017, https://www.outsideonline.com/2234616/life-after-near-death-cory-richards.

122 "after suffering a possible . . .": Ted Chamberlain, "Everest Helicopter Rescue Saves National Geographic Photographer," *National Geographic,* April 2012, https://www.nationalgeographic.com/news/2012/4/120428-everest-rescue-helicopter-photographer-world-science/.

123 was projecting a facade: Max Ritter, "Caught Inside: How Cory Richards Battled Depression at the Top of the World," *Teton Gravity Research,* https://www.tetongravity.com/feature/adventyre/caught-inside-cory-richards.

124 "I had a sense that things . . .": "The Line," Roam Media video, March 21, 2019, https://www.youtube.com/watch?v=dW43Df9Du_I&list=PLk_c-vLEH_HBGZh_Nu_-zNgldu2rV7POz.

124 partying with eighteen-year-olds: Cory Richards, "After Summiting Mt. Everest, He Returned Home to Face His Demons," *National Geographic,* March 30, 2017, https://www.nationalgeographic.com/adventure/features/athletes/cory-richards-explorer-photographer-everest-personal-challenges/.

127 "murder the impossible": Reinhold Messner, "The Murder of the Impossible," *Mountain* 15 (1971), http://web.mit.edu/lin/Public/climbing/Messner.txt.

127 "damnable heresy": David Simpson, "Damnable Heresy," *London Review of Books* 34, no. 20 (October 2012), https://www.lrb.co.uk/the-paper/v34/n20/david-simpson/damnable-heresy.

128 Cory's odds of dying: Andrew Bisharat, "What's Harder than Summiting Everest? Getting Climbers to Respect It Again," *National Geographic,* April 2019, https://www.nationalgeographic.com/adventure/2019/04/cory-richards-attempts-everest/.

CHAPTER SIX: INTO THE ABODE OF SNOW

Sources for the section on the Great Trigonometrical Survey include *The Great Arc: The Dramatic Tale of How India Was Mapped and Everest Was Named* by John Keay; *Into the Silence* by Wade Davis; and *Everest: Eighty Years of Triumph and Tragedy,* edited by Peter Gillman. I also corresponded with Keay and Clifford Mugnier, chief of geodesy at the Department of Civil and Environmental Engineering at Louisiana State University. Mugnier fact-checked this section of the manuscript. See also: Michael Rand Hoare, *The Quest for the True Figure of the Earth: Ideas and Expeditions in Four Centuries of Geodesy* (Farnham, UK: Ashgate, 2005) and Matthew H. Edney, *Mapping an Empire: The Geographical Construction of British India 1765–1843* (Chicago: University of Chicago Press, 1990).

137 can make up to $500: Tom Vater and Laure Siegel, "Belt and Road Reaches Nepal's Wild North, Winning China Influence," *Nikkei Asia,* March 9, 2019, https://asia.nikkei.com/Spotlight/Belt-and-Road/Belt-and-Road -reaches-Nepal-s-wild-north-winning-China-influence.

143 "miserable man, venomous and cantankerous": Wade Davis, *Into the Silence: The Great War, Mallory, and the Conquest of Everest* (New York: Knopf, 2011), 46.

144 chains to expand or contract: Tom Middleton, "The Great Trigonometrical Survey," *Bluesci,* January 29, 2011, http://web.pdx.edu/~fischerw/proj_pub /humboldt_project/docs/0126-0150/0143_GreatTrigSurveyIndia_BlueSci.pdf.

145 deducing that XV was 29,002: John Keay, *The Great Arc: The Dramatic Tale of How India Was Mapped and Everest Was Named* (New York: Perennial, 2000), 166. According to Keay, it is likely that Waugh knew that XV was the tallest mountain on Earth as early as 1850 but wanted to be absolutely certain, so didn't announce it until 1856.

145 suggestion met with considerable resistance: Peter Gillman, ed., *Everest: Eighty Years of Triumph and Tragedy* (London: Little, Brown, 1993), 12–13.

146 peg the difference at 26.5 miles: These figures come from Clifford Mugnier, chief of geodesy at the LSU Center for GeoInformatics.

147 "the Chinese Dream": Xi Jinping, *The Goverance of China* (Beijing: Foreign Languages Press, 2014), 35. See also: Michael Pillsbury, *The Hundred-Year Marathon: China's Secret Strategy to Replace America as the Global Superpower* (New York: Henry Holt, 2015).

148 outmaneuvering the US economically: Graham Allison, "What Xi Jinping Wants," *Atlantic,* May 31, 2017, https://www.theatlantic.com/international /archive/2017/05/what-china-wants/528561/. See also: Andrew Miller, "China's Hundred-Year Strategy," *The Philadelphia Trumpet,* August 2016, https://www .thetrumpet.com/14006-chinas-hundred-year-strategy.

148 China Three Gorges Corporation: Sylvia Chang, "Power Projects Face Himalayan Task," *China Daily Asia,* April 22, 2016, https://www .chinadailyasia.com/asiaweekly/2016-04/22/content_15421122.html.

149 policy called Comfortable Housing: Max Fisher, "Satellite Images Show Entire Tibetan Villages 'Relocated' under Controversial Chinese Program," *Washington Post,* July 18, 2013, https://www.washingtonpost.com/news

/worldviews/wp/2013/07/18/satellite-images-show-entire-tibetan-villages-relocated-under-controversial-chinese-program/.

150 **subordinating Tibetan culture to Chinese:** Lawrence Davidson, *Cultural Genocide* (New Brunswick: Rutgers University Press, 2012), 89–111. See also: John Bragg, "A Diminishing Tibetan State," *Fair Observer,* October 13, 2013, https://www.fairobserver.com/region/asia_pacific/diminishing-tibetan-state/.

154 **". . . looked a very uninviting place":** Herbert Carr, *Irvine Diaries* (Goring Reading, UK: Gastons-West Col, 1979), 91.

CHAPTER SEVEN: THE MIRACLE HIGHWAY

155 **Sherpa . . . is a specific ethnic:** Jamie McGuinness, "Sherpa vs sherpa," Project Himalaya, https://project-himalaya.com/info-trek-climb-job-roles.html. This footnote was fact-checked by Norbu Tenzing Norgay, vice president of the American Himalayan Foundation. Norbu is the son of Tenzing Norgay.

157 **"a prodigious white fang":** C. K. Howard-Bury, George Mallory, and A. F. R. Wollaston, *Mount Everest: The Reconnaissance, 1921* (London: Edward Arnold, 1922), e-book: location 2694.

158 **"Suddenly our eyes caught glint . . .":** Magdalene College Archives F/GM/III/1 GM to Ruth June 15, 1921.

158 **". . . gave the impression of tremendous . . .":** Herbert Carr, *The Irvine Diaries* (Goring Reading, UK: Gastons-West Col, 1979), 87.

158 **"They unfortunately haven't taken . . .":** Julie Summers, *Fearless on Everest: The Quest for Sandy Irvine* (Seattle: Mountaineers, 2000), 174.

159 **wrong size taps and dies:** Sandy Irvine Archive, Merton College, Oxford, letter from Sandy Irvine to Lilian Irvine, April 17, 1924.

159 **"I'm awfully glad . . .":** Carr, *Irvine Diaries*, 87.

162 **For complex reasons:** Sources for the discussion of the jet stream include an interview with Michael Fagin. See also: www.weather.gov/jetstream/jet and www.everestweather.com.

168 **According to Alan Arnette:** Alan Arnette, "Everest 2019: Stories to Watch This Season," AlanArnette.com, March 25, 2019, www.alanarnette.com/blog/2019/03/25/.

177 **knee-length jacket insulated:** Wade Davis, *Into the Silence: The Great War, Mallory, and the Conquest of Everest* (New York: Knopf, 2011), 386.

179 **story of Malavath Poorna:** Anoo Bhuyan, "Youngest Girl on Everest Wants to Be Role Model for Tribal Children," BBC News, May 28, 2014, www.bbc.com/news/world-asia-india-27599570. I made contact with Poorna and requested an interview several times, but she declined to speak with me.

179 **"to prove girls can achieve . . .":** Ila Ananya, "Poorna Malavath: 'My Reason for Climbing Mt Everest Was to Prove Girls Can Achieve Anything,'" Firstpost

.com, April 1, 2017, https://www.firstpost.com/living/poorna-malavath-my-reason-for-climbing-mt-everest-was-to-prove-girls-can-achieve-anything-3363538.html.

181 The "miracle" is not: Mark Horrell, "Everest's Magic Miracle Highway," MarkHorrell.com January 8, 2014, https://www.markhorrell.com/blog/2014/everests-magic-miracle-highway/.

182 "Had a terrible night . . .": Carr, *Irvine Diaries*, 98.

185 "yellow brick road": Jon Krakauer, *Into Thin Air: A Personal Account of the Mt. Everest Disaster* (New York: Anchor Books, 1997), 66. From a quote from the late Scott Fischer: "These days . . . we've built a yellow brick road to the summit."

CHAPTER EIGHT: FANI

195 snow terrace at 26,770 feet: Elevation according to Jochen Hemmleb.

195 hundreds of high-resolution photos: Renan's drone images will eventually be displayed in an exhibition about the exploration of Mount Everest at the National Geographic Museum in Washington, DC.

195 a total of twenty-six wide-angle: Find the image here: www.nationalgeographic.com/adventure/2019/06/mount-everest-aerial-north-side-drone-photography/.

197 begun padlocking the bottles: Grayson Schaffer, "A Beating on Everest," *Outside*, June 20, 2012, www.outsideonline.com/1929221/beating-everest.

199 None exist, to my knowledge: According to Jochen Hemmleb, no 1924 oxygen sets still exist. The set that Noel Odell brought back from the mountain and gave to the RGS was lost in the late 1960s (one can't help but wonder if it is sitting on the mantel in someone's house), and the only known 1924 oxygen cylinder is one that Percy Wyn-Harris found in 1933 and gave to the Alpine Club, which now uses it as a gong. Another was found and photographed by the 1953 expedition at Tengboche Monastery in Nepal, but its current whereabouts are unknown.

200 Jim Gile, a software engineer: Jim Gile, "Climbing with Supplemental Oxygen: By the Numbers," *8K Peak Technologies*, January 14, 2015, www.8kpeak.com/blogs/sneak-peak/18637335. Jamie McGuinness, for one, does not agree with Gile's conclusions. As someone who has climbed high with and without supplemental oxygen, he thinks that anecdotally, Gile's numbers feel off, probably because Gile has overestimated the efficiency of the masks, which don't always seal well onto one's face.

201 I had written an article: Mark Synnott, "The Everest Moral Dilemma," *National Geographic*, April 21, 2015, https://www.nationalgeographic.com/adventure/adventure-blog/2015/04/21/everest-fixed-lines-or-fair-means/#/179704376.jpg.

201 Odell called the "Oxygen Debate": Alpine Club Archive, Noel Odell Papers B75.

202 spoke at the Alpine Club in 1908: Ian R. Mitchell and George W. Rodway, *Prelude to Everest: Alexander Kellas, Himalyan Mountaineer* (Edinburgh, UK: Luath Press Limited, 2011).

202 "The natives whom we found . . .": Mitchell and Rodway, *Prelude to Everest*, 89–90.

203 "Coolies have a very keen . . .": Mitchell and Rodway, *Prelude to Everest*, 98–99.

203 "A Consideration of the Possibility . . .": Alpine Club Archives, 1922/C108. See also: John B. West, *High Life: A History of High-Altitude Physiology and Medicine* (New York: Oxford University Press, 1998), 170–75.

204 pilots during World War One: West, *High Life*, 175–76.

204 Kamet breathing "English Air": C. G. Bruce, *The Assault on Mount Everest, 1922* (London: Edward Arnold, 1923), e-book: location 2650.

204 "Kellas I love already . . .": Magdalene College Archives F/GM/III/1 GM to Ruth May 17, 1921. See also: Wade Davis, *Into the Silence: The Great War, Mallory, and the Conquest of Everest* (New York: Knopf, 2011), 204–6.

205 "the most incredibly dirty warren . . .": Magdalene College Archives F/GM/III/1 GM to Ruth June 5, 1921.

205 stony hillside outside the: David Robertson, *George Mallory* (London: Faber and Faber, 1969), 155. "Stony hillside" is quoted from a letter written by Mallory to Geoffrey Young. "I shan't easily forget the four boys, his own trained mountain men, children of nature, seated in wonder on a great stone near the grave." See also: Davis, *Into the Silence*, 227–29.

207 Prakash had tried twice: Out of all our climbing sherpas, I formed the strongest bond with Prakash. In addition to the time we spent together on the expedition, I also conducted a long interview with him in Kathmandu after the expedition. We continue to keep in touch.

210 "It is no use pretending . . .": Magdalene College Archives F/GM/III/1 GM to Ruth August 22, 1921.

210 "time the breathing regularly . . .": C. K. Howard-Bury, George Mallory, and A. F. R. Wollaston, *Mount Everest: The Reconnaissance, 1921* (London: Edward Arnold, 1922), e-book: location 3538.

212 In the Andean highlands: Cynthia M. Beall, "Two Routes to Functional Adaptation: Tibetan and Andean High-Altitude Natives," *PNAS* 104 (May 15, 2007), www.doi.org/10.1073/pnas.0701985104.

212 UC Berkeley named Rasmus Nielsen: My primary sources for the discussion of Sherpa genetics include Rasmus Nielsen, Peter Hackett, and Andrew Murray. This section was fact-checked by Nielsen and Hackett.

213 studying "the Tibetan question": Xin Yi, Yiu Liang, Xin Jin, et al., "Sequencing of 50 Human Exomes Reveals Adaptation to High Altitude,"

Science 329, no. 5987 (July 2, 2010): 75–78, www.doi.org/10.1126/science .1190371.

213 archaic human called the Denisovan: Emilia Huerta-Sánchez, Xin Jin, Asan, Zhuoma Bianba, et al., "Altitude Adaptation in Tibetans Caused by Introgression of Denisovan-like DNA," *Nature* 512 (July 2, 2014): 194–97.

213 Denisovans lived in Asia: David Reich, Richard E. Green, Martin Kircher, et al., "Genetic History of an Archaic Hominin Group from Denisova Cave in Siberia," *Nature* 468 (December 22, 2010): 1053–60, www.nature.com/articles /nature09710.

213 or 8 percent of Han Chinese: Pontus Skoglund and Mattias Jakobsson, "Archaic Human Ancestry in East Asia," *PNAS* 108, no. 45 (November 8, 2011): 18301–06, www.doi.org/10.1073/pnas.1108181108.

214 their physiology was studied: Edward Gilbert-Kawai, Adam Sheperdigian, Thomas Adams, et al., "Design and Conduct of Xtreme Everest 2: An Observational Cohort Study of Sherpa and Lowlander Responses to Graduated Hypobaric Hypoxia," *F1000Research* 4, no. 90 (April 10, 2015), www.ncbi.nlm .nih.gov/pmc/articles/PMC4448741.1/.

217 "This is a thrilling business": Magdalene College Archives F/GM/III/1 GM to Ruth June 28, 1921.

220 According to the *Irish Sun*: Sarah Slater, "Bray Mourns Irish Climber Seamus Lawless . . . ," *Irish Sun*, May 27, 2019, www.thesun.ie/news/4143997/.

CHAPTER NINE: THE DAY EVEREST BROKE

All the actions, thoughts, musings, dialogue, impressions, and emotions detailed in the stories of Reinhard Grubhofer, Kuntal Joisher, Rolfe Oostra, and Dolores Al Shelleh come from the transcripts of my interviews with them. Thoughts attributed to them in italics are direct quotes I got from them. I corresponded with Alex Abramov, who was in Moscow, electronically. To re-create the events of May 23, 2019, I reviewed photos and video from various summiteers, social media posts, weather forecasts, and the list of who summited when in the Himalayan Database. I also monitored and took notes on radio transmissions from various teams throughout the day. Cory's story and the dialogue with him and Topo was re-created from my notes and a subsequent interview.

226 photograph of the traffic jam: Megan Specia, "On Everest, Traffic Isn't Just Inconvenient. It Can Be Deadly," *New York Times*, May 23, 2019, www .nytimes.com/2019/05/23/world/asia/deadly-everest-traffic-jam.html.

226 Gurkha soldier named Nirmal Purja: Megan Specia, "World's 14 Highest Peaks in 6 Months: Nepali Smashes Climbing Record," *New York Times*, October 29, 2019, https://www.nytimes.com/2019/10/29/world/asia/nirmal -purja-record-climber.html.

227 "energy loss" and "heavy traffic": "Thane Mountaineer Dies While Descending Mt Everest," *Times of India*, May 24, 2019, www.timesofindia .indiatimes.com/city/thane/thane-mountaineer-dies-while-descending-mt-everest/articleshow/69473426.cms.

227 "Mount Mid-Life-Crisis": Teresa Kubacka, "Mount Mid-Life-Crisis," TowardsDataScience.com, December 23, 2019, https://towardsdatascience .com/frostbite-stories-part-1-mount-middle-life-crisis-97df574d58d7.

230 Grubhofer felt no joy: Joshua Hammer, "Chaos at the Top of the World," *GQ*, December 4, 2019, https://www.gq.com/story/mount-everest-chaos-at-the -top-of-the-world.

234 "Come on, you can do . . .": This and the other sherpa dialogue re-created as per Joisher's recollection.

237 "Only Sherpas and Bhotias killed . . .": T. Howard Somervell, *After Everest: The Experiences of a Mountaineer and Medical Missionary* (London: Hodder and Stoughton, 1950), e-book: location 860. See also: Wade Davis, *Into the Silence: The Great War, Mallory, and the Conquest of Everest* (New York: Knopf, 2011), 444.

237 Today, the death benefit: According to Alan Arnette.

238 disaster struck on Manaslu: Kelly McMillan, "After Avalanche, Record Climb Is Bittersweet," *New York Times*, October 13, 2012, https://www.nytimes.com /2012/10/14/sports/after-avalanche-record-climb-is-bittersweet.html.

239 "For more than a century . . .": Grayson Schaffer, "The Disposable Man: A Western History of Sherpas on Everest," *Outside*, July 10, 2013, www .outsideonline.com/1928326/disposable-man-western-history-sherpas-everest.

243 In addition to killing seventeen: There does not seem to be a consensus on how many people died in the avalanche on Everest in 2015. *The New York Times and The Washington Post* both reported seventeen deaths. Wikipedia lists eighteen, and the Himalayan Database lists fourteen.

CHAPTER TEN: KAM

The details of our meeting with the climbing sherpas in ABC on May 23 were re-created from my notes, an audio recording made by Jim Hurst, and video footage of the event. All the dialogue is verbatim from the transcript. My sources for Kam's story include hours of interviews I conducted with her while she was recuperating in India after the expedition. I also interviewed Rolfe Oostra, Sheena West, Arthur Prestige, and Di Gilbert. Oostra and Gilbert were instrumental in helping me to reconstruct the exact timeline of Kam's descent and subsequent rescue. I attempted to make contact with Bir, but the outfitter in Kathmandu for whom he works told me that he was locked down in his village due to COVID and unable to communicate. I was, however, able to review a statement written by Bir in which he recounted his side of the story. Bir and Kam's accounts differ on some important points. To be fair, I left out anything on which there was disagreement about the facts. I did not interview Jamie Ironmonger, but I was able to review a written statement that he prepared in January of 2020. The exchange between Ironmonger and Kam, during which he asked her to turn back with him, comes from this statement. For the record, Kam refutes Ironmonger's account and says that he never asked her to turn back. There is disagreement amongst Kam's team about what time she summited. I came up with 11:15 A.M. as a best guess based on the time stamp on photographs she shared with me and by cross-referencing with the people I could see in the background of the photos. The Himalayan Database incorrectly lists her as having summited at 9:45 A.M. Both Kam and Rolfe read and fact-checked the manuscript before publication. Each of them gave me their blessing to share their stories.

284 "Fight for your life": Di Gilbert, "The Dark Side of Everest—A Personal Reflection," Scarpa.com, June 20, 2019, https://www.scarpa.co.uk/blog/the-dark-side-of-everest/.

286 tragic story of David Sharp: Peter Gillman, "Left to Die at the Top of the World," *Sunday Times*, September 24, 2006, www.thetimes.co.uk/article/left-to-die-at-the-top-of-the-world-pb7shlbt8r0. My primary source for the David Sharp story was Jamie McGuinness, who gave me a long interview on the subject. Jamie knew Sharp and had previously guided him on both Cho Oyu and Everest. And Jamie was on the north side of Everest in 2006, listening on the radio and communicating with climbing sherpas as the Sharp tragedy unfolded. See also: Nick Heil, *Dark Summit: The True Story of Everest's Most Controversial Season* (New York: Henry Holt, 2008).

287 "The poor guy's stuffed": Allen G. Breed and Binaj Gurubacharya, "On Top of the World, but Abandoned There," *Washington Post*, July 30, 2006, www.washingtonpost.com/wp-dyn/content/article/2006/07/29/AR2006072900922_pf.html. The quote from Sharp's mother on page 295 is also from this article.

287 "the whole attitude towards climbing . . .": Tom McKinlay, "Wrong to Let Climber Die, Says Sir Edmund," *New Zealand Herald*, May 23, 2006, www.nzherald.co.nz/nz/news/article.cfm?c_id=1&objectid=10383276.

288 "cut him up": This quote is from Jamie McGuinness, who was in ABC closely monitoring the situation. Jamie gave me a first-person account of Lincoln Hall's story. See also: Lincoln Hall, *Dead Lucky: Life After Death on Mount Everest* (New York: Tarcher, 2007).

289 "I imagine you are surprised . . .": Hall, *Dead Lucky*, 195.

289 "Lincoln only has one life": Jack Broom, "Olympia Guide Helped Save Life of Everest Climber Left for Dead," *Seattle Times*, May 30, 2006, https://archive.seattletimes.com/archive/?date=20060530&slug=climber30m.

290 Pollard has his own story: Over the course of several interviews, Thom shared with me his tale of the dying Indians he encountered in 2016. Many of the details are recorded in his journal.

291 "Sherpas can't use force . . .": John Branch, "Deliverance from 27,000 Feet," *New York Times*, December 19, 2017, www.nytimes.com/interactive/2017/12/18/sports/everest-deaths.html. This article was an important source of information on the timeline and other details about the Indians.

291 A video later surfaced of Ghosh: www.youtube.com/watch?v=d6rpnN29vug.

293 soldier named Leslie John Binns: Mario Cacciottolo and Natasa Simovic, "Briton Leslie Binns Abandons Everest Peak to Save Fellow Climber," BBC News, June 2, 2016, https://www.bbc.com/news/uk-36437937.

294 "I owe my life . . .": Nimi Kurian, "He Won Hearts," *Hindu*, June 16, 2016, https://www.thehindu.com/features/kids/He-won-hearts/article14424007.ece.

296 came across the mystery man: Kam's guardian angel has never been identified. Kam and Oostra believe they saw him lying dead outside of camp, but officially there were only two confirmed deaths on the north side during the spring 2019 season: Ernst Landgraf and Kevin Hynes. It is possible that the man was Chinese and his death was not reported.

CHAPTER ELEVEN: ENGLISH AIR

297 awoke feeling so "seedy": Herbert Carr, *The Irvine Diaries* (Goring Reading, UK: Gastons-West Col, 1979), 105.

298 a "council of war": E. F. Norton, *The Fight for Everest 1924* (London: Edward Arnold, 1925), 74.

298 the preliminary "monsoon current": Christopher Norton, *Everest Revealed: The Private Diaries and Sketches of Edward Norton, 1922–24* (Cheltanham, UK: History Press, 2014), 108.

299 "A dead numbing cold . . .": C. G. Bruce, *The Assault on Mount Everest, 1922* (London: Edward Arnold, 1923), e-book: location 2710.

300 "scrap the oxygen altogether": E. F. Norton, *The Fight for Everest 1924*, 76.

301 "Geoff's plan was voted": Carr, *Irvine Diaries*, 106.

301 "It is 50 to 1 against us . . .": Magdalene College Archives F/GM/III/4 GM to Ruth May 27, 1924. See also: Wade Davis, *Into the Silence: The Great War, Mallory, and the Conquest of Everest* (New York: Knopf, 2011), 526.

301 Bagwan died of "dehydration, exhaustion . . .": Prachi Bari, "Pune Man Conquers Everest, Dies during Descent," *Hindustan Times*, May 25, 2019, https://www.hindustantimes.com/pune-news/pune-man-conquers-everest-dies-during-descend/story-PwG71cetsHxDTmEb7ExdKL.html.

302 "Her legacy in mountaineering . . .": Staff reporter, "Kalpana Dash, Odisha's First Woman Mountaineer, Dead," *Hindu*, May 24, 2019, https://www.thehindu.com/news/national/other-states/kalpana-dash-odishas-first-woman-mountaineer-dead/article27231811.ece.

307 "We struck gold here boyo": From a Facebook post by Rolfe Oostra, "Three Everest's," Facebook, May 28, 2019, www.facebook.com/RolfeOostra360/posts/three-everestsperhaps-not-unreasonably-i-thought-of-mallorys-camera-and-how-it-w/2379087088994830/.

313 "Another porter sick—paralysis . . .": Carr, *Irvine Diaries*, 101.

316 "Odell and Irvine gave such . . .": E. F. Norton, *Fight for Everest 1924*, 81.

316 "Very cold and disagreeable job . . .": Carr, *Irvine Diaries*, 109.

317 "I really hate the thought of oxygen": Carr, *Irvine Diaries*, 125. The line is quoted from a letter that Irvine wrote to Peter Lunn.

317 "A most unpleasant night . . .": Carr, *Irvine Diaries*, 109.

318 ". . . shall appear in letters of gold . . .": E. F. Norton, *The Fight for Everest 1924*, 86.

319 Norton's base layers: E. F. Norton, *The Fight for Everest 1924*, 82.

320 "much of the beauty . . .": E. F. Norton, *The Fight for Everest 1924*, 88.

322 "one last almighty push": T. Howard Somervell, *After Everest: The Experiences of a Mountaineer and Medical Missionary* (London: Hodder and Stoughton, 1950), e-book: location 1685. See also: Davis, *Into the Silence*, 536.

322 for Mallory's "indomitable spirit": E. F. Norton, *The Fight for Everest 1924*, 92.

323 ". . . has any real guts": Davis, *Into the Silence*, 532.

CHAPTER TWELVE: ABOVE THE BRINK

331 "Jamie, if you come down . . .": Thom recorded most of the radio transmissions during the summit push. The dialogue with the CTMA is verbatim from transcriptions of these recordings.

338 ". . . bulky inconvenience of the whole apparatus": E. F. Norton, *The Fight for Everest 1924* (London: Edward Arnold, 1925), 99.

338 torn from Mallory's pocket notebook: Alpine Club Archives, Last Letters, uncataloged. See also: E. F. Norton, *The Fight for Everest 1924*, 100.

339 "savagely wild jumble of peaks": Wade Davis, *Into the Silence: The Great War, Mallory, and the Conquest of Everest* (New York: Knopf, 2011), 542. See also: E. F. Norton, *The Fight for Everest 1924*, 100.

340 "sudden clearing of the atmosphere . . ."; "My eyes became fixed . . .": "The Mount Everest Dispatches," *Geographical Journal* 64, no. 2 (August 1924): 164.

342 "Nothing would have amused him . . .": E. F. Norton, *The Fight for Everest 1924*, 103.

349 Mallory discussed two options: J. B. L. Noel, *Through Tibet to Everest* (London: Edward Arnold, 1927), 275.

351 Hahn put Anker on belay: This account comes from an interview with Anker. See also: Conrad Anker and David Roberts, *The Lost Explorer: Finding Mallory on Mount Everest* (New York: Simon & Schuster, 1999), 150–53.

352 "Could Mallory have scaled . . .": Eric Simonson, Jochen Hemmleb, and Larry Johnston, "Ghosts of Everest," *Outside*, October 1, 1999, https://www.outsideonline.com/1909046/ghosts-everest.

352 scenes for a documentary film: *The Wildest Dream: Conquest of Everest*, National Geographic documentary, 2010, https://www.youtube.com/watch?v=lpwBQlOSJ3I&list=PLZY8_SfbfJPccVGvlu0xdH8Csd3EnfUlI.

353 documented free ascent: According to Jochen Hemmleb, the Second Step has seen three other "free" ascents besides Anker's: Catalan Oscar Cadiach in 1985, Austrian Theo Fritsche in 2001 (solo), and Nickolay Totmjanin in 2003. Only verbal testimonies exist as proof of the first three ascents. Cadiach and Fritsche rated the pitch 5.7–5.8; no rating is documented from Totmjanin. Leo Houlding, who seconded Anker's lead, rated it 5.9.

356 "We didn't know them . . .": Jon Krakauer, *Into Thin Air: A Personal Account of the Mt. Everest Disaster* (New York: Anchor Books, 1997), 251–54. See also: P. M. Das, "The Indian Ascent of Qomolungma by the North Ridge," *Himalayan Journal* 53 (1997), https://www.himalayanclub.org/hj/53/7/the-indian-ascent-of-qomolungma-by-the-north-ridge/, and Richard Cowper, "The Climbers Left to Die in the Storms of Everest," *Financial Times* (May 18, 1996), http://richardcowper.com/site/exped/ever_article1.html.

356 someone finally moved his body: The Chinese have been discreetly removing dead bodies from high on Everest for a number of years. We'd heard rumors that a major such cleanup had been planned for the spring of 2019 but was later canceled due to problems getting permission from the victims' relatives. We know this grisly work has been ongoing because guides have reported that well-known bodies scattered along the route, like Tsewang Paljor, nicknamed "Green Boots," are no longer there.

CHAPTER THIRTEEN: HIGH ENDEAVORS

360 eleven people had already died: Two more deaths occurred on the south side on May 25 and 27, 2019, both after summiting: Briton Robin Haynes Fisher, forty-four, at approximately 28,500 feet, and Coloradoan Christopher Kulish, sixty-two, on the South Col.

365 on a Chinese chain gang: We had all worried that there might be repercussions for my leaving the fixed lines to go to the Holzel spot, but when we met up with Dechen, the CTMA official, in Base Camp after the climb, he only wanted to offer his congratulations, nothing more. Dechen, who is in his early thirties and speaks perfect English, is an experienced climber who completed the Explorers Grand Slam, a variation of the Seven Summits that includes tagging the North and South Poles.

366 "Very dangerous, very dangerous": The dialogue with Lhakpa comes from video footage of this scene shot by Matthew Irving. See the documentary film

Lost on Everest, National Geographic (2020). The trailer is available on YouTube, https://www.youtube.com/watch?v=PxqEu9HvIgc. The full film is available on Disney+.

367 "little more fatiguing . . .": E. F. Norton, *The Fight for Everest 1924* (London: Edward Arnold, 1925), 105.

368 ". . . inevitable that disaster has overtaken . . .": Christopher Norton, *Everest Revealed: The Private Diaries and Sketches of Edward Norton, 1922–24* (Cheltenham, UK: History Press, 2014), 112.

369 ". . . when a darkened atmosphere hides . . .": E. F. Norton, *The Fight for Everest 1924*, 108. See also: Wade Davis, *Into the Silence: The Great War, Mallory, and the Conquest of Everest* (New York: Knopf, 2011), 547–50.

372 He was done running sweep: When we got back to Kathmandu at the end of the expedition, Lhakpa Tenje Sherpa came to my hotel for a long interview and debrief of the expedition. He said he had already forgiven me my indiscretion in the Yellow Band. His comment was essentially "no harm, no foul." We parted as friends.

CHAPTER FOURTEEN: HOME

373 MALLORY IRVINE NOVE REMAINDER ALCEDO: Royal Geographical Society (with IBG), Everest Expeditions special collection; planning documentation: EE/25/2/1. Control no. rgs213342. According to Jan Turner, the word *Obferras* was a typo. The telegram should have read *Obterras*, which is a reference to the society's motto at the time: *Ob terras reclusas* ("for the discovery of lands").

374 they "all cried together": Peter and Leni Gillman, *The Wildest Dream: The Biography of George Mallory* (Seattle: Mountaineers, 2000), 260. The quote is from Clare, Mallory's daughter, seventy-five years after the fact.

374 "a deeply sensitive person": Julie Summers, *Fearless on Everest: The Quest for Sandy Irvine* (Seattle: Mountaineers, 2000), 17.

375 ". . . the hole in our hearts": Summers, *Fearless on Everest*, 259.

376 a folded-up newspaper clipping: Sandy Irvine Archive, Merton College, Oxford, Box 2, Wallets and Rucksack patch.

376 "Is this right for Llanfairfechan?": Herbert Carr, *The Irvine Diaries* (Goring Reading, UK: Gastons-West Col, 1979), 30.

378 I told this man: For obvious reasons, I have chosen not to reveal this person's identity.

378 sixty-six single-spaced pages: I ran the entire document through Google Translate, then selected the most relevant sections to be professionally translated by Stacy Mosher of Mosher & Ran. All the quoted material comes from the professional translation.

381 because the Great Leap Forward: Fan Hong and Lu Zhouxiang, *The Politicisation of Sport in Modern China: Communists and Champions* (Abingdon, UK: Routledge, 2013), 17–19.

383 a letter from Arthur Hinks: RGS/IBG Collections: ar RGS/CB9/Odell.

385 ". . . that Mallory and Irvine succeeded": E. F. Norton, *The Fight for Everest 1924* (London: Edward Arnold, 1925), 113.

ACKNOWLEDGMENTS

When it comes to this story, there is no one to whom I owe a greater debt of gratitude than Thom Pollard. Were it not for Thom's Everest obsession, the 2019 Sandy Irvine Search Expedition would never have happened. By the same token, I am indebted to Tom Holzel, whose decades of dogged research laid the foundation for this story. I also owe a huge thank-you to Renan Ozturk and his wife, Taylor Rees, who worked tirelessly to get this project funded and off the ground. Renan shared my vision for this story from the start, and I am fortunate to have had such a talented and creative partner for this venture. From the moment our team first gathered together in Kathmandu, it was clear to all that this expedition had soul, and that had everything to do with the sterling individuals who made up our team: Matthew Irving, Jim Hurst, Nick Kalisz, and Jamie McGuinness. It was an honor and a privilege to share this experience with such a talented and easygoing group of people.

I can say the same about our climbing sherpas and camp staff, without whom we would not have gotten far. As Thom said many times during the expedition, getting to know these guys was one of the greatest rewards of our Everest experience: Lhakpa Tenje Sherpa, Prakash Kemchay, Bal Bahadur Lopchan, Kusang Sherpa, Pasang

Kaji Sherpa, Lhakpa Tenje Sherpa, Ngati Sherpa, Pemba Nuru Sherpa, Pema Kancha Sherpa, Sonam Sherpa, Pemba Tenzi Sherpa, Pasang Gomba Sherpa, Dawa Dendi Sherpa, Karma Sherpa, Da Gejie (Dawa) Sherpa, Bire Tamang, Dapa Sang, Dorje, and Chhumbi.

I am grateful to National Geographic for believing in all of us. If you enjoyed this book, you will also find great interest in the July 2020 special Everest issue of *National Geographic* magazine entitled "Journey to Roof of the World," as well as the hour-long television documentary, *Lost on Everest*, which is available for streaming on Disney+. Also not to be missed is Renan's behind-the-scenes documentary, produced by Sony Alpha Films, *The Ghosts Above.* Special thanks to my editor Peter Gwin, who is one of my staunchest supporters, as well as Sadie Quarrier, Bengt Anderson, Drew Pulley, Fred Hiebert, and Martin Gamache. Deep gratitude is also due to Sony Alpha and the North Face for their generous financial support of our expedition. At the North Face, I would like to thank Matt Sharkey, James Kelly, Dave Burleson, and Samantha Petrie. Thanks also to additional sponsors including La Sportiva, Lenz, Good To-Go, ProBar, Revo, Julbo, and outerU.

In Britain, I owe thanks to the staff of the Foyle Reading Room at the Royal Geographical Society, most especially librarians David McNeil and Jan Turner. At Merton College, Oxford, I am indebted to librarian Julia Walworth, who arranged my visit and has been a huge help ever since. I'd also like to thank archivist Julian Reid and deputy librarian Harriet Campbell Longley. Special thanks to the Sandy Irvine Trust and the Warden and Fellows of Merton College, Oxford, for permission to quote from the letters and documents from the Sandy Irvine Archive. Thanks also to the Master and Fellows of Magdalene College, Cambridge, for permission to transcribe from the Mallory letters in the Magdalene College Archives. Archivist Tilda Watson, librarian Catherine Sutherland, and Jemma O'Grady were a huge help in procuring and sourcing these letters. Nigel Buckley, former librarian at the Alpine Club (now at Balliol College, Oxford), was not only a most gracious host during my visit to the Alpine Club headquarters but was also instrumental in helping me to find primary sources for my historical research on the early Everest expeditions. I hope to return the favor one day when Buckley heads to Baffin Island on an exploratory climbing expedition.

Inspiration comes in many forms, and I would be remiss not to acknowledge the many writers whose gift at crafting prose has caused me to pull my hair out many a day as I sat at my desk trying to live up to their example: Wade Davis, Julie Summers, Peter and Leni Gillman, Jon Krakauer, David Grann, Sebastian Junger, Erik Larson, Laura Hillenbrand, John Vaillant, and Robert Pirsig, to name a few.

John Climaco, Shaun Pinkham, Spencer Salovaara, Jeff Achey, Peter Gwin, Jim Zellers, Greg Child, Hampton Synnott, Cory Richards, Conrad Anker, Tom Holzel, Thom Pollard, Alan Arnette, and my father-in-law, Alan Kew, read the manuscript and offered valuable edits and feedback that helped to improve the story.

Jochen Hemmleb, who is, in my opinion, the world's leading authority on the mystery of Mallory and Irvine, could not have been more supportive while I was writing this book, and my conversations with him about the many nuances of this story were instrumental in shaping this narrative. Hemmleb was also an early reader of the manuscript, and I am deeply indebted to him for his thorough fact-checking of my work.

I also owe a huge thank-you to all the many people who graciously shared their stories, insights, knowledge, and expertise—and trusted me to share their information accurately with the world: Conrad Anker, Peter Hackett, Cory Richards, Rolfe Oostra, Kamaldeep Kaur, Reinhard Grubhofer, Dolores Al Shelleh, Alex Abramov, Arthur Prestige, Adrian Ballinger, Emily Turner, Topo Esteban Mena, Jake

Norton, Eric Simonson, Andy Politz, Graham Hoyland, Di Gilbert, Sheena West, Pete Poston, Olivia Hsu, Hal Hallstein, Ben Phipps, Kuntal Joisher, Parth Upadhyana, Shekhar Babu Bachinepally, Vamini Sethi, Michael Fagin, Alex Tait, David Mencin, David Lageson, Peter Athans, Norbu Tenzing Norgay, Scott Johnston, Brian Oestrike, Andrew Murray, Rasmus Nielsen, Clifford Mugnier, Reinhold Messner, Noel Hanna, Gonbu, Navin Trital, Lhakpa Tenje Sherpa, Prakash Kemchay, Mingma Sherpa, Frank Campanaro, Scott Woolums, Bartek and Andrzej Bargiel, Julie Summers, and Peter Odell.

For contributing to the photo insert, I would like to thank Renan Ozturk, Matt Irving, Thom Pollard, Jamie McGuinness, Tom Holzel, Clare Mallory Millikan, Rolfe Oostra, Reinhard Grubhofer, Kuntal Joisher, Mark Ballard, Caroline Gleich, the Sandy Irvine Archive, the Royal Geographical Society, Getty Images, and Baidu Baike. Huge thanks and kudos as well to Clay Wadman for the wonderful maps. Thanks also to Tor Anderson for his design help on the maps.

I worked closely on this book with my old friend Jeff Chapman. His meticulous edits, insights, analysis, and big-picture view of where I was going with this story played a huge role in every step of its creation. I cannot thank him enough for helping to make this book eminently more readable than it would have been without his input. I am also indebted to Peter Miller and Ben Ayers, both of whom gave the manuscript a careful read and provided valuable insights and edits.

My agent, Gillian MacKenzie, never ceases to amaze me with her fierce dedication to my cause. She is not only one of my greatest advocates but also a dear friend and trusted advisor. The talented team at MacKenzie Wolf, including Kirsten Wolf, Rachel Crawford, and Renee Jarvis, is truly one of a kind.

At Dutton, I have found many kindred spirits, most especially my extraordinary editor and friend, Stephen Morrow, who is undoubtedly one of the best in the business. If there is anyone in this world who cares more about this book than me, it is Stephen, and as usual, his deft touches with the manuscript have made me look like a far better writer than I am. I would also like to thank publisher Christine Ball, editor in chief John Parsley, as well as Yuki Hirose, Amanda Walker, Emily Canders, Katie Taylor, Hannah Feeney, LeeAnn Pemberton, Alice Dalrymple, Hannah Dragone, Tiffany Estreicher, Katy Riegel, and Dominque Jones.

I owe everything, of course, to my family, who have always supported and loved me unconditionally, despite the unconventional path I have followed in life. My in-laws, Sherman, Meredith, Rauni, and Alan, all ooze with talent and are ever ready with sage advice when I need it. And I have long drawn great strength from my sister, Amy Synnott, who is a brilliant editor and writer; and my dear mother, Suzanne, who will fight for me to the end. As I mention at the end of this story, I believe that our greatest endeavors are less about what we set out to do than what we bring back. And I hope that what I've brought back to my children, Tommy, Lilla, Matt, and Will, over the course of my travels, is the lesson that we give our lives meaning and purpose by caring deeply about things—regardless of whether those things make sense to other people or not.

Finally, I'd like to thank my wife, Hampton, who held my hand both literally and figuratively throughout this project. Without her deep love and support, I never would have had the courage or the fortitude to see this mission through. In her, I have found a partner who understands the siren call of the mountains as well as anyone I know. And I know she will agree that our greatest adventures as a family still loom on distant horizons.

INDEX